'Glorious insights . . . It is warm, responsive and good-humoured . . . gloriously candid' *Scotsman*

'Few memoirists are imbued with as perfect a commixture of funny and serious as Ferdinand Mount' *Sunday Times*

'*Cold Cream* is a pleasure to read. It is the richest, most intelligent autobiography of the decade' Edward Pearce, *Tribune*

'Mount conveys perfectly the bizarre, part-official, part-domestic atmosphere of Thatcher's Downing Street . . . An impressive panorama of Britain's fairly recent history, poignant, even tragic and fabulous good fun' *Times Literary Supplement*

'Unlike so many political writers he has a light Wodehousian touch' *Oldie*

'The whole thing is written with such delightful self-deprecation – a bad of the super-toff if ever there was one – that you stop worrying about whether you've been played and simply enjoy the ride' Kathryn Hughes, *Guardian*

A NOTE ON THE AUTHOR

FERDINAND MOUNT was born in 1939, the son of a steeplechase jockey, and brought up on Salisbury Plain. After being educated at Eton and Oxford, he made various false starts as a children's nanny, gossip columnist, bagman to Selwyn Lloyd, and leader-writer on the doomed *Daily Sketch*. He later surfaced as head of Margaret Thatcher's Policy Unit and then editor of the *Times Literary Supplement*. He is married with three children and three grandchildren and has lived in Islington for half his life.

Apart from political columns and essays he has written a six-volume series of novels, 'A Chronicle of Modern Twilight', which begins with *The Man Who Rode Ampersand*, based on his father's racing life, and includes *Of Love and Asthma* (he is a temporarily retired asthmatic), which won the Hawthornden Prize in 1992. He also writes what he calls 'Tales of History and Imagination', including *Umbrella*, which the historian Niall Ferguson called 'quite simply the best historical novel in years'.

COLD CREAM

My Early Life and Other Mistakes

FERDINAND MOUNT

BLOOMSBURY

LONDON · BERLIN · NEW YORK

First published in Great Britain 2008

This paperback edition published 2009

Copyright © by Ferdinand Mount 2008

The moral right of the author has been asserted

Letters from Isaiah Berlin quoted with permission of the Isaiah Berlin Literary Trust.
Letter from Philip Toynbee quoted by kind permission of his literary executors. Quote
from 'Sir John Piers' by John Betjeman © John Betjeman by kind permission of the
Estate of John Betjeman. *Animal Farm* by George Orwell (copyright © George Orwell,
1945) by permission of Bill Hamilton as the Literary Executor of the Estate of the Late
Sonia Brownell Orwell and Secker & Warburg Ltd. Quote from 'Right Royal' by John
Masefield reproduced by permission of the Society of Authors as the Literary
Representative of the Estate of John Masefield. Quote from 'Died of Wounds' copyright
Siegfried Sassoon by kind permission of the Estate of George Sassoon. Drawing on page
183 reproduced by kind permission of Nicholas Garland and the *Daily Telegraph*.
Drawing on page 333 reproduced by kind permission of Peter Brookes and *The Times*.

Bloomsbury Publishing Plc
36 Soho Square
London W1D 3QY

www.bloomsbury.com

Bloomsbury Publishing, London, New York and Berlin

A CIP catalogue record for this book is available from the British Library

ISBN 978 0 7475 9647 9

10 9 8 7 6 5 4 3

Typeset by Hewer Text UK Ltd, Edinburgh
Printed in Great Britain by Clays Ltd, St Ives plc

All papers used by Bloomsbury Publishing are natural, recyclable products made from
wood grown in well-managed forests. The manufacturing processes conform to the
environmental regulations of the country of origin.

For Francie,
who will remember it all differently

MY EARLY LIFE AND OTHER MISTAKES

Finally in Florence in 1904, I hit upon the right way to do an Autobiography: start it at no particular time of your life; wander at your free will all over your life; talk only about the thing which interests you for the moment; drop it the moment its interest threatens to pale, and turn your talk upon the new and more interesting thing that has intruded itself into your mind meantime.

Mark Twain

Actually it may not be the right way at all. It seems a bit confusing, not to say self-indulgent. But it is the way I have fallen into, and so I am quoting Mark Twain to show I am not the only one. At least if I jump about like this, I cannot pretend to be growing as a person. In fact there is not much evidence of personal growth here at all. On the contrary, I feel more like Rupert Bear in the strip that ran for ever in the old *Daily Express*: always exactly the same in his bright red jumper and matching yellow-and-black check scarf and trousers as he bumps into a succession of magicians, pirates, manikins and greedy princesses. I probably have quite a bit in common with the anxious, impatient little bear. Unlike Rupert's adventures, though, my unsporting sketches will not be told in rhyme. There is always something to be thankful for.

F. M.

CONTENTS

An ill-advised adviser – The Falklands – Ian Gow and
Dr Bodkin Adams – The geography of Number Ten –
Back stairs and their uses – The intolerable Alfred
Sherman – Whitelaw's gloom – The Family Policy
Group and other leaks – Bombing in Cabinet – Ridley's
secret plan – Mrs Thatcher and the Redoxon – Jeffrey
Archer's joke – The speechwriting team – The hole in
the manifesto – Ascot and the election date – The
Parkinson Affair – My autumn of discontent – The
leaving party – Dinner at the Metropole – 'We should
have gone on'

LAST SEPTEMBER

I HAVE A KEY or think I have. But the door is unlocked. In fact it yields to a push (the tongue of the latch is worn away so it won't shut unless you slam it). The hall inside is as dark as ever. I can feel the brown lino bend under my feet as if my feet were bare. In the dining room beyond the hall the light is faint, almost silvery, just-before-dawn light, but it is enough to see the dust over everything. As far as I can make out, nothing has changed. The oval mahogany table is still too big for the room and you have to squeeze behind the chairs to get round it. On the cheap sky-blue sideboard – a strange colour, nobody else had a sky-blue sideboard – there still sits the ugly silver cup, a little tarnished now, for the Wylye Valley Hunt Members Race that my father won on the big dark horse originally called Shaggy Boy, which for some reason he had rechristened Colonel Overdraft. There were only three horses in the race, and I don't think the others made it to the finish in the heavy going, but hadn't he popped the cup years ago? Over the sideboard hangs the picture of *Vesuvius by Day* – 'Eruzione de 2 Gennaio 1839' it says underneath – with the fishermen hauling in their nets not stopping to look at the lava trickling down the mountainside. *Vesuvius by Night* (same *eruzione*) hung the other side of the room but I don't stop to look at it. I unlatch the old flimsy door to the steep stairs. They are so steep that when my father fell up them as he did later on with distressing frequency he still seemed to be standing more or less upright.

At the top of the stairs there is the passage leading to our rooms, my sister's and mine. But instead I turn right on the landing, sharp right, back on my tracks, and open the door at the end. The light is silvery in here too but a little duskier than in the dining room, so at first all I can see is the curved glass top of the dressing table with the hairbrushes and jars of Pond's cold cream and I can hardly make out the shape of the big double bed with the rose brocade counterpane.

Then I see that there is someone in the bed and I see that it is my mother. And she turns towards me and raises her head so that her long tawny-gold hair falls across the pillow and she says, quite coolly but with the hint of amusement which is her standard way of speaking: 'Oh there you are. I've been in France. I'll see you in the morning.' And she opens her arms to me and I – but I don't know what I do because that is where it stops and even as she is speaking I know that I shall not see her in the morning.

That is the dream I have towards the end of April 2005. I am sixty-five years old and my mother has been dead for nearly fifty years. I have other dreams too, roughly once or twice a year. Sometimes I meet her, by arrangement I think, in a teashop which appears to be in some out-of-the-way seaside resort, though the teashop itself is just like the House of Steps in Salisbury where my mother and I meet her sister, my aunt Pansy, after I have been to the dentist next door. Mr Robson's surgery is a few yards short of the gateway to the Cathedral Close and when I lean back in the chair for the injection before yet another lot of fillings I can see the spire of the cathedral above the hedge at the end of his garden. Or I can turn my gaze a fraction sideways and look at the photos on the bookcase of Mr Robson's two fair-haired freckled children Peter and Susan who don't look at all like him because they are adopted and I wonder what it must be like to be adopted. It is always a relief when Mr Robson has finished with me and we can go next door and have scones and strawberry jam and watch Aunt Pansy put the next cigarette in her amber holder before continuing with her latest topic which is usually something to do with Dickens, like bus services in Dickens's London (there were dozens of them apparently, with the buses painted in different colours and competing fiercely against each other, which sounds very odd to me and I wonder if she has got it right).

Aunt Pansy is not in my dreams, only my mother, who looks pale and tired and speaks with difficulty. In fact I am not sure I actually hear her speak. It is more as though her words are being reported to me by some invisible third person. She has been away, she says, she had to go away although she did not want to and she is sorry she did. I ask her politely where she has been, but her answer seems rather vague, although I get the impression that again France may be the answer or part of it.

There is another dream too, when I am walking down a leafy street actually in France and I catch sight of my mother at a table on the pavement. She is wearing a pale raincoat and a headscarf. The raincoat looks a little too small for her, so I think it must be her old one, although coats often look too small on her. There is someone else at the table, an inconspicuous tidy sort of man. But I don't think she has run off with him – he seems more to be part of some kind of mission which is what has taken her away. She seems a bit embarrassed to see me, though pleased too. Yet even as I am dreaming this dream, I can feel that this is not really happening and it is too much like an old Hitchcock film I have seen recently.

But the first dream, the one about going home, is not like any film and I wake up exhausted and soaked with sweat when it is over.

The summer I was sixteen my mother took me to Italy – Milan, Florence, Siena. We went at the end of the holidays, the beginning of September, to avoid the worst of the heat. 'Florence can be extremely oppressive in July and August,' I told my mother, who knew that already. She knew a lot of the things I told her, but I had just memorised the entire Blue Guide and I had to tell someone. The other book my head was full of was *Wonders of Italy*, edited by Joseph Fattorusso, or Giuseppe as he called himself on the flyleaf. He also published the book, from his premises at 17 via Vigna Nuova, Florence – even the address was thrilling. I imagined the ancient courtyard hung with bright green vines and the clatter of the type-setters. The book had a black cover embossed with a lattice design and the arms of the Italian cities enclosed in each diamond. I knew those too – the suckling wolf of Rome, the lion of St Mark's, the

pawnbroker's balls of the Medici. I was insufferable. On every page
there were smudgy little passport-sized photos of every worthwhile
sight there was in the country and I was determined to see them all.
The text supplied by J./G. Fattorusso was woodenly translated from
the Italian or perhaps it was wooden to start with: 'Whoever is in
quest of health has at his disposal all kinds of summer and winter
resort, all kinds of mineral springs besides the charm of pleasant
surroundings. Little wonder therefore if Italy has been called the Land
of Wonder.' But who cared about the text? It was the pictures I
squinted at for hours on end, then plotted our preambles so that we
should not miss a single cloister or Madonna.

We sit on the hard green couchettes, folded back into the wall
after our restless night. The sky is already bright blue and there are
the first cypresses and the orange roofs and the classical belltowers. I
stare out of the window with my long bony nose pressed against the
misty pane, and the sour train-taste in my mouth and my eyes
watering with the effort of taking it all in. And there opposite me is
my mother slowly brushing out her long tawny-blonde hair with her
cheap pink hairbrush and looking at me with that amused, sidelong
look. It is years after this fresh September morning that someone of
her age says to me (I cannot now remember who it was), 'I always
found your mother's squint so attractive.' Is what she had a squint or
a cast in the eye, I wonder, or do they come to the same thing?
Frances Partridge, the last of the Bloomsberries, writes in her diary in
1949 when my mother is in her mid-thirties, 'Julia has the Pakenham
bloom and charm, and the soft husky lisping voice. She is in fact very
pretty in spite of having an outward squint, so that one of her eyes
seems to be flinging itself skywards in amazement or abandon while
the other looks straight at you. The effect is quite fascinating in a
curious way, like a permanent gesture.' I never notice any of this,
that is just how my mother looks, amused, faintly conspiratorial and
encouraging, as though any moment I too will see the joke which so
far only she is on to.

She is tall and plump. She laughs when she is described as
Junoesque because she knows perfectly well that what they mean
is fat. Like all her siblings except her eldest sister Pansy, she is large-
boned and not naturally graceful. 'Pakenhams have no spring' is one

of her pronouncements about her family. 'Pakenhams are too odd to get into Parliament' is another. So far both claims have proved correct. She has always been that shape. I have seen her in photographs as a schoolgirl and then at Oxford and she looks just as she does now in September 1955. The novelist Barbara Pym was at Somerville with her and wrote in her diary for 27 January 1934: 'In the afternoon I went shopping by myself. I saw Julia Pakenham looking superb in a turquoise blue frock and new halo hat. She was wearing a fur coat, so one couldn't see how fat she was.' I like to think of my mother swinging along the High Street or more probably the Cornmarket where the clothes shops are, dolled up in her turquoise frock and halo hat with her fur coat flapping (otherwise how could Barbara Pym have seen the frock?).

That summer Barbara Pym, then aged twenty-one, began to write a novel featuring her sister Hilary and herself as spinsters in their fifties – an odd project and oddly prescient, for they were to live together spinsterly most of their lives except for the period when Hilary was married. The novel's publishing history is as odd as its subject matter. It was rejected by Chatto and Gollancz, at first accepted then rejected by Jonathan Cape, then put aside and revised after the war, and finally accepted again by Cape and published in 1950. It was called *Some Tame Gazelle*, and it is the only one of her novels whose characters were drawn directly from life. My mother features as Lady Clara Boulding. I hoped that Barbara Pym's sharp eye would tell me something about my mother at the age of twenty-one. But the book turns out to be a sprightly spoof. The two sisters, Harriet and Belinda, spend their time knitting their own underwear and spooning over the local clergymen, while Lady Clara has only a walk-on part as a stately widow who finds solace in opening the village garden party.

I am sure my mother would not have minded if she had lived to read Barbara Pym's diaries. I would like to ask her what she thought of Barbara who in her photographs looks not totally unlike my mother – or perhaps that is just the period look, the way the hair flops, the cut of the jacket – but that too is not possible.

What I do have is a photograph of the 1934 New College Commem Ball where my mother is trying the fur-coat strategy again. Although the ball is being held in high summer, on 22 June, there she

is in the front row with a dark fur cape thrown around her shoulders. None of the other fifty girls in the picture is wearing anything of the sort, so it is clearly not the fashion. My mother is sitting in a characteristic half-turned posture with her eyes shying away from the camera. I am not sure whether she is genuinely nervous or half flirting with the lens. Next to her is a young man in spectacles who appears almost equally ill at ease. He is dark, a little plump, owlish, certainly not handsome, and looks as if he would much rather be somewhere else. This impression, like my mother's shy look perhaps, is misleading. Isaiah Berlin loves parties and gossip and intrigue and is already a legend for these qualities as well as for his intellectual brilliance. After taking my mother out, he sends her little notes datelined 'All Souls 2 a.m.', going over the events of the evening and embroidering the points of interest. The dateline suggests that he cannot get to sleep for thinking of her, but he does not actually say anything of the sort because he is shy with girls and adopts a certain formality of address – addressing them as Miss so-and-so, partly as a joke and partly as a kind of protection.

My mother is just taking her finals at the time and to her chagrin is placed along with the dregs in the third class. Isaiah, or Shaya as everyone calls him then, writes to her in a state of high indignation:

49 Hollycroft Avenue, Hampstead, NW3
August 1st
Dear Lady J (you don't, I hope, mind this slightly Regency style of address?)

I want principally to express my horror, amazement and sympathetic indignation at the act of the PPE examiners. I approached Mr Sumner, whom I met shortly after seeing the *Times*, and succeeded in giving him a very considerable sense of guilt: he admitted that were he to have had his time again he w'd have acted differently perhaps, and pleaded weakly that the enormous brilliance of a certain Hitch, of Worcester College, I am told, blinded him to your merits. To show some independence of judgment he asked if I knew a Miss R. Walker? I did? He thought she was in some respects the most interesting person in the whole examination, yes, including his colleagues; (will you be kind and pass this on to the relevant quarter? please).

I am sure that my mother is grateful to Isaiah for taking up her cause with the austere and scholarly Balliol historian Humphrey Sumner and forcing him to concede that perhaps she ought to have been awarded a second. Sumner is later to become a distinguished Warden of All Souls, to be succeeded in turn by the mischievous and altogether more lightweight John Sparrow – which occasions Maurice Bowra's wisecrack 'One Sparrow does not make a Sumner' – so his approval is certainly worth having. But I wonder how pleased she is at having to pass on Sumner's rare gush to her great friend Rachel Walker, always known as Tips.

There is another photo of the New College Commem, this time showing only their party of ten rather than the entire company. In this one Isaiah is again posing as the alienated foreign intellectual with his index finger stroking his chin in *Penseur* mode. Tips is next to my mother, looking sidelong at the camera with her sharp pointed face. I see that she too has a fur cape round her shoulders, a white one, so perhaps they have made a pact about this, or perhaps it is just chilly at 5 a.m. when these photos are taken. She is already visiting Isaiah's rooms in All Souls for philosophy tutorials, and after she graduates and goes to Paris to continue her studies, principally of logic, she writes letters of increasingly violent passion to her 'darling, darling Shaya'.

Tips writes to my mother too, from chez Mme Fuchs, 7bis rue Cassini. It is a peculiar letter, brilliant in passages but visibly disordered and shaken by the passions passing through her. The letter starts abruptly, without a Dear Julia, by saying how funny she thinks the letter she is enclosing from Nest, my mother's old schoolmate, now at home in Chepstow and writing to tell Tips of her engagement to someone called Storky who is in the Army. It is comically ponderous, Nest's letter, but somehow sending it all the way back to England for my mother to laugh at is a little chilling. 'I wish awfully you were here,' Tips goes on, 'for on the terrace at St Germain there is a fair with a round-about (not too violent) that swings out over the view to the tune of the Gold and Silver waltz. I went on it for two hours solidly with Jacqueline trying to soothe my nerves after a scene with M. Cavaillès when I had said finally that I wouldn't and he had broken a chair and most of the things in my hand bag and produced a pistol, a frightening dark bulbous little thing, oh so little. I HATE SCENES.'

Jean Cavaillès is her philosophy tutor. He is later to become a Resistance hero and is shot in 1944 by the Gestapo, rather than shooting himself or indeed Tips after she rejects his proposal of marriage. She writes to another friend that 'I love him but he is austere and mathematic to the point of frightening away all of me that Shaya stimulated.'

Isaiah ends the letter to my mother by saying that he hears she is going to Salzburg and hopes she will be there on the 23rd because he may be passing through on his way to Palestine to hear a Toscanini concert and will attempt to give her lunch. The trip to Palestine is his first of many and he says marks a turning point in his life, particularly in his attitude to his Jewishness. But the Toscanini concert is important to him too. In a letter to his parents he describes it as 'the greatest experience of my whole life'. He has kept the stop-over in Salzburg secret from his parents until after he is safely out of Nazi territory, because he thinks they might have worried. My mother is indeed in Salzburg on the 23rd because he describes her to his parents as 'making me an ovation when I arrived'. Presumably she goes to the concert with him but it is unlikely to be the greatest experience in her life too because she is as near tone-deaf as I am. Music means almost nothing to her. We do have a radiogram, a huge thing as big as a wardrobe which was left behind by a young officer stationed near us just before D-Day from which he never returned to reclaim it. But we only have about half-a-dozen records, viz. Peter Pears singing 'The Foggy, Foggy Dew', Paul Robeson singing 'Old Man River' and 'Swing Low, Sweet Chariot', Heddle Nash's version of 'Il Mio Tesoro', Doris Day's 'Buttons and Bows', the ballet music from *Rosamunde*, and Frank Sinatra belting out 'Sunflower'. When in my first term in College at Eton I have to perform standing on an old round table at Chamber Singing, as all the new boys in this scholars' hothouse have to, it is 'Buttons and Bows' I sing in my tuneless monotone because I know no other popular song. The music aside, though, a memorable experience it must have been to sit next to a transported Isaiah with the stormtroopers in the streets and probably in the concert hall too, listening just as rapturously as he is to the programme – Mozart, Brahms and Beethoven.

After Salzburg, while Isaiah goes off to Palestine my mother goes on to Vienna where she meets Tips and then on to Budapest. They photograph each other looking out of their hotel window. With the light flooding in on them they look quite fancy-free as if their lives had only just started and they might go anywhere and do anything. When Tips returns to Paris, her letters become odder still. There is a strange note of exaltation that alarms her friends. Isaiah flies over to Paris to see her. She takes him for a walk in the Zoological Gardens, and to his horror proposes to him. He is agonised by the ordeal of extricating himself. In fact he is so stricken that he never gets this close to a woman for the next ten years. But it is doubtful how serious Tips is about either of her admirers, because even before Isaiah comes to Paris she gaily declares to another friend, 'Whisk hey and with a pirouette I discard them both and stay free. Genius is within me and for its burning alone I stay.'

But sadly other things are burning in her too. She goes home, becomes seriously depressed, flies into violent rages, attacks her widowed mother, and then is hospitalised for most of her long life (she lives until she is nearly eighty), enduring first electric-shock

treatment and then a lobotomy, which reduces her to a near-vegetable state. It is hard to get out of one's mind the picture of the elegant, sharp-faced girl who has so captivated the cleverest men in Oxford and Paris swinging out high over the terrace at St Germain with the whole of Paris spread out beneath her.

My mother really likes Austria and southern Germany, and the German language too, which she went to Munich to study before going to Oxford, fancying that she might do modern languages, though in the event she reads Politics, Philosophy and Economics – which turns out to be a mistake, one which I am to repeat thirty years later. Her sister Violet joins her in Munich and they do the Okto-berfest and watch the prostitutes touting within yards of Hitler's Brown House. My mother goes skiing at St Anton too, with her friends Ralph and Coney Jarvis, and Boofy Gore and his fiancée Fiona Colquhoun. Boofy is like a character out of P. G. Wodehouse, Pongo Twistleton to be precise, who works his way up from being a mere younger son to become the irrepressible Earl of Ickenham, 'one of the hottest earls that ever donned a coronet'. In the 1960s I often see Boofy (I never discover his proper name), now the Earl of Arran, and now an elderly clubman with a puce face and a carnation in his buttonhole, trotting around Fleet Street where he earns a crust as a sprightly columnist for the *Evening News*. In the House of Lords he pilots through two famous bills, one to protect badgers, the other to protect homosexuals. So he alters the ecology of Britain more than many a sober and solemn citizen. After the war Ralph Jarvis inherits the great house of Doddington Hall, Lincs, and lays down wild gardens and avenues of old roses which he breeds, and sweeps away the sombre evergreens the Victorians

planted and restores the house and its policies to a glory that its Elizabethan creators would have appreciated. So he also impacts on the ecology.

Also on the skiing trip, dwarfing the elfin Boofy, is a young man of six foot four with buck teeth and hair like an ocean wave, who is probably meant to be my mother's partner. This is Donald Maclean who has just joined the Foreign Office. A year earlier he also joined the NKVD, the forerunner of the KGB. After the war he is stationed in Washington where he has access to the secrets of the atom bomb

which he passes to his Soviet handlers. So he too has quite an impact on the ecology.

Donald Maclean gets very drunk on the skiing trip, though not nearly as drunk as he gets after the war. My mother knows that Maclean is a Communist. There is no mystery about it. Nobody thinks it at all odd that he should be enjoying the après-ski life at St Anton. Quite a few of my mother's friends are Communists, like her Oxford friends Sheila and Maire Lynd (Maire, also known as B.J. or Baby Junior, is the dark girl next to my mother in the picture of the New College Commem) and the equally drunk but much more delightful Philip Toynbee, but virtually none of them, except for the occasional Mitford, has anything resembling a soft spot for Hitler. Certainly my mother doesn't, though her political opinions remain unvoiced. But she loves *Eiskaffee* and baroque architecture and German poetry. She even tries to teach me a little German as well as French, and we struggle through the opening passages of Gustav Freytag's novel *Soll und Haben*. I don't make much headway but the taste does come back to me later on.

Isaiah writes my mother at least one more letter, four years later, when she gets engaged. It is a marvellously convoluted affair, in which he gets diverted from his opening theme, which is his tardiness in writing to congratulate her, by a sudden parenthetical spasm of loathing for Henry James and his world (or works, the precise minuscule hand is not always easy to read). Anyway he says her new name seems to him 'gay and very distinguished' and he wishes to give her a gay and distinguished wedding present and what would she like. But what touches me is the postscript which is scrawled across the All Souls letterhead because there is no room on the other side of the page: 'If you ever have a son, will you send him to Eton and New College and let me send courtly messages to you by him? I have a clear, rather attractive concept of that, a quarter of a century or so hence.' Parts of that concept do turn into reality twenty-five years later, others sadly do not.

My mother is, I think, extraordinarily happy at Oxford, happy to join in the babble of clever young people, happy to be courted for the first time. It is a further stage on the liberation trail, after the restrictions of her girls' boarding school, St Margaret's Bushey, Herts.

SMB is a sound academic establishment, founded to cater for the orphan children of indigent clergymen. By the time my mother goes there, the clergy orphans are easily outnumbered by the children of the well-to-do and even the fashionable, such as Clementine Mitford and her cousin Unity. My mother likes SMB too, glad of proper sustained teaching after the erratic input of a succession of governesses. She and her sister Violet have implored their mother to be allowed to go away to school, unlike their elder sisters. This is a minor triumph, making them the first women in their family to go to school, just as my mother is the first to take a university degree (women were only admitted to degrees at Oxford a few years before she goes to Somerville). 'You have gone where no Pakenham woman has gone before,' booms her aunt Georgie Gough when she graduates, although my mother would have preferred to have gone a little bit further, like into the second class. Anyway she enjoys SMB enough to send my sister there, who twenty-five years later finds a large tapestry by J. Pakenham still hanging in the school hall where they held the concert at which my mother insisted on reciting, with her fair hair streaming down her pink cheeks, James Elroy Flecker's 'War Song of the Saracens':

> We are they who come faster than Fate; we are they who ride early or
>   late;
> We storm at your ivory gate; pale Kings of the Sunset beware!

The next performer opted for 'Christopher Robin had squeezles and wheezles'.

My mother even goes back to SMB after she is married, in 1938, for the Christmas sale which is always held in the first week of December. She is accompanied by Unity Mitford whom she grew quite fond of when they were taken swimming together as children. Unity, or Bobo as she is known in the family, is a year younger than my mother. The Mitfords are near neighbours in Oxfordshire and even more so in London; they live at 26 Rutland Gate, the Pakenhams at Number 12. Unity has not lasted long at SMB, being sacked after a year, she claims for reciting before the entire school plus governors and parents, 'A garden is a lovesome thing, God wot rot.' In fact this seems to be

WEDDING GUESTS

Miss Clementine Mitford, her cousin the Hon.
Unity Mitford, and Lady Julia Pakenham
leaving 21 Arlington Street after attending the
Campbell-Ormsby-Gore wedding reception.
Lady Julia Pakenham, Lord Longford's youngest
sister, put the final polish on her education at
Somerville College, Oxford, and took a B.A.
degree.

apocryphal, as does her father Lord Redesdale's parthian shot after the expulsion to the headmistress, the formidable Miss Boys: 'Madam, your shape suggests a measure of self-indulgence totally unsuited to the religious position you pretend to hold.' Another version of the expulsion is that Unity has sent Miss Boys a coffin full of lilies. This seems to be apocryphal too. In fact she is just one of those girls who cannot see a school rule without breaking it.

This quality is fully operational during her visit with my mother, who sees to her horror that Unity is wearing a swastika in her lapel. She is also wearing the old SMB badge to which she is not entitled. When they get to the school, she is asked to remove both. In the train back to London, Unity announces, 'I want to have a lot of sons for cannon fodder.' Julia, outraged, retorts, 'I expect you'll only have one and die in childbirth.' It is commonly believed by the Pakenhams that the Mitfords will cry if you say something rough to them, and Unity now begins to cry, sobbing, 'I don't think I shall, I've got very wide hips.' Julia replies, 'That doesn't count, the outside measurements don't count.' As it happens, she is already two months pregnant with me.

For my mother, life at SMB is a good deal livelier than back home in Rutland Gate. This is mainly because my grandmother is an invalid who has suffered ill-health most of her life. As a young woman, she permanently damaged her knee after falling over a dustpan and brush left in a passage by a housemaid. She never walks far without a stick or crutch. She is also so crippled with arthritis that she cannot play games with her children, which is deeply frustrating to her, as she is sporty rather than intellectual by nature. Ironically she becomes a spoilsport, always anxious about propriety or health and quick to put a stop to any fun. She is only really at ease with babies and small children, which is perhaps why she has so many of them.

Now most of her children are grown up and she is dying of colon cancer and spends most of her time lying on a chaise-longue. She has had the tumour removed and her colon joined up again, but the cancer has already spread and there is little they can do for her. This is a particularly unfortunate complaint for a woman who is so phenomenally reticent about bodily functions. She conceals all evidence of her illness as best she can, just as she dislikes any mention of nudity or anything indelicate. As the fatal nature of her illness becomes apparent, she sends Julia and Violet, the only children still at home, on a frenzied tour of visits to relations in England, Wales and Ireland, so that they may not have to witness her decline, of which they remain only dimly aware. When she has to go off to a succession of nursing homes for various treatments and operations, she even conceals the address of the nursing home from her own mother (who is much less inhibited, indeed has a remarkably robust attitude to the physical side of life). When she returns from these medical forays, she retreats further into the fortress of her sitting room. Her children have to make appointments to see her. Her illness entrenches her emotional inhibitions too. She devotes much of her remaining strength to devising new methods of keeping out harmful draughts or improving her children's diet. Despite deep, even obsessive love for her children, she finds it harder than ever to express her feelings by word or gesture. No doubt partly as a result, her family never learn how to embrace, at least not in public, with any semblance of affection or enthusiasm. The day at 12 Rutland Gate begins at the breakfast table with what Violet calls 'the crash of skull against skull which passed for a morning kiss in my family'.

My grandmother dies in the November of my mother's last year at Oxford. Four days before her death she writes to Somerville in a quavering hand, enclosing a receipt which she thinks my mother might need and enquiring whether she has yet come to terms with her spectacles and recommending frequent wiping with a soft cloth – anxious to the last, desperate to omit no precaution. All this may well be why my mother, who is a mark-grubber like me, does so badly in her finals. Certainly her tutor Lucy Sutherland, later to become a

much-loved principal of Lady Margaret Hall, thinks so. She writes a
sweet note hazarding that 'all the disturbances of your last year did it
and I wished your luck had helped a little, as the result would have
been more accurate'. A slightly curious phrase, the one about your
luck, but a good one. Luck never is my mother's strong suit.

But it is the shadow of an earlier death that hangs over Rutland
Gate, a shadow that never quite leaves my mother and her brothers
and sisters. She is the youngest of six, she and her sister Violet being
known as the Babies, because of the four-and-a-half-year gap after the
birth of their elder sister Mary. Their father is a professional soldier,
now a brigadier and nearly fifty when my mother is born. She is only
sixteen months old when he comes up to the nursery in the spring of
1915 to say goodbye to his children before going off to Gallipoli. At
first she is frightened by this big bald untidy man – he is said to be the
worst-dressed man in Ireland or England, whichever country he
happens to be in. He has already been away a lot since the outbreak of
the war and so is pretty much a stranger to her. But then just as he is
going, she relents and warms to him and kisses him goodbye and he
turns back from the open door to answer her. The next day he writes
a note to her from his barracks in Norfolk in his bold careless
Edwardian hand (or is he writing in such large letters because he
is writing to a small child?):

April 7 1915
Dear Julia,
    Good bye till we meet again, when I hope you will not be
frightened by me.
Your loving Dada
Longford

He used to command the 2nd Life Guards but now he has a
Yeomanry Brigade, the 2nd South Midland Mounted. For four
months they sit in Cairo with their ten thousand horses, waiting
for instructions from General Sir Ian Hamilton in his yacht moored in
Suvla Bay. The Australians and New Zealanders who led the invasion
have scarcely managed to shift from the scrubby little beach that is to
be immortalised as Anzac Cove. Every time General Monash has

them scamper up the sandy crumbling cliffs, the Turks safely entrenched on the heights above mow them down. The only answer is to open up a second front to the north across the salt lake which will be dry by the summer. That is a job for infantry. So the ten thousand horses are to be left behind in Cairo and Longford is given barely a fortnight to turn his cavalry into footsoldiers. The no-longer-mounted brigade sails across the wine-dark sea past the plains of Ilium. In the distance Longford can just see the small mound that is now believed to be the site of old Troy. There is a Turkish machine-gun post on the top of Priam's citadel. They come ashore a little south of where Lord Byron swam the Hellespont. Longford's head is full of allusions – he read classics at New College and keeps them up when he is campaigning. But he is under no illusions as soon as he sees the terrain: the great glittering expanse of salt lake with the line of pine woods on the hills beyond and the Turks dug in all along the horizon.

Just after landing, he is talking to his second-in-command Fred Cripps, an irrepressible boulevardier, very different from his brother, the future Chancellor of the Exchequer Sir Stafford. At this moment a shell comes over rather close, blowing up a wagon behind them. Cripps ducks. Longford doesn't move except to turn to him and say, 'What on earth are you doing, Fred, are you frightened?' Yes, says Cripps. 'Please,' says Longford, 'even if you are, try not to show it quite so obviously to the men.'

Two days later they are ordered to advance. After briefing his officers, Longford beckons to Fred and says quietly, 'I wanted to say goodbye to you, as we shall both inevitably be killed this afternoon.' At 4 p.m., much later than they had planned, they set off across the plain. In the spring the lake is a shimmering mirror and the grass round it is carpeted with anemones and dwarf irises but now the whole place is a crusty white expanse, quite pitiless and barren. Almost immediately they are deafened by the enemy fire across the entire front. The firing is so fierce that bullet meets bullet in the air, forming little squashed shrapnel crosses as they hit the ground. Longford carries a map in one hand and a walking stick in the other. They manage to get across to the scant shelter of a bluff known as Chocolate Hill. The white dust on their boots turns to heavy cocoa-coloured mud. They pause to regroup and look to the dead and wounded. Cripps is hit in the leg and cannot move. As the Westminster Dragoons come up alongside, a Lieutenant Ferguson hands over his troop and picks up Cripps. They stagger up arm in arm through the blizzard of bullets and shells. When they are in the lee of the hill, Cripps takes out his cigar case and lights a huge Corona. The men around him let out a cheer. Longford presses on towards the Turkish outpost on Scimitar Hill twelve hundred yards away. By now dusk is gathering and a thick mist, unusual for August, mingles with the smoke. They blunder on through the scorched gorse until they reach the Turkish trenches and see the Turks scrambling out of them. But they are still under constant fire from the communication trenches. And as they stumble out of one trench and into the next, they are easily picked off. When he hauls himself out of the last trench, in the mist and the smoke and darkness Longford is killed. So are twenty-one of his twenty-eight officers and all his staff. Fred Cripps survives another sixty years.

The regimental history calls the action at Scimitar Hill 'the most costly in proportion to its size, the least successful of all the Gallipoli battles'. In his apologia disguised as a history of the Great War, Churchill puts it more grandly: 'The British losses were heavy and fruitless. On this dark battlefield of fog and flame, Brigadier-General Lord Longford, Brigadier-General Kenna VC, Colonel Sir John Milbanke VC, and other paladins fell.' The resonance of these phrases did not save him from my grandmother's fury. Like thousands of others bereaved by the venture, she never forgave him.

Longford's body remains where he fell, too close to the Turkish guns to be recovered. The corpses remain *in situ* for three years until the Armistice. To help identify his body, Longford has his coat of arms and his family motto – *Gloria Virtutis Umbra* – tattooed on his chest. So there he lies with his map, slightly out of date (nobody in the War Office expects to be going to Gallipoli), and his Irish blackthorn stick and his pale blazoned chest: quarterly or and gules, in the first quarter an eagle displayed vert for Pakenham. But by the time they come to look for the bodies the muddy craters are overgrown with camel thorn, thyme, saltbush and myrtle, and even those bodies they do discover are only skeletons. Of the 3,000 tombstones in the cemetery on Scimitar Hill, 2,400 including Longford's are inscribed 'believed to be buried in this cemetery'.

For nearly a year he is listed as missing in action. My grandmother persists in thinking that he may have been taken prisoner. She even calls on her daughter Mary to write to him, in the belief that somehow a letter from a child will get through. But the letter is sent back. It is not until the following July that she gathers her children together and tells them he is dead. A memorial service is held in St Mary's Bryanston Square. Among the hymns she chooses is 'Within the Churchyard, Side by Side', not known to me but popular at the time for sad occasions. The hymn is one of those composed for the young by the Victorian hymn-writer Mrs C. F. Alexander, who wrote 'All Things Bright and Beautiful'. It used to be in *Hymns Ancient and Modern*, but has been excluded from recent editions, on grounds of sentimentality I imagine. Thomas Hardy might have done something with the theme, but Mrs Alexander is off form here:

> They do not hear when the great bell
> Is ringing overhead;
> They cannot rise and come to Church
> For they are dead.

Besides, the words do not meet the case in hand, because my grandfather is not lying within any churchyard. So with that resourcefulness with which she sometimes startles her children, my grandmother composes an extra verse:

> And those who die away from home
> Their graves we may not see
> But we believe God keeps their souls
> Where'er their bodies be.

As though in obedience to her own lines, she refuses to visit the site of her husband's death for nearly a decade. Then in 1925 she sets out with a friend, gets as far as Istanbul, but cannot face it and turns back. The next year, accompanied by her daughter Mary, she makes it. I still have my grandfather's little Army prayer book, bound in khaki cloth with a gold Union Jack embossed on the front. It is small enough to fit into a battledress pocket, but he cannot be carrying it as he walks up

Scimitar Hill or I would not have it now. Inside it is inscribed in my
grandfather's hand (more minuscule than his farewell message to my
mother): 'Longford 2nd Mtd Bde Oct 26 1914' and underneath in my
grandmother's more spidery writing 'Returned from the Dardanelles
1916' – with his other kit presumably – and underneath again
'Revisited Dardanelles September 4th 1926.'

Her numerous brothers and sisters and brothers and sisters-in-law
do their best to comfort and support the shattered family. At
Christmas 1915, my grandfather's sister Aunt Georgie sends them
a rhyme of her own composition:

> 'With apologies to the Author of Ten Little Nigger Boys'
> Six Pakenham children
> All in a row,
> 'Are they down-hearted?'
> Oh dear no!

Then follow six more stanzas, each more excruciating than the last,
describing the children in order of age, ending with my mother:

> *Six* One last, not least,
> Another Pakenham daughter,
> Fat fresh and pink and fair
> Full of smiles and laughter.

I do not imagine it did much to cheer them up. It is poor stuff even for
an aunt of the period. At least my mother is too young to mind the
seemingly obligatory reference to her being fat.

We are booked into the Albergo Porta Rossa which the guidebook
says is the oldest working hotel in the city, for all I know the oldest
working hotel in the world, although it does not work very well.
Stendhal, Byron, Goethe, Dickens, George Sand and Alfred de
Musset all stayed there and now we are staying there too. It is a tall
cavernous prison-like building in a grim dark street, the via Porta
Rossa, as dark and shabby as *Wonders of Italy*, which only adds to its
enchantment. The hotel, or *albergo* (I ask my mother the difference

and she is slightly miffed because she doesn't know the answer and in her quiet way she is a bit of a know-all like me), is dark and shabby inside too and the plumbing makes clanking noises all night and the coffee has a taste which is not exactly burnt, more as though some small animal has died in it. The room we are sharing is also dark and cavernous, which is just as well because my mother and I are both physically modest, almost obsessively so. When she is a debutante, although she and Violet have both read a copy of *Lady Chatterley's Lover* smuggled in from abroad, my mother will not allow Violet in the room when she is dressing, even though she needs help in fixing the green-lined train to the white net dress in which she is to be presented at Buckingham Palace. Her mother has passed this modesty on to her, and now she has passed it on to me, so we dress and undress in semi-darkness with our backs turned to each other. Only now and then I inadvertently catch a glimpse of pale flesh in the umbrous light and hear the silky slither of her undressing, or the pop of a suspender.

I had no part in the choosing of the hotel, although I would certainly have chosen it if I had known it was so old and so full of celebrity links. My mother has chosen it because it is the cheapest of the decent hotels, which is also why we are sharing a room. I know that at the age of sixteen I ought to complain about this but I don't really mind at all, because in an embarrassed muddled way I am very pleased to be going on this trip alone with my mother. Being away at boarding school so much makes it hard to re-establish our old intimacy even in the holidays. In any case I am delighted to be going. In fact I was amazed when my mother suggested the trip in the first place, because I did not think we could afford such an excursion.

Is this why my father has not come with us, to save money? Or is it because he does not like rubbernecking round museums? I do not dream of asking the question. There are too many questions I do not dream of asking. Some will, literally, come back to haunt me. There are people who talk about the unanswered questions in their lives. I never get as far as asking them. If there is one quality I envy in other people, apart from the usual ones like a beautiful singing voice or effortless virility, it is having the free-springing impulse to ask questions: 'Why have you done that?' 'What do you really feel?'

'What do you want?' I would have got so much further into life, and got more out of it, if I had only known how to ask.

My mother isn't one for asking too many questions either. A couple of years after her sister Pansy marries the painter Henry Lamb they take her over to lunch at Fordingbridge with Augustus and Dorelia John. Augustus is Uncle Henry's oldest painter-friend, though much more famous, in fact then probably the most famous painter in England, which can't have made things any easier when Uncle Henry had his long affair with Dorelia. As they go into lunch, my mother finds herself next to a little man she has not met before. Oddly for such a famously bohemian household there are name-cards set out in each place at the dining table and the little man remarks to my mother:

'I wonder whether they have put Shaw on my card.'

'Why do you wonder that?'

'Because I have several names.'

'Oh have you?' my mother says and lets the matter drop. This is her only meeting with Lawrence of Arabia, who is then in the RAF and going around as Aircraftsman Shaw. As far as my mother is concerned, Shaw he would remain, except that on the way home over the downs Uncle Henry, who does not care for show-offs, says how much he dislikes that fellow Lawrence.

One question I would like to know the answer to is how do my parents live? Neither of them works, nor ever has done, as far as I can see, at least not in any sustained way. After taking a fourth at Oxford, in military history (both the course and the class no longer obtainable), my father was put into a merchant bank called Brown Shipley, a company long since assimilated into larger, more voracious banks (Ted Heath worked there for a time before it was swallowed up). 'Put into it' is, I think, the right phrase, suggesting fairly forcible intro-mission. He managed to pop out again soon enough, and I do not think was gainfully employed until he joined up just before the war and for two or three years had his Army pay until he was invalided out with TB. After the war he managed to keep a clean sheet as far as employment was concerned, although he did write a few articles for *Punch* when Malcolm Muggeridge was editing it before he became a television star and a born-again Catholic. Yet the family trusts on which they survived, their shares of marriage settlements made for their mothers, were minuscule – not surprising, since my father was one of three and my mother one of six and neither of the grand-mothers had much to start with. Occasionally ruffling through a pile of old papers I come upon a few lines of my father's handwriting, usually on bits of paper other people don't normally make serious notes on, like the bill from Axtells the butcher or the Carter's seed catalogues. My father's handwriting is unique – at least I have never seen another like it. He almost never joins up the letters and there are flourishes on the descenders – p, g, f, y, j, especially j – while the ascenders, the h's particularly, bristle like spears. At his most casual it looks a bit like Chinese calligraphy. It also takes more time to do than ordinary joined-up writing, and even the letters he has taken trouble over tend to be rather short. His numerals are just as distinctive as his letters and could only be his too, and these stray notes tend to repeat simple sums, going over and over how much money he has left and how much he can hope to leave my sister and me. It is as though he can scarcely believe how little there is and if he does the figures one more time they might come out higher, but the total is never more than £7,000, and in the event when he dies there is barely half that much. His only other known source of income, his disability pension from the War Office – £175 a year when it was first granted in January 1942 after he had been invalided out – has already long ceased. The post-mortem shows that his lungs are in perfect condi-tion, his liver too, which is surprising.

Bills remained unpaid until the last possible moment, and beyond. In the morning the doormat was thick with brown envelopes, mostly stamped REMINDER and FINAL WARNING. Once a bailiff came out from Warminster because my father had not got around to paying the rates. He was a squat man with a moustache and a bowler hat, like Thomson and Thompson in the Tintin books.

'Is your father in?' he asked, peering round the murk of the hall, as though hoping to find him hiding under the table which was the only furniture.

'It's just me here,' I said. 'Would you like to come back later?'

'I'll wait. I'm afraid I'll have to distrain,' he said, looking round the hall again. I had no idea what the word meant, but it sounded painful.

'Would you like to sit down?' I said and fetched a chair from the dining room and he sat there in the gloom, with his bowler hat on his knees, his boots planted on the bendy lino. I looked in on him every now and then, pretending to be passing through the hall on some other errand. I could see no sign of him doing any distraining, but then I did not know what to look for. He just sat there. It seemed an eternity but it was probably less than an hour before my father came back from, I think, the butcher and settled up. The amount involved was £27-something.

My father was lackadaisical about filling in forms too, and, when he got around to it, liked to read them out to the rest of us, as though this was a traditional social activity like charades. He read out the questions from the census, 1951 it must have been, followed by the answers he had given. Against trade or profession he had put 'gentleman', with a snort as he said it, and against source of income he put 'of independent means'. Why don't you put 'inadequate means'? my mother said. But she said it as a joke. I never heard them quarrel about money or suggest ways in which either of them might earn some. If they were unhappy, it was not poverty that made them so, or not directly. Their relative poverty, like their idleness, seemed to come naturally to them.

So just as naturally I was born fretting. My earliest memories are of wanting to get on with things. I was either in a fever of impatience or worrying about what I was going to be impatient about next. When I was eight and nine, I used to take my mother's breakfast up to her, thrusting the spoon into the square blue Earl Grey tin, then jabbing two teaspoonfuls into the cracked Crown Derby teapot with its pretty cornflower pattern, squinting under the grubby old electric grill to make sure the toast wasn't burning, not because I feared my mother's displeasure (she would never be cross about something like that) but because scraping the toast or, worse still, having to make it all again would take up time and I would be late for school – all this done at breakneck speed – then rattling up the steep stairs to her lying under the rose-brocade counterpane. I would stay a minute or two hovering by her bed to accept her thanks and pass the time of day. But even in that brief pause I was already beginning to fret. Why did she always put on a little bit of butter at a time, then a matching smear of marmalade on a corner of the toast, rather than save time by covering the whole surface at once? I am the original time-and-motion freak. In my impatience I do not stop to wonder why my father does not sleep in this bed but dosses down in the dark spare room the other side of the bathroom.

Sometimes, though not often, my mother is already half up when I bring her breakfast. She is sitting in her dressing gown at her glass table with its three mirrors, slowly working Pond's cold cream into her face. The cold cream is almost the only beauty aid she has or needs because her complexion looks after itself, and so I attribute magical qualities to those chunky white jars with their sea-green lids. Now and then she allows me to help her and my stubby little fingers draw white streaks across her warm cheek. When I complain that my skin is chapped, she sits me down at her glass table and rubs cold cream into my face too, and it seems like the coldest feeling in the world as I look into the three mirrors and watch from different angles my mother's strong fingers slowly working on my pink cheeks. The cold cream has a very faint fragrance, like the smell of a rose that hasn't got much scent. It may be that my mother's allegiance to cold cream is not just because she thinks it does her skin good. When she was in her early twenties, Pond's had a long-running publicity campaign which used titled girls as models and endorsers. My aunt Mary got in first and she handed the franchise on to my mother. 'Lady Julia Pakenham says she owes her flawless complexion to Pond's Cold Cream,' and there would be a picture of my mother looking flawless. It was rather well paid and accompanied by a year's supply of free cold cream, which cemented her lifelong loyalty to the product. I am not so keen and find it hard to sit still beside her while she massages the stuff into my flaky cheeks, but then I never like sitting still having things done to me.

Even now I am older and we no longer have these sessions with Pond's cold cream and we are two adults on holiday together I am still anxious. We have been walking all morning and, although my mother is a keen sightseer like me, she is beginning to flag. We are in Santa Maria Novella, the big barn of a church next to the railway station. We have seen the Ghirlandaio frescoes in the Tornabuoni chapel and carefully identified the marvellous portraits of all the scholars and fashionable ladies of the time, we have sorted out the Strozzi chapel, and gawped at the vertiginous Last Judgment by Andrea Orcagna which covers the whole of the altar wall. Finally we have seen the big Masaccio fresco of the Trinity which is deeply satisfying because I can see how it is the first painting to absorb Brunelleschi's system of linear perspective, just as it says in Berenson. My mother thinks the fresco is a bit muddy. She also thinks it is time for lunch.

'We must see the cloisters first,' I say. 'They aren't open in the afternoon.'

'Must we?'

'It's the famous *chiostro verde*, all done in green.'

'I know what *verde* means. There was a nice-looking tratt the other side of the square.'

'The green paintings are by Uccello. I wonder if they are like the ones in the National Gallery.'

'We could always come back tomorrow,' my mother says.

'We shan't be in this part of Florence tomorrow.'

So we pay the extra to get into the green cloister and while my mother is fishing 200 lire out of her scuffed black handbag I look again at the guidebook and see it says that the frescoes are much damaged. Which they are. Adam seems to be climbing out of a scummy bog and it is hard to tell Eve from the Serpent. Round most of the cloister there is a noisy party of French schoolchildren blocking our view. They are as bored as my mother and emit shrill confident cries to make it clear they don't think much of the green cloister or possibly of the Land of Wonder as a whole.

My mother does not bear a grudge against me for dragging her round the green cloister. She does not bear grudges much. Perhaps it would be better if she did, it would give more of a shape to her life, though naturally I do not think this at the time.

'I'll have the mozzarella and tomato,' I say, crunching two grissini at once.

'Didn't you have that yesterday?'

'Never change a winning game.' I am rather proud of this new phrase, which I have recently acquired from Big Bill Tilden's *Tennis A–Z*. The great American player has retired from the game before I start learning it, but some unpleasant miasma still clings to his name. Is it that he sometimes cheats or is nasty to ballboys? It is only after his death that it comes out about the string of catamites he exploits, many of them recruited while ballboys.

My mother has the spaghetti bolognese which I point out she had the day we arrived, so we are quits, but then she is not competitive for the same reason that she does not bear grudges. All her sisters and sisters-in-law write books – biographies, novels and later on memoirs. She says that it is her proudest boast that she never wrote a book; she might even have it put on her tombstone, but she doesn't.

I never choose spaghetti or pasta of any description, although I don't think we use the generic word pasta to describe all those varieties of slimy yellow wriggles which seem to me such a poor apology for food. In School Hall there are three types served up to us – the vermicelli which comes in a soup of sorts, watery and glabrous like some dim species of seaweed, the spaghetti itself which comes chewy and slithery with a sickly tomato sauce, and worst of all macaroni cheese, the vilest of the lot, made of industrial-strength rubber with the cheese sauce so overpowering and nauseating that you can scarcely taste the macaroni, which is no great loss. At teatime where we gang together in our own rooms we never have any of that muck or any of the revolting tinned stuff that they have in other messes – that is the term for these little groups, like messes in the Army. We have boiled eggs, toast and Tiptree's strawberry jam and two or three times a term a Fuller's walnut cake which we have to go over the bridge into Windsor to buy. We fancy ourselves as a discriminating quartet – Hope, Reade, Harrod and I. Francis Hope's parents are donnish Oxford people, though in fact his father Michael makes metal windows in the family firm in Birmingham and Francis claims that his parents already have him booked to marry Harriet Crittall, the heiress to the other great metal-window factory in the Midlands. Years later Hopes and Crittalls do merge (before being taken over and asset-stripped by Slater Walker), but Francis and Harriet do not. Julian Reade's father has a red beard and worked for SOE during the war, though in the 1920s he had been Britain's first Trotskyist. Julian himself is pale and slight with the face of a chilly cherub and he is the only one of us in our year who has divorced parents. His mother is remarried to a dentist and lives somewhere near Sloane Square. The dentist is, I believe, nice to Julian who can be tricky (we have nicknamed him Gloom, although we suspect he is one of those professional Eeyores who conceals an inner cheerfulness). Henry Harrod's father is the famous economist Roy Harrod and his mother Billa is writing the Shell guide to Norfolk and knows more about Norfolk churches than anyone else, even John Betjeman whom she was engaged to briefly, though she says they never went all the way. When I go to stay with Henry in the holidays, she takes us to tiny forgotten churches with round flint towers standing in the middle of cornfields. In her old age, forty years later, she shows the Prince of Wales the same churches, because although he has spent half his life in the county he has never seen any of it except the bit you see while pheasants are being beaten out of a spinney for you to shoot at.

So we all come from intellectual families and think that dentists are comic and that we ourselves are incredibly clever, though the other three of us agree that Francis is the cleverest person we know (we are just turning sixteen now and we have started to use Christian names). He is so clever in fact that he produces an argument to prove that the earth is flat after all and none of us can see the flaw in it. The next evening he tries the argument on his tutor Giles St Aubyn, who cannot pin down the flaw in it either. Giles is languid and charming in a nasal sort of way. He is also rich beyond the dreams of schoolmasters, although he is only the younger son of a lord. He has a flat in Holland Park hung with Piranesi prints which favoured pupils are invited to see. He also owns an island called St Tudwals off the coast of North Wales which even more favoured pupils are invited to visit (I have seen the flat but not the island). But Giles is a historian and so cannot be expected to have geography at his fingertips.

Francis is beaky-nosed with curly black hair and a curling lip. He likes to tell us that in spite of looking very Jewish he is not Jewish at all, which impresses us greatly. Then at the end of one holiday he comes back and announces proudly that he has asked his parents and he is relieved to discover that after all he is Jewish, which impresses us even more. We are not, however, impressed by Michael Yudkin, the son of the famous nutritionist, who is in the year above, because he is so obviously Jewish and has to shave twice a day. We are anti-Semitic in a vague, dismal way, perhaps because we are ignorant of the subject, although we know perfectly well what Hitler did. Most of us are the sons of distinguished people, except for me because my parents are distinguished for not doing anything. Luke Hodgkin's mother is going to win the Nobel Prize for helping to discover the secret of life. Luke is quite capable of winning the Nobel Prize too except he is not a chemist.

'You've started talking again,' my mother says suddenly. 'You were such a talkative little boy and then you went away and when you came back you didn't utter a word.'

'Really, didn't I?' I am completely taken aback by this. I had imagined that I had been talking roughly the same amount ever since I first learned to talk. It is disconcerting to see myself in this new light: silenced by the shock of boarding school, reduced to a near-catatonic state by being separated from my family. The last thing my mother wants to do is upset me. She is simply startled by my rush of school gossip, startled and pleased too.

'I was quite a cheerful little boy then, was I?'

'Yes, you were rather jolly, but proud too, definitely a rather proud child.'

This thought too tickles my self-love, though being proud by nature is nothing to be proud of. It is nice to have discovered a topic that interests us both so much, me for obvious reasons and my mother, I think, because it brings back a time that was nearer the idyll she had hoped for: children playing under the apple trees and my father back from the war.

Her pleasure is contagious, so I carry on babbling and tell her the story of the last school play but one, which was *Julius Caesar*. Calum Robertson, Robertson major, a large, clumsy boy who is both rather popular and liable to teasing, as clumsy boys often are, is playing the part of Pindarus, servant to Cassius. It is an unexacting role. He hardly appears at all until halfway through Act IV when Brutus and Cassius are out of Rome waging war on Mark Antony. Someone comes in to tell Brutus (played by Andrew Sinclair, who looks suitably tough for the part, rather like the Michelangelo bust of Brutus) that Cassius is on his way and says, 'Pindarus is come to do you salutation from his master.' Nothing happens because Calum Robertson has missed his cue and is somewhere down in the bowels of School Hall finishing a snack. So there is this terrible long pause, until finally, brilliantly, Duff Hart-Davis who is playing some other hanger-on of Brutus' says, 'He cometh not, my lord, but here cometh Cassius instead.' And Cassius (played by Bamber Gascoigne, I think, no, he was Mark Antony) has to scurry on half a scene early. 'He cometh not, my lord' becomes a catchphrase which everyone in College starts using.

As I finish this story, I think, how strange, is this perhaps the first anecdote I have told my mother for eight years? Even while I am laughing at my own story, a little tide of sadness trickles in at the thought of what both of us have missed – not my brilliant stories, I mean, but all the conversations that we might have had together. Something like this happens, I suppose, to all mothers whose children go away to boarding school, but the sudden deprivation must have been sharper for my mother because she has been my only teacher for so long. I didn't even go to a day school until I was eight and a half. I don't imagine that my parents formally applied for me to be educated 'otherwise', in the terms of the Butler Education Act. I just didn't go to school. There was talk of the school inspector coming out to visit our village but nothing happened. In those early post-war years a lot of things that were officially supposed to happen didn't happen. The petrol shortage was one excuse that you used to hear, but looking back I suspect that shortage of energy would be nearer the mark. We forget now how tired everyone was after the war. In any case, if the inspector ever should appear, Tinty Maxton who lives in the Grange up the road and has hair down to her waist allegedly cannot read although she is two years older than me and her mother writes poems which are published in *Country Life*.

My mother does not bother to set up anything resembling a schoolroom. Most of the time we just sit next to each other on the sofa with the cabbagy-rose chintz and amble through Janet and John and the multiplication tables, then on to French irregular verbs and a bit of algebra. She allows frequent breaks, and we knock off at lunchtime. In the breaks and at lunch we chat about any old thing. Ever after I cannot help secretly wondering why people make such a fuss about education. So it is a cruel cutting off for both of us when I am sent away to school, and poor consolation when I am shipped back every three months, green in the face and succumbing to a violent and prolonged asthma attack as soon as I get home.

But now sitting opposite her in the trattoria I do not think how awful the whole thing has been for my mother. Instead I concentrate on the thought of my own emotional crippling – a tragic, not unbecoming light to see myself in. It is sad, though, that we should have stopped communicating all that time because there is no question of our not getting on. We agree about most things (I am too full of myself to contemplate the possibility that she may have influenced me). We love books, music leaves us cold. We love gossip and gardening, we have no interest in anything mechanical. We are as happy in art galleries as we are ill at ease in cinemas.

My earliest memories of film-going are not like most people's. The moment the house lights dim I am not rapt in an enchanted world. On the contrary, I am gripped with nervous impatience as soon as the Pearl and Dean Parthenon fades and the film starts. My attention begins to wander from the screen to the wonderful internal decoration of the Gaumont Salisbury. Outside, the cinema is the replica of a black-and-white medieval guildhall; inside, its walls are covered with the most amazing plaster turrets and prancing knights. So it is a disappointment when the film my mother has chosen for us happens to be on at the Regal in the market or the Odeon, which are boring and ordinary inside. I must be the only ten-year-old who goes for the decor in the cinema rather than the movie. Why do we go at all? Well, my mother thinks we need an outing and everyone else goes to the cinema, so we don't want to seem like freaks. But the truth is that we are freaks because what we really enjoy is walking out before the end. The best moment is always when my mother turns to me and says, 'Do you mind awfully but I think that really is enough.' The first film we walk out of is *Red Shoes*, starring Moira Shearer. Its ghastliness lives with me to this day. The last one we walk out of is *Marcelino Pan y Vino*, an insufferable weepie about a little boy who sees Jesus which wins all the prizes. Some films we do sit through, but these do not stick in my memory much. We sit through Olivier's *Henry V* because it is Shakespeare although it seems childishly bad. For the same reason we sit through *Macbeth* at the Salisbury Arts Theatre. All I can remember is the pathetic cardboard goblets in the banqueting scene. But the escaping out into the delicious fresh air is the thing, and the toasted teacakes with strawberry jam at the House of Steps afterwards.

Later we walk out of the Festival of Britain, or rather the Dome of Discovery, which we agree is the dullest place on earth, showing that my indifference to the natural sciences is already entrenched at the age of eleven, before I have learned any science.

My father does not walk out of films or plays. The difficulty is rather to persuade him to take his seat in the first place. He says, 'I always like to give the play a twenty-minute start, it makes the plot more interesting.' Coming in after twenty minutes, he argues, you have at least the challenge of trying to work out what is going on. On the other hand, so many plays run out of steam after the first act, and he risks missing the only good bit. Another reason my father rarely watches the curtain go up is that it enables him to have a quiet drink or two in the bar unjostled by his fellow theatre-goers. During this he sometimes manages to extract interesting information from the bar staff. Thus meeting us no earlier than the interval at one of the first performances of *The Mousetrap*, he is able to tell us who did it and he does. In theory, this should ruin my precious half-term outing (my first visit to a West End theatre). In fact, though I pretend to be annoyed, I am secretly proud of my father's subversive behaviour.

Then I suddenly remember another thing about Calum Robertson. Although sweet-natured, he has a feral temper when roused and one lunchtime when he is being baited beyond endurance, he throws a whole plate of spaghetti in tomato sauce at his chief persecutor, which shows how angry he is because he has a legendary appetite (see the Pindarus incident above). Most of the disgusting muck misses whoever it was and splats against the panelling. Marks of congealed spaghetti and tomato sauce never quite disappear, which we think proves that it contains some toxic preservative or colouring, although it may only be that the maids cannot be bothered to clean that high up. I don't suppose that my mother is really interested in these tales about Robertson major, whom she has never seen. But she is delighted to watch me prattling, and I am delighted by her delight.

'Shall we share a zabaglione? It says you need *due persone*.'

'I think we've earned it.'

The next morning we take the number 25 bus north up the via Bolognese and ask for the nearest stop to Number 120, which is the Villa La Pietra where my uncle Tony's schoolfriend Harold Acton lives. I have never met him because he seldom leaves Florence now. Well, I don't suppose I would have met him even if he did. My mother has never met him either, but Uncle Tony has dropped him a line. The invitation to lunch that came through to our hotel was very friendly, my mother says. Even so, I get off the bus in quite a nervous state, which is not helped by the long jangling of the distant bell and the slow response time of the servant who comes down the steps to lead us up to the villa.

This is all just how I imagined it, the steep path between the dark cypresses, only a sliver of the villa's high stucco façade visible between them, some old coat of arms in high relief above the arched door, the zizzing of the crickets in the long grass, and the servant in white gloves scurrying on ahead of us, suggesting by his White Rabbit *empressement* that we are late which we aren't, my mother having said she expects Harold Acton is fussy about time, that sort of person always is, and so we must allow a good hour from the hotel.

But he, our host, is not at all how I imagined him. I expected a person of infinitely refined appearance, a little frail too, in retreat from a coarse unfeeling world. He is, after all, just about the most famous aesthete there is, the last Englishman to live in Florence in the style of a Victorian milord, the author of *Memoirs of an Aesthete*, who puts as his recreations in *Who's Who* 'jettatura [whatever that may be] and hunting the Philistines', the champion of Chinese classical theatre who has lived for seven years in old Peking, the original of Anthony Blanche in *Brideshead Revisited*. And there he is on the doorstep to welcome us, but he looks like the master of ceremonies at a boxing match, big and almost burly, light on his feet but not mincing, as though he himself had danced around the ring in his time and his pleasant, homely mug had stopped a few punches. The well-cut cream suit and the light tan suggest Miami rather than Florence, perhaps even gangland connections.

How dark it is in the hall – all you can see of the famous early Italian pictures is the dim glimmering of the frames, the odd halo of saint or Madonna. Our eyes have had no time to adjust from the noonday sun outside and there is a stifled exclamation from my mother as she knocks into some large piece of Italian furniture, an armchair as it turns out when she sends it into a brief skid in my direction and I find my outstretched hand grasping the tasselled brocade of the arm. Harold Acton is quick to rescue her, quick too in his apologies for the darkness.

'The Tuscan light is so cruel, you know, and one must protect the pictures.'

Ah the voice – at last a tremble of the exquisite. He speaks in a strange, careful Italian accent, as though he were an Italian with perfect command of English idiom who has not heard the language spoken for some years. But no, that is not quite how it is because I have already heard some Italians speaking near-perfect English and they do not have this sort of delicate accent at all but give a rough, even raucous edge to their consonants.

'And have you been to the Pitti? It is so empty.' He makes Pitti and empty sound as if they were the same word with a little plosive puff on the p and the tongue tonking the teeth on the t before the exaggerated sign-off eee.

'Ah Mother, here they are.'

He draws us into a much lighter room, a drawing room, fairly large, and there at the end of it, small and upright in another tasselled-brocade chair, is an elderly woman in a blue cocktail dress with blue butterfly specs and permed hair the same blue, a shade more silvery perhaps. I mentally call it a cocktail dress, although I do not have much clue about what a cocktail dress looks like, only because as soon as the greetings are over she enquires where the cocktails are. Her voice sounds harsh and startlingly American – Chicago perhaps – or it may be partly by contrast with Harold's fluting Florentine English.

'I was just bringing in the martinis when they arrived. Mother loves martinis. I hope you do too.'

'So do you, Harold, don't pretend you don't.'

Here we are then, two pairs of mothers and sons, although Harold, as I now think of him but would not dream of addressing him, insists that we are no such thing.

'It is a gross imposture. They must be brother and sister, Mother, don't you think so?'

My mother blushes at the compliment and so do I, while I am marvelling at his articulation of the word imposture, which I cannot hope to render on the page.

Harold's mother lets us know that her name is Hortense, because she tells us an anecdote about a friend who is a trustee of the Met which involves her saying, 'You won't believe what they've done now, Hortense.' By the time she has finished the anecdote she has finished her martini and enquires whether there is any more in the jug, which there is luckily because I see that I have finished mine too, and so has my mother. It is the first time I have had a proper dry martini and the sharp tingle of it down the throat is glorious. The second is just as good. 'Some people like olives in them,' Mrs Acton says. 'Can't abide the things myself.'

By the time we step out on to the terrace for lunch, I am in heaven. There is the table beautifully laid under a tangerine awning and the man who let us in is already there standing behind Mrs Acton's chair.

'Where is that wonderful lemony scent coming from?' my mother asks.

'Ah, that is my *limoniera*. We bring them indoors for the winter.'

We follow his pointing hand to the tall bushes further along the terrace with their pale yellow-green fruit dangling like lanterns and behind them a classical conservatory with its doors flung open. I am about to ask some intelligent question about the cultivation of lemons, but I cannot take my eyes off the steaming first course, the pasta, that the waiter is bringing round on a scalloped silver dish. What a delicate primrose colour, how gleaming white the waiter's gloves.

'This is fettucine Alfredo. You know Alfredo's of course – it used to be the best place in Rome, but sadly declined now, I fear. Alfredo's, Mother, you remember Alfredo's.'

'Of course I remember Alfredo's. Never was much of a joint,' Mrs Acton snaps.

The waiter has reached me now and with a deft twirl of his silver serving fork he raises a tangled globe of the pasta and deposits it with a flourish on my – but as the fork is about four inches away from the target area he notices that there is no plate in front of me and with an equally deft twirl he whisks the pasta forkful up and away back to the scalloped silver dish. The dexterity of the manoeuvre and his wholly impassive mien while executing it almost make me think that he has done it on purpose to demonstrate his skill, like the preliminary twirl of the matador's cloak. With another dextrous flourish he lays my plate and repeats the twirling exercise, landing the pasta with the most feathery of touches.

The fettuccine are every bit as feathery as his touch. In fact I have never tasted anything like it before. Hard to imagine that this wonderful stuff is any sort of culinary cousin to Calum's spaghetti. It melts and curls on the tongue, and the parmesan is hardly like cheese at all, it is so fresh and light and airy.

'With your marvellous complexion you must beware of the sun, my dear. September can be so deceptive. It is still dangerous to take a *sun bath*.'

My mother says she does not care to be in the sun too long anyway. Mrs Acton agrees. I would agree too except I am too bowled over by the phrase 'sun bath' and make a note to adopt it myself.

'And what are your plans?'

'Well,' I say, plans being my department, 'we haven't been to the Bargello yet or Santa Croce.'

'Good, good, and the Museo Horne? I recommend the Museo Horne.'

I have not heard of the Museo Horne.

'Herbert Horne was a collector of the utmost distinction.'

'Did you know him well?'

'He died when I was twelve.'

'Was he sort of like Berenson?'

'Not entirely.'

'It would be wonderful to meet Berenson.'

'I fear that would be difficult to arrange. He gets very tired these days, and besides, he is rather exclusive.'

A chill, sudden but unmistakable, has descended on the arbour. It has been gathering, I dimly recognise, during the last few exchanges, but now it is here.

'B.B.'s a snob,' says Mrs Acton.

'Mother,' says Harold with a smile, benign again in an instant. When he smiles, he has a Chinese look. Perhaps he learned it from

living so long in China. But then he also seems to have a sunny disposition. As lunch goes on, I notice how seldom he says anything biting or unkind. Any snap in the conversation seems to come from his mother. Perhaps he is different when she is not there. Or perhaps he is not the original of Anthony Blanche at all.

After lunch we walk down the terraces at the back of the villa and admire the statues lurking in the high laurel hedges and under the tall ilex trees, gods and shepherdesses frozen in their antics against the dark green leaves. Each avenue and flight of steps brings us to a fresh surprise and then, when we turn at the corner of the last avenue, there is the greatest surprise – the view of Florence below, so close I feel I can almost touch the Duomo.

I take a photo of Harold pointing to one of the statues, his pointing hand following the outflung attitude of the statue, and my mother looking on in her flowery dress with a large handbag. There is another photograph – they are both in my sister's album now – taken by my mother of him and me and he is looking at me with his Chinese smile.

How gawky I look with my fluffy hair and awkward posture – not in the least attractive, but then perhaps sixteen-year-old boys do not come to lunch very often.

'Was the garden always like this?'

'No, my father really made it, or at least restored it. He bought most of the statues and had vast quantities of earth brought in to shore up this *belvedere*. It was, I like to think, his finest achievement.'

I agree warmly, but somehow the news that it is a reconstruction is rather disappointing.

There are two more occasions when I see Harold Acton. The first is about ten years later when I am being taken out to lunch in a London club, and I suddenly see him on the far side of the room waiting while his companion pays the bill. I mumble an explanation to my host and I hurry across the room to catch him.

I tug at his sleeve and he turns. Not the faintest sign of recognition. In a breathless babble I explain who I am and how kind he was to us in Florence.

'Ah yes,' he pronounces in that slow exquisite voice, looking at me closely like a doctor inspecting a patient for giveaway signs. '*Much* changed.'

The second time is twenty-five years later, when he must be getting on for eighty. We are on holiday in Florence and it comes into my head that my children ought to see this ancient monument of civilisation. We arrange to come for a cup of tea, which he says over the telephone with infinite regret is all he can offer because there is trouble with the servants. A decidedly surly young man brings crisps and peanuts for the children. This time the room we sit in is so dark I cannot remember whether it is the room we sat in the first time. I am not sure if he is aware quite how dark it is because he says his sight is going. He has just had cataracts removed, in Geneva – the journey was most fatiguing but you cannot trust Italian eye surgeons, they are so corrupt. Corrupt seems an odd word to use of eye surgeons, but it is the word that years later an Italian eye surgeon who has married a friend of ours uses too.

What is certainly going, if not gone, is the garden. After the hard frosts of the preceding winter, large parts of the terracing have toppled down the hill. The place where you see the whole of

Florence from is closed off, *in restauro*. Nothing is for ever, not even the view.

But this is not quite the end of the story. When Sir Harold – knighted for services to what? Florence? Civilisation? Why not? – finally dies in 1994, he leaves La Pietra to New York University. He toyed with the idea of leaving it to Oxford, but the Oxford dons, indolent and unhelpful by turns, failed to respond. Anyway, American universities are the ones that are rich enough and eager enough to take over these crumbling pleasure palaces. So Harvard is looking after Berenson's I Tatti, Georgetown has the Villa Le Balze, Johns Hopkins the old Spelman place. They are the rightful heirs to the vanished generations of Anglo-American dilettantes.

But for NYU there is a snag. Out of nowhere comes a woman claiming to be Arthur Acton's illegitimate daughter and so Harold's half-sister and under Italian law automatic heir to a large slice of the estate, including La Pietra and the palace on the banks of the Arno that now houses the British Institute in Florence and once also belonged to Arthur and Hortense. Liana Beacci, as she is called, says her mother Ersilia would come up to La Pietra and act as Arthur's secretary and went on from there to other duties. They had met originally at a dentist's surgery in Florence. I am not sure whether Ersilia was another patient or part of the team, a receptionist or hygienist perhaps, if dentists in Florence had hygienists then.

Anyway the appeal court throws Liana's suit out, but eight years later, after Liana herself has died, her children get the case reopened – and not just the case. A couple of years on they get the graves of Arthur, the scarcely cold Liana and the not much colder Sir Harold reopened too. And there is a DNA match between the three of them, although NYU's lawyers refuse to accept it, on the grounds that Arthur's corpse is half a century old now and in poor shape. Not much of an argument this, considering that scientists these days are finding DNA matches with prehistoric bog-men, but the NYU lawyers have a better defence than the corruption of Arthur's corpse, which is that La Pietra was never really his in the first place, because it was Hortense who bought it with her own money – just as her brother, the dilettante Guy Mitchell, bought the Villa Il Giuliarino just up the road from the Spelmans.

Guy and Hortense were the children of William H. Mitchell, president and founder of the National Trust Bank of Illinois. Quite appropriate really, because La Pietra was built for the Medicis' bank manager Francesco Sassetti. So Hortense is a link with the stench of the Chicago stockyards in the gilded age of American capitalism, just as Sassetti was the archetypal consigliere when the Medicis' agents were screwing the last maravedi out of every debtor in Europe.

Nobody seems to remember much about Hortense when she was young. But from some old photographer's archive on the Internet I manage to pull down two photos of her taken just before the Great War, both in fancy dress. She looks dumpy and unsure of herself, loaded down with frills and flounces. The costumes are a weird mixture of Aladdin and the Mikado. Plain girls often get photographed in fancy dress, I think because it is a leveller. Perhaps Arthur liked to see her that way, because she didn't come up to his standards in expensive gowns by Worth or Fortuny.

Even before the Liana affair, Arthur had a reputation as a bit of a chancer. He was supposed to be a painter but supplemented Hortense's funds by shipping Italian works of art across to his dealer in New York, who was none other than the legendary architect Stanford White, designer of the Washington Arch, the Century Club and much else in old New York (most of it demolished now). Their promising partnership was brought to an untimely end in 1906 when White was famously shot by his lover's husband Harry K. Thaw. Stanny's warehouses were bulging with all the treasures of old Europe. When one on Broadway went up in flames, Stanny was pretty near bust because he bought most of the stuff on credit and hadn't insured it. He bought girls with the same insatiable gusto as he bought antiques, preferably girls just past puberty. He had seduced Evelyn Thaw when she was barely sixteen, but then Harry Thaw shared Stanny's taste in showgirls twirling more or less naked from red velvet swings. Not exactly the New York of Henry James – or Harold Acton.

I don't know anything about Ersilia's husband. Perhaps he wasn't grand enough to go about shooting his wife's lovers. Possibly Arthur used some of Hortense's money to hush him up. I don't know either whether he would have found an illegitimate child extra embarrassing because he was himself born out of wedlock, the son it is presumed of Harold Edmund Acton, the tenth son of Captain Charles Acton, one of those innumerable Actons who made their career in the service of the kings of Naples and who eventually spawned Lord Acton, the famous historian who said that 'all power tends to corrupt and absolute power corrupts absolutely'. Harold Junior wrote a book about the Bourbons of Naples, two volumes in fact, and collected any Acton memorabilia he could lay his hands on, as though if his collection was fine enough it might make his father legitimate.

When you look at it, La Pietra doesn't sound a very happy ship. And it is curious too that Arthur Acton and Bernard Berenson, those two most civilised men living those exquisite lives in the Florentine hills – lives which I envy so much in my precious adolescence – were in fact picture dealers and neither of them overly scrupulous ones at that. Arthur Mario Acton did not have B.B.'s European reputation as a scholar and so was in no position to bump up the price of a painting by giving it a more distinguished attribution, however optimistic or fanciful, as Berenson did so often for his dealer Joseph Duveen, but I bet he did his best. S. N. Behrman's life of Duveen has a wonderful account of how the old rogue seduced B.B. into selling his expertise for lucre. From Behrman I discover that Berenson, a Lithuanian Jew from Boston, speaks English in this pseudo-Italian way like Harold: 'When I was a jun-ee-or at Har-vard, I formed a pas-sion-ate de-vo-tion to Bell-ee-nee.' Not at all like Hortense then, though she too had spent most of her adult life in Florence. Did the voice grow on them slowly over the years, or did they consciously adopt it to show how cultivated they were?

At the time of course no such cynical thoughts cross my mind. I am swimming in pleasure. The next morning we are standing in the high hall of the Bargello, once the conference chamber of the city's chief constable, which I now see from the dictionary is what Bargello means. For years I thought it meant little boat and tried to see something boat-shaped about this grim fortress. But for me this is not a grim fortress at all. In fact I think this great airy place is the most wonderful room there is. There are tremendous Michelangelos downstairs in the courtyard, including the bust of Brutus that looks like Andrew Sinclair and is said to have been chiselled off by some other sculptor. But here is where the sculptures I love best in all the world are. The museum closes at 1.30 p.m. every day and this strikes me as quite right because these statues – Donatello's St George and his David and Verrocchio's David – are of the morning, figures of our dawn. When I am anxious and restless in the night, it is one of those phrases that comes to me with a strange calming effect – 'the Bargello is only open in the morning'.

These are the first statues which stand free. They step out of their niches and they step down from the ideal to the individual, vulnerable, living, capable of reflecting our sympathy. St George stands resolute high on the wall here, as he used to stand outside in all weathers on the wall of the market hall. His mailed arm is draped over the cross on his shield in a conventional pose of defiance. But this is not a conventional pose of defiance with every sinew strained like Michelangelo's gigantic David. St George looks untried, a little apprehensive even – is this his first time in action? And he looks like someone at school, Marsham perhaps, Patrick Marsham in Mr Wilkinson's house who dies young, though of kidney disease not in battle. Donatello's David too with his amazing provocative smile and his naked body thrust forward and his hips jiving to the right, he looks like – who is it? His right hand is bent at the elbow in a slightly camp gesture with his fingers loosely holding a stone. Is this the stone he brained Goliath with, that he has picked up, bloodstained probably, to take home as a souvenir, or is it another one he had in reserve in case he missed with the first? And why is he wearing that absurd hat with flowers or ivy leaves plaited round the brim? Because this is a bronze statue, you cannot tell whether it is a summer straw hat or a bronze helmet like the one Mercury wears in the Interflora logo. Ah I know now who he reminds me of, but I cannot quite tell my mother because what reminds me of S – that's unmistakably who it is – is the way S stands in the shower, so that his buttocks have this taut look. S is quite innocent, I think, though the rest of us are not and our sex-starved fancies steam up around S like the steam in the showers which have no ventilation to speak of and which we freely compare to the gas chambers.

Verrocchio's David – let us get back to art – has exactly the same pose, the hips a little canted to the right, the torso thrust forward, the left elbow crooked and the hand resting on the hip (no stone in it, though). But it is not seductive like Donatello's, not magical in this sated, almost post-coital style – in short, not like S or our fantasies about S. I saw S the other evening; he is more or less bald now and he tells me he is active in the Liberal Democrats. I would not quite dare to say that art starts to go downhill after Donatello, but secretly that is what I think – never glad confident morning again, no going back to the Garden of Eden. As soon as you know, something is lost. That canted hip, that sated smile, they won't last long.

I am dizzy with looking. Exhilaration is sliding into exhaustion. And because I am getting tired I fail to notice that my mother is tired too. She asks if we can go back to the hotel – we can get a sandwich on the way. But because it is our last day I insist we have a proper lunch and we stop at a big draughty trattoria just opposite the niche on the market wall where the copy of Donatello's St George now perches. The waiter is a large man with a black moustache that looks painted on. He talks a cockney English because he used to live with his cousins in Clerkenwell. There is some stuff in the guidebook I have to catch up on, so I don't really notice how quiet my mother is. The food is strangely greasy, not like Italian food at all, everything seems doused in a sweaty broth. It is a relief to get back to the Albergo Porta Rossa which is luckily only 200 yards away because it is raining now, hard. Florentine rain slanting down the narrow streets and darkening the dun stucco and the rusticated stonework on the grim palaces of thirteenth-century merchants.

We lie on our beds and listen to the rain sliding down the glass roof in the courtyard outside our window. Quite soon I start wanting to go out again, because there is a two-star monastery we have not yet clocked up – I have forgotten what it is called, all this is a long time ago – and my mother says she does not feel up to it but why don't I go and tick it off?

'The trouble with you,' I say, 'is that you have no soul.'

As soon as I have said it, I realise what a terrible thing it is to say. I cannot think why I have said it – it's not a phrase I would normally dream of using.

A minute or two later, while I am still trying to think what to do next, how to repair the damage, although I am too confused to make any kind of apology because I am still tired and irritated as well as appalled, I hear my mother crying. I cannot remember ever having heard or seen her cry before and I cannot see her crying now because it is late afternoon and it is dark in our hotel room at the best of times – there is only a small window on to the inner courtyard and the sun never reaches it. And of course I still do not know what to do. After all, as she has pointed out, I have only just learned to talk again, so I am nowhere near being able to do the normal thing which would be to go over to the iron bedstead and take her in my arms and hug her. So we just lie there in silence until the rain eases off and enough time has passed for us to be able to pretend that nothing much has really happened and we can go downstairs and look for a late cup of tea.

After Florence we go to Pisa, only for the morning. We have a lot to fit in – Siena, Arezzo, San Gimignano and Bologna – before we fly home from Milan on the 17th.

We are standing about twenty yards across the grass from the Baptistery. My mother is resting by the white stone bollards which look like chess pawns. I am looking back at the voluptuous rusty-pearly shape of the Baptistery, like some swollen fruit (pomegranate?) encased in its gothic prickles. Beyond are the Cathedral and the Leaning Tower and the long arcades of the Campo Santo, all in dazzling white marble quarried from the mountains behind, which are hazy mauve now in the September light.

'Julia!'

'Anne, how amazing!'

The two Englishwomen fall on each other's necks. Embracing there on the grass with the white marble pillars all around, in their calf-length skirts and their headscarves they look like one of those quattrocento biblical scenes we have seen so many of, which feature women meeting and embracing like this, slightly awkward, bending forward with their lower bodies quite far apart.

'And you know Richard?'

My mother does know Richard, but not so well, it seems, because they shake hands. Richard has an intense look in his dark eyes. He has the air of a professor and it turns out that he is a professor or soon will be, of philosophy with special reference to aesthetics. He is friendly, even charming, and in the small talk that passes between us you can tell how clever he is. My mother usually likes that type of person, she likes to see them do their stuff while she listens with a half-smile and doesn't feel she has to contribute, although she may be quite mordant afterwards. But on this occasion she seems a little ill at ease and I am not sure why, because I don't think she has taken an instant dislike to him and Anne is obviously a friend of hers whom she would normally be pleased to see. So this unease is puzzling. And I notice that none of them shows much enthusiasm for prolonging the meeting by suggesting a drink in the café just behind us, let alone joining forces for lunch.

'He's called Richard Wollheim,' my mother says afterwards. 'They haven't been married long. She used to be married to Philip Toynbee. You remember Philip, don't you?'

Of course I remember Philip. He is one of the most memorable figures in our childhood. Tall and muscular with a sallow, long-jawed face and a sardonic twist to his mouth, he is a wild and warm character, who seems to my sister and me lovably childish, more childish than we are. He comes to stay with us at the Malt House, Chitterne a lot, often with his friend Ben Nicolson who looks not unlike him, only a bit more frail and gaunt with the hollow Spanish eyes of his mother who is Vita Sackville-West. Philip at this stage is a foreign correspondent as well as writing novels and reviews. Ben is an art historian who has just become editor of the *Burlington Magazine*, but for my sister and me they are a pair of Punchinellos on the loose, endlessly falling up and down our steep stairs as though on purpose to divert us. 'I couldn't decide whether to wake up Ben to give him his sleeping pills,' Philip announces at breakfast, and we collapse in giggles at their hopelessness. When they have been shovelled on to the train at Westbury, my sister says wistfully, 'I love Philip's green face.' Philip is especially fond of my mother and when pissed is liable to throw his arms round her and declare undying love which nobody takes very seriously, and when he is in low spirits which is quite often at this period he writes letters to her, usually awash with self-pity and/or self-disgust.

'Philip says he's at the end of his tether,' my mother says to my father.

'Philip hasn't got a tether,' my father says. My mother reports this back to Philip who is delighted at the thought. He is especially on the loose when he comes to stay with us, because Anne has left him to go off with Professor Wollheim who looks like a steadier prospect. So our encounter in Pisa is my own first encounter with the awkwardness of meeting old friends with new spouses, that uncomfortable period of acclimatisation to the new arrangements while the happier memories of the old ones are still green and the wounds of the break-up are still raw. During this painful period, 1949–50, Philip takes up with the *Observer*, or rather is scooped up by the proprietor David Astor who likes finding hutches and fresh straw for lame ducks. Philip is despatched to the Middle East. He is fascinated by the progress of the new Jewish state and there are plenty of coups to report on all over the region. He lodges in Cairo with Donald Maclean and his American wife Melinda. Maclean has just come from Washington to be Counsellor in the British Embassy, the youngest in the diplomatic service to reach this rank – he is only thirty-six. It is not from the Macleans, though, that Philip writes to my mother, presumably in answer to an earlier letter of hers to this hotel or another:

Metropolitan Hotel, Cairo

May 9th

Darling Julia,

You have a prophetic soul. No, I hadn't been turned out by Melinda. It was simply that they had a compulsory foreign-office guest. But now, after three weeks snuggery, I am out on my ear, and no mistake about it. Poor Donald has indulged in a wild crescendo of drunken, self-destructive, plain destructive episodes – and his wife has made me responsible. Actually I've done my honest best to control him, but, as you can imagine, not with much to show for it. Last night we smashed to pieces the flat of the American ambassador's secretary (God knows why). This has caused a major diplomatic incident. Anyway Donald is being sent back to England for treatment, and I mean to run off to Transjordan – until *that* becomes too hot to hold me.

Frankly, this is about the end. I loathe and dread hotel life, yet cannot, it seems, survive very long chez amis. What next? My whole journey will be a series of escapes from the frying pan to the fire and back again. Ugh! But for the intelligent affection of a young Egyptian, a new friend, I would really have got to the end of my mythical tether. And only three days ago I was beginning to feel thoroughly smug and convinced that I was after all a super-journalist. I now learn that there's been a coup d'état in Syria while, so to speak, my back was turned. Bugger! I expect I shall be back with you before much longer. After all, bad as England may be, one is at least cushioned by dear friends. Here there are not enough to go round.

I have also got into trouble for dancing with the Princess Faisa in my braces and outraging a great many important pashas. I am mad about her – and not only because she is beautiful and kind, but also, alas, because she is a princess.

There is no such thing as sex here. The Egyptians don't believe in it, and I'm beginning even to doubt whether I do. Certainly one can't have sex, drink and talk. I prefer drink and talk. Though I hate them too!

How is everyone?

I nearly resigned from my paper, because they added several things to my article. Horrors like 'What a scoop!' and 'But, for *my* Egyptian . . .' But they've apologised very nicely – and are being kind to me in every way. (The pianist has started playing Buttons and Bows – and I could weep for lovely Chitterne).

Goodbye and best love to you both

Philip

Xoxo xoxo

People writing home often lay it on a bit to amuse the people they are writing to. But Philip is if anything underplaying what happens. The night before, 8 May, Maclean wakes him up at three in the morning, already drunk and fierce, insists they go off together to a series of all-night bars, still won't go home. Philip, at his wits' end, drags him to the flat of an Embassy official to sleep it off. They both pass out. At midday Maclean gets up, drinks a bottle of whisky, demands more, goes down to the flat below which happens to belong to the secretary of the American Ambassador, dances round the room breaking mirrors and vases and chairs, tears a heavy marble mirror from its wall brackets and throws it into the bath. The bath breaks in half, the mirror amazingly does not. He then stuffs all the secretary's underwear down the lavatory. This is by no means the Counsellor's first rampage but it is to be his last. The long-suffering British Ambassador is forced to send him home. But it is not much worse than the trip up the Nile when an equally pissed Maclean seizes Melinda by the throat and makes as if to strangle her, then threatens to drown the chief boatman who is asking for double fare, then seizes the boatman's loaded rifle and says he'll bash his skull in. When Lees Mayall, First Secretary at the Embassy, tries to restrain Maclean by pinning his arms behind his back, Maclean lurches backward jamming Mayall against the Nile bank and breaking his leg. Lees, a man of the most saintly temper, refuses to bear any grudge and continues to believe that Maclean is being harshly treated. Nor is Maclean's violence when drunk his only drawback. He also roams all over the parks of Cairo into the small hours picking up pretty Egyptian boys and reeling into the smart hotels and swearing undying love to the bellboys. Philip by contrast is merely getting drunk and making passionate advances to King Farouk's sister in his braces.

Back in London, Maclean is given six months' leave and sent to a series of shrinks who offer conflicting diagnoses of his condition. Another form of therapy is also made available. In August his friend Mark Culme-Seymour puts him up for membership of the Gargoyle Club. Guy Burgess joined in 1943 and is never out of the place. Kim Philby was a pre-war regular though he now deems it prudent to stay away. But for Maclean the Gargoyle is perfect, the mixture of posh and louche, the tolerance of unspeakable behaviour, the ideal place to crash out in. He takes up where he left off in Cairo. In no time he gets so drunk that he seems to be having an epileptic fit on the floor and Culme-Seymour has to squirt him with a soda syphon to bring him round. Then he refuses to go down in the lift unless the lady who looks after the ladies' cloaks comes with him. When really drunk, which despite Dr Erna Rosenbaum's therapy he usually is, he insists on telling all and sundry that 'I work for Uncle Joe'. One night in the club, seeing Goronwy Rees, a fellow of All Souls and a former Communist, he snarls, 'I know all about you, you bastard, you used to be one of us but you ratted.' Years later after the end of the Cold War,

Goronwy's daughter Jenny (a friend of mine from *Daily Mail* days) discovers from a former KGB agent, Oleg Tsarev, that her father really was briefly a Soviet contact through Guy Burgess, though he resigned after the Nazi–Soviet pact and remained haunted for the rest of his life by what he had done. Jenny seems almost relieved to establish the true facts. We are the generation that likes to clear things up.

Nobody in the Gargoyle takes much notice of all this. Nor, it seems, does the Foreign Office, because in September Maclean is appointed head of the American Department. A couple of months later Philip reappears from the Middle East. He too takes up where he left off, returning to his habits of wartime when he used to come in to the club after fire-watching and start throwing pepper pots about. Soon after his return, over in New York the supposed Soviet agent Alger Hiss is found guilty of perjury and sent to jail. Philip writes a piece for the *Observer* conceding that there may be some truth in the accusations against Hiss. A few days later he bumps into the already blind-drunk Maclean in the Gargoyle. 'I am the English Hiss,' Maclean mutters in his most menacing manner and pushes Toynbee, pint-glass in hand, backwards into the band – a slight contradiction with his claim to be working for Uncle Joe, since the party line is that Hiss is entirely innocent. In May, Guy Burgess is sent home from Washington in disgrace, and he and Maclean take the boat from Southampton to St Malo and are never seen again in the West.

These are the Gargoyle's declining days. For twenty-five years the upper three floors of 69 Dean Street, Soho, have provided a refuge and a playground for high bohemia. The club is a weird mixture of styles. After the reception hall you come into a fusty country-house sitting room with vaguely Tudor panelling. Then to the left leading down to the main L-shaped room there is a brilliant staircase lined with mosaic tiles cut out of looking-glass. The dazzling effect is the brainchild of Henri Matisse, whose eldest daughter Marguerite is married to the gay and tempestuous critic Georges Duthuit who loves to dance the night away. Downstairs there is a little cockpit of a dance floor and red-and-gold banquettes and tables. The room is dominated by two great Matisse paintings, *The Red Studio*, roughly six foot by seven (it's now in MoMA), and *The Studio, Quai St Michel*, now in the

Phillips collection in Washington. These were bought for £600 the pair from Matisse's studio by David Tennant, the proprietor and inventor of the Gargoyle Club.

David is my father's best friend. For more than thirty years their eyes light up when they see each other – the last time shortly before David's death which is a year before my father's. I am startled by the exuberance of their embrace, they crash into each other like waves breaking. David and my father are companions in mischief, letting off fireworks at every opportunity – including real fireworks. They cannot get enough of gunpowder. David is always laying on *feux de joie*, sometimes in fancy dress, at the mill house in Sussex which he rents as a kind of Gargoyle in the country. Years later I meet a stately hostess called Carol Dugdale who recalls being accorded a salvo of gunfire as she and her new husband Eric, an affluent insurance broker, are driving away from a weekend party with the Tennants. My father and David fire their shotguns in the air, then they think it will be more amusing to shoot out the Dugdales' rear tyres but my father succeeds only in peppering Mrs Dugdale, leaving several pellets embedded in her scalp. 'We didn't want you to go,' he says weakly when cornered by the indignant Eric. She bends over to show me the scars which she still carries from this fusillade thirty years earlier, but her hair is too thick and piled up for me to see. As I am peering at the braided grey strands, I realise that she is positively proud of these scars. They are stigmata of her long-buried past as a Bright Young Thing.

During this bizarre ceremony I see her younger daughter Rose, whom I am supposed to be partnering for the dance later, staring at us with one of her wicked derisive grins. At this stage Rose is still playing her mother's game, wearing white gloves to church and being Hon. Treasurer of the Oxford University Conservative Association. Only in her mid-twenties does she break out in dramatic style: first by burgling her parents' farmhouse down in Devon, this being only a dry run for the IRA raid on Sir Alfred Beit's art collection in Ireland, where she and her gang leave Beit and his wife, my mother's old schoolfriend Clemmie Mitford, both already elderly, bound and gagged, and finally after being jailed for nine years being sprung from the prison yard by a helicopter. It is as though she has chosen to repeat her mother's parabola from the wilder shores of bohemia to the buttoned-up bourgeoisie only in the opposite direction. I cannot help liking Rose – she has such a merry subversive way with her. So when years later I meet the Beits, by now very frail, I cannot help saying that I used to be fond of Rose, and Sir Alfred murmurs, almost apologetically, 'Oh dear, that's what everyone says. You must forgive me if I cannot entirely share your opinion.'

David and my father even look rather alike, at least before my father's hair goes white so early. There is a Henry Lamb portrait of my father painted the year he marries my mother and as a child I think it is a portrait of Big David (so called to distinguish him from Little David, his son by his first wife, the actress Hermione Baddeley) because I do not remember my father with such black hair. But David is bigger and stronger than my father, and more reckless. Above all, although they are both younger sons of rich landowners, David is himself rich while my father is anything but.

David's grandfather Sir Charles Tennant founded a great industrial combine, starting with bleach but then bleaching the proceeds into banking. The Glasgow skyline is dominated by his factory chimney, 'Tennant's Stalk', just as his baronial palace dominates his glen in the Borders. So David can do as he fancies and does. What he does first is to create his own pleasure palace in the dark heart of Soho where spies and poets and painters and idlers can drink and fight and argue in loud voices all night. How violent they all are, these umbrageous musketeers, how easily aggrieved, how nervy.

My father falls into this company as easily as a raindrop falling off a roof. He is just entering his heyday as a jump jockey, effortlessly riding winner after winner at point-to-points and steeplechase meetings around the country. He rides in flat races too, and hurdle races and two-horse matches like in the eighteenth century. He will take any ride where he can make the weight, which being just on six foot tall and well built is not always easy. So in the season, like other jockeys before and since, he lives on champagne and dry toast and not so much of the toast. Even after the war when he is hard put to make twelve stone seven at the Larkhill point-to-point I can see how graceful he is in the saddle, how still he sits until he needs to make a move, how urgent he is when he lets the horse go. Up at Manchester one October he gets the ride on Golden Miller who is about to become the greatest chaser of all time. Normally the champion jockey Ted Leader rides him, but this is an amateur hurdle race, to warm up the Miller who is still only four years old and has yet to win the first of his five Cheltenham Gold Cups. Carrying twelve stone one, the horse is elbowed into third place by a couple of lightweights, but it remains the experience of my father's racing life – 'like sitting in an armchair'.

Sometimes he drops in at the Gargoyle and after several drinks goes on to the Turkish Baths in Jermyn Street to sweat off a few pounds so he can make the weight for the horse he is riding in the next day's race. After a doze in the cooling room alongside the other jockeys he drives out of London down the Bath Road at first light, to exercise a couple of horses for Captain Bay Powell, up on the Wiltshire Downs at Aldbourne. He gets to Aldbourne a good deal quicker if he is driven by his friend Derek Jackson, who is a speed maniac and a millionaire. Jackson has half a dozen horses of his own with Bay Powell, which he rides with the reckless panache of a self-taught horseman, his knees up to his chin and his elbows pumping. Derek and his identical twin brother Vivian inherited a quarter share in the *News of the World*. Both of them are brilliant physicists and rampant bisexuals as well as fearless horsemen. 'I wide under both wules,' says Derek in his peculiar gravelly voice with its difficulty on the 'r's, referring to his love life rather than the different codes for flat racing and steeplechasing. Deep down, the twins care for no one in the world but each other. My mother is in a nightclub with Vivian when a fortune-teller prophesies that he will meet death in snow. Not long after, Vivian is killed in a horse-drawn sleigh which he has insisted on taking the reins of and driving furiously across frozen snow. Derek is never quite the same again and hands out a rough time to each of his seven wives, but despite this and his flagrant fascist views, my father cannot resist the Horse, as he calls him, though he says 'it's always a mistake to confuse the Horse with a human being'. Derek is as fearless in war as in peace. After flying sixty combat missions in Beaufighters, he leads the crucial trials of Window, the anti-radar device, himself chucking handfuls of silver tinfoil out of the cockpit window to see how much is needed to confuse the ground radar.

During the war, Bay Powell gave over his stables as a temporary billet for Able and Easy Companies of the US 101st Airborne Division while they were preparing for D-Day. The exploits of Easy Company in France became legend, perpetuated by Steven Spielberg's series *Band of Brothers*. As a memorial, in 2004 the entire stables were shipped over, stall by stall, to be reinstalled as a museum at the paratrooper training base in Georgia. So Bay's stables are gone, and so are the Turkish Baths at 76 Jermyn Street, obliterated in the Blitz a fortnight after they had closed down.

This is the background my father comes from, racing and hunting and beagling. His own father dies out hunting, not jumping a fence but falling off his horse with a heart attack in the middle of a wood while the hounds are snuffling around. When my father is at Oxford, he brings the Magdalen beagles home for the holidays and runs them through the woods at Wasing. Not on Sunday of course. On Sunday the family goes for a walk in the woods to break the monotony between matins and evensong. On weekdays there are family prayers in the sitting room. The three boys kneel behind the servants. All my father can see is the striped bottom of the butler between the parted tails of his tailcoat.

My father is always known as Robin. He was christened Robert Francis after his uncle Robert, a lieutenant in the 60th Rifles who had died of a fever at Gibraltar aged twenty, and another uncle, Frank, who was killed at the Battle of Loos – the combination giving my father a cheerful start in life. His best friend is his cousin Pam, who comes from the same background, horsey, churchy, just over the Wiltshire border. Pam has a melting oriental beauty and a slender figure and a silky chuckling voice, none of which she wishes to waste on the local curates and farmers. She persuades her parents, Uncle John and Aunt Winnie (the only woman I have met who really does say huntin', shootin' and fishin'), to let her go to London with an allowance of £1 a week. She models for Liberty and appears in films as an extra wearing her one evening dress, once as the dancing partner of Stewart Granger in a film nobody can remember the name of. My father recruits her as a model for a fashion show at the Gargoyle to replace a girl who has gone sick. While Pam twirls her frock around the tiny ballroom floor, she catches the eye of the art dealer and bon viveur Freddy Mayor, whose gallery is the first to show Max Ernst, Rouault, Miró and Klee in London and who is also the original of the dealer Reggie Frott in Anthony Powell's early novel *Agents and Patients* (Powell, like his friends Evelyn Waugh, Malcolm Muggeridge and George Orwell, is also an occasional Gargoyle visitor, mostly, I think, before he marries my mother's sister Violet and becomes my uncle Tony).

'Who's that girl, looks like a bit of all right.'

'Robin's cousin – you'd better talk to him.'

Pam and Freddy arrange to meet the next day for lunch. He fails to recognise her – a remarkable achievement considering her exotic appearance, hangover perhaps. Still, off they go together and are married for the rest of their lives, with only the occasional insignificant slippage.

Pam adores my father, he is the Regency buck girls dream of, but she knows his fragility too. 'David led darling old Robin astray. Not very difficult.' My father has no more of a tether than Philip. There they all scamper down the glittering gold-and-silver staircase: my father from Wasing Place, Aldermaston, Berks, Goronwy Rees from a Calvinistic Methodist manse in Aberystwyth, Philip from the plain living and high thinking of Professor Arnold Toynbee's Yorkshire farmhouse, Dylan Thomas from Cwmdonkin Drive, Swansea – all slipping what tethers they may ever have had. Dylan has just married Caitlin Macnamara and it is anybody's guess which is the wilder. One evening at the Gargoyle my father is knocked clean off his seat by a powerful blow to the head and he looks up from the floor to see an inflamed Mrs Thomas shouting at her husband, who managed to get out of the way in time leaving my father in the firing line.

Into this resort of mayhem and misbehaviour comes the surprising figure of my mother. Unlike many of the other Gargoyle habitués, she no longer has an oppressively respectable home to escape from. The gloomy establishment at 12 Rutland Gate is dispersed after her mother's death five years earlier. Like her sisters she can go where she pleases. I think she merely wants to see what is going on. She too is charmed by Big David, his gift for making a party go, his beguiling restlessness, his delicacy unexpected in such a big strong bony man. He doubles as an announcer on the Third Programme. My father likes to mimic him saying over the air late at night, having already called in at

Mrs. Peter Quennell and Lady Julia Mount

The Hon. David Tennant gave a party at the Gargoyle Club, of which he's the moving spirit. With him below is his fiancée, Virginia Parsons, daughter of the late Alan Parsons and Viola Tree. Mrs. Peter Quennell is the wife of the author and poet; Lady Julia Mount is the Earl of Longford's youngest sister, and married Robin Mount in March

The Hon. David Tennant and Miss Parsons

the Gargoyle, in infinitely refined but already somewhat pixilated tones, 'And now we are going to play a little courante by Lully.'

Perhaps it is my father who first takes her to the club. Anyway there she is standing at the bar after they are married, seeing the 1930s out, looking entirely at her ease with Peter Quennell's latest wife, as though she had been a resident of high bohemia all her life. She is already pregnant. What an interesting and varied life I seem to have led in the womb, going to a bazaar with Unity Mitford, out on the razzle with Dylan Thomas and Philip Toynbee, possibly Burgess and Maclean too. Perhaps this explains my lifelong quest for respectability.

My last year at school we have a new German teacher. Mucus Lucas, the previous incumbent, proves unable to control the tough eggs in the back row and retires hurt to go and teach in a girls' school. 'This one won't stand any nonsense,' my tutor prophesies. At first sight the new master looks quite innocuous, with a mop of corn-

coloured hair and a soft, hesitant, slightly insinuating voice as though
he means you to read between the lines of what he is saying. But from
the beginning of the first lesson he is in control, apparently without
making the slightest effort to exert authority. He switches on charm
or menace at will and when the yobs at the back start to make trouble
he delivers merciless and exact parodies of their arrogant, languid
voices. For me David Cornwell also has the marvellous freshness of a
born teacher who is teaching his subject for the first time (he is barely
twenty-five). He takes me up partly because I am quite good at
German but also, I think, because I look a bit down in the mouth. He
invites me out to supper in his cottage at Dorney with his elfin-pretty
wife Ann who illustrates children's stories. She shows me some of her
illustrations which somehow seem to be rather like the cottage we are
actually in, with their two little boys tumbling round the fireside and
David (we are old enough now to call the masters by their Christian
names) talking about anything that comes into his head. One of the
things that I like about him is his irreverence towards the school and
its encrusted traditions but at the same time his fascination with the
place as though he was marking it all down for future use: 'Really,
only Upper Boys are allowed to walk on that side of the road? I heard
that but could not believe it, and tell me, the business about who
can wear the bottom button of his waistcoat undone, amazing.' Then
we talk about Goethe or Schiller while Ann puts the children to bed
and I feel I am at home – something I have been sorely in need of
lately.

His end-of-term reports on my progress sometimes have a sharp
turn – 'Ferdy must try to curb the Cyril Connolly tendency in him'
– but I do not resent this: it seems like a sign of intimacy. In any
case, by now I am accustomed to being ticked off for being a
smartass. Almost every term, Stephen McWatters, the Master in
College who has to look after all the scholars, complains in his
report that I am aloof or supercilious or both. Towards the end of
my time at school, McWatters, known to me as McOcean for his
generally drippy disposition (which I suppose only confirms his
criticism of my snootiness), tells my father that I 'have largely
outgrown my superciliousness'. My modern languages tutor, the
redoubtable Oliver Van Oss, does not agree, quoting the French

master Serge Cottereau, according to O.V.O. one of the thirty cleverest men in France:

> The French intellectual is really alarmingly perceptive! Cottereau puts his finger unerringly on Ferdy's weaknesses when he warns that his nil-admirari-irony-cum-fantasy speciality – in which more than a hint of the old snootiness recurs – is (i) too unreal to satisfy for long, brilliantly pyrotechnic as it sometimes is ('fatigue un peu à la longue') and that (ii) it probably betrays a form of mental laziness ('une aimable paresse d'esprit'). This last seems to me a sound criticism of a basic English weakness.

True then and probably truer now, fifty years later, certainly of me and probably of the English too. Supercilious, snooty, cynical, wearisome, mentally lazy – and this was supposed to be a good end-of-year report. How they see through you, the best school-masters, and how little the seeing-through does to change you.

As he has warned from the start, David does not stay long at the school. In fact he leaves only a term or two after I do. He is going to join the Foreign Office but somehow words gets round that there is more to it than that. 'Corns is going to be a spy.' Waste of a good teacher, I think. He adopts the pen name of John le Carré for his first book, a thriller set in a public school, one or two of the characters being immediately recognisable, notably Grizel Hartley, the ebullient Brunnhilde married to a famous ex-housemaster.

He comes back into my life after his tremendous success with *The Spy Who Came in from the Cold* when he is living near Wells, only a few miles from my uncle Tony Powell's house in Somerset, and he and Ann come over to dinner. To make up the party, Aunt Violet has asked my mother's old friend Mary Mayall and her husband Lees, the one who had his leg broken by Donald Maclean in Cairo and who is currently Vice-Marshal of the Diplomatic Corps, though a more bonhomous, less stuffy soul it would be hard to imagine – as Uncle Tony points out, another example of the Foreign Office's gift amounting to genius for misjudging character, e.g. Burgess and Maclean *passim*. Kim Philby has defected and the hunt is on for the Fourth and Fifth Men.

'Did you ever know Philby?' Cornwell asks.

'Oh yes, I used to meet him with Malcolm Muggeridge, at the Gargoyle before the war,' my uncle replies.

'What was he like?'

'Quite an amusing fellow but obviously a complete crook.'

'And Burgess and Maclean, did you know them at all?'

'Burgess was the most ghastly type of BBC pansy, quite insufferable. Not as bad as Maclean though.'

'My mother went skiing with Maclean,' I volunteer.

Then Lees Mayall pipes up: 'Donald Maclean was my boss in Cairo. He broke my leg when he was drunk. We remained great friends until he went off.'

'It was *your* leg, was it?' David is enthralled. In fact, as Lees and Mary continue to describe what a struggle they had in Cairo to cover up for Donald, an unholy glee comes over him, which even such a master of concealment is unable to suppress entirely. Here he is at the very core of the Establishment and it is turning out to be every bit as rotten as he always said it was.

It is a pity for him that he remarries and moves to Cornwall, for as the spy scandals continue Uncle Tony reveals further connections. The latest to be suspected of being a double agent is Sir Roger Hollis, who as head of MI5 granted Blunt immunity from prosecution.

'Did you ever know Roger Hollis?' I ask.

'Oh yes, I was at Oxford with him. Dullish as far as I remember, drank a fair bit, sort of chap who would go to bed with anybody.'

This is thrilling news. So far nobody has suggested that Hollis was anything other than a model of propriety. Now he appears to be easy meat for any blackmailer.

'On the whole, I preferred him to Blunt,' my uncle continues, 'who was dreary even for an art historian. All right on Poussin, I suppose.'

It is my wife's turn: 'Anthony Blunt used to be sick in my mother's lavatory. She had only just learned to cook and he was her spare man when she gave dinner parties.'

'I imagine he was a rather cold fish.'

'No, he was incredibly kind. In fact he got me my job at Christie's and he used to ask me to tea at the Courtauld, which can't have been any use to him at all.'

This apparently motiveless kindness of Blunt's to young girls remains a mystery. At the height of his prolonged interrogation by the security services, Frances Butlin – a friend of ours who was working at the Courtauld, then in her early twenties – was asked to stand in as switchboard operator on a Saturday morning. She could not get the hang of the system at all and kept on putting Sir Anthony through to himself. Eventually he came down from his office and in the kindest possible way gave her the rest of the day off while he settled down to man the switchboard himself. I like to think of that long chilly figure with his ears clamped in headphones hunched over the switchboard, plugging in leads to get through to some unsound Poussin scholar in Rome or square an ex-boyfriend who might talk or even perhaps synchronise stories with an old KGB control now in retirement in Portugal.

Perhaps he just had a kindly streak in him. His elder brother Wilfrid, the artist and calligrapher, was the kindest of men. He taught us drawing at school, or rather he let us wander out into the fields behind the drawing schools and set up our sketchbooks beside the Willow Brook. The more dutiful of us gossiped and occasionally pencilled in the outline of the nearest pollarded willow. The more daring found a spot in the longer grass well hidden from the playing fields and lit up. Towards the end of the lesson, Wilfrid wandered out from the schools, himself with a Turkish cigarette drooping from his lips (you could smell its intoxicating bouquet a hundred yards away), and from further along the sedgy brook you could hear his voice uplifted in the mildest possible complaint: 'Oh really, Serocold, this is too bad. I don't think I can let you out again.' Himself a deliciously relaxed and indolent figure, he inspired those qualities in others. He taught us to write italic too, those of us who had no talent for drawing, and for years my writing looked like a page from a medieval missal, until hurry drove it downhill again. Wilfrid was miserable when he learned of Anthony's treachery which he could scarcely believe. In his charming autobiography *Slow on the Feather*, he constructs the most charitable explanation for his beloved brother's behaviour, but you feel that he never quite swallows it himself.

My parents' courtship is leisurely, not at all like Freddy and Pam Mayor's whirlwind. I do not mean so much the length of time it lasts,

not quite a year from their first walking out to their marriage at St
Peter's Vere Street the following March. What I mean is that they
take these last bachelor months as some kind of final holiday. Without
career or prospects or much money to speak of between them, their
engagement seems one long golden suspension of time, like a spider's
thread glistening in the morning sun.

They go to stay with Pansy and Henry Lamb in a fold of the downs
beyond Salisbury. This is when Henry paints my father's portrait, the
one that makes him look like Big David. While he is sitting, the two
sisters pick strawberries or go into Salisbury to have coffee at the
House of Steps. In the evening Henry plays the piano. He could have
been a professional pianist if he had not decided, quite late on, to
become a painter. But he was a doctor first of all. Somerset Maugham
remembered seeing his golden head crossing the yard at St Thomas's
when they were both medical students. In the Great War Henry was
sent to Mesopotamia and was awarded the MC for tending the
wounded under fire. After the war when he becomes attached to the
Bloomsbury Group, they never refer to this, being more interested in
his green faun's eyes. Lytton is hopelessly in love with him and he has

an affair with Dorelia, and Margaret Kennedy puts him in her bestseller *The Constant Nymph* as the irresistible Lewis Dodd. When I see him years later he is a little dry old man (he was twice Pansy's age) and all this is hard to imagine. But when he starts talking I begin to see. He is beady, so full of spark. And the old embers are still burning. 'How sensible that you can see girls undressed on the films now,' he says to me, aged fifteen, apropos of nothing. He keeps up the old Bloomsbury sport of nude bathing too. 'Haven't you ever seen a grown man naked before?' he says to my teenage cousin Antonia, catching her startled eye as they splash across the river.

Then my parents cross the Irish Sea to Tullynally, or Pakenham Hall as it is then called, the enormous gothicky castle in the dimmest bogland in the middle of Ireland. On the writing paper it says 'Station Inny Junction', but visitors are advised not to get off there because there is no proper road across the bog. My father claims that when he is waiting to change trains at Inny Junction during the war the stationmaster receives a telephone call to clear the line because the delayed 8.10 from Sligo is finally on its way and the stationmaster ripostes down the line, 'Let her come, she'll meet her match.' Pakenham in these years between the wars is a realm of innocent enchantment, where my uncle Edward Longford reigns like Babar in the kingdom of the elephants. He is already prodigiously fat, though not yet up to his post-war weight which must approach thirty stone. For the last twenty years of his life he must be the fattest peer in Ireland by a distance. His wife Christine is as slight and skinny as a whippet. She is a curious mixture of sharp and fey, as if her witty comments on people and places come from somewhere a long way off. They have painted the great hall and its surrounding passages bright scarlet and blue and replaced the old country-house furniture with immense Chinese and Japanese pots and vases. Edward's siblings and their assorted friends turn up without warning or invitation, particularly those asked by his brother Frank, the future campaigner for prisoners and against pornography and Edward's heir presumptive (Edward and Christine never looked much like having children). Frank does write to say he has asked one Oxford friend to stay but his handwriting is so bad that no one can read the invitee's name. Violet and Julia are deputed to greet the mystery guest. The two girls, aged

eighteen and seventeen, take him all round the house, up to the battlements and the flag tower and then down to the enormous kitchen garden to pick up fallen fruit. The guest chatters away non-stop, chuckling and exclaiming with delight at everything, and in the kitchen garden begins to quote Marvell, 'The nectarine and curious peach, Into my hands themselves do reach,' but still gives away no clue to his identity. At their wits' end the girls ask him to write his name down in the visitors' book – 'It's an Irish custom to write your name down at the beginning of your stay, in the hope that you may stay for ever.' But he is on to them and writes his name in quavering Irish letters which they cannot decipher. Only next day when Frank appears do they discover the name of my father's Magdalen friend John Betjeman.

John does indeed stay pretty well for ever, spending the summer holidays at Pakenham throughout the 1930s, even after he gets married to Penelope Chetwode and she has to stay behind to look after their baby son Paul (a reluctant Penelope not exactly designed for the home-fire role). And he is there the first summer my parents go there together. My father rows John and my mother across Lake Derravaragh. Also in the boat is a young Irish actress, Cathleen Delaney, whom John flirts with. They go to watch the hurling matches at Castlepollard. They botanise in the flower meadows beside the lakes. In the evening they play gramophone records of Protestant marching songs – 'The Sash My Father Wore', 'The Old Orange Flute'. They wander through the deserted demesnes of West Meath: Portloman and Belvedere, Tristernagh and Bloomsbury, once the residence of one of Betjeman's favourite dim peers, Lord Trimlestown, whose brother he claims now lives in an upturned wheelbarrow by the roadside.

John likes to pose as an even dimmer Irish peer, Lord Massey, and persuades Edward to ask some other moth-eaten lords to dine. It is, he

claims, the greatest moment of his life when Lord Cloncurry or possibly Lord Kilmaine holds open the door to the billiard room after dinner and says, 'After you, Massey.' He and my father also spend a lot of time getting tanked up at the medical hall in Castlepollard, the two of them standing next to the groceries in their battered brown hats, melting into the small towns of Ireland which they both love.

From all this jaunting round West Meath comes Betjeman's delicious epic in the manner of Tom Moore, *Sir John Piers*, which he persuades the *West Meath Examiner* in Mullingar to publish that summer. It must be Cathleen Delaney who inspires the barcarolle of Part Two:

> I love your brown curls, black in rain, my colleen.
> I love your grey eyes, by this verdant shore
> Two Derravaraghs to plunge into and drown me,
> Hold not those lakes of light so near me more.

I still have the copy John gave my parents and inscribed in cod Irish script 'Julia agur Robin o Mount o Seon O Betjeman 1938'. It is at Pakenham, I think, that John first perfects his role of impresario–magician, teasing and flattering the dull out of their dullness, gilding not the lily but the dustiest dandelion, keeping the show on the road to the very end of the road. Not everyone takes to his carry-on, suspecting a touch of charlatanry. Tony Powell is always a little leery of him and is delighted to catch him out when Betjeman, the supposed technophobe, makes my cousin Alice drive him to the doctor's house to find an adequate electricity supply for his electric razor. But I find him irresistible, and as the years go by come to revere him more and more as a teacher of the eye and heart, who makes us see not just the charm but the moral splendour of the dim and disregarded. One evening in the 1960s he takes a gang of us down to an evening of old-time music-hall at Deptford Town Hall. On the bill are some of the greatest stars of thirty or forty years ago, delighted to be back on the boards again, amazingly preserved in voice and limb, in fact their vigour and grace all the more striking now that they are into their seventies: Wee Georgie Wood, the cheeky schoolboy, Randolph Sutton, the crooner who was the first to sing 'Bye Bye Blackbird' in London, Wilson, Keppel and Betty the contortionist acrobats, Billy Brown the British Working Man, and Hettie King who comes on rouged to the eyebrows in a sailor suit and sings the song that made her famous nearly half a century earlier, 'Every Nice Girl Loves a Sailor'. In the interval, still a little out of breath from their exertions and the sweat showing through their make-up, they crowd round Betjeman. He is their Diaghilev for the evening, enchanting them all just as he enchants crabbed clergymen and pernickety architectural historians, making them feel that theirs is the only universe which counts and that they are the kings of it.

Edward is himself a serious amateur of the Irish language, and translates old Irish poems into a pleasant springy English verse. Long after his death I read one of these translations to a literary gathering in Lisdoonvarna, Co. Clare, and am pleased to find how green his memory is in his adopted land. From the moment he is ducked in Mercury Pond at Christ Church, Oxford, for taking the nationalist side, that is the side he unwaveringly supports. In his later years he scarcely ever crosses over to England, except once or twice to take the Gate Theatre company on tour. He inherits a considerable fortune, owning the town of Longford and half the port of Dún Laoghaire, and he pours much of it into the theatre, selling works of art off his walls to keep the Gate going. No doubt it is partly for that dedication to the Gate that his funeral procession winds for several miles, with the Anglo-Irish family up at the front in mourning dress (I even hire a top hat) and Brendan Behan and Joan Littlewood bringing up the boozy rear. But in between, I fancy, are hundreds of the plain people

of Ireland who never go near a
theatre and who simply want to
honour Edward for his passionate
allegiance to the land of his fortune over the country of his
birth.

But oh he is greedy. At meals
the lord's plate is stacked high
with the produce of the kitchen
garden, said to be the largest in
Ireland (it is as though the
enormous kitchen garden has somehow bred the enormous Earl,
much as a well-mulched cold frame will bring forth a prize
pumpkin). Once Edward's austere Protestant butler Andrews
switches the plates as though by accident and gives the lord's plate
to me. It is a cruel jape, as Uncle Edward begins to expostulate,
paws trembling, 'Andrews, Andrews, I think, I think . . .' Silently
the plates are switched. He is a gentle man. I cannot remember an
unkind thought coming from him, spoilt and indulged beyond
reason of course, but his indulgences are mostly in the cause of
giving pleasure to others.

It is while staying at Pakenham Hall that Henry Lamb paints all his
brothers- and sisters-in-law while they are still in their twenties. These
portraits in their unmistakable pinks and greens and browns hang all
along the passage and up the stairs. Uncle Henry's mild magic enfolds
the whole orphaned family. In Edward and Christine's misty kingdom of lake and bog he is their gentle, caustic Prospero. When Violet
is sitting for him, a new visitor, Tony Powell, like Betjeman scarcely
known on first arrival, is called in to entertain her. In no time they are
engaged and not much later married.

I must myself have been ten or eleven when I first meet my uncle
Tony. He and Violet are living in a painfully tall and narrow house at
the entrance to Regent's Park, 1 Chester Gate. Unlike the rest of the
Nash terraces around it, it stands more or less on its own since one of
Hitler's bombs has burned its twin next door down to the ground
floor. Everything about the house is novel to me because I have never
been inside a London town house before (in fact I don't think I have

been to London before), and so I am fascinated by the endless twisting stairs, the dumb-waiter creaking up from the kitchen with the decanter, and at full length on the Regency chaise-longue my uncle, a shortish, dapper figure, wearing a bow tie and a jacket which if not actually made of velvet gives the decided impression of being a smoking jacket, a garment which I know only from books. I always think of him reclining thus like Madame Récamier with a favoured cat strolling impertinently across his cavalry-twill trousers throughout our long conversations over the next fifty years at the house they are soon to move to, the Chantry, a Regency house near Frome and quite near us too. My father spotted the property for them and they got the whole lot, stables, lakes and grottoes, for something like a song. The Chantry is the same style and date as the Nash ex-terrace they have just quitted and they have of course taken all their furniture with them, including the chaise-longue, so it is to me as though he has never moved an inch in all these years. Only the name of the cat – a Burmese or a scrawny Cornish Rex – changes (Albert, Trelawny, Fum) and even that at very long intervals. As far as longevity goes, for cats the Chantry is like the Caucasus for human beings, a sad comparison with the lifespan of our own cats who are usually mown down in the road outside, so that during the period when I am naming them after Australian tennis players, Hoad, Rosewall and so on, we manage to use up the entire Davis Cup team.

The only time I ever remember conversing with Uncle Tony when he is actually sitting upright is in his extreme old age when, frail in body and increasingly in mind too, he is pushed about the house in a wheelchair – the reversal of the normal pattern of life in which we sit up for the best part of it and only lie down at the beginning and end.

My mother has brought me up to London to see the Sherlock Holmes exhibition which is a few hundred yards away from 1 Chester Gate at 221B Baker Street, although no such address ever existed and the exhibition is held in part of the enormous modern building which houses the Abbey National and which would include 221B if it had existed. I am especially keen to see the Persian slipper which the great detective keeps his tobacco in, because my aunt Mary has lent it to the exhibition. But I cannot remember much else about the show and in my mind Holmes's bachelor quarters become hopelessly confused with 1 Chester Gate with its old portraits of Welsh ancestors and the gilt sphinxes and eagles of the Empire furniture for which my uncle Tony has such a penchant. Something of the cool curiosity, the interest in exact particulars, in getting things right, seems to link the fictional sleuth and the real-life novelist. Holmes not only takes in details that most of us miss, he also notices people whom we all too often don't give a second glance to: the boy who delivers a message, the woman who answers the door. Powell too has a marvellous evenness of curiosity. He is always eager to know exactly where someone comes from. As the fame of his books grows, he is often accused by his detractors of being an incurable snob, whose novels focus on an effete society which is already smouldering on the scrap heap of history. My uncle is certainly interested in family trees. The old green volumes of the *Complete Peerage* are on a handy shelf and the conversation makes regular pit stops to look someone up. But he swears that if there were a Burke's of Bank Clerks he would buy that too. Nor are his fans all nostalgic Tories. They include the playwright Dennis Potter, the Marxist historian Perry Anderson and the socialist firebrand Tariq Ali, all responding, not to the saga of a closed caste but to the way Powell evokes the remarkable anarchic openness of English life, its quicksands and eddies and backwaters, indeed the ups and downs of life generally.

Round the corner from the Sherlock Holmes exhibition and so not far from Chester Gate lies the Wallace Collection and Poussin's picture *A Dance to the Music of Time* which gave the title and set the theme for Powell's twelve-volume novel sequence: 'the Seasons, moving hand in hand in intricate measure: stepping slowly, methodically, sometimes a trifle awkwardly, in evolutions that take recognisable shape; or breaking into seemingly meaningless gyrations, while partners disappear only to reappear again, once more giving pattern to the spectacle: unable to control the melody, unable, perhaps, to control the steps of the dance'. Some time after Powell's death, when I was giving a lecture about him, to remind myself of the picture I pulled down from the shelf the magnum opus on Poussin by Sir Anthony Blunt – referred to by my uncle as 'the traitor Blunt'. To my surprise I found that scholars now say that the clumsy maidens dancing their measure are not the Four Seasons at all but rather the figures of Poverty, Industry, Richness and Luxury through which man passes in an eternal series of revolutions. It's a sort of wheel of fortune in fact and one which would have done just as well for the gyrations in the books. One should also not ignore the two putti in the picture, one holding an hourglass to show that it's later than you think and the other blowing a bubble to indicate, well, by now even the dimmest stockbroker knows what a bubble is.

On looking at the picture again, I also detected a certain resemblance in the figure of Time to the author. If you subtract Time's whiskers and ignore his nakedness, there is something about the figure – his ironic smile, the way he watches the figures dancing with such amused detachment while plucking his lyre – which recalls Powell's relationship to those around him. Perhaps all authors are a bit like that.

As a young man, he frequented the Fitzrovia pubs and grazed the pitiless pastures of Soho. He lived in Somerset for the last fifty years of his life without becoming in the least countrified, venturing out only for a stroll down to the lakes or to chop a few logs. Indoors he bottled a cask of wine once a year, ventured into the kitchen to make the mildest curry I ever tasted and covered the walls of the basement with a scrap mural of almost Sistine Chapel proportions. On Christmas Day our old Morris panted up Chantry hill for lunch and later on, after our family had scattered, I would stay there for the whole holiday and became aware how strict his regime was; for all his geniality and his generosity as a host, never a morning away from the desk, never a day lost.

He could be touchy. His friendship with Malcolm Muggeridge never recovered from the latter's supercilious review of *The Valley of Bones*, one of Powell's best novels. In my introduction to the American edition of Powell's memoirs, I said that the review was of an earlier and not quite so good novel in the series, *Casanova's Chinese Restaurant*. My aunt Violet, then nearly ninety, wrote swiftly to point out my error and its significance, namely that it was with *The Valley of Bones* that Powell began to be more generally recognised as a formidable writer and that is why Malcolm Mugg, who was not so recognised, was provoked to sabotage.

My uncle never cared to admit to being wounded and he acted as if the breaking off of relations meant little to him. Yet his friendship with Muggeridge and Orwell had been one of the key things in his life after the war. The three of them lunched together in Soho once or twice a month and he was Malcolm's literary editor at *Punch*, while my father also contributed articles on country matters, such as horse trials, Hadrian's Wall and myxomatosis. For a time Malcolm and his enchanting and forgiving wife Kitty

Muggeridge at Chitterne, 1955

were regular visitors to the Chantry and to Chitterne too. Malcolm became especially fond of my father and remarked with pleasure how alike our voices were. After my mother died, almost alone among my parents' friends he kept up with me, sent me the odd book and took me out to lunch at the Garrick (it was he who was giving me lunch when my erstwhile hero Harold Acton failed to recognise me because I had lost my youthful bloom). I hugely enjoyed the extravagance of his vowels and his self-disgust: 'You cannot imagine, my dear Ferdy, how ghaastly it is to be recognised in the street after one has appeared on television. It is like being accosted by a prostitute. But then appearing on television is the vilest form of degradation' – which of course did not deter him from appearing on it with relentless frequency, just as his denunciation of the sins of the flesh did not slow him up much. Yet behind all the puckish–puritan poses there was a genuine good nature which warmed even those who had decided in advance to take against him.

By contrast, Powell's friendship with Orwell ended only with Orwell's death. Tony procured the smoking jacket which Orwell wore when receiving visitors during his last days in hospital (an untypically flamboyant garment for Orwell, more suited to my uncle in fact). And at the funeral, he chose the hymns and read the lesson from Ecclesiastes.

When *Animal Farm* came out in 1945, my parents had an early copy and soon after I learned to read I picked it up, imagining from the title that it must be a book for children, though the green and grey jacket and the lack of pictures were not obviously alluring. I read the book through almost without stopping, at first enthralled by the heroism of the animals in breaking free of Mr Jones, then disgusted by the treachery of Snowball and Napoleon. My sister was still too young to read, but I taught her the words of the animals' marching song and together we sang it as best we could to the tune of 'Clementine', as instructed by the author:

> Beasts of England, beasts of Ireland,
> Beasts of every land and clime,
> Harken to my joyful tidings
> Of the golden future time.

I was surprised and a bit annoyed when my father told me that the book was really an allegory which I was too young to understand. None the less, my aunt Violet reported to Orwell how much I had enjoyed the book especially because 'there were no difficult words in it'. Orwell was delighted to hear that he had written so simply and clearly that a child of seven could love the book.

Like Orwell, Powell liked to explode received literary opinion. He denounced *Lolita* as 'Hollywood tinsel' and *War and Peace* as a soap opera. In his Journals, his willingness to point out where some celebrated author had gone off the rails became a ripe mannerism, brilliantly parodied by Craig Brown – '*Hamlet* is a not uninteresting play, but the plot is flawed.' But at the same time he had unexpected favourites who didn't write the way he wrote – Hemingway and Dostoevsky, for example. And he was always eager to bring out the qualities of a new or neglected writer, accepting their flaws – 'with every writer there is always something you have to put up with'. He was quick too to spot and make friends with younger writers such as V. S. Naipaul, Philip Larkin and Kingsley Amis. He easily outlived Larkin and Amis and so lived to read their letters in which they referred to him as 'the horse-faced dwarf', often in the course of reporting on a recent visit to the Chantry. He took this stoically.

When it came to willpower – a subject in which he was much interested – he was a curious mixture. My father used to say, not altogether admiringly, 'Tony has the strongest will of anyone I've ever met.' Yet he felt not the slightest urge to interfere in anyone else's business. In this he claimed he was utterly unlike the Pakenhams who were always eager to give advice (not my mother) whereas 'The Powells won't tell the people in the same carriage that the train is on fire.' Vidya Naipaul said that he had never met anyone except himself who was so utterly absorbed in the life of being a writer. For me tiptoeing along the edge of that life, this was a sympathetic quality. Those outside the literary world could sometimes find his company uncompromising, even chilly. But then it is hard to think of a single good novelist of whom this is not true. The icicle in the heart which Graham Greene said every novelist needed does not improve the ambient temperature.

When I came to write novels myself, I found his influence the most difficult of all English novelists to get away from – this may sound like a backhanded compliment but it is a compliment none the less. I know that when I start a story I have always his shadow behind me, insisting on the importance of dwelling, of giving full value to a place, however superficially unmemorable, to a person, however dim or marginal they might be in the eyes of the world, to a moment which seems so inconsequential.

Well into his late eighties Powell was a remarkable advertisement for not taking exercise. But there succeeded a long unhappy period of frailty. And at three in the morning he took a turn for the worse, and the doctor was summoned. The doctor was new, youngish, and he turned out to be called Powell too. On the way in, my cousin Tristram chatted to him about what part of Wales his ancestors came from. It was a typical Powellian moment: unexpected, genealogical, comical, melancholy. Powell died later that night. He had left instructions that his ashes should be scattered on the lake below the Chantry. While the rest of us gathered on the bank, Tristram and his other son John rowed the ashes out to the middle of the water. As he scattered them, Tristram read 'Fear no more the heat o' the sun'. The moment was in fact less reminiscent of *Cymbeline* than of Tennyson's 'Morte d'Arthur', a favourite of Powell's. Snow was gently falling, as it does at the beginning and end of *A Dance to the Music of Time*.

★   ★   ★

Is it in the course of that languorous summer at Tullynally or only after they are married that my parents decide they must live in the country? My father will do something with horses, or they will run a smallholding, or perhaps he will become a land agent. But they must get out and away, somewhere on the downs, in Wiltshire or Berkshire, where there is room to breathe and the view goes on for ever.

They find a small white house, a cottage really, in a straggling village a few miles west of Stonehenge. It only has two up and two down plus a lean-to kitchen with a window that opens directly on the farmyard next door. The best thing about the Malt House, Chitterne, is its garden, which has two old cooking-apple trees that have been allowed to grow into writhing Rackhamesque shapes and a little avenue of box that separates the lawn from the kitchen garden and the potting shed. At the end of the garden there is a steep hill and beyond are the downs where you can walk or ride for miles without seeing anything except the odd hill fort. They buy the Malt House for £900 from a Miss Woodley and their life together begins. My father joins the Wiltshire Yeomanry and my mother becomes my mother.

While she is waiting for this to happen, she designs a modest extension to the far end of the house: a long sitting room with French windows into the garden and, above, two more bedrooms, grandly known as the day nursery and the night nursery though they turn out to be just the bedrooms for me and two years later my sister.

In the autumn term after our trip to Italy I start taking classes to prepare me for being confirmed. These are voluntary, and there are not many volunteers, not among my friends anyway. They mostly come from stout atheistical families and would regard being confirmed as letting their parents down. But I sign on with enthusiasm and gobble up the catechism like a pound of cherries. I am a closet ritualist and love putting on my freshly laundered white surplice on Sundays before filing into chapel. One of my first purchases when I get to Oxford is a new surplice – £1 17s 6d from Shepherd and Woodward in the High Street. While other freshmen are buying cravats and brothel-creepers and packets of Durex, and the richer ones Morris Minors or even small sports cars, I am buying a surplice. It hangs still in my cupboard, preserved from periodic clear-outs on the grounds that it might come in handy for charades or other dressing-up games, although we never play any such games. I just keep it as a souvenir of past pleasures, just as keen sportsmen keep on their walls an old hockey stick or the paddle of an oar.

The sad truth is that at this stage I am really more interested in church than in sex. The steamy hankerings for S occupy only a small puzzled corner of my thoughts. As far back as my prep school, more advanced boys have tried to stir my interest in the facts of life, without much luck. I remember Iris Bond, a chunky boy who happens to have the initials I.R.S. and who is actually a year younger than me, attempting to fill me in about what bulls do to cows and his baffled rage when I refuse to be enlightened. My notion of the mechanics remains hazy, in fact mistaken on important points, until long after the age at which these days a normal programme of sex education would have put me right. My knowledge of the female body is not much better than John Ruskin's, nor, come to that, am I much clearer about my own body. This is partly due to being a late developer on all fronts. Wet dreams are a mysterious hazard of adolescence that happens to other boys, on a par with verrucas except I know you do not report them to matron. Nor am I especially keen to remedy the gaps in my understanding. When the Master in College catches me reading under the bedclothes after lights out, I am reading Henry James (*The Wings of the Dove*, I think), which shocks him almost as much as if it had been *Lady Chatterley*. 'I can't get on with that stuff at all,' he mutters.

By contrast, standing in chapel I exist in a state of something approaching bliss, not unlike that perfect freedom recommended by the Second Collect, only in my case attained not by the service of the Lord but rather through my remarkable capacity to exist for long periods in a moony vacancy of mind. This vacancy overcomes me at frequent intervals throughout my childhood and youth and is extremely vexing to everyone. 'What are you staring at?' my father asks at meals as I go into trance mode. To keep the grown-ups quiet, I usually fudge up some answer – the butcher's van going by or one of the Misses Feltham in a new hat – although in truth I am not looking *at* anything at all. This is why I choose to stare out of the dining-room window, so I can appear to be gazing at some real object of interest. Otherwise I have to mumble sorry and switch back on.

At school my staring in class begins to irritate the masters. D. G. Bousfield, the maths master, a ferocious footballer and general tough customer, is so disconcerted that he breaks his chalk on the blackboard while expounding elementary trig and cannot stop himself shouting, 'Mount, will you stop staring at me.' 'Sorry sir, I was just concentrating' – which of course I wasn't at all.

The advantage of chapel is that nobody can tick you off for staring into the middle distance because that is how devout people look. In fact quite often my trance morphs into some more concrete and immediate topic like which member of sixth form has the largest adam's apple. In my view, the winner is clearly Fearnley-Whittingstall, although when checking this verdict with Henry Harrod he suggests that F.–W. may be deriving an unfair advantage from his head being stuck in the air so far as he processes into chapel. It is a sadness to find on meeting Robert Fearnley-Whittingstall years later that this mighty protuberance has shrunk into a relatively ordinary neck.

When reading articles about transcendental meditation, I wonder whether I have been meditating all my life without knowing it. Certainly my trances do manage to empty my head of any identifiable train of thought, but I cannot honestly claim that they make me a better, more rounded person. All I am is rather irritated when the trance is interrupted. I expect Coleridge felt the same when the person from Porlock broke in, except that I could not possibly have written 'Kubla Khan' or anything else when entranced, but then nor, I suspect, could Coleridge.

What also irritates me is when my atheist friends attempt to quiz me on my beliefs. It hardly seems proper to explain that belief does not come into it. It just isn't the right sort of question, any more than it would be reasonable to ask whether you believe in tennis just as you are about to serve. 'Well, why do you recite the Creed then?' which is a good question that I let slide. Uncle Henry Lamb also likes to quiz me on such matters when he comes into the House of Steps. Like all the Bloomsberries he is mystified why people go on bothering with this mumbo-jumbo. What do you think of Pascal, he will say, or why do you go to Communion? Oh I don't know, I say blushing, I just find it, er, refreshing. Like a bath? he enquires with a glint of mockery behind his cruel specs. I grunt in a non-committal way and butter another toasted teacake.

Among the atheists in our class is Quintin Hoare, the languid and clever offshoot of the banking family who later becomes a buttress of the *New Left Review*. His languid manner is almost more annoying to masters than my staring. He manages to nettle D. J. Graham Campbell who is endeavouring to teach us divinity into expostulating, 'But, Hoare, don't you believe in the Holy Ghost?' 'Yes sir, of course I do,' replies Quintin in his most languid, accommodating manner, 'but he just doesn't interest me very much.' I am the other way round. I could not say for sure what I believe in or don't believe in but I find it all very interesting. By contrast, most of the time I feel about the natural sciences the way Quintin feels about the Holy Ghost. Darwinian theory, for example. It sounds vaguely implausible, but I'll let it go. What I can't get the hang of is the post-facto logic, what Professor Steven Rose calls the Just-So element. If the goldfinch has to be this brilliant scarlet and gold in order to attract a mate, then why doesn't the wren? And if the wren has to be this drab brown to avoid detection by predators, why doesn't the goldfinch? It now seems that the goldfinch would have done better to adopt the low-profile strategy as the buzzards and the red kites are picking them off in droves. Besides if there is no deliberate agency at work, isn't it an intellectual confusion to attribute any sort of *strategy* to genes, let alone to Professor Dawkins's elusive memes? Not surprisingly with this attitude I finish second from bottom in biology and not much higher in physics and chemistry.

Actually what I am more interested in at this period is not survival, whether of the fittest or not. I am more interested in non-survival, or in other words death. Sometimes I am a little surprised that not everyone shares my interest in the subject. In the midst of life we are after all in it and nowhere more so than here. From the moment you walk in under School Arch you see the names of the dead in blackened bronze stretching in long columns all along the arcade and the words from *Samson Agonistes* that I sometimes mutter to myself to ward off an asthma attack: 'Nothing is here for tears, no weakness, no contempt, dispraise or blame: nothing but well and fair and what may quiet us in a death so noble.' The names carry on across the far side of School Yard in the cloisters, in a trickle of individual tablets put up by grieving families, occasionally breaking out into a broader eddy where brothers are remembered next to one another: Robert Septimus Grenfell, 12th Lancers (what my father calls one of the fractional regiments) killed in action at Omdurman, Francis Octavus Grenfell VC killed in action in France, Riversdale Nonus, his twin, killed in action in France nine months earlier. John Buchan wrote a book about the Grenfell twins – in its way it was a contribution to the war effort.

At the top of the winding stairs in the antechapel and in the chapel itself there are more plaques in bronze and marble in Latin and Greek and English remembering masters and provosts and boys who died untimely deaths, many of them young men in their early twenties who never recovered from being wounded or gassed in the Great War.

Even the great elephant dome of School Library across the road and the massive School Hall next to it are memorials, to the Etonian dead of the South African War – the first large-scale slaughter to erode the self-confidence of the English upper class. Exploring the recesses of the library in my first week at school, I stray into some part that is off-limits to small boys.

'What are you doing there, boy?'

A very old man whose bony skull and gnarled hands are covered in freckles is glaring at me.

'Just looking, sir.'

'What's your name, boy?'

'Mount, sir.'

To my amazement tears begin to run down his ancient freckled cheek. For several minutes he cannot speak. Then seeing my startled face he pulls himself together.

'I used to share lodgings with your uncle, no, it must be your great-uncle.'

There is a brass in the chapel to George Mount who taught at the school and died in 1901, just before he was thirty, of typhoid, I think. The inscription reads *Nunc scio vere quia misit Dominus angelum suum* – now I truly know why the Lord has sent his angel. At school Uncle George was known as the Angel. A contemporary master, not Tom Cattley the retired School librarian who burst into tears, but Hugh Macnaghten who became Vice-Provost, wrote a poem about Uncle George which is too awful to quote. He also wrote this: 'I remember meeting him, when he was a master, as he came back from a solitary run, near the gate of Agar's Plough, and thinking that I had never seen any sight more glorious. He might have been one of Botticelli's archangels.' I wonder what became of the angelic gene. Uncle George must have taken the same route for his solitary run as Widmerpool is described as taking twenty years later.

My uncle Grig is really called George, after the Angel, just as my father is named after two other dead uncles. We all live in the shadows of the dead. In his wonderful book *The Stripping of the Altars* Eamon Duffy paints a picture of an England that lost communion with the dead at the Reformation. Not here we haven't. The whole place is one huge chantry for departed souls.

Even when as little boys we are munching tea and jam in the shabby canteen known as the tea room, there looking down grimly at us is the portrait of Godfrey Meynell VC who bought it on the North-West Frontier in 1935 in a war we have never heard of, the Mohmand Campaign. We are a little awed by the thought of winning the VC posthumously in a battle nobody remembers at all.

'Restless natives, I expect.'

'Very restless natives.'

Even when we have a drink, it turns into an act of remembrance. The school has a little pretend pub called Tap, a tiny bar-room hidden behind the High Street where senior boys can learn to drink beer. David Cornwell thinks it is the most civilised thing he has heard about the school. All round the walls of Tap are the leaving photographs of old boys dating back to the Edwardian era. Half of them seem to have perished in one war or another. Mrs Hobbs, who pulls the half-pints and brings out delicious little sausage croquettes known as Durhams, can tell you all about them because she has been serving there since she was eighteen.

'Oh he was a lovely boy, killed on the Somme the first day. There were three more of my boys went in that one.' How handsome Mrs Hobbs is. We can imagine her flirting chastely with the boys and then only a few months later hearing the news of their deaths.

In our very first term, Edward Hussey and I are taken up to St George's Chapel in Windsor on 6 December, the birthday of the school's founder Henry VI, to lay lilies on his grave. It is an eerie outing. The two of us shivering in the darkened chapel, only half lit by candles, Edward carrying the lilies as the top scholar and behind us Ian Davidson carrying roses to represent our sister foundation King's College, Cambridge, which he is destined for and bringing up the rear the Vice-Provost, old Charlie Rowlatt, whose stomach is reputedly made entirely of tin after he was disembowelled in the Great War. Just us and the flickering lights and the limp banners of the Garter knights hanging above us in the chilly night air. Talk about living in Holy Henry's shade. But then I have a lot to thank our Founder for. He intended his new foundation just across the Thames for seventy poor scholars, not for the hundreds of gilded youths who later flocked into nearby boarding houses, and I am one of the relatively few among the seventy whose parents do not have to pay a penny in fees. Their combined income passed the College's means test without breaking sweat. So all they have to fork out for is my tennis racquet and my surplice. This subject is never mentioned by my parents, nor by my schoolfellows. For we are as delicate about money as about the other facts of life.

Only a week before the lilies business, on St Andrew's Eve, we have for the first time watched the loving cup pass from hand to hand among those who are to play for College in the medieval scrum known as the Wall Game the following day. One after another they chant 'In piam memoriam J.K.S.' This is the annual homage to J. K. Stephen, Virginia Woolf's first cousin, renowned classical scholar, light poet and football giant. J.K.S. went crazy in his late twenties, either from receiving a blow on the head at Felixstowe from something thrown at him from a passing train or from syphilis, according to which story you believe. He later made terrifying advances to Virginia's half-sister Stella and died raving aged thirty-three. It was from J.K.S. that Virginia derived her fear that her own insanity was hereditary and incurable. Here he remains an unblemished demigod.

These ceremonies already seem a little ludicrous and antiquated to us although we would not want them gone. We amuse ourselves in speculating who will be toasted half a century hence and try out our own initials, though this is extremely unlikely since none of us is any good at the Wall Game. In practice of course, as I checked the other day, fifty years on it is still J.K.S. who is remembered, though now at the grand supper after the game rather than on its eve. I cannot help being beguiled by these continuities and feel myself heir to something or other as I file up to the Bishop of Lincoln behind my fellow confirmands and kneel for him to place his bony hand on the top of my head (we have been told that the Bishop does not care to be patting pomaded heads, but my rebellious hair is slicked down with a few drops of Eau de Portugal which John Spicer in the year above says is the only stuff): 'Defend, O Lord, this thy child with thy heavenly grace that he may continue thine for ever.'

I feel like a penitent in one of the fifteenth-century wall paintings that run round the chapel. They were painted by an artist nobody has ever heard of called William Baker. He and his assistants were paid £8 7s 4d for their work. When Queen Elizabeth came to the throne, the local barber was paid 6s 8d to whitewash over these popish images. For nearly three centuries the paintings lay hidden behind the whitewash and later on behind classical wainscoting as well. In the 1840s they were briefly and partially revealed when stalls carved in the new gothic taste were being installed. Provost Hodgson considered these scenes of miracles wrought by the Virgin Mary unfit for the eyes of Anglican schoolboys, and remained deaf to the pleas of Prince Albert, the only civilised man in England, that the paintings could remain accessible to art-lovers if they were kept on hinged or sliding panels. It is not until the 1920s that the gothic canopies are removed, and even then to the fury of old Etonians who have got used to staring glassily at the canopies for five years of their life. So there they are around us, the most wonderful wall paintings in our desecrated northern islands, depicting these unseemly miracles: devils riding on horseback, Jews being converted, merchants selling their souls, empresses having visions. The great Victorian architect G. E. Street who had glimpsed them briefly in 1847 thought they might be the work of a pupil of the Blessed Angelico. But we know they are only the work of William Baker, who probably never left Berkshire. Anyway Provost Hodgson need not have worried. The boys haven't a clue what is going on in the paintings. But how beautiful they are and how miraculous to have them round us every day. Perhaps we too could recover our souls if only we could remember who we had sold them to.

As I come back from the Bishop's throne, I still cannot see my parents anywhere in the congregation. I am used to this. The Morris Ten is not a good runner. Sometimes it will not start at all, but more often it conks out after thirty or forty miles leaving us becalmed by the side of the Bath Road somewhere near Avebury while my father walks to the nearest pub to call the AA and my mother settles down to the *Daily Telegraph* crossword. Neither of them seems much fazed by these hiccups, regarding them as a normal part of motoring life. But I already know that this is not how other people live. The Lane Foxes' Humber Super Snipe never breaks down.

I pass back between the lines of parents who are seated in the pews normally occupied by the boys, which makes them look out of place, cruelly reduced, as if by some hideous trick they have been returned to their old school places but still wearing their grown-up suits and frocks. And I see my father after all. He too looks somehow reduced, his ruddy complexion turned pale in the grey November light dropping down from the long windows, his fierce leonine figure no longer standing out from the crowd, which is perhaps why I have missed him. I was looking for someone altogether more extraordinary. He is alone.

'Mummy sends her love. She had to go to hospital. Just a few tests, nothing you need to worry about. I've got a present for you.'

We stand in Upper School while the other parents push past us to get at the drinks, impatient and thirsty after the service. My present is the Phaidon *Michelangelo* with the head of the Madonna in the St Peter's *Pietà* on the jacket. I stare glumly at the inscription on the flyleaf in my father's weird Chinese-style hieroglyphs, not one letter joined up to the next. Perhaps my mother cannot write any more. 'To Ferdie with love from his parents on the occasion of his confirmation by the Bishop of Lincoln. 26 November 1955'. It seems a cold, remote message, like an announcement you might put in a newspaper. I do not dare to ask what is wrong with my mother, and my father does not want to tell me. He is conscious of my anxiety but cannot think what to do about it.

'It's all right if we come to the school play, is it?' he says after a bit.

'Oh it really won't be worth it – I've got a tiny part, I'm only in one scene really.'

'We wouldn't dream of missing it,' my father says with enthusiasm, but as I know he doesn't much like the theatre and they never normally come to school events he only strengthens my suspicions. Then my father has to go because he has to hare across country to St Margaret's Bushey to see my sister confirmed which is happening on the same day and of course he is late.

The play is *Danton's Death*, the first production ever in English. A friend of Raef Payne's has translated it from German and someone quite important is going to come and see it, an agent or producer, but Raef does not know on which night, or perhaps he just says this to make us try harder. Raef is a dreamy bachelor master with a lick of brown hair and a drowsy voice and a total absence of keenness which enchants us all. He happens also to have been brought up in Chitterne which creates a bond between us.

'I don't think acting is really your thing,' he says in that reflective way of his after I audition for him, which suggests that he has given a lot of thought to the matter. I cannot disagree. Hard to say exactly what my biggest thespian deficiency is: lack of physical self-confidence certainly, also absence of enthusiasm for the stage. Anyway the part of Legendre, an enraged deputy in the assembly, is about my limit. Julian Reade is Robespierre, but then for some reason Raef decides that Francis Hope should share the part, each doing two nights. Along with being brilliant at everything else, Francis is not only a brilliant actor but also a brilliant memoriser and learns the demanding part over a weekend. Both Robespierres are mesmerising: Francis is volcanic, outraged, unforgiving; Gloom is pale, icy, contemptuous. Everyone agrees that between them they make up the perfect Robespierre.

By contrast, I am dismally bad on all four nights. Sometimes I shout too loud for my words to be understood. One night I get stuck between the benches so that I cannot rush forward with the rest of the infuriated mob to save Danton from Robespierre's implacable wrath. On the third night I forget the middle bit of my few lines so that what comes out makes no sense at all.

But none of this matters to me because there they both are on the last night jostling among the other parents in School Hall. I jump down from the stage without first going behind to remove my greasepaint as we were told.

'What did you think of it?' I say breathless but trying to sound negligent, expecting 'Darling, you were wonderful,' though knowing perfectly well I was not.

'It made you realise how long the French Revolution went on for,' my mother says. 'I never heard of Legendre. Is he supposed to look like an angry sheep?'

'Everyone looks like an angry sheep in these wigs. Anyway Bayne major says I look like a dilapidated teddy bear.'

'No, more like an angry sheep, I think,' says my mother looking at me in a mock-serious way as though judging a competition. I am delighted to see her so sharp. I am delighted to see her full stop, although it is so near the end of term and I shall be home soon anyway.

She is pale but that is only to be expected when she has been ill, and in the past tense is where I put her illness. And when I do come home for Christmas nothing seems very different. We go for Christmas lunch over to the Chantry and we go to the meet of the Wylye Valley Hunt in front of the pub at Horningsham. Most of the time, though, I am upstairs on my own listening to my green rexine-clad portable radio, especially at the weekend when I can listen all day to the comedy shows and then the repeats on Sundays, starting at lunchtime with *Educating Archie*, which isn't my favourite, then going on to *Life with the Lyons* and *Ray's a Laugh* until we come to the assuaging tones of Richard Dimbleby introducing *Down Your Way* which I switch off for, returning for the supreme treat of *Take It from Here* (or in the summer *Much-Binding-in-the-Marsh*), then off again for *Grand Hotel* with Max Jaffa and his Palm Court orchestra, usually coming back on once more for *Variety Bandbox* with Al Read (my all-time favourite), Terry-Thomas and Arthur English. Never before or since do I listen (certainly never view) with such intense pleasure as I do to the Light Programme through these years. Any moment now pop music really begins, with Elvis's debut (1956, just as sex starts in 1963), and I get a blue-and-grey record player for my birthday, also clothed in slinky rexine, and I buy the first Presley albums and Sinatra's *Songs for Swinging Lovers*, but they don't mean half as much to me as the Light Programme comedy orgy every Sunday. While I am listening, out of the window through the bare branches of the big nut tree I can see my mother slowly brushing the dead leaves off the lawn in her heavy straw-coloured mac, a riding mac I think it is called, though I don't think she has been on a horse since she was sixteen. Beyond the box hedge my father is digging over the vegetable patch. He takes the wheelbarrow round the side of the house and crosses the road to the other farmyard opposite where Mr Stratton keeps a couple of carthorses. After promising the farm foreman a drink at the King's Head he wheels a barrowload of the finest manure back in triumph. The helpful outdoors type of boy would be eagerly helping his father send forkfuls of manure thudding into the silver barrow, would perhaps even remember to bring over a few sugar lumps for Dobbin or Flossie or whatever they are called. But I have now become an early prototype of the couch potato, although as a small child I had enjoyed helping my parents in the garden, so I stay upstairs listening to the Glums and then in the breaks for the news and the shipping forecast try a bit of *Madame Bovary* which is the set book for French A-level. In fact it turns out to be the set book for French S-level too and then the set book for university French, so by the time I stop being educated I know *Madame Bovary* better than any other book in the world. Flaubert is so beastly to all his characters that with each reading I become increasingly fond of them all. I begin to think that Charles

Bovary is probably quite a good doctor really, certainly no worse than Dr Falk who leaves the business end of a hypodermic syringe stuck in my bottom, and I think Emma must be rather fun to be with. First time round, though, I am struggling with the French and have no time for forking manure and other horticultural tasks, which if challenged I can always claim bring on my asthma. Because of the smell of the manure or because of the physical effort of forking it? Either or both. That is the beauty of being asthmatic. Since the doctors don't really know what triggers an attack, the patient is king. From an early age I have mastered the art of self-diagnosis, managing to get myself excused all runs and swimming lessons. I am already one of the senior non-swimmers in the school and experience a little throb of pride every time the list goes up at the beginning of each summer term, 'Non-Nants' as they are called in the cod Latin that hangs around the place like the smell of the fog from the river. Although this naming and shaming has no effect on me, for form's sake I protest at such public harassment of an unfortunate minority. But Francis Hope points out that public ridicule is an essential feature of all despotic systems. After all, putting up the exam results on the school notice board is only posting a list of Non-Intelligunts.

On Boxing Day we go over for drinks to Lees and Mary Mayall at their house Sturford Mead, a Regency villa in honeyed stone just beyond Longleat perched above the road from Warminster to Frome. From the lawn in front of the house you look through the trees to Cley Hill, whose rounded top is visible for miles around. The house is full of their children from this marriage and their previous marriages. Tony and Violet Powell are there too and our cousins Tristram and John. I know the house from childhood because Henry and Daphne Bath lived there before they were divorced. My father suggested buying the house to the Mayalls, in fact seems to have made a tidy commission on the sale, which annoyed Henry Bath. It must have been the only commercial transaction my father ever made a profit on.

It is the headquarters of Wiltshire high bohemia, the place where my parents have had a good time ever since they came to Wiltshire. Sturford smells the same whoever is living there – that swimmy fragrance of gin and cigarettes and the flowers in big vases on the

marble table in the hall. Now it is my
mother's best friend Mary Mayall who
is at the centre of the good time,
standing in front of the fire with her
legs wide apart drawing the cigarette
smoke through her bright scarlet lips
down into her lungs and bringing up
great liquid chuckles at her own jokes,
or anyone else's, for she is stingy with
nothing, certainly not with drink or
laughter. After lunch – on second

thoughts, have we had lunch? No, I don't think we have – lunch is
probably there somewhere and may well be served towards dusk, but
at Sturford drinks are the main meal of the day – so then, after drinks
we troop out through the big French windows to air the gin and catch
the last rays of the sun.

My mother lines everyone up so she can take a group photograph.
Because it is late December the sun is low in the sky, only just above
the yew hedges which Daphne planted years ago and which have now
grown to head height. But it is as bright and startling as winter sun
often is and the picture comes out better than many of my mother's
photos, certainly better than some of the ones we took in Italy. When
the film comes back from being developed (for some unexplained
reason my mother sends her photos all the way to Roses' laboratories
in Chester), in the left foreground there is a black shadow reaching
across the paving. It is the shadow of the photographer.

My mother times her treatment to start after we have gone back to
school, in order that we remain unaware that she is having these spells
in hospital. My father drives over to Bath every day to see her. Every
time he passes under a railway bridge on the way when there is a train
going under it, he wishes with all his heart that she will be all right. I
have never heard of this custom of being granted a wish if you pass
under a bridge when a train is going over it. My father says that he
used to do it when driving to a race meeting before the war, wishing
that he would win the big race. I do not ask whether it worked for
him then. Perhaps he has invented this superstition himself. By the
time he tells me about it, its track record is not looking so hot.

At school I am starting to specialise in modern languages and am learning all about passion, which is what French literature, and German literature too, seems to be mostly about. Apart from *Madame Bovary*, there is Racine whose plays are all about women boiling with irrepressible passions which get all the more stoked up, we are told, because of the extreme formality of the alexandrines in which they are expressed. I find something harsh and repellent in these European classics. There is a rank odour about them, like fox urine. And I always take against the heroine who is supposed to be on the side of Life, which is a side I am not at all sure about. In *Anna Karenina* I am on the side of good old reliable Karenin. In *Middlemarch* I long for Mr Casaubon to discover the key to all mythologies so he can say snubs to the ghastly Dorothea. As for Lady Chatterley, when we finally get hold of a copy, my sympathies are entirely with Sir Clifford. The master who tells us all about passion is Oliver Van Oss who is now my specialist tutor. O.V.O. is a large rubicund man in a navy-blue cardigan, of vaguely Napoleonic appearance, with an expression that is both sardonic and menacing. He was at Magdalen College, Oxford, with my father, but they treat each other with that unexplained reserve of people who have been together in the same place for quite a while but have never really taken to each other. O.V.O. is a mesmerising teacher, on a par with David Cornwell; he also paints flowers and collects things like porcelain and Rembrandt etchings. He is also a bullshitter of Olympic class. One of his poses is of a man who is himself no stranger to passion. To shock us he says things like 'Once you've had a black woman, you'll never want a white' or 'The French go on about sex the whole time, but it doesn't mean they are always doing it.' There is more passion too on the German side because the period we are doing is *Sturm und Drang* which is all about love and violence and death, especially suicide.

All this only increases my fondness for the mild, the quiet, the cool. I become even more sceptical and withdrawn than nature intended. Reserve is my habitat – I am a one-man reservation. This attitude is not just to do with the books we are reading, although in my view literature has a lot to answer for. I am also trying to keep out of my mind the thing that I do not want to think about, and not thinking about unwelcome subjects is a skill that unlike swimming and drawing I have a natural gift for. In the corner of my photograph no black shadow is permitted.

My mother and I are photographed together one more time, on the school's summer feast day, the Fourth of June. Instead of having a picnic on the cricket field and wandering round the boundary, we go over for lunch at Holthanger, the house that my uncle Grig and aunt Betty have just bought on the Wentworth estate, although Lennard's the shoe factory my uncle owns and manages is miles away in Bristol. My mother sees her sister-in-law as little as possible, so to come to Holthanger at all is quite an effort for her at the best of times which obviously this is not. But the advantage of Wentworth is that it lies inside the five-mile radius of the school within which we are permitted to roam when we go out with our parents. I don't know why we are so dutiful about observing this limit. At this date, the masters are scarcely equipped with long-range monitoring equipment. Holthanger is a modern low house designed in the shape of a ship with its portholes peeping through the shrubbery on to the third fairway of the Burmah Road golf course.

After the leg of lamb and the crusty apple pie we go out into the garden. My sister takes the first photograph and there is my mother just in front of me flinching from the camera as usual, looking downwards and to one side. As always she looks ten or fifteen years younger than her age, which is now forty-two. Into her thirties pub landlords would ask her if she was eighteen yet. She looks untouched by life, although she has never been this thin before. Then she takes over the camera and lines up another group photograph. This time we are standing on the verandah. On the wall behind us there hangs a big grisaille painting by my father's great friend Adrian Daintrey. It is a strange painting, much stranger than anything else he did. It shows three young women in sleeveless dresses sitting outdoors round a table on what is obviously a hot summer's night. The three young women are Mary Mayall, Augustus John's daughter Poppet and my mother. Adrian must have painted it about twenty years earlier when they were all twenty-two or thereabouts. How luscious and nonchalant they look. Or perhaps the strangeness is not all in the painting itself but in the fact that my mother is photographing a black and white image of her younger self, the ghost of summers past.

What comes through to me now, all this time later, is not so much how reluctant my mother is to be photographed (that is nothing new) but how eager she is to do the photographing. She already sees herself, I think, as somehow detached from the scene, like a kindly stranger passing along the prom who offers to take the picture so we can all be in it together. A few days after the Fourth of June, she and my father go off on holiday, the first time for years they have done this, just the two of them. They go to Lake Como and she snaps my father rowing her across the lake just as she snapped him rowing across Lough Derravaragh when they were engaged. Does Charon like to be photographed, I wonder idly. No, there would probably be a notice on the bank of the Styx forbidding flash photography. They go to Verona too, and the last photograph of all shows my mother in front of Juliet's balcony. Perhaps that is another omen too, though obviously it is my father taking the picture. But all I know of their time in Verona is that they bring me back an unbelievably gaudy tie as I have a taste for gaudy ties. This one has a pattern of slashes of orange, crimson and scarlet and is called Il Fulminante, the Thunderbolt. Apparently in this shop in Verona the ties have names, which I have never heard of anywhere else. I immediately fall in love with Il Fulminante and wear it at every opportunity. I am wearing it when my uncle Henry paints a portrait of me a year later. There is a depressing contrast between the reckless gaiety of the tie and my lugubrious expression, the sort of look that provokes annoying strangers to say 'Cheer up, it may never happen.'

Anyway, all this stuff about photographic omens is fanciful. The truth is that it is my mother's camera and she automatically takes pictures as people do when they are on holiday. What is not fanciful is that from roughly now on, or perhaps from a month or so earlier, she begins to withdraw from life, and from my sister and me. It is a staged and graceful withdrawal, begun out of love for us, to spare us pain, sorrow, even anxiety. And my father acquiesces, partly I think because he has no confidence in his ability to look after us, to hold us up. And so we are despatched around the country, my sister and I, to stay with our relations, Francie mostly to Uncle Grig and Aunt Betty and to the Mayalls because she and Lees's daughter Elizabeth are best friends at school, I to my mother's sisters Mary and Violet in Herefordshire and Somerset. We do not fully understand what is happening to us, we do not grasp that this is, in the gentlest and best-intentioned way, a breaking up of home which is final and not to be retrieved.

I am staying with my aunt Mary. We are just going to have lunch and I am standing by the bow window in the library which serves as the dining room. She is on the telephone and we are waiting for her.

'I've just been talking to your mother,' she says. 'She's going up to London to have an operation which the doctors think will be very good for her. She sounds very pleased about it.'

'Oh,' I say, trying to sound steady. 'Did she say what sort of operation exactly?'

Aunt Mary is not a great one for covering things up.

'It's on her head,' she says and cannot really think of much to add.

'Ah yes,' I say. 'That's good.' Meaning that's so bad that even I can see what must follow, but all that matters now is that I do not cry because there are quite a few people standing around waiting for their lunch.

'So you'll be able to see her before you go to Germany.'

Which I do. She is lying on her side in a little room in the Maudsley, more like a hutch than a room, and she is not breathing at all well. There is a bandage somewhere round the back of her head, or perhaps it is just the way the pillowcase has rucked up. The light is dim and I do not wish to look as if I am peering. The room seems so strange and anonymous. There is nothing in it except her bed and the table with some medicines on it. I have a weird fancy that she has been

brought here by force, against her will, and I am somehow relieved
when I see a jar of her Pond's cold cream in among the medicines, as
though its presence proves this really is her room. She says she is sorry
about the breathing and now she knows how I must feel when I have
an attack. How she envies me going to Munich, it was so lovely
before the war strolling in the English Garden which is where her old-
school-not-really-friend Unity Mitford shot herself and of course I
must not miss Salzburg either. Then quite soon I have to go because I
have been told I must not tire her out, though in truth I am not sure
how much longer I can hold out myself, and we embrace, awkwardly
as we always embrace, and I feel her warmth and refuse to believe
what I know I must believe.

Number 50 Zugspitzstrasse is a medium-sized, cream-coloured
villa in Gauting, which is a suburb on the way out from Munich to
the Starnbergersee. The house does not seem large enough to
accommodate all the foreign students that Frau Jarolymek is packing
in. Besides me, there is a tall boy from school called Robin Heathcote
whom I know only by sight, two Belgian sisters who seem like twins
but aren't, a Scottish girl called Maureen who irritates Frau Jarolymek,
me too a little though I am not quite sure why, but anyway not nearly
as much as I am annoyed by the French boy who is one of those
undersized runtish French boys who manages at the same time to look
about five years old and to bear a weird resemblance to the poet
Baudelaire in his last years. The infant Baudelaire talks non-stop on
every subject with an air of unchallengeable authority. If thwarted in
any way, he begins to scream and rushes to his room. Frau Jarolymek

seems strangely tolerant of his tantrums, as though she is privy to some special reason for humouring him, such as him being a haemophiliac. He is not interested in talking German, let alone English, which means that it is the Belgian girls who are his captive audience while Robin and I play endless ping-pong under the big willow tree in the garden. Maureen sometimes plays ping-pong too but she is not much fun to play with. When the ball bobbles in his direction, the infant Baudelaire thinks it amusing to pretend that he has accidentally squashed it. I write about these things to my mother, but mostly what I write about is culture: about going to see *Figaro* for the first time at the Bavarian State Opera which is now at the Residenztheater because our boys bombed the old opera house flat along with other large portions of the city, and about how the Figaro is not as good as whoever it is on one of our few gramophone records at home, though how would I know. Then I go on in my newly acquired italic hand which makes everything look more pretentious:

On my way back from the opera I had an attack of asthma (Bavaria is very oppressive. Ach, das Klima . . .) and undid my collar and loosened my tie. But the last few steps to the Starnberger Bahnhof were too much for me and I curled round the post for support. Half the population of Munich gathered round to look at this drunken reveller, who was wheezing so heartily.

Then I turn to discuss the monuments of the city, with special attention to Bavarian rococo:

The Asamkirche ranks first, followed by the Theatinerkirche, which is entirely white inside and of extreme magnificence. A couple of moderate Tintorettos keep up the tone. I apologise for being a tourist bore, but we connoisseurs must show off our culture to someone because most of the pensionnaires are too half-witted. Besides, little scandal has happened bei Jarolymek, except that the Infant Baudelaire has left amid a flurry of screams.

I shall miss the Oktoberfest by a few days but as according to Frau J it consists mainly of beer and dancing, I shall not be very sorry.

Lots of love Your affectionate Münchner Ferdie

What an appalling letter to write to anyone at any time but in the
circumstances the intellectual snobbery, the preening hypochondria,
the callous self-absorption leave me, well, breathless. That it should be
my last gasp which holds the floor . . . Two days before I post this
letter from Munich, my uncle Henry also writes to my mother, from
Ireland:

Darling Julia,

Ever since those sadly abbreviated moments of my visit to you at the
Malt House I have been longing for a chat in a less hurried style to try
and make up for what there was no time for on that occasion, and then
I remember that I *never* had a chat with you that didn't seem too short
– for the simple reason that there seems to be no subject nor topic
which interests my mind or heart on which I would not like to have
your opinion.

We arrived here on Sept 1st – my first visit for more than 20 years,
and everything seems so little changed that it is exactly like a drop
straight back into 100 fascinating memories of you all which I had
foolishly neglected. But our thoughts were keenly turned towards you
from the moments of driving up the Wylye past the Codford Milk Bar
(the usual turn off for us going to Chitterne) through Warminster
where, on a busy corner, we got a glimpse of Francie and Mary Mayall.

Edward and Christine welcomed us in the porch here just as a pair of
under teenagers might receive their beloved parents after a long
absence; most convincing and really warming to my cynical heart.
I don't know when you were last here, but Pansy and Val [their son,
my Wiltshire playmate, a few months older than me] claim that
Edward is no fatter. My view is that it has all gone on *below*, though
face and hands seem little different, surely the fore and aft measure-
ment has doubled. Any way they seem to me like a pair of very
generous innocents and make me rather ashamed of ever having
thought otherwise. According to custom they left us on Monday
morning. Edward was superb, at the top of his form, and in a splendid
black coat for Dublin and a scarlet carnation, went on to a triumphant
burst of song in his best old style.

Unfortunately the weather remains unsatisfactory for though there
have been some fine half-days allowing several long walks the air is

filled with a silly cottonwood sort of fluffiness which takes all force out of the colours. I had armed myself with oil sketching materials but it has only been possible to try some sous-bois close ups and now these are held up by rain and the same grey mist. The rations as ever are massively impressive.

Well Julia darling, I do hope all this little chronicle won't have tired you. I did so much want to send you a message of love and I know Pansy and Val want to be joined in it. Please give my love also to Robin. Yours ever Henry.

Henry Lamb is aged seventy-three when he writes this letter. I am sixteen. It is not hard to see whose heart is the fresher. The visit to Pakenham turns out to be his last. I think of it as Prospero's return to the enchanted isle.

It is a consolation of sorts that my mother may have received Uncle Henry's letter and not mine, because three days after I wrote it Frau Jarolymek comes out into the garden with a telegram for me.

VERY BAD NEWS. MUMMY DIED PEACEFULLY THIS MORNING. YOU AND I MUST LOOK AFTER FRANCIE. ALL LOVE DADDY

Frau Jarolymek leads me upstairs to my room and briefly embraces me in the doorway, without much warmth. I don't think expressing her feelings comes naturally to her either. She smells faintly of – is it cinnamon? – perhaps she has been baking a cake when the telegram boy comes. She draws the curtains without my asking because that is what you do when death passes by (we do it in Chitterne too, but I am not up to telling her this). She asks me if I would like her to stay with me, but I say, 'Nein, danke.' I lie on the bed but cannot break down and cry because I am deep-frozen. Outside, the Belgian girls are playing ping-pong and giggling and crying 'Oh la la!', then I hear Frau Jarolymek's voice and the clucking of the ball stops, so she must have told them about me. Because I cannot weep, I pretend to myself that I am falling into a light doze, although it is only about midday and the sunlight is coming in between the curtains.

I am not sure how much time passes before Frau Jarolymek knocks
on my door.

'Are you all right? There is another telegram for you.'

REGRET TO INFORM YOU MUMMY IS DANGEROUSLY
ILL. WILL WIRE AGAIN LATER. LOTS OF LOVE DADDY

My head is whirling so fast that I cannot pin down exactly what my
reaction is, not hope, or not only hope, more a sense of bewilderment
and exasperation. Perhaps the wires are so totally crossed that the next
telegram will say 'Mummy making amazing recovery', but I don't
really allow myself to think this because I know it isn't true. After a
minute or two my wits are collected enough to compare the despatch
times of the two telegrams and see that the second was sent off three
hours before the first – so much for German efficiency. And somehow
this discovery opens some sluice-gate and I begin to cry at last.

The next thing that happens, which doesn't seem surprising at the
time, is that I don't go to the funeral. Apparently my mother has said
quite firmly that she does not want me to interrupt my stay on
account of her, and my father is too poleaxed to think of going against
her wishes and I am too inhibited to ask, because as explained earlier I
am no good at asking questions. So she dies just as she wishes to die,
causing minimum fuss and attracting as little attention as possible. We
know that she wanted to live as long as she could, otherwise she
would not have come up to London for an operation which promised
at best no more than a brief extension and could not guarantee even
that. But she did not wish to stage anything that could be described as
a fight for life if it meant upsetting those whom she loved. None of
her brothers and sisters is anywhere near. Henry and Pansy are in
Ireland with Edward and Christine. Mary (in some ways the closest to
her, certainly her most faithful correspondent) is at home in Herefordshire. Violet and Tony are abroad.

I realise now that she deals with her illness much in the way her
mother dealt with hers, by reticence, withdrawal and solitude. The
word 'cancer' is not mentioned to me as it was not to her and her
brothers and sisters when her mother was dying (or not until right at
the end). Even when years later, looking for something in my father's

desk, I come upon her death certificate and see under cause of death 'Carcinoma of the breast', the words come as a shock, as though this was still news to me. Would she have been cured these days? I do not know whether her cancer was of a particularly invasive type or whether neglect came into it, either her own or the doctors'.

For me too there is another echo in her dying, not of my grandmother's death but of the death of my grandfather, the Paladin of Gallipoli. I think of the verse my grandmother added to the hymn at his belated funeral:

> And those who die away from home
> Their graves we may not see.

Except that in this case I am the one who is away from home. And this strange sheltering from any direct experience of my mother's death continues. She is buried in the churchyard at Wasing, where all my father's family are buried. It is a peaceful wooded spot on the top of a gentle slope overlooking the Kennet Valley. It is no great distance from Oxford or London or any of the other places I live in over the next ten years. Yet I do not visit her grave until I have to in order to see my father buried beside her nearly thirteen years later, by which time I am married and have a baby son. This cowardice does not go unpunished, for my mother's ghost still comes and goes in my dreams, never properly laid to rest.

For a time in the 1970s and 1980s there is a fashionable theory that reticent types like my mother are especially prone to cancer, breast cancer in particular. Keeping your troubles buttoned up inside you is bad for you. It sounds a slightly primitive, almost medieval theory – are there really worry-rats gnawing away inside you? But it is not a new theory. D. H. Lawrence talks of some unhappy woman, his mother perhaps or her fictional equivalent, having cancer 'brought on by fretting'. And in Chekhov's story 'Three Years', Nina Fyodorovna is convinced that because her tumour is in her breast the cause of her illness must be to do with love and family life, specifically her faithless husband Panaurov. But Chekhov is a doctor and he means Nina to be a silly goose. For a time, though, I take some interest in this psychogenic theory and read any article that mentions it, but then the theory seems to peter out and the doctors fall back on the genetic explanation, otherwise known as bad luck.

I was brought up all wrong and so was my mother. I know that now and I am glad that my children are brought up quite differently. We should not have flinched from the camera's gaze, my mother and I, or been so modest about our bodies. We should have said yes to the flesh and looked the sun in the eye. We should not have needed a jar of cold cream to touch one another's cheek. Yet there is a part of me which does not regret the reticence.

In any case, I see that I have given the wrong impression. I have told too sad a story. I have not shown how gay my mother was, how caustic, how charming. Perhaps the frontispiece to this book will redress the balance. Uncle Henry was flitting through a Parisian phase at the time – there's a splash of Modigliani, even Matisse. The phase faded, but his affection for his sister-in-law did not. And you can see why. Look how the empty glass is cocked towards the viewer. There is time for another quick one before they close.

THE CODFORD ROAD

O N SUNDAY AFTERNOONS in summer the whole village used to go for a walk. They always go down the Codford road. There are three other roads out of Chitterne but each of the other roads soon hits a steep climb up to the downs. Quite a few of the walkers are elderly, which is why they stick to the Codford road because it stays on the level as it meanders in sync with the winter bourne that runs for four miles until it meets the River Wylye at Codford St Mary (which is also our telephone exchange, we are Codford St Mary 265). The winter bourne is called the Cut. I always hoped to discover that it once had a sweeter name like the Babble or the Ripple. But the Cut it is, after the channel that was cut through the water meadows years ago. It looks all right in winter when it brims up to only a few feet lower than the road. But in summer it is not a fetching sight. You can see the bulges of the sandbags that shore up the banks and at the bottom the weeds fail to hide the old saucepans and broken white enamel basins that were used to force rhubarb under until they became too broken even for that. After the first bend out of the village, though, the water meadows broaden out and the Cut looks pretty enough as it loses itself in the rushes and buttercups.

Of course it is not the whole village that goes walking, only a dozen families or so even on a sunny day, thirty or forty people altogether, but the whole village is what it looks like as I wobble round the corner on my bike and there they are strung out across the road, as unconcerned as if it had been officially closed to traffic: the women in summer frocks, the older women wearing close-brimmed navy-blue straw hats, the men in suits of a brighter blue or chocolate brown, both with a faint chalk stripe, the kind of suits you only see on country Sundays, ordered mostly off the Littlewoods catalogues that Mr Goodsell brings to the kitchen window.

The window opens directly on to the farmyard. Mr Goodsell would not think it proper to call at the front door or even the back door because to get to the back door you have to walk the whole way round our house past the sitting-room windows and the terrace. So he has to dance across the cow muck in his bright brown brogues and poke his head through the little window to negotiate with Mrs Herrington. The green paint on the window is peeling and flakes fall on his shoulders as he crouches to get down to her level. Mr Goodsell has a much smarter blue suit than the ones in his catalogues. He is altogether an elegant figure with piercing blue eyes and perfect white teeth such as you do not see in Chitterne. He looks and sounds a bit like Cary Grant and, as he comes from Bristol, I wonder whether he may not be related to Cary Grant who comes from Bristol too, but perhaps he has just modelled himself on the great man.

Mrs Herrington is not smart at all. She has an unruly bird's nest of white hair and about three teeth in her head, none of them at all white, and her apron is somewhere between grubby and filthy. She has been in service all her life, starting only about twenty miles away at a village called Damerham the other side of Salisbury. Now she cooks for us and helps to look after my sister and me. Once or twice a year my parents have some people in to dinner and she cooks for that too. Because she has to walk two miles each way from her tied farm cottage up on the downs, she arrives in wellingtons and in wellies is how she serves dinner to the guests. She is abounding with love and when I go away to boarding school she is the one who cannot stop crying. When her daughter Joyce marries a man in the RAF, Francie and I are bridesmaid and pageboy, my only appearance in this role and an excruciating one, in a red velvet suit that Little Lord Fauntleroy might have rejected as too sissy. Joyce made the suit herself but on out-of-date measurements so that it nips viciously at the armpits and crotch, making the torture physical as well as social.

Even less often than they give a dinner party, my parents go abroad on holiday (twice or perhaps three times during my entire childhood, I think). They go for a week at most because the travel allowance is only £25. During these weeks we go and stay with Mrs Herrington. We walk home with her up the village street, carrying our little brown cardboard suitcases which don't begin to look like real suitcases. Halfway up the hill on the Shrewton road, we turn left on to a track. In a couple of hundred yards we are walking across empty downland where the only noise is the larks and there are red poppies growing on the chalky path. After we have gone over the first rise, there is not a house to be seen in any direction, only endless rolling downs. This is how I imagine all open country, the sort of country you read about in Zane Grey's stories of life on the prairie which I am already reading, or, much later, the steppes of Tolstoy and Turgenev.

Walter and Mabel Herrington's cottage at New Barn is one of a huddle of farm buildings set in a faint hollow in the middle of absolutely nowhere. It is a journey back in time too. Nothing inside seems to have moved since the Boer War. The upright piano with its ornate carved stand for the music, the doilies on top of the piano to protect the veneer from the cut-glass vases, the oleographs on the wall, the scalloped mirror, the sturdy square mahogany clock – all look as though they came with the cottage. My sister and I sit beside Mrs Herrington feeding her bits of cloth for the rag rugs she never stops knotting. We have badgered her into making one for each of us to put beside our beds. I am already imagining my bare feet sinking into its caressing squudge. Even the most expensive pile does not quite give the deep pleasure of a rag rug.

Being something close to a saint, Mrs Herrington's dealings with Mr Goodsell are not on her own behalf but to please her daughters Phyllis and Joyce. I like nothing better than to balance my feet on the edge of the big pottery jar under the table, so I can make myself tall enough to squint over her shoulder as together we debate whether one of these spring blouses would suit Joyce, the prettier of the two girls, or whether Phyllis would like this pop-up electric toaster, a popular novelty line according to Mr G., certainly one that has not come our way before. Sometimes in my excitement my sandals lose their grip on the edge of the jar which is full of eggs being preserved and my toes dip into the cold liquid that is preserving them. The liquid is called isinglass, Mrs Herrington tells me, which sounds mysterious and legendary like something to do with King Arthur. Mr Goodsell, being a master of his art, knows that he must suck up to me too if he is to clinch the sale: 'I can see the young man has excellent taste' or 'Now, sir, which of these skirts would you say is the more stylish?'

One morning I meet Mrs Herrington coming back from the sitting room. To my amazement she is in tears and she is dabbing her eyes with her pinny. Of course I would not dream of asking what has caused this. It is only a few days later that my mother explains to me that Mrs Herrington has got into trouble with Mr Goodsell. She has ordered too many blouses and toasters from his catalogues and cannot pay off the instalments that are due and my parents have had to bail her out. As my mother tells me this, I am distraught. We have been had for suckers, Mrs Herrington and I. In fact my enthusiasm for the top-of-the-range items may be responsible for her downfall. Mr Goodsell is a smiling villain and I am delighted when my mother tells me that the correct term for him is a tallyman, which sounds suitably demeaning. I am further delighted when she points out the aptness of his surname, which she says is like something out of *Pilgrim's Progress*. I know about *Pilgrim's Progress*, though I haven't read it, because the March girls in *Little Women* are each given for Christmas a copy in a different-coloured binding (it is the only Christmas present they get because they are so poor) and I like *Little Women* very much as I do many books intended for girls such as the Pullein-Thompson pony books, although I don't like ponies at all.

As they walk down the Codford road in their Sunday frocks, the women gather flowers from the hedgerows. In the late spring the flowers are mostly blue and white, bluebells and stitchwort and white campion. In high summer they are more often purple and yellow: knapweed and ragged robin and rosebay willowherb and toadflax and bird's-foot trefoil and wild honeysuckle. Walking along in their finery with these blowsy bunches they look like a wedding party. Later on, when I see Stanley Spencer paintings of Cookham disguised as heaven or heaven disguised as Cookham, I am reminded of these Sunday walks at Chitterne. Those effects of his which critics describe as naive or fantastical seem to me strictly realistic depictions of village life as it used to be. The odd thing is that I have never heard other people mention Sunday walks of this sort in their own villages. Was Chitterne in its remote nook of Salisbury Plain merely a little backward? When listening to friends describing the most enchanting paseos or passeggiatas that they have witnessed in foreign cities, I do not dare to say that I remember seeing the same thing at home for fear of being greeted with disbelief.

The walking tails off in September. Only a handful of families carry on until autumn is unmistakably here. By then Stan Grant will have scythed the roadside banks. He does his scything in a smart white collarless shirt and grey waistcoat and trousers. He inclines slightly to finish each stroke and the sun catches the silken sheen of his waistcoat backing. It is as though he came down the road in his immaculate three-piece suit and suddenly took it into his head to take off his jacket and hang it on a branch and do a little scything. He is equally nonchalant when fielding at cover point for the village cricket team which my father captains for a couple of seasons. I remember him standing there in his waistcoat, kneeling gracefully to stop the ball and return it to the keeper, all as though he is not actually part of the team but just happens to be passing when the ball comes his way – but this must be nonsense because now I think harder Stan wears flawless whites, is famous for them in fact, and anyway the pitch is tucked high up on the sloping field some way from the road. The slope is so acute that the canny batsman will always aim to work the ball to the downhill side where it moves fast over the bumpy ground and the fielder's best hope is that it will cannon into your shins, which is not much of a hope really.

The field which is used for cricket is also where the Bomb falls on Chitterne, or to be precise, where the Bomb falls a good half mile from the village. We inspect the chalky crater the next day. My father explains to me that, contrary to my assumption, the Germans have not actually been aiming to hit us. The pilot was probably dumping his load on his way back from the big raid on Bath. My confidence in total victory for the Allies, already of near-Churchillian proportions, is further reinforced by this evidence of wastefulness and incompetence on the part of the Luftwaffe.

Usually, though, I do not go cycling down the Codford road on Sundays. The truth is that for years I fail to cycle unassisted. Everyone else my age, not to mention my sister who is two years younger, is pedalling away on their own, some with their hands off the handlebars or their feet on them, but I am still insisting that Olive Furnell who is our au pair equivalent should run along with me holding the saddle. As with my non-swimming, I am curiously free of shame about this, although I have never seen any boy nearly as tall as me having his saddle held. The only reason I do not care to meet the Sunday walkers is because they are so strung out across the road and I am not confident of being able to avoid them, my steering being no better than my balance. Olive is a pale, almost olive-complexioned girl who looks a bit austere but is in fact amiable and obliging beyond the call of duty, assuming that my mother has ever spelled out what her duties are, which is unlikely, ours not being a house for mission statements. So I do not hesitate to whistle her up as saddleholder whenever it suits me which may be when she is halfway through the ironing or the washing up. As a result she may still be wearing her apron as we fly down the Codford road together. Luckily Olive is a fast runner, always finishing well up in the hundred yards at the village sports. It does not occur to me how odd we must look together, me and my bicycle maid in her pinny. Although officially classified as shy, I have an imperious streak and am not as self-conscious as shy people are meant to be.

But then on a weekday nothing much is coming the other way. Nobody has any petrol except the doctors and so if there is a car it is usually Dr Falk or Dr Graham Campbell bumping along in their old saloons on their rounds. Now I think of it, in fact it is Dr Graham Campbell not Dr Falk who leaves the hypodermic needle in my bottom. Tall and cadaverous in a dark blue pinstripe, Ronald Graham Campbell is my usual medical attendant. When I have a bad asthma attack, about once a week at this period, he comes over from Warminster without a murmur. Together we go through the motions, I hitch up my pyjama jacket, he listens to my chest, depresses my tongue with the little wooden spatula before peering down my throat and then into my ears. All this I regard as merely the formal preliminaries before the real business of handing over the box of little yellow ephedrine pills – half a pill under the tongue magically soothes the tubes, nothing else works, certainly not the breathing exercises the nurses are always teaching me. After this ritual he goes downstairs and has a glass of sherry with my parents. I can hear the rumble of their chat through the floorboards. I like to think they are discussing my condition but they are probably making small talk about less interesting topics. I wonder whether all his patients give him sherry, because if so he must be plastered by the time he gets back to his surgery, or is it only because he was at school with my father? Much later my father tells me how kind and sympathetic Ronald was when my mother was ill, though he could do nothing for her.

More often it is the clop of horses' hooves that we hear from the bend beyond the cricket field. In these quiet years after the war horses are still used to save petrol. When I hear the hooves, I turn into the bank, the tall grass flicking my bare leg, while behind me Olive recovers her breath pressing her hands on her knees and then wiping her face with her pinny. Round the corner comes old Jack Stratton on his big chestnut. He owns most of the land between here and Codford and he likes to ride over his land. To me he seems as old as the downs. I suppose he must be seventy but looks twice as ancient because he is very nearly blind which is why he is wearing dark glasses on a string and his black bowler hat is on a string too in case it falls off. His tweed jacket is the colour of fresh rust. As he passes us, he rises to the trot and seems more awesome still as though he has suddenly been called to an appointment with death or destiny and when he barks good afternoon at us we are struck too dumb to answer.

'Good job that horse knows its way home,' Olive says as the sound of the hooves dies away behind us.

'Perhaps he isn't blind at all, just pretending.'

'I'll give you perhaps,' says Olive. 'Now see if you can do this next bit without me holding on.'

But even after I have gone away to school and Olive has gone away to get married I am still unsteady. Luckily my bike won't fit in the Morris, so I cannot be forced to take it around without Olive behind me. Unfortunately when my mother drops me off to stay with my new friend from school, Nichol Fleming, his father has borrowed an extra bike for me to ride through their beech woods above Henley-on-Thames. Colonel Peter Fleming is a famous explorer, much more famous both as an author and adventurer than his younger brother Ian. I have already read his *Brazilian Adventure*, though not *One's Company* or *News from Tartary*. He is a deeply bronzed, pipesucking figure radiating fitness and manliness. He is as awesome in a different way as Jack Stratton. So though I am dreading the cycling, it is almost a relief when five minutes after my mother's car has disappeared up the gravel sweep he sends us off into the woods. Giddy with terror, I pedal over the rutted tracks, dreading a crash at each turn and counting the minutes until we can honourably go home. As we come off the muddy path on to the gravel leading back down to the house, which is called Merrimoles, I take terminal fright at the terrifying angle of the slope and try to brake but go sideways over the handlebars on to the pitiless pebbles. As I wheel the bike down the slope, trying to sob quietly, Peter Fleming emerges from a nearby bothy carrying a couple of those plaster ducks that are used to lure other ducks on to ponds to be shot at. The blood streaming from my forehead makes a fine show.

'You poor chap,' he says, clenching his teeth around his pipe, dismayed at the bad start my visit has got off to, but also stirred by the prospect of action.

He brings out a handkerchief and wipes my face, inadvertently smearing the decoy ducks with my blood – there is plenty to go round – so that we look as if we have all been involved in some complicated sporting accident.

Almost simultaneously his wife, Nichol's mother, the actress Celia Johnson, comes out of the front door and runs towards us across the gravel looking more wholeheartedly distraught than her husband (it is less than an hour since my mother entrusted me to her care).

'Oh darling, how awful, what will I tell Julia?'

At Saturday film night the preceding term we had *In Which We Serve*, which Celia stars in opposite Noël Coward and I immediately feel like one of the survivors limping down the gangway after being rescued from Mountbatten's latest fiasco at sea. I am deeply moved by the sound of Celia's extraordinary voice which is at once exaggeratedly refined and unbearably poignant, making the simplest sentence sound as if it comes from an irreparably broken heart. The doctor is called and he stitches up my forehead. I am rather brave during this operation. I am always rather brave when I am the centre of attention. I wonder hopefully whether I might not bear a scar to the end of my days (which I do, smack between the eyebrows), but I am also thinking the delicious thought that there will be no more cycling and we can stay indoors and listen to the radio.

This turns out to be false optimism because the Colonel has plotted an elaborate plan for Nichol and me the next day to canoe down the Thame, a tributary of the Thames. Although Nichol is captain of the rugger fifteen at school and perfectly good at lessons, his father is haunted by the fear that he is both a milksop and an idiot. He cannot leave his son alone, constantly referring to him as 'the Korean refugee' and reminding him of his poor marks in some Latin or maths exam. By contrast, Duff Hart-Davis, the son of the publisher Rupert Hart-Davis who lives near by and is two or three years older than us, is Peter's Golden Boy, an Oppidan Scholar, a brilliant shot, etc. It is Duff who jumps into the breach and pipes up 'He cometh not, my lord' when Pindarus alias Calum Robertson lingers in the bowels of School Hall and misses his cue. Duff is admirably resourceful and he and another older boy are to go ahead in another canoe to show us the way.

I suppose I must have been in a boat of some kind before, but I have not grasped the principles of boarding one, so while the Colonel looks on from the bank sucking his pipe I find myself with one foot in the canoe and the other sploshing around in the mud. The canoe swings around into the current and my foot slides out of it so I am up to my waist in water being sucked out into the middle, frantically clinging to what I remember from *Captain Hornblower RN* must be the gunwale if canoes have gunwales. Colonel Fleming, having perhaps put my bike crash down to some piece of daredevilry which failed to come off, the sort of thing Nichol ought to be imitating, now begins to realise that he has a proper dud on his hands, compared to whom his son is Captain Marvel. With a brisk tug on the rope he pulls the canoe back to the bank and me with it and then holds it steady while I clamber in before he wishes us bon voyage and disappears up the bank to the station brake he brought us in.

All this has taken some time and Duff's canoe is already out of sight. As we splash round the first bend and disentangle the boat from a half-submerged log, we see a bridge ahead and a familiar figure leaning over the parapet brandishing a pipe.

'Try to keep in time,' he shouts down to us.

Then there is a long straight stretch and the sun comes out and dapples the water and I begin to see how paddling might become enjoyable. Through the overhanging trees I see another bridge and a figure leaning over it. Is he going to be coxing us from every bloody bridge?

But this time the figure turns out to be several small boys who throw a volley of sticks and stones at us. Peter is, however, on the next bridge.

'Duff and David are twenty minutes ahead of you,' he calls, tapping his watch.

Later on we stop and get out of the boat to eat our sandwiches and I fall in twice more, once when getting out of the boat and once getting back in it again.

Eventually we come out of the Thame and swing left downstream into the Thames which to my exhausted eye looks about as wide as the Amazon at this point and rather more dangerous because of the vast river cruisers steaming up and down and rocking us silly with the wash they leave behind. By now being totally muddy and sodden, I am beyond caring when bucketfuls of water start cascading into the canoe. But Nichol, clearly fast developing a river sense, says, 'I think we'd better get into the side and bail some of this out.' So we tie up at an overhanging willow tree and I get out of the canoe to try and dry off a bit and I fall into the Thames in precisely the same manner as I have been falling into the Thame except that the Thames is about four feet deeper and I am in up to my neck for the first time.

Peter picks us up at the mooring belonging to a riverside pub and dripping from every limb I help to carry the canoe back to the station wagon. Duff and David landed an hour ago and have gone on home to shoot pigeons. Back at Merrimoles I have already used up the clothes I brought with me and Celia finds me some of Nichol's old clothes. It is a sunny evening now and I experience the delicious sensation of being warm and dry as I wander across the lawn, admiring the lovely rolling view across the cornfields with the woods beyond stretching to the skyline, until I trip on the low coping surrounding the Flemings' new swimming pool. Or perhaps it is the hose pipe I trip on because luckily the pool has just been filled as I fall head first into it and go all the way down to the bottom skinning my knuckles on the unpainted concrete (Peter only consented to install this pool on condition that it should exhibit a Spartan lack of frills). There is no one there to see me struggle back to the surface and clamber out and trudge back indoors to ask if there are any more of Nichol's clothes I could borrow. Within twenty-four hours I have thus put up a remarkably consistent display on wheels, water and foot.

'I never knew the Thames Valley was so full of pitfalls,' Peter Fleming said, ruefully tamping down his pipe.

'Ferdy does seem to be rather accident-prone,' Celia said to my mother when she came to pick me up.

Clearly I am not a suitable companion for the outdoor life, but the Colonel and I become strangely fond of each other. His dissatisfactions are remote from mine or Nichol's, yet there is something greatly appealing about him. He is obsessed with keeping fit – then quite an eccentric obsession for middle-aged men. He is at this moment preparing for Territorial Army camp, his head filled with lists of kit and plans for exercises. Yet even aged ten as I am or perhaps eleven, I cannot help noticing his self-mockery about the part he is playing. That is what makes his travellers' tales readable still, not to mention his historical books and columns for the *Spectator*. He takes a genuine interest in my own boast that I am going to be a writer of some sort, and it is in a column for the *Sunday Times* that he gives the first ever mention in print to something I have written. Nichol and I, both aged twelve, have started a school magazine called, not very alluringly, *School Chat*. We write out the copy in painstaking longhand and then duplicate it on slabs of gelotype which reproduce in a fetching if erratic shade of purple, which the assistant matron has to scrub off our hands. I contribute a serial spy thriller to the first issue which comes out shortly after the defection of Burgess and Maclean, a fact delicately alluded to by Peter in his résumé of my work:

'Our serial Part I' is called 'The Ambassador'.

Jack Hale lay back in his chair and contemplated his *Morning Post*.

'Oh why doesn't Galford have an election, defeated on the taxes bill again,' he thought.

But his ruminations are intruded on. 'My name is Haxe, minister of the interior of Goestad.' Hale is a bit weak on foreign affairs. 'Excuse me, but I do not know where Goestad is,' he says. The Minister of the Interior is not offended. 'I shouldn't think many people do, it is in the middle east,' he explains understandingly.

In no time at all, Hale has been flown to Goestad, and Haxe, aware no doubt of the reputation for eccentricity recently gained by His Majesty's Foreign Service, is unfolding his plan. 'Now I have heard you are an accomplished ambassador are you prepared to go to the British Consulate and ask for the post of Ambassador to the Hadavian Government? For a man of your ability and fame it should not be difficult.'

From now on events move swiftly. Hale, who objects strongly to being used as a spy, is locked in a room and all seems hopeless. 'Then he remembered that he had a penknife. He started to cut through the door. It was a long and tedious job.' But he gets out, dodges 'two, thin, lean men' and finds 'a limousine waiting by the sidewalk'. The suspense is unbearable when the narrator breaks off in the approved style and the reader has to content himself with 'The rules of our puzzles' (three sweets for the quiz and four for the crossword). *School Chat* seems to me an interesting and well-conducted periodical.

My reaction on being shown this piece mirrored the reaction of every writer down the ages: disappointment at not being mentioned by name, ability to skate over any ironic comment and to concentrate on the favourable and quotable snippet. I wanted to put ' "an interesting and well-conducted periodical" – *Sunday Times*' on the masthead of our next issue, but something stopped me, possibly a faint intimation that a little kindly mockery might be intended. Yet my thriller was just the kind of adventure that Peter would himself have liked either to write or to star in. I would not be surprised if it was he himself who put it about that when Celia and he were first married and had just built Merrimoles he found climbing the stairs so suburban that he used to swing up the creeper (wisteria, I think) festooning the balcony outside their bedroom.

But he remains hard on Nichol, always comparing him unkindly with other boys including me, and Nichol suffers permanent damage, although twenty years later he becomes as keen on country sports as his father. A little before then, when he is nearly thirty, he comes out and we all think it is something to do with the way Peter has treated him. But then fashion changes and by the time Nichol dies young in his fifties of a heart attack (Peter dies of one too, when out shooting grouse in Scotland, but he is in his late sixties) we no longer think that being gay has much connection with having a father who is harsh, weak or absent, but everything to do with genes. As with explanations of cancer, nurture goes out of style and nature comes back. And yet I still remember that feeling of danger in the offing – or is it only embarrassment? – when Peter says to me, 'Nichol can't get anywhere with algebra – I'm sure you sail through.'

There are no such snags to Celia. She is marvellously restful to be with. We sit and do crosswords and jigsaws together as though we were an old married couple. And she tells me things, not about acting – you could be with her for a week and never guess her profession – but about ordinary details of life, like how the waists of mannequins in the shop windows are six inches less than the waists of real women and how tradesmen's entrances are always situated so that the tradesmen never pass the windows of the gentry's part of the house, which explains to me why Mr Goodsell has to crouch at our kitchen window. But though I do not realise it at the time, it must be her voice which gives these plain facts their haunting mesmerising quality.

My father seems to feel little inclination to make a man of me. Perhaps those hours watching by my bedside while I struggle for breath make him feel it would be tempting fate to try. So he never puts me on a horse, though in the album he keeps of his riding exploits there is a picture of him on a large pony when he can't be more than seven. This suits me – riding is the last thing I have in mind. The thought of it no more occurs to me than I dream of riding a camel when I see pictures of Bedouin crossing the Sahara.

But I like watching, I am a born spectator. In the flat field next to our house, the farm boys sometimes ride the carthorses bareback, slapping their rumps to make them buck in a galumphing sort of way so the boys can pretend they are in a rodeo. Now and then the Strattons give my father a yearling to break, because he has a name for being good at it, which isn't always the case with steeplechase jockeys.

My mother has planted a little row of beech saplings to hide the barbed wire of our boundary fence. Quite a few of the saplings haven't taken and I stand in one of the gaps listening to the shrivelled leaves rustling and the barbed wire singing in the wind. In the middle of the field my father stands in pale grey flannel trousers and a mushroom-grey jersey with a shawl collar like the stable lads wear. The trousers are thin and the wind blows them against his slender thighs as the yearling trots in a circle round at the end of the rope my father is holding. Even I can see how delicately he keeps the tension balanced, not too tight to frighten the horse but not so slack that it can just stop and put its head down and start eating the grass. When the wind drops, I can hear my father clucking encouragement. How long it all goes on for, how patiently my father lets the yearling settle to the routine, my father who has so little patience for anything else, certainly not the routine business of life.

This must be in the winter because I remember how cold it is and how shrivelled the beech leaves are. In the spring we follow my father as he rides in point-to-points all across our part of the West Country – the Avon Vale, the Beaufort, the Blackmore Vale, the South and West Wilts, the Cattistock, the Vale of the White Horse – but most of the meetings we go to later on are on the rolling plain of Larkhill which is the nearest course to Chitterne and less than a mile from Stonehenge, closer still to Woodhenge, that equally mysterious monument which is now only a circle of postholes with modern wooden stumps to mark them. It is on this pitiless steppe that the greatest dramas of my childhood are played out. My father, by now well over forty and not exactly taking care of himself, is riding almost

exclusively a pretty chestnut gelding with white socks called Wheat-sheaf who in horse terms is as old as he is, probably older. Wheatsheaf belongs to a long-distance lorry driver called Mr Jones, who likes to stand in the paddock with a fag in the corner of his mouth grinning with delight that he should possess such an animal. Wheatsheaf has no proper stable but is kept in a shed next to the post office in Edington, a village in the lee of the downs a couple of miles from the Westbury White Horse. This arrangement is to enable Mr Jones's daughter Pat who keeps the post office to look after Wheatsheaf. It is an arrange-ment which suits my father's love of the unorthodox, although he does not think of finding out Mr Jones's Christian name, or if he does we never hear it.

The extraordinary thing is that Wheatsheaf, aged though he is, turns out to be the most beautiful surefooted jumper, probably the best point-to-pointer my father has ever ridden, and would need only a little more speed to have made a serious steeplechaser. It is on his back that my father wins thirteen or fourteen races, his last wins before giving up the game at the age of forty-seven, and we all huddle together for the camera, my mother and me, my father grinning all over his face which like his yellow jersey and red cap is spattered with mud, Mr Jones in his belted tweed overcoat and flat cap and his daughter Pat holding Wheatsheaf's head and giving him a big kiss.

Only once or twice does my father come off Wheatsheaf. Usually it is at the last fence where we are all standing and the crash of birch twigs and the crunch of horse and rider hitting the churned-up turf ring sharp in my ears even now. It is never the horse's fault. My father says he was getting tired himself and did not put him at the fence properly. He says this sort of thing as we are bumping over the downs in the back of the ambulance off to Salisbury Infirmary and he is wincing with the pain, having broken his collar bone for the sixth time in his career, not to mention cracking a rib or two.

He says much the same, though with far less reason, when he comes off the horse my mother has been persuaded to buy for £100 which was called Shaggy Boy and which my parents rechristen Colonel Overdraft. The Colonel is a big black horse and not reliable at all. His only achievement is to be the sole finisher of three in the Wylye Valley Hunt Members Race and to win the ugly square-handled silver cup which used to stand on the pale blue sideboard in our dining room until my father popped it, though I cannot imagine he got more than a fiver. The colours my mother registered with Wetherby's for this brief ill-judged excursion into ownership (which she could not begin to afford) were rather pretty: sky-blue and silver stripes with a sky-blue cap. I suspect that in fact it was my father who chose them, copying as far as he was allowed by Wetherby's the colours carried by Right Royal, the horse-hero of John Masefield's narrative poem which he loved:

> Under the pale coat reaching to his spurs
> One saw his colours, which were also hers,
> Narrow alternate bars of blue and white,
> Blue as the speedwell's eye and silver bright.

The story of the poem is that Right Royal's rider, Charles Cothill, has a dream the night before the race that Right Royal wins the cup and he plunges his all so that he may marry his fiancée 'bright Emmy Crowthorne' on the proceeds. Right Royal does eventually win, coming from last to first in this gruelling steeplechase which is as long as the Grand National though the terrain looks more like Chelten-ham to judge from the illustrations to the poem, copious line drawings and colour plates by Cecil Aldin, the artist whose work adorns the back passages in every hunting household. Unfortunately the bookie welshes to America and Cothill hasn't a bean left. All the same,

> Charles married his lady, but he rode no more races;
> He lives on the Downland on the blown grassy places,
> Where he and Right Royal can canter for hours
> On the flock-bitten turf full of tiny blue flowers.

This, I suppose, was my father's dream too. It is not Masefield's fault that the reality did not turn out quite so happily. My sister and I used to wear the blue-and-silver silks for dressing-up games, the jacket doing nicely as a princess's dress or a vizier's robe.

If my father did not give up racing after marriage, he did more or less give up betting. In fact he never gambled seriously after he had piled up a sizeable debt to the bookies in his twenties. He did not dare to approach his own father, who was a keen racing man but would never have got into such trouble. So he went to his uncle by marriage, the Rev. Harvey Thursby, the Rector of Mortimer, only a few miles from Wasing. Uncle Harvey was the heir to large coal deposits somewhere in the North, and also devoted to the turf. He lived in a rambling white villa with peacocks calling on the terrace and the largest collection of paperweights in Berkshire. He was as saintly as a man burdened with such advantages can be and instantly made out a cheque, advising my father in the sweetest possible way never to do it again, which he didn't.

'Right Royal' was one of the many poems my father read to me at bedtime and I came to know much of it by heart, as I did also 'When I Am Dead, My Dearest' by Christina Rossetti, 'The Bells of Shandon' by Father Prout, the pen-name of that rascal Francis O'Mahony, 'Sleep Is a Reconciling' attributed to John Dowling, and, most tear-jerking of the lot, Adam Lindsay Gordon's ballad 'The Sick Stock-rider':

> Hold hard, Ned! Lift me down once more and lay me in the shade;
> Old man, you've had your work cut out to guide
> Both horses, and to hold me in the saddle when I swayed,
> All through the hot, slow, sleepy, silent ride.

Gordon was educated at Cheltenham College and sailed for Australia at the age of eighteen where he became a wandering horsebreaker and then the most famous steeplechase rider in Victoria, but money troubles enveloped him and his mind was never the same after a bad fall when staying on the farm of his friend Harry Mount. Six months later he shot himself, after seeing his last book of poems through the press. He became for a time regarded as the national poet of Australia. It was said that if either Harry Mount or Harry's brother Lambton had been on hand Gordon would never have thought of suicide. My father and I were both much moved by this thought (though the brothers were no relation of ours, so far as we knew) and we were both near tears as we reached the final quatrain of 'The Sick Stockrider':

Let me slumber in the hollow where the wattle blossoms wave
With never stone or rail to fence my bed;
Should the sturdy station children pull the bush flowers on my grave
I may chance to hear them romping overhead.

Action and melancholy were what my father craved, in literature as in life. His favourite book was Lermontov's *A Hero of Our Time*, and he loved Tolstoy's tales of life with the Cossacks and Turgenev's *Sportsman's Sketches*. He shared with his brother-in-law Tony Powell a taste for Alfred de Vigny's *Splendeurs et misères de la vie militaire*. Tony kindly sent my parents each volume of *A Dance to the Music of Time* as it came out, but my father could not get on with the series at all. He complained that nothing much happened even in the volumes covering the war and that the only people who liked reading them were women at the hairdresser, a strange verdict considering that the usual complaint is that *Dance* appeals only to men.

Even when going for a stroll in the country, my father would try to inject some excitement by vaulting a five-barred gate or getting down on his hands and knees by a stream to see whether there was a trout he could tickle. Once, when walking off Christmas lunch at the Chantry, he saw a derelict pram overturned in the ditch in Mells Lane and immediately took out his matches and set fire to it. He said it would make a good diary entry: 'Christmas Day: burnt a child's pram.' He did not keep a diary. Both the effort and the self-regard would have been alien to him.

He joined the Wiltshire Regiment as a Territorial in 1938. His view of Munich has stuck with me so fast that nothing I read now will shake it. He remembered being sick to his stomach when he heard the news of the Agreement, his gloom deepened by the frantic general rejoicing that greeted it. And yet at the same time he could not help thinking that Chamberlain, whether he intended it or not, had given us a breathing space to prepare for the war that was bound to come.

When the Commandos were being formed, a notice was sent to all infantry regiments appealing for volunteers for hazardous special duties. My father put his name down, imagining that this was the thing to do and thinking no more of it, and was startled to discover that he was the only man who had signed up. So he came to join that motley crew of buccaneers, blowhards and three-bottle men who tumbled out of White's Club and on to the night train: Randolph Churchill and Evelyn Waugh, the Stirling brothers Bill and David, Harry Stavordale, the heir to Holland House and half of Dorset, and his intemperate younger brother John whom my father loved, Robin Campbell, Reuter's correspondent and painter who was married to my mother's friend Mary Ormsby-Gore, Edward Stanley, yachtsman and serial marrier, Bob Laycock, professional soldier and already their superior officer although thirtyish like the rest of them, and quieter and more thoughtful than the others, and Nic (I never heard his other name, but he came to be my father's best friend in the Army). As their training camp moved from one desolate stretch of bog and moorland to the next, country-house hotels accustomed to lodging bachelor fishermen and ladies on walking tours had to cope with this rowdy invasion which was probably worse than if the Boches had been billeted on them. Up in Ayrshire, Nic and my father lived off the land poaching the Duke of Montrose's rabbits and pheasants on the isle of Arran and sailing back to the hotel in Girvan, sodden, unshaven and exhilarated, ready for a hot bath and a few drinks. In theory women were not permitted to join the subalterns while they were in this rigorous training mode, but the Colonel had smuggled his mistress into the hotel, and so my father did not see why his wife should not come up too, which is how my sister came to be conceived, thanks to the Colonel's mistress. But my mother could only stay for the weekend and this is the letter my father sent after her:

My darling Julia,

I have seen your train leave the station and I feel terribly low, darling it means so much if you are even near and now that you are going so many miles away I know how much I am going to be sad. I love you darling so much that I hate to hear you talking to anyone else. When we are together I know that often I am stupid to you. It is because I am worried because I know that soon I shall start fighting and I am not certain how I shall acquit myself and all this makes me unsure. However I love you so well that I dare hope all will pan out O.K. I will write often to send you and F my love and I hope he will like the rabbit.

Best love R.

It would be nice to think that I treasured the toy rabbit for years afterwards but I have no memory of it.

They managed one more leave at Chitterne before my father set sail for North Africa. The troopship HMS *Glengyle* had to sail all the way round the Cape to reach its destination because the Luftwaffe commanded the western Mediterranean. As the *Glengyle* lumbered through the tropics the odyssey began to lull the senses. Only the endless brutish chaff of Randolph Churchill broke the velvet silence of the sea and the stars: 'Robin says he has two brothers, they must be very dim.' 'Bill Mount's not dim at all,' piped up Godfrey Nicholson, a somewhat humourless heir to Nicholson's Gin who in very much later life became Father of the House of Commons – but by then Randolph's attention, as fleeting as the flying fish that skimmed across the *Glengyle*'s decks, had moved on to a fresh target. 'Here's Johnny Fox,' he bellowed. 'Is Harry still paying your debts, John?' Now and then my father managed to escape to a quiet corner of the deck and read *Vanity Fair* or *Lavengro* out of the ship's old-fashioned library and write letters home of an almost incoherent sweetness.

Monday(I think the 16th) January 1941
My darling and sweetest Julia,

Just off to swing in my hammock – darling I feel I love you so dearly. All my memories of our life together seem so happy to me tonight, from the moment we first met from our wedding day till the

time we said au revoir at Salisbury. Darling I remember nothing amiss
– can you say so too, now I think only of lovely times together, the
morning in the sunshine, the day after we were married, in Paris – the
Spanish Steps – our flat in London – sweaty days in the garden, the trip
to Greenwich. I have arranged not to have this letter censored (it is on
parole) so I can say how much I love you and I don't think darling it
will be so long before we are in each other's arms.

By now they were steaming into the southern hemisphere:

We have crossed the line and tho it is warmish it wasn't too bad. I had a
good ducking which was photographed I will send it you in due course
and a good time was had by all. The gambling has increased in the heat,
you won't be surprised to hear, and someone the night before we
reached port lost £700 at a sitting. I managed to win 5 West African
shillings off Harry Stavordale at bridge.

When we reached our first port, niggers came alongside and dived
for sixpences – they were too rich to dive for pennies. Their canoes
were called *HMS Nelson, The Lord Is My Help*, etc. The crew of the
latter offered his daughter to me for 1s/6d; however I entered into
negotiations for a monkey but when I went down the ladder the
man was covered with a loathsome white deposit either a disease on
his skin or just dirt. So immediately all one's liberal ideas about the
natives fled, also desire to purchase the monkey. I nearly bought a
bad-tempered looking canary but in the end bought a banana which
a naval officer sd. was probably contaminated with yellow fever so I
didn't eat it.

The nicest thing is the evening – usually very pleasant, then no half
light and then the night – millions of stars – from the boat deck you see
the decks littered with soldiers and sailors sleeping, some singing – and
the other ships ploughing through the sea – then the Last Post – climb
into my hammock and so to sleep.

Much boxing goes on here but I only spectate tho I have done a
little sparring but feel a bit [he does not complete the sentence]

Write to me often sweetest and I'll be back to kiss you soon darling
best love. I am very well Robin. I look a terrific planter in my tropical
kit.

There is a gap of nearly two months in the letters until the next one which comes from Egypt and explains the gap and also the broken-off sentence about the boxing on the *Glengyle*.

Luxor Hotel 31st March

My darling,

I haven't written a letter to you for ages. I will explain why. After leaving Capetown I was almost continually ill and had a rather miserable time with fearful pains in my stomach and coughing blood and one thing and another. So when we arrived in the desert I was sent up to Cairo to be examined. Directly I got on land I felt much better and I stayed for a couple of nights at Shepheards [hotel] while I consulted various doctors and hospitals. Finally it was decided that I should go back to bed in hospital – a very good military one and I was Xrayed etc and all the usual mumbo-jumbo. I was suspected of having TB but I shd have thought that my sanguine complexion alone wd have shown that diagnosis to be wrong. Finally they found what they called a lesion in my lung, which they thought was possibly the result of a steeplechase fall. Apparently this had shown in the Xray and had made them suspect TB. I have now been discharged completely fit for duty and all that it has really meant is that I have avoided 3 or 4 weeks very dull and extremely uncomfortable time with the Regt. This darling I am afraid is a very dull account of a very dull subject – my health.

N. Africa is simply wonderful. You get the blue of the Sea, a small green cultivated belt – greener than Tipperary – and then the Desert. The Desert is terrific. 'It is impossible to deny Allah in the Desert' (the Koran).

Despite the upbeat ending, my father does not sound entirely reassured and I imagine his letter must have sent my mother into a state of agonised anxiety – one which was not soon to be dispelled.

A few weeks after he was passed fit again for duty, his Commando, No. 7, undertook its first operation – in fact the first Allied raid anywhere in North Africa, a night raid against the port of Bardia on the Libya–Egypt border, just east of Tobruk. The enemy's positions were well dug in and heavily fortified on a sandy cliff above the

harbour, and from the start things went awry. The Folbot canoe, piloted by Captain R. J. Courtney RN, which was meant to paddle ashore from a submarine and guide the Commandos in, was damaged on launching and unable to fix its guiding lights (the Folbot works became notorious for late delivery and poor workmanship and later went bust). Not much damage was done and several Commandos wandering about in the dark failed to find the re-embarkation point and were taken prisoner. Others halted or lay down as soon as the Germans opened fire. My father got back safely. He remembered only chaos and confusion and firing at random and mostly at shadows, although he thought he might have fired once at a German sentry.

However, it turned out that the Germans were not the greatest threat to his health. This is the letter he wrote a month after the raid. The top left-hand corner of the air letter has been torn off but I hope I have filled in the missing bit accurately:

25th May
Darling Julia,

I was lying in bed this morning when a lovely letter from you was brought me which cheered me up no end. I don't know what the last letter you had from me said so I will make a fairly brief summary. We went into action recently which is said to have been a success, 'G' troop is thought to have done much the best which is a feather in Nic's cap. We had no casualties in our troop but Guy Ruggles Brise, Brian Ashford Russell and several others were taken prisoner, which was very sad. I am now in hospital again which is very disappointing. I have got slight chest trouble and I am being sent on a four month's cure to Durban and then back to Blighty. You know how I always make the most of my symptoms so darling please believe me when I say that there is nothing to worry about. The doctors just don't think that my chest will stand up to a long campaign at the moment and so they are sending me to a place with a wonderful climate where they think a few months complete rest will do the trick. I felt pretty rotten a fortnight ago but a weeks rest in this hospital has set me up and I look my blooming self again.

Of course it means my leaving the Regt and I am very disappointed at having done so little. Colvin [his commanding officer] seemed genuinely sorry at my leaving and I dislike leaving the troop and Nic who was much the nicest chap I've come across in the war.

I've had time to read a lot and even before I was ill I used to go into the local town [Alexandria perhaps] and spend hours in an excellent club library; chiefly reading very nostalgic literature eg Soapy Sponge, Highways and Byeways in Wiltshire (Chitterne – there is hardly anything of interest here) and Country Houses of England. This week I read Sense and Sensibility, a book by Edith Wharton, Oblomov a strange Russian book, and a book on education by Shaw written years ago.

It is very sad poor John Fox Strangways is missing. He was wounded in an attack, in the thigh. His batman carried him as far as he cd and then deposited him in a shell hole; next morning they sent a patrol to the spot but there was no sign of him – so it is hoped he is a prisoner.

I am thinking of growing a beard as it will give me something to think about. The most satisfactory part of my confinement is that I shall be home in the not very distant future but I reckon not before yours. Rather ashamed to be starting home without any medals but it cant be helped.

The 'slight chest trouble' from which my father was suffering as he stormed the cliffs of Bardia had nothing to do with an old steeplechase fall. It turned out to be TB, as no doubt the doctors, and my father too, had suspected all along. He had, after all, had it before when he was sixteen and had been laid up for months. I imagine he did not wish to reveal the diagnosis until he got home, although my mother would not have had to be a genius to guess. Tuberculosis at that time was still a terrifying word. The miracle cure, streptomycin, did not come in until 1944, though M&B, a sulpha drug, was turning out to be effective at containing the infection if not at directly attacking the bacillus. It could bring off a cure if the disease was still in its early stages and not of the galloping sort. Anyway it did the trick in this case. When he got home my father recuperated for a few months at a sanatorium in Bath and by the following year was well enough for ordinary life, though not for soldiering.

Still, he was all in one piece, unlike John Fox-Strangways who had indeed been taken prisoner but had to lose a leg and spent the rest of his life in constant pain, which partly explains why, in a notorious incident after the war, he kicked Nye Bevan down the steps of White's Club with his good leg, although the drink might also have had something to do with it. Robin Campbell lost a leg too and gained a DSO, in the Commando raid on Rommel's HQ, and was also taken prisoner. Bob Laycock led 7 and 8 Commando into Crete, accompanied by Lieutenant Evelyn Waugh who later was dropped with Randolph Churchill into Yugoslavia. The Stirling brothers became a legend in the desert. They were said to strangle German sentries as easily as they strangled rabbits. David Stirling went on to found the SAS. Admiral Keyes, whose son Geoffrey had been killed in the raid on Rommel's HQ and won a posthumous VC, set up a Special Boats Section under Captain Courtney whose canoe had provided such an uncertain light for the raid on Bardia. And Nic, the one whose other name I never heard, was killed. Everyone else had such an exciting war.

My mother's confinement was not due until September and my father was still a long way from home when my sister was born. The telegram reached him when the hospital ship was anchored off Freetown, Sierra Leone, which is why she was given the name of Frances Leone.

While he was still in hospital in Egypt, he was not short of news from the war.

Being in hospital I missed the battle of Crete. I am not really allowed out of bed but I usually make a short tour in the morning to discover the hospital gossip. Johnny Mills, a Lt from our lot, arrived in the middle of the night with 2 bits of a mortar shell in his bottom. He gave a good description of this desperate encounter. The whole time our lot were on the island they were given no rations and were short of water. Watched ceaselessly from the air and dive bombed at the least movement, they had to retreat during the night. 'G' troop apparently did a marvellous bayonet charge, killed ten boche and captured a machine gun. Everyone is overcome with admiration for the New Zealanders – the best soldiers in the world is how they are described. Nic when last heard of was all right. One chap from our troop was killed – he hadn't been with us long and 2 corporals from my section were wounded in the arms both by the same parachutist – the parachutist n'existe plus. Colonel Bob was in the picture a good deal and Johnny Mills on his nightmare walk to the beach – he was walking wounded – was fortified at Bde HQ with some wine. At one time he was lucky to get some water in which the Maoris had been boiling potatoes.

When I get to England I shall be invalided out of the army. I'm really rather sorry about this but still it will be rather nice not being in the power of redfaced majors. But then I've spent nearly 2 yrs in the army and it seems rather wasted time if I have to chuck it now. Still it will be lovely to be with you again – the prospect one of limitless bliss. I shall have to get a really open air job – it's lucky we've settled in such a healthy spot. You might keep your ears open for anything. Some Wiltshire grandee I feel sure wants an agent or something. I shall tackle Geordie Herbert and of course there shd be a good chance of war work of some kind on Salisbury Plain.

I've met an old friend in this hospital Tommy Weston the jockey. We have great racing gossip. He has an appraising and intensely practical mind, a very tough little Yorkshireman. You know how badly professional sportsmen come out of a war. Tommy must be 40 but joined the Navy and is in the same racket as I was . . .

It was so lucky my chest trouble was discovered before Crete as I shd never have lasted the campaign as the physical endurance required was terrific and I shd either have had ignominiously to have come back with the walking wounded after 2 days as those did who were taken ill or else 'missed the boat' home. To many people's surprise apparently, some people did very well, others quite the reverse; in no instance among the officers at any rate was I in the least surprised.

I wish we were together darling and after this bloody war we will be.

Your loving husband Robin

I'm v. interested in F's talking.

So the last gasp of my father's war coincided more or less with my first chirrups just short of my second birthday. For some of this time during her second pregnancy my mother was staying with her mother-in-law at Wasing Lodge, a quiet dower house of Berkshire bluenose brick by the gates of the park. Hilda Lucy Adelaide, as her granddaughters liked to call her, was a formidable figure with a fuzz of white hair and a misleadingly kindly expression. She could have been the old lady in an Ealing Studios comedy who turns out to be a match for the baddies. She was a magistrate for twenty years or more, the terror of the Berkshire bench, her mauve velour hat being regarded by the local villains as the equivalent of the black cap. She was also an obsessive fisherman, a classical pianist and the last woman to serve underarm at the Berkshire lawn tennis championships. None of these accomplishments made her any easier to get on with. Nor had widowhood lessened her tendency to lecture and interfere. After the war my father rationed his visits to her, and my mother saw as little of her as possible. Hildegarde, as my parents referred to her, had never quite lost hope of leading my father into soberer ways.

To me, though, perhaps because I was the only boy among her grandchildren, she was sweetness itself. She looked on benignly as I rode the ebony elephants that were as tall as I was and that her father had retrieved from his years in the Indian Civil Service. She pointed out the wild strawberries that grew in the cracks on her terrace and kept watch as I splashed in the little stream which ran along the wood at the end of her garden. Sometimes I would play in this watery glade with my older cousins Clare and Mary under the vigilant eye of Gwen Hoare their nanny who was a local girl then in her later teens. When Mary grew up and married Ian Cameron, Gwen went and looked after her children, Alexander, Tania, David and Clare, until they too were grown up. When David Cameron hit the headlines and was first

being interviewed on television, my wife detected a surprising undertone in his pleasant fruity tenor, which she described as an almost rustic burr, and listening carefully I thought I caught it too. I like to think that this is Gwen's voice coming through. After two generations of devoted service, it is only natural that her forceful character should leave its mark. The hand that rocks the cradle . . .

While always severe on her granddaughters, Hildegarde even managed to contain her displeasure when I grabbed a fistful of the gentians that she grew as a commercial sideline. Her butler, who was confusingly called Mr Butler, drove a consignment of them up to Covent Garden early on Monday morning. I cannot imagine that the proceeds paid for the petrol.

As a child and even later on, I was unaware of the family estrangements which for most of the time good manners kept under wraps. I did not know, for example, that my father and his elder brother Bill had been best friends right up to the time when my grandfather fell off his horse stone dead. He was sixty-five years old, not so young for the period I suppose, but he had not yet made any financial provision for his younger sons which might have dulled the pain of Bill copping the entire estate – 4,000 acres of mixed arable and woodland between Newbury and Reading, including a fine pedimented Adam house with Victorian extensions and delightful Georgian gothick outbuildings, not to mention a rich library derived from the family's origins as stationers on Tower Hill and a collection of mostly Dutch pictures which turned out to be not as good as had been fondly imagined. None of this came the way of my father or his younger brother Grig.

In fact it is only now that I realise that there was not a single object in our house that came from Wasing. In the English upper classes, it is only the younger sons who are expelled naked from the Garden of Eden. When we take the train up to London, my father rushes to the window as we rattle through the Kennet Valley, desperate to catch a glimpse of Wasing up on its gentle slope beyond the river and the canal. In the summer, the house is hidden by the trees. It is as though he is barred from his lost demesne and this is his only chance of seeing it again.

Nor did it help that, as a colonel in the Berkshire Yeomanry, Uncle Bill had played a glorious part in the days immediately after D-Day, leading his troops from a tank plunging into the *bocage*, shouting 'Let's go kill some boches,' or words to that effect. My father could not resist remarking sourly that when Bill was eventually wounded, it was in his bottom (in fact the thigh). His normal generosity deserted him when referring to any military exploit of his relations. His cousin Chris Mount flew all the way through the Battle of Britain and beyond, becoming almost the only man to command both a squadron of Spitfires and a squadron of Lancasters. Mickey or Mouse Mount, as he was known in the RAF, was an inoffensive, sweet-natured man who eventually became a solicitor in Maidenhead, but all my father would say of him was 'Chris saved his pay all through the Battle of Britain.'

When my grandmother died, she left us the ebony elephants which

I have to this day. She died in 1950 in the London Clinic, where I also happened to be a patient, having my sinuses swabbed in the hope that this might cure my asthma, though I could not see much difference afterwards. My parents took me along the passage to see her, lying frail in her bed in a very frilly white nightie. I remember thinking that the nightie was somehow unsuitable. I was only allowed to stay for a minute or two but was deeply proud of having seen her when, a week or so after I had returned home, my mother showed me the notice of her death in the *Daily Telegraph*. She was the first dying person I had seen, also the only grandparent I had known, not exactly a role model perhaps, but she was all right to me.

Only now and then in my father's letters from the war do I catch a glimpse of the resentments he managed to hide from me. My father's playmate, the art dealer Freddie Mayor, the one who married cousin Pam, told me that he used to refer to Uncle Bill as 'Sir Stuff-It-Up'. Although I was already nineteen or twenty I was shocked to hear this and didn't really believe it. But the nickname does crop up in my father's letters, and very much later on I came reluctantly to the conclusion that, for all Bill's genuine benevolence and sense of duty the nickname was not entirely undeserved. The defining moment happened outside the premises of Messrs Walford, solicitors to the gentry, of Bolton Street, Piccadilly, after a meeting to decide whether to pay off my father's debts by releasing a modest sum from the minuscule trust fund which was my mother's legacy to my sister and me. Francie and I were only too eager that this should be done but Uncle Bill and Mr Walford insisted on due form. So we sat there, the five of us, my father an embarrassed spectator, for what seemed like hours surrounded by intimidating black legal boxes labelled 'D. of Norfolk', 'E. of Sefton' and so on. Eventually the release of this tiny sum was agreed – my father's debts were inconspicuous and would have melted into oblivion if only he had had a job of any sort – and we came out into the sunlight. While my father went off with Francie, Uncle Bill took me aside and said to me, 'I'm sorry about all this business. Of course I could let him have some money from the estate but it would all go' – and with his elbow he mimed a drinking motion, rather furtively in case my father should see, although he was already halfway down Bolton Street. It would be nice to record that I said something sassy like 'Well, you could give it a try all the same,' but all I could manage was a weak 'Yes, I see,' though I remember trembling with anger as I hurried off down the street to catch up with Francie and my father.

From a good way back the Mounts had been rather Low Church and very highminded. Richard Mount, the boy from a Kentish farm who married the boss's daughter and became a partner in the City stationery firm which made maps for Pepys's Admiralty, had distinct Puritan tendencies. Frugal to the last (his motto was *Prudenter et Constanter*), Richard decreed that the £60 which would otherwise have been spent on his funeral be divided among his poor relatives back in the Kent village of Elmstead. Modest his funeral might have been as a result, but there was a sermon preached at it by the celebrated Presbyterian divine John Newman in which he described Richard as 'a hearty friend to the Societies of Reformation of Manners and Suppression of Vice who did greatly lament the growing wickedness of the Time and Place in which he lived'. Many of Richard's descendants carried on lamenting in the same vein.

They diversified from marine charts and stationery into publishing and cleaned up by publishing pamphlets from both sides in the great dispute over longitude. They also went into soap and vitriol (then a key component in the manufacture of ink and dyes), property and probably slaves too. By 1760 they were prosperous enough for Richard's grandson to decamp from the City and buy a handsome estate in Berkshire, building himself a fine mansion in the new style overlooking the Kennet Valley. A generation or two later they were making their way into Parliament, first for the Isle of Wight and then for the local seat of Newbury. They were modest Tory backbenchers who left little mark on proceedings – far outshone by their descendant David Cameron. But a high moral tone came naturally to them. My uncle Bill was firmly in the tradition.

As in all families, there were exceptions. The original Wm Hickey's Diary records an encounter with John's son, the first William Mount to live at Wasing, in about 1780:

> The fourth of the party was a gentleman dressed in the very extremity
> of fashion, having a valuable diamond ring upon one of his fingers. He

also arrived in his own carriage, and was introduced to me by the name of 'Mount'. I afterwards found him to be the only son of the great stationer upon Tower Hill, under the firm of Mount and Page. His father, being immensely rich, allowed this young coxcomb to squander what he pleased. I soon discovered Mr Mount was no small favourite of Emily's.

The dinner and wines being of the best, and Mr Mount no flincher at the glass, by seven o'clock we had disposed of a considerable quantity of champagne. We therefore adjourned to the playhouse, going in Harriet Powell's carriage, and returning in the same to supper. At a late hour we broke up, and I was preparing to go home, when Emily said she must speak to me. Mr Mount at that moment drew her aside; when a whispering conversation took place between them. He seemed angry. In a few minutes she wished him goodnight, and coming up to me said, 'I have so much to say to you we must not part yet.' She then led me, not to the chamber I had before slept in, but her own, where I passed a night that many would have given thousands to do.

Some of William's genes may have transmitted themselves to my father. And 'no flincher at the glass' became a family phrase, not to say motto, certainly a more apposite one than 'prudently and constantly'.

If my father made any sustained effort to get a job after the war, no word of it ever got through to me. In Chitterne we were surrounded by military establishments of one sort or another: the School of Infantry at Warminster, the big camp at Larkhill, the Regular Officers Selection Board at Westbury, more sprawling barracks across the downs at Bulford and Tidworth. But the project of finding work at one of these places was never heard of again. Even less was heard of his other idea, of becoming land agent to some Wiltshire grandee. Instead my father went on more or less where he had left off before the war, finding a decent ride where he could and finding a drink almost anywhere.

Almost the first thing I was aware of about him was how much he was at ease in any kind of company, perhaps because I was so intensely aware of how I myself was sometimes miserably ill at ease and sometimes wasn't and never knew which it was going to be, so I was always apprehensive meeting anyone new. It seemed to me too – although this cannot have been quite true – that he talked in exactly the same way to my literary aunts and uncles as he did to whoever happened to be in the bar at the King's Head across the road. My parents' immediate circle was neither of these. The people they saw most of belonged to what, a generation later, came to be called 'Hobohemia', a raffish subdivision of the upper class which, like some rare blue butterfly, was to be found only on the Wiltshire Downs. The species centred round Longleat and Henry Bath and his two wives, Daphne and Virginia, both adored by my father and quite liked by my mother: Daphne bright and dashing, Virginia dreamy and drawling behind a curtain of long hair – the Veronica Lake 1940s style which she kept all her life. She had been married first to my father's best friend David Tennant. My sister and I became quite hardened to the regular change of partners on Salisbury Plain, Mary Campbell becoming Mary Mayall, Mary Dunn taking on the now one-legged Robin Campbell in her place and so on. We took divorce among our parents' friends as a matter of course, regarding them, I think, as belonging to a species that was somehow different from us, but we would have been horrified if any member of our own family had split, which they never did, at least not in that generation.

This version of La Ronde on the downs seems to me looking back almost dreamlike in its lack of contact with the age of austerity the rest of the country was living in. Almost nobody in my parents' circle did any work, although they might have been memorably brave in the war, like Robin Campbell or Daphne Bath's second husband Xan Fielding who with another Hobohemian Paddy Leigh Fermor had led the guerrilla operations on German-occupied Crete recounted in *Ill Met by Moonlight*, later turned into a film starring Dirk Bogarde.

Those who were employed at all worked mostly in the Foreign Office, like Lees Mayall and Tony Rumbold, and even that employment seemed to involve, not the pompous decorum usually associated with the FO but heroic drinking bouts which ended in broken legs and desperate escapades, like the Rumbolds using diplomatic immunity to smuggle their friends' children and valuables out of Prague. This misleadingly glamorous picture of the diplomat's life lingered long enough in my mind to make me fancy when I was sixteen or seventeen that I might like to go for the Foreign Office, but soon a distaste for anything resembling a serious professional career swept over me, and I forgot all about the idea, just as my father forgot about the idea of becoming a land agent.

The trouble was that Hobohemia was a country for grown-ups. Children did not figure, although there were plenty of them. Those affected by their parents' splitting had to shuffle up and down the Wylye Valley from the old household to the new. My sister and I found ourselves parked in huge nurseries with strange children and step-children who had scarcely got to know each other, with a frosty and often bemused nanny inherited from some earlier ménage attempting to persuade us to try the cucumber sandwiches or the fairy cakes. From downstairs the scent of gin and cigarettes and the noise of uproarious talk and pre-war drawls – my dear, how absolutely frightful – floated up to us. How slowly those afternoons in those chilly undecorated playrooms (for children's rooms then, like the servants' quarters, tended to be left out of the make-over by fashionable decorators) wore through until our parents burst upstairs, laughing as they came and took their wooden little children home.

During our trip to Ireland my parents took me to lunch with Derek Jackson and his latest (third) wife, the glamorous Janetta (he being her fourth husband), at Gaybrook, the house they had rented outside Mullingar because the Horse was in tax exile. He was as generous and welcoming as he knew how, but his glittering eye and his strangely hurried, gravelly speech was unnerving. I could feel how impatient he was, how short his attention span, especially for children, whom he resented as competitors almost as much as he resented God – 'that greybearded monster' as he called him – and for the same reason. It was a relief when I was sent off into the Gaybrook woods to play with Janetta's daughter Nicky, who was a couple of years younger than me. In the damp, silent shrubbery I developed a fantasy that we had been abandoned in a trackless forest like children in a Victorian story, but Nicky did not much care for the idea, perhaps because it sounded too much like real life. A year later, Janetta had a baby (Rose, Derek's only child by any of his wives). Within hours of the birth, Derek told her that he was running off with Janetta's half-sister Angela, to become her fourth husband too, though he never actually married her.

At Christmas we stood glumly under the enormous tree at Longleat while Henry Bath in full Santa rig handed out presents to the children of the tenantry, which seemed to include us. Henry, a natural show-man, the first of the stately-home showmen in fact, normally dressed like an Edwardian fairground barker in a loud check jacket with a scarlet handkerchief frothing from his breast pocket. With his broken nose and haughty mien he bore something of a resemblance to the Iron Duke when young. His clipped, impatient way of talking suggested the military – he had been wounded in the second war, his elder brother had been killed in the first. Like many grandees he alternated between endearing generosity and anxious cheeseparing, finding it easier to be genial to the children of his friends than to his own sons, resembling Peter Fleming in this but not much else. He would slip me a fiver and say how intelligent I was although I had given not the slightest evidence of this: 'My boys are no good at all, utterly useless.' In the background, one or two of his tall, handsome, pugnacious sons (they had all been captain of boxing at school) would lounge, visibly seething. Being such a performer, never happier than when appearing on television or being recognised by visitors to Longleat as he loitered by the ticket desk, he might have been expected to enjoy playing Santa Claus but in fact the only part he really enjoyed playing was himself and he thrust the presents into our hands in a brisk and peremptory manner: 'Here, this one's yours – take it, boy.'

I was more at ease with the older generation when I was on home ground, especially if I was in bed with asthma and highly scented women from the literary end of Hobohemia – Sonia Orwell, Glur Quennell, Pauline Gates – would come up to my room and lean over my bed and kiss my fevered cheek or brow, murmuring 'Darling' as they did so. Best of all was Pauline's brother Robert Newton, fresh from his triumphs as Bill Sikes in *Oliver Twist* and Long John Silver in *Treasure Island*, who would sit down heavily on my bed and do his part in an outrageous but none the less terrifying Mummerset accent, clasping me to his bosom and leering hideously at me: 'Arrh Jim lad, stick tight to old John Silver and tha'll come to no 'arm.' I had been given a pair of red metal stilts that Christmas and Bobby used them to hop round the room wreathing himself in Christmas paper chains and filling the room with pissed enchantment. I was a starveling boy at this period, looking pretty much like the boy who played Oliver Twist in the David Lean film, a resemblance remarked on by Bobby as he rolled his eyes with his murderous burglar glare, 'Ay, Robin, your boy should have had the part,' although he was of course smashed at the time.

My father had a theory, which I eventually came round to myself, that going for a drive in the Morris would do wonders for my asthma, perhaps because the bumps and rattles would shake up my tubes or because the engine fumes would numb them, or both. So we would embark on long excursions across the downs. Sometimes we would go to look at a horse that my father had ridden or might ride or a garden shed that he might buy. Sometimes we would go for some medical attention – like the strange practitioner at the far end of Warminster near the golf course who gave my feet electric shocks to cure my fallen or rather non-existent arches. A couple of times we went fishing on Uncle Bill's water on the River Kennet, but that meant asking his permission which I now realise stuck in my father's throat. But all these expeditions, whether long or short, required refuelling stops on both the outward leg and the return journey. Much of my time was spent reading in the car waiting for my father to emerge from the saloon bar, children in those benighted times not being admitted to licensed premises. So I became familiar with the car park of almost every pub in Wiltshire – the crumbling tarmac, the buddleia sprouting from the garden wall, the crates of empties stacked by the back door, the smell of disinfectant from the gents. How well I knew them all: the Angel at Heytesbury, the George at Codford, the Bath Arms and the Old Bell at Warminster, the Station Hotel at Market Lavington where we would pick up my mother from her rare excursions to London, the George at Shrewton, the County Hotel at Salisbury where my father would stiffen his nerve before the interview with the manager of Barclays Bank next door, the famous Bear at Hungerford (a compulsory staging post on the return from Wasing), the good Wheatsheaf at Andover and the bad Wheatsheaf at Virginia Water. These stops were never protracted, long enough for me to finish a chapter of *Barnaby Rudge*. They were an advertisement for the cheering properties of alcohol, since my father got back in the car, not by any means drunk, but decidedly debonair. Later I was old enough for him to bring me out a glass of cider, though still not old enough to go inside. Nothing could exceed the pleasure of sitting unmolested in the passenger seat with *Scoop* or *Tess of the D'Urbervilles* and a half-pint of that rotten-sweet fizz in my hand. Ever since, I have been happier outside pubs than inside them.

Now and then we would bump into old racing acquaintances, trainers and jockeys he had known in that unimaginable period before the war: short, bow-legged men who somehow still managed to look wiry even if they had put on a pound or two. Often their teeth flashed gold when they smiled which gave them a sort of gipsy allure. I don't know whether this was a fashion among jockeys who had prospered or just a fashion in dentistry at the time. Once at Salisbury races, high on the downs overlooking the cathedral, we met my father's old friend Tommy Weston who had been in hospital with him in Egypt. 'Oh being in the war was nothing,' he said. 'If you'd been down the pit and then a stable lad you knew what having it hard was all about.' But there was no hint of boasting or complaint about him and I gazed with total adoration on the tough little man who had won the Derby on Sansovino and on Hyperion, both owned by Lord Derby himself and trained by George Lambton, author of my father's favourite horse book *Men and Horses I Have Known*. Not only were Tommy's two Derby winners among the greatest racehorses of their day, the beauty of their names tingled in my ears.

As time went by, my father began to think that here we were in the depths of the country and that, although I was clearly the bookish sort, I ought to be taught the rudiments of country sports. He had already taught me a bit about coarse fishing. Now perhaps – I was fifteen or sixteen – it was time for me to learn how to shoot. My father had of course no land to shoot over and, though a fine shot in his youth, no longer had a gun. So as usual he had to cadge. He managed to borrow an old twelve-bore from one of the Strattons. It was a rickety weapon whose lock, stock and barrel were only loosely acquainted. He then asked his neighbour Siegfried Sassoon, who lived in Heytesbury, the village beyond Codford, whether we could loose off a few cartridges in his woods.

They had become friends through a shared love of steeplechasing, cricket and poetry. These days they both preferred to ride long distances over country rather than submit to the fussy disciplines of foxhunting. My father once rode twenty miles and back over the downs to inspect a house which David Tennant was thinking of buying. Siegfried would often ride down the hill to Greenways School, Codford, to see how his only child George was getting on – visits which became so frequent and so embarrassing that George had to beg him to stop. Perhaps their shared experience of war had brought them together too, although my father's experience had been so much briefer and less horrific. Or perhaps not so much because of the actual experience of war as because of feeling spare and out of place and let down after it.

Siegfried gave his blessing and for a couple of hours on a misty November afternoon we patrolled the undulating ornamental woods that he had planted up behind Heytesbury House. He had bought the huge house after he got married in the mid-1930s – his own late forties – to the astonishment of his friends. He was flush for the first time in his life because his wife Hester had money. 'Sig's impaled an heiress,' my father would say as we drove past the gates with the newly painted coats of arms which showed a smaller shield in the middle, the heraldic method of advertising that the holder has skewered a rich bride, but for all I know these may well have been the arms of the previous owner, only now standing out so vividly after being repainted. Sig and his brothers belonged to the branch of the family which was known as 'the poor Sassoons'. They had been cut off when his father married out. On hearing the news, old Mrs Sassoon had rushed straight to the synagogue and cursed any children that might be born of this unholy union, declaring her son officially dead, saying the funeral prayers and observing the correct period of mourning. Perhaps not surprisingly in these circumstances, Siegfried was ambivalent about his half-Jewish ancestry – his 'oriental side' as he called it – and was apparently content that even people who knew him quite well, like my father, should go on thinking that his Bombay merchant forebears were Parsees.

There was not much wildlife about, though it was soothing to stand in the long grassy rides and watch the mist creep up over the orange and purple foliage of the beeches and maples. We were thinking of heading home when a plump cock pheasant whirred across the ride looking for a place to roost in the firs higher up the hill. I raised the gun, but while I was still fiddling with the safety catch, an elderly figure leaped out with startling agility from the bend in the avenue. He wore a battered felt hat and a bright scarlet scarf thrown round his neck and even at that distance – a hundred yards or so – I could see how handsome he was. He moved towards us stumbling into a run and waving his hand in agitation. 'Please don't shoot, he's so beautiful,' he cried, almost at the same moment as my father called back, 'Hullo, Sig.'

I had not yet read *Memoirs of a Foxhunting Man* or I might have been reminded of the narrator describing how as a boy on his second day out hunting he sees a fox run across his path. Someone holloas and before he can stop himself he exclaims, 'Don't do that, they'll catch him.' The narrator tells us later that before he went to France to fight he had 'never shot at a bird or an animal in my life' – so his first targets were humans.

Sassoon's attitude to blood sports, like his attitude to his Jewishness, indeed his attitude to most things, was not without its complexities. All I felt myself at that moment was extreme annoyance at the in-and-out running of the adult world. If he was going to deny me the only decent shot of the day out of his reverence for life, why on earth had he let us come at all? I could not be expected then to understand that it was Siegfried's besetting trait to repent of any gesture almost as soon as he had made it, to start wanting to extricate himself from a love affair or any other allegiance (to socialism, to pacifism) the moment he had embarked on it. He lived in a haze of dissatisfaction, abnormally sensitive to outside influence but repelled as quickly and violently as he had been attracted.

He asked us to drop in for tea when we had finished, but to come in by the servants' entrance because he was alone in the house and there was no one to answer the front door – again a characteristic carry-on, suggesting both poverty and solitude but also an unshed grandeur. There appeared to be no question of him answering the front door himself. My father and I wandered around the back of the house, trying several locked doors before coming on a peeling green door which opened and led us through a series of dank and empty passages painted the same indifferent green. Somehow we managed to end up in what was clearly the drawing room which seemed empty too until our eyes focused enough to see the celebrated gaunt hawk's profile outlined against the dying light through the long windows. Thus discovered – I saw from later visits that this was how he liked to be come upon – he pushed a plate of dry cucumber sandwiches at us and began to talk in a shy undertone. At first I thought this awkward way of speaking was because he was out of practice in company. Hester had been turfed out several years earlier and George was away and for the moment estranged too. But this turned out to be Siegfried's normal way of talking. His poetry readings at the height of his fame had often been more or less inaudible. His undertone was no obstacle to a formidable eloquence when he got going. He talked in a way I had never come across before, without any reserve or hesitation, roaming across all sorts of subjects: verse techniques, the difficulty of finding servants, staying with Max Beerbohm, the current Test series against Australia, his first meeting with Thomas Hardy, the shortcomings of his wife/son/daughter-in-law, his neglect by the critics – this last a recurring theme. 'They don't understand what a talent I have for light verse' and then 'George has just got married, he's much too young, you know, and she isn't suitable for him at all' – although later when he was ill and George's first wife who was a nurse by training looked after him, he changed his mind and decreed that it was George who wasn't worthy of her. His initial objection had been, I think, as much to do with snobbery as with the young couple's age. He had a prickly sense of his social position, despite being, on and off, a declared socialist. To the end of his life he liked to be known in Heytesbury as Captain Sassoon.

I liked his lack of *pudeur* about expressing both his resentments and his enthusiasms, his lack of a protective skin. His self-centredness too was much more sympathetic than it sounds when written down. But it must have been wearing to live with, not least for himself. I knew nothing then of his vigorously gay years between the wars when he had a string of affairs or near-affairs with celebrated lovers – Ivor Novello, Rex Whistler, Noël Coward and above all the unbearable Stephen Tennant with his pearls and tantrums. Siegfried, though, gave as much hell as he got in these tortuous episodes and he had now returned to the chastity of his youth, I am sure with relief. He had always found his sexuality something of a burden – 'trouble down there' he called it – and he had told Edward Carpenter, the pioneer of free love for all sorts, that he was still 'unspotted' at the age of twenty-five. Even though I had no clue about any of this, I could not fail to be aware of the dissatisfaction that never ceased to nag his soul.

Why was Sassoon like this? In the public mind, after all, he remained not only one of the most celebrated poets of the Great War but also an abiding emblem of courage and protest against the carnage. There are few more memorable gestures of dissent than his throwing the purple ribbon of his Military Cross into the Mersey. He was indeed a legend that you were surprised to find still alive, a fact he was not slow to comment on with his habitual self-irony. Though his later poetry had never been in fashion (because most of it was as bad as his pre-1914 verse), the first two of his fictional autobiographies, *Memoirs of a Foxhunting Man* and *Memoirs of an Infantry Officer*, became instant minor classics, soon added to every English Literature syllabus. On rereading *Foxhunting Man* recently, I found it rather too easily nostalgic and sometimes clichéd (it was his first effort in prose), but *Infantry Officer*, published two years later in 1930, reads as well as ever, crisp and caustic and lyrical. Some of the setpieces – his return a year later to the network of trenches where he had first seen such horror and which were now a harmless, empty warren several miles behind the Allied lines, or his watching his company trudging back from the Somme an hour before daybreak – are unsurpassable. As for the war poems, I was recently driving down the M4 listening to a selection of recordings retrieved from the British Library archive and found it hard to keep on driving as I heard that unobtrusive voice, only just audible, reading 'Died of Wounds':

> The ward grew dark; but he was still complaining
> And calling out for 'Dickie'. 'Curse the wood!
> It's time to go, O Christ, and what's the good?
> We'll never take it, and it's always raining.'

My shooting career trickled on, though my father was too distraught after my mother died to give me any more lessons and quite soon he had abandoned Chitterne for London. Once or twice a year I was asked to go shooting at Wasing or in my cousin George's woods in Herefordshire or with his sister Alice down in Cornwall. I liked standing at the edge of a covert with the frost still on the grass listening to the jaunty cries of the beaters as they worked their way through the undergrowth or watching the mist gather on the estuary below us at

Port Eliot, but I never became even half adequate with the gun, not having learned the essentials properly. All the same, I was pleased when my father gave me a second-hand twelve-bore for my twentieth birthday. Like the gun he had borrowed for me four years earlier, there was a certain looseness in the fit between lock, stock and barrel, but the stock had some pretty silver chasing on it and it went nicely with the green suit of plus-fours I had just bought from E. M. Whaley, outfitters, of Salisbury. My pretensions to be a gentleman were then reaching their sad little peak, although no money except my university grant was coming into my Barclays account, and that erratically because my father had failed to fill in the form.

As he instructed, for safety I stowed the three parts of the gun separately – the barrels in a locked hanging cupboard, the lock and stock in among my socks and shirts and the cartridges in a drawer in my desk. By then it was my third year at Oxford and I was out in lodgings up the Woodstock Road with Henry Harrod. I had explained to our landlady Mrs Margolyes, a doctor's wife who owned several properties in the area, that we only needed two rooms. 'It's the three rooms or nothing,' she said firmly. 'They're very nice rooms. I'm sure you can get someone else.' While this conversation was going on, Mrs Margolyes's fourteen-year-old daughter Miriam was lying on the hearthrug, an opulent tumble of dark curls and puppy fat. 'I'm going to be an artist's model,' she told us while her mother was fetching the agreement form. 'I'm going to pose for Augustus John. I've written to him and he says he's very interested.' As it happened, Augustus John died only a few months later, so his last hours may have been spent dreaming of the nubile nymphet who was about to come and pose for him. Perhaps it was his death that decided Miriam to become a great comic actress instead. Anyway we took the rooms at 122 Woodstock Road, which were every bit as good as her mother claimed. Most of our friends had already found a place to live, but someone said that James Stobo was looking for a room. Neither Henry nor I had met this tall, handsome, shy undergraduate who was in another college, Lincoln, I think, but the moment we did we could see he would be ideal. For some reason – our standoffishness, his shyness – we never got to know him much better, although he was by no means a recluse and went out with two enviable girls whom we did know, Mary Curzon and Mary Lambert. So we went on, the three of us, for months, saying hullo on the landing, keeping our cereals separate but sharing the milk and taking our baths at different times. We remained shadowy to one another, though I did lend James a volume of Rilke, *The Notebooks of Malte Laurids Brigge*, which I never actually read, though I was reading German and he wasn't, so we must have had some conversation beyond the housekeeping. Rilke's book purports to be the musings of an impoverished Danish poet living in Paris. It is not a cheerful work. The opening lines give something of the flavour: 'People come here, then, to live? I should rather have thought that they came here to die.'

I had been out all day doing nothing very much. Number 122 Woodstock Road was a fairish bike or bus ride from the centre of Oxford, so having once got into the city centre I tended to stay there, dawdling in the library or the Kardomah café or the rooms of friends who were still in college. So it must have been latish afternoon when I scrunched across the gravel of the forecourt and was startled to see a policeman. He was talking to two friends of mine who turned to look at me with shattered faces.

'I'm afraid I have some very bad news for you, sir. Your friend Mr Stobo, he appears to have shot himself. And we think it must be your gun he used.'

They had taken the body away and locked his room, which was next to mine. I did not ask to go in. There was a lot of blood apparently.

'The body was discovered by a Mr Picarda who says he's a friend of yours.'

Even in my horror, the glacial part of my brain registered that if a body had to be discovered in a pool of blood there was no more suitable person than Noel Picarda to discover it. Uproarious, relent-less, witty, disgusting in both speech and person, lecherous, indifferent to all considerations of good taste, he was the only person I have met who can truly be called Rabelaisian. Already a Liberal candidate, he later became one of the dubious fairy godmothers at the birth of *Private Eye*, and later still, rebranded as Noel Picarda-Kemp, got within a few hundred votes of becoming a Tory MP, whiling away the interim performing in night clubs, haunting pubs in Soho and the Inns of Court and perpetually failing his Bar exams. Later on, Noel was beset by family lawsuits and mental distress and he came to an end of protracted sadness, but at this moment in his life he possessed an unnerving bravura and it was typical that, after James's room had been cleaned up, he had not the slightest hesitation in renting it himself.

James had broken into my cupboard and ferreted out the other parts of the gun and put them together. At the inquest it emerged that he had only recently recovered from glandular fever and was still subject to recurrent fits of depression as a result. One of the girls who had come to the inquest thanked me for not mentioning her name in the evidence I gave. But in truth the idea of referring to any possible disappointment in love had not remotely occurred to me. On the question of James's motives, as of most other things about him, my mind was a blank. The coroner was very gentle and assured me that I was not to blame but of course I thought I was, not so much for failing to lock up the gun more securely (I had done what I could and in fact I could not help feeling resentful that James should have taken it) as because I had not even been aware that he had had glandular fever and that he was overcome by these terrible bouts of melancholy in the next room. What had seemed to me a civilised relationship was unmasked as a ghastly example of English cold-heartedness and lack of human curiosity. And though James's distraught parents could not have been kinder to me, they must surely have thought so too. I sold the gun to a back-street dealer near Paddington. But I cannot say that I never fired another one. It was quite a few years later that I gave up shooting for good, and then not because I had come to hate the sight of blood but because I had grown tired of missing. There was, I suppose, a weird parallel between Siegfried who had never fired at a living thing until he started firing at Germans and my gun which, in my ownership at least, had killed virtually nothing except James. But it was not a parallel that occurred then even to my frozen heart.

Siegfried's vigilant but unpredictable sensibilities showed them-selves in other ways too, in his generosity with money when he had it, for example. He would hand out large sums at surprising moments, among others to his old wartime friend Robert Graves, but only after they had ceased to be real friends, in fact after a coolness had sprung up between them.

There was another example of Siegfried's generosity which was to have an indirect effect upon my life. Towards the end of the war, a month before D-Day, Hester announced that she was leaving him to go back to her mother. This was not the first such walk-out, nor was it to be the last, but it came at a moment when he had just sent off George, not yet eight, as a weekly boarder at Greenways School, Codford, only a couple of miles down the Wylye Valley. Desperate with loneliness, in the course of his rides over to see George which were to become so embarrassing to the boy, he struck up a friendship with the school's owner, Vivien Hancock. Mrs Hancock was herself in a sad state. She had already lost her husband and now her eldest son had just been killed in the war. Not surprisingly in those grim days, the school was struggling. Siegfried lent her £8,000 to buy the freehold of the place – say, £100,000 in today's money. Equally unsurprisingly, Hester assumed that they must be having an affair. Quite possibly Mrs Hancock did have her eye on Siegfried. She had a literary side and had chosen as the school's motto 'A Green Thought in a Green Shade', a line from Marvell's poem 'The Garden', the poem Betjeman quoted in the kitchen garden on his first visit to Tullynally. The motto probably bewildered some of the parents then but it would go down a treat in today's eco-climate. Besides, Sassoon was not only the most famous living war poet, handsome at all times and charming when he wanted to be, but he appeared to be streaming with cash (though most of it was Hester's). For his part, he liked her enough to waive the interest on the loan when she couldn't pay it, but no more than that, I fancy. And he must have breathed a quiet sigh of relief when she took up with a Mr Gibbons who was to be her second husband. All the same, if he was to have any hope of getting his money back, the school had to fill its classrooms. So without having more clue what the school was like than that George did not seem to be too miserable there (it was probably better than being caught in the screeching match back home in Heytesbury whenever Hester returned, which was all too often), he began enthusiastically recommending the school to all his friends.

My father, equally unversed in such matters, seemed to be the only one who took the bait. Nobody else we knew had a boy at Greenways and none of our neighbours' sons followed George and me there. I'm sure my father sent me because he rather worshipped

Siegfried, and Siegfried for his part was recommending the school (a) to convince himself that he had done the right thing for George and (b) to get his money back.

So in the September of 1947 my father and I bumped along the Codford road in the Morris Ten, turning right at the milk bar and left just before the George (where the assistant masters crept out to get tanked up) and down the sodden gravel sweep of Greenways School, to be greeted on the steps of the portico by the statuesque figure of Mrs Gibbons (as she now was), always dressed in some shade of scarlet, cerise or fuchsia with a beautifully permed head of steel-grey hair. No mark of the tragedies she had so recently suffered clung to her, still less any hint of her present state of indebtedness. On the contrary, she radiated authority and composure. In fact she was by some way the most terrifying woman I have ever met, leaving far behind, for example, Dame Antonia Byatt, Margaret Thatcher and Baroness Mary Warnock. For one reason or another, Mr Gibbons failed to stay the course and rather soon, I think in the next summer holidays but two, she traded him in for a Mr Clark, who, long after I had left, became headmaster. My father fantasised that this would become an annual occurrence, possibly involving human sacrifice, comparable to the rapid turnover of priest–kings in *The Golden Bough*. To this day, the word 'man-eater' instantly brings Mrs Gibbons to my mind.

She was economical too. My first school report was headed 'Greenways School, Bognor Regis' with the Bognor Regis crossed out and 'Codford' inked in. The school had left Bognor several years before, so she must have had a stack of old report forms to use up.

Yet, for all her hypnotic powers, the Scarlet Peril, as she was known in our house, failed quite to dispel a certain air of chaos and impermanence that clung to Greenways, even a faintly sinister ambience. The atmosphere had about it something of Llanabbas, the prep school in *Decline and Fall*, but also something of a gulag in some distant region of the USSR just this side of Siberia. You would occasionally come upon groups of senior boys, the Pioneers as they were called, marching off in a working party armed with picks and scythes and shovels to clear some area of virgin scrub at the extremities of the estate. The millpond the far side of the railway from Bath to Salisbury appeared on school postcards as 'The Bathing Pool, Greenways School', which gave a false idea not only of ownership but also of propinquity and suitability for bathing. The muddy approach fouled with cowshit from the surrounding thistly meadow, the pool's weedy depths and stony bottom, the menacing tug of the millrace if you went in too far – all combined to initiate my long career as a non-swimmer. Some way down from the handsome late-Georgian mansion were the classrooms, a bunch of whitewashed huts which might have been either agricultural or military in origin, again suggesting some sort of penal camp whose inmates needed to be kept far away from civilisation, perhaps for health reasons. A draughty barn behind the classrooms served as a gymnasium where Sergeant Fry taught us boxing. We were so cold in our white singlets and shorts that at least the thump of a left jab in your chest from Weedon or Billings two warmed you up a bit. The other boys tended to be the children of Army officers stationed somewhere on Salisbury Plain or overseas. They were already toughened by knocking about from one posting to the next and hardened to life in the pack. I made nothing resembling a friend there, merely trying not to incur the contempt of those boys who could inflict the sharpest rabbit punches and the worst Chinese burns. It was for this reason that I invited Weedon and Billings two to come home for my birthday tea. Not a great success. I was saved from being beaten up on home territory only because my parents had given me for this birthday a handsome leather punchball on an iron stand and my guests spent the afternoon sinking their sharp little fists into it.

At least I was only a day boy, although I did regret not being a boarder for the night that several of the classrooms were burned down. Even the sight of their smouldering ruins the next day was thrilling enough. Mrs Gibbons speedily announced that the blaze was caused by an electrical fault, but we knew better. My own suspicions fell on a gangly Smike-like boy known as Lofty, who seemed particularly ill at ease. I was delighted to have my suspicions apparently confirmed when Lofty did a runner and got as far as Trowbridge station before the police picked him up. Nothing in my brief career at Greenways gave me more pleasure than being on hand in the panelled hall when the coppers brought back Lofty shivering with fear and exhaustion.

The headmaster, Bernard Ince, was a disciplinarian with a black moustache and a volcanic temper. He held up boys by their hair when they vexed him. His nickname was Funf after the sinister German spy in *ITMA*, played by Jack Train talking into a glass tumbler. The character's catchphrase was 'This is Funf speaking' – a take-off of Lord Haw Haw's greeting, 'Germany calling'. Naturally Funf appeared only in the wartime episodes of the long-running radio show and the earlier ones at that, well before my time, so that, although I was addicted to *ITMA* as to all the radio comedy shows, I had never heard Funf and regarded the nickname merely as a brilliant onomatopoeic rendering of Mr Ince's explosive qualities. I don't remember learning anything much at Greenways, but I don't remember not learning anything either, so the teaching probably wasn't too bad, though it does seem significant that the only members of staff I can now remember are Funf and Sergeant Fry, suggesting that the principal lesson I learned there was the art of survival. Still, it was typical of Mrs Gibbons's entrepreneurial spirit that she stuck my name up in gilt letters on the school honours board although I was only there for a couple of terms and won the scholarship after more than three years at another school. History does not record whether Siegfried ever got his £8,000 back.

Why was I transferred to another school? Had my parents lost confidence in Funf and the Scarlet Peril? They were not in the least competitive on their own behalf, but, as often happens with people who have no ambition for themselves, they were eager for their children to do well. So from the backwoods of Greenways I was shipped away to Sunningdale School, Ascot, Berks, a low redbrick villa surrounded with pale green ironwork verandahs in a forest of rhododendrons, which specialised in preparing boys for Eton or, at worst, Winchester.

My first term my parents drove me there. The school trunk, specially bought in Salisbury for the purpose, had been squeezed into the boot. My father had started up the car to make sure it would go. The three of us came down the little crazy-paving path to the gate in the yew hedge that my father had planted to deaden the noise of the tanks rolling by from Warminster to Larkhill. I looked back to the front door. Mrs Herrington and Francie were standing on the step in the shadow of the jew's mallow that framed the doorway, with Olive just visible behind them. Through my own tears I noted that they were crying too and I looked up at my parents' faces in the hope of scoring a full house. My mother just looked strained – as I have said, she did not cry easily – but my father was in difficulties. He was inclined to tears, unashamed of them in fact. 'I have no time for a man who cannot weep,' he said, I think quoting someone, Churchill possibly. I remember being precisely aware at the time that this was a final separation.

Sunningdale is no more than sixty or seventy miles from Chitterne, but the drive seemed endless as we bumped over the blank wastes of the eastern plain, now in mid-January a sullen ploughland stretching to the horizon. One part of me dreaded the usual breakdown and us arriving humiliatingly late, perhaps after the other boys were all in bed so that I would be plunged directly into some terrifying dormitory rag. On the other hand, perhaps a breakdown would trigger some marvellous chain of events which would make it impossible for me to go away to the new school at all – an accident which would bankrupt us or cripple me or both. I would become a heroic Tiny Tim figure who would be universally acknowledged as a genius without ever having to leave home. But by now we were chugging through the even gloomier heaths of Hampshire, scene of the darkest deeds in every thriller I had read from Wilkie Collins to Bulldog Drummond and Dennis Wheatley. By the time we reached the pine woods and nursery gardens of Bagshot my senses were dulled with despair.

New boys and their parents were ushered into the drawing room on the private side of the house through French windows under one of the pale green verandahs. The headmaster, George Devereux Fox MC, a grave narrow-shouldered tortoise rather below average height, dressed in gravel-coloured tweeds, his hair slicked down like wet tarmac, greeted us with a sombre courtesy which I was to discover never left him even when my distant cousin Spencer Lyttelton kicked him up the bottom as he bent over to retrieve some papers, not out of any special animosity but because a bending headmaster presented an irresistible target and Spencer had learning difficulties. Mr Fox was as unflappable as a gravedigger. Mrs Fox offered us tea. Her grey hair had a perm every bit as formidable as the Scarlet Peril's (much in the style worn then and now by HM the Queen) and her personality was only marginally less commanding, though she preferred to dress in a misty blue wool. The room was deeply carpeted and full of expensive-looking china, Meissen I was told later. In the corner the bridge table was set up ready for play (the Foxes were bridge fanatics, G.D.F.

eventually dying as he would have wished at the table after having landed a tricky four spades). There was no suggestion that anything as rough and noisy as a school lay beyond the heavy panelled doors. We were unmistakably in the land of Posh.

Mrs Fox enquired after my current state of health, being well briefed on my delicateness. She hoped that the air would be good for my asthma, most boys seemed to thrive there and there were wonderful long walks over the heath. Mr Fox knew of my father's racing life and shared his passion for the turf. I concentrated on preventing my cup from chattering against the saucer and now and then furtively eyed the other boys who were standing with their parents in glum little clusters. Mrs Fox began to introduce us to our cell-mates and to break us into the surname drill: 'This is Clarke, he's come all the way from California, and this is Doble and this is, yes, Morton Evans, and Langton who's going to be Langton minor although it's his cousin not his brother who's already here.'

By now I was longing for my parents to go and leave me alone to face this ordeal, which they could do nothing to help me with. But I could see my father beginning to succumb to his instinct to make any party go, even an occasion like this which wasn't really meant to be a party at all. And oh horror, he turned out to know Mrs Morton Evans and embraced her warmly and called her Ginette and beckoned my mother to say hullo which I could see she was not all that keen to do. Then a fresh bunch of parents came in sweating badly under the weight of their son's trunk, and Mr Fox had to explain to them that trunks were meant to go in by the school entrance and then he had to restrain them from lifting the trunk up again because a man would come and take it. So the trunk sat there while the parents went on apologising and this cheered the rest of us up a bit and also helped to break up the party and at last my parents began to say their goodbyes. I embraced my mother in the usual awkward way and my father gave me one of his bristly kisses which I rather liked, perhaps because he was better at kissing.

I cried myself to sleep for the first ten days, and for the first four or five days of the following term, then not at all. I can remember the first night that I felt no inclination to sob and thinking how peculiar this was. Then the life of the school began to possess me in all its nerve-racking, consuming intensity. Those first few nights I could hear the other boys too snuffling into their sheets and the little furtive bedspring noises as they shifted about. We slept in the end as small boys always do sleep, but I at least was usually awake to see the grey dawnlight creep round the edges of the curtains and kiss the top of the silver or leather frames of the parents' photos which the other boys had propped on their bedside lockers. I had not seen proper posed photographs like these before, usually with the scrawly signature of Lenare under them, the mothers seen through a fine mist, often bare-shouldered with several rows of pearls, the fathers in sharper focus in pin-striped suits and regimental ties. On sports days and at half-term I try to recognise the parents from their pictures, but the photographs resemble each other more than they resemble the real-life parents. I would quite like to have a photograph of my parents to put up. But it is safer not to ask for one because I know that it would not be the right sort of photograph. In the same way when our parents' cars come up the drive to take us out for the day, though I fret in case my parents do not turn up at all, I am not entirely distressed that the Morris Ten should stutter round the bend in the rhododendrons half an hour after everyone else. At least it will have the gravel outside the library window to itself and not be shamed by the Lane Foxes' Humber Super Snipe and the Blofelds' Armstrong-Siddeley. And by then there will be no other boys left to peer out of the window and exclaim, 'I say, have you seen Mount's father's car?'

There is nothing like the sense of desolation on waking up your first few days at boarding school and discovering you are not at home in your own bed with the picture of the ducks over the fireplace, especially in January with the wind rattling at the window panes and not the friendly old nut tree swishing outside. Sunningdale is tucked away in its dripping woods beside the railway line from Wokingham to Waterloo and is certainly not on a proper street, although Dry Arch Lane which it is on is gloomy enough, but it was of those first few mornings at Sunningdale that I immediately thought when later I read those lines in *In Memoriam*:

> The noise of life begins again,
> And ghastly through the drizzling rain

On the bald street breaks the blank day.

But then every morning something wonderful happens – at least I thought it wonderful that first morning and it never ceases to give me a lift. At a quarter to eight Ruby comes in with her big jug of hot water to fill the basins on the washstands lined up along the middle of the room. Ruby is a rangy girl, part Irish I suppose though she doesn't sound it particularly, with lots of lipstick and hips that jiggle as she throws back the curtains and fills the basins to a depth of about four inches, and as she does this she sings, in a wild, clear voice, whatever she has just picked up off the radio. She sings 'Let Him Go or Let Him Tarry', 'Red Sails in the Sunset', 'She Wore Red Feathers and a Hula Hula Skirt', and 'Don't Fence Me In'. The songs are mostly about being carefree and not giving a fig for men who are not good enough for her, which is somehow thrilling and cheering for us lying there in our striped pyjamas rubbing the sleep out of our eyes and trying to put the night behind us.

But homesickness, we soon learned, was not the only peril of the night. In between the main dormitories on the upper floor there was a modest flat, barely more than a bed-sitting room, inhabited by the deputy headmaster, Mr J. B. Burrows, a lean, hatchet-faced bachelor with a moustache that boded no good. By day he taught French and history with implacable rigour. Even when he handed out a chocolate if you had conjugated *avoir*, *devoir* and *recevoir* without a mistake, there was a vulpine gleam in his eye. He never slept. No matter how late the bolder spirits like Lane Fox and Hall minor started their midnight feast or began to tease some sleepy innocent, Mr Burrows was there in a moment, gliding silently into the room and seizing the guilty boy by the scruff of his pyjamas to lead him down the passage. The terrible thump of his cane could be heard all too clearly through the thin partition walls, usually followed by the screams and whimpers of the victim. No less horrific to me was the ritual which required the victim on return to his dormitory to pull down his pyjamas and exhibit the dreadful purple-black stripes across his bottom. All this was, I suppose, part of Sunningdale's brief to prepare boys for Eton, which at that time was an inferno of corporal punishment, little altered from the unrestrained brutalities of the eighteenth century. For the seventy scholars in College, there were at a rough computation half a dozen distinct forms of beating, ranging from the 'siphoning' administered with a rubber tube by the captain of Chamber, the junior boys' dormitory, through the various canings handed out by the Captain of the School, the Master in College, the Captain of the Boats and the President of the bloods' Olympus, the Eton Society or Pop, to the 'swiping' carried out under the medieval beams of Lower School by the headmaster himself. Unlike the abrupt and terrifying irruptions of Mr Burrows, there was at least a semblance of formality about these occasions (I do not suggest this was much of a consolation). Some sort of indictment would be drawn up, witnesses were required, a chalk line would be drawn across the victim's striped trousers.

Some of the fiercest beatings were handed out to those who had shirked games. During the autumn term, in theory the whole of College was in training for the great Wall Game against the Oppidans on St Andrew's Day, even those too small or too maimed to have the faintest hope of making the team. Every day some form of physical exercise had to be recorded on the time sheet, half an hour's desultory squash being the softest option and the easiest to fake, the squash courts being at the far end of the playing fields. This Stalinist regime was overseen with intense passion by Conrad Russell, the youngest son of Bertrand by the last of his wives. His strange hissing voice comes back to me at odd moments: 'You cannot posssibly have played ssquash between three and four on SSaturday afternoon because all the courtss were booked for the match againsst SStowe.' In later life, Conrad transformed the history of the Civil War from a story of class warfare to a struggle between the three kingdoms. It was hard to recognise this relaxed, rather puckish historian from the martinet of the sixth form, still harder to imagine that this fitness obsessive was to die from smoking too much. His successor, a boy called Gordon Clark, was, if possible, even more fanatical. He revived College Sports, which he claimed was an ancient festival although no one could actually remember it, and insisted that every boy should compete in at least one event. This provoked a rebellion among the more radical younger element, led by Hope and Reade. They claimed, equally spuriously, that exemption from this grisly occasion could be obtained by attending evensong in College chapel instead. This groupuscule of non-runners, almost all of them declared atheists, accordingly sat through the Nunc Dimittis, as the rest of us sweated round the running track while Gordon Clark enjoyed himself with a megaphone. He was, however, faced with an unmistakable challenge to his authority. The defection of the Evensong Six could not be overlooked. On the other hand, corporal punishment did not seem quite right. In the event, each of them was made to copy out a whole book of the *Iliad* with Greek accents, surely a unique example outside the Communist bloc of people being punished for attending divine service.

In the case of a swiping, the sixth-former on duty, known, quite absurdly and incredibly, as the Praepostor, has to summon the victim from his class and lead him across School Yard, preceded by the school verger with his wand or Holy Poker, by which name the verger is also known. I once have to do this and march a boy called Shelburne into the presence of Dr Birley. Then and now Robert Birley is regarded as one of the greatest educationists of modern times. Not merely is he a memorable headmaster of Eton, reviled for his modest reforms by reactionary Old Boys as Red Robert. He has also reformed and denazified the German education system after the war and when he leaves Eton he goes on, not to some cushy billet at Oxford or Cambridge, but to Witwatersrand University to fly the flag for liberal principles in the worst days of apartheid. Yet there he is, this great man, faced with this boy Charlie Shelburne, who has let another boy finish his algebra sums for him and refused to reveal who the boy was and the only way to resolve the impasse is to send him up to the Head Master to be birched, so here is Lord Shelburne taking down his trousers and the Holy Poker handing the Head Prune a bundle of birch twigs and Dr Birley measuring out his run between the gnarled inky desks defaced by the graffiti of earlier no-goods such as Shelley and Pitt the Younger and coming in at an angle with his characteristic heavy limp – he is a big ungainly man – and letting fly with his sawn-off besom at the rosy buttocks held down by the hunched figure of the Holy Poker while I stand by simpering in my fancy waistcoat with a sanguine carnation in my buttonhole.

But my shame is not confined to standing idly by. For it is in this term that I have outstayed all my contemporaries and risen by virtue of no other merit to be Captain of the School. This is perhaps the first occasion on which my lack of leadership qualities comes to the fore. My reign belongs somewhere in the class of Ethelred the Unready or the feebler Merovingian kings. Like all weak monarchs I strive too late to impose my will. My chief tormentor is a boy called Nicholas Wade, who has the knack some boys have of infuriating the authorities without actually breaking any definable rule. Once or twice I try to pin something on him but nothing sticks until the final week when a fire practice is held. Something about the way Wade slides down the canvas chute – too fast, too slow, too noisy? I cannot now recall – fires me up to administer the only beating of my consulate, for the offence, not often equalled in the history of trumped-up crimes, of sliding down the fire escape in an insolent manner. As I slink down the passage from the library after handing out four or five limp-wristed thwacks, I bump into the Matron in College, Naomi Johnston, a big-breasted, good-hearted, bright-eyed character. 'Congratulations,' she says with an ironic twinkle, 'now you're a real Captain.' These were the character-building experiences which parents then paid thousands of pounds to have beaten into their children, though my parents had it all done for free.

But, grotesque as these episodes are, they pale into nothing beside the headlong savagery of the midnight thrashings administered by Mr Burrows. It is precisely because it is all so terrifying that we do not think of telling our parents, certainly not those of us who snuggle deeper under the sheets when the door flies open and the grim avenger appears, for we are those who have resolved at all costs to learn the art of staying out of trouble (which I master effortlessly, because terror lends me outsize wings). Everything is, I suppose, a lesson in something and even then I dimly appreciated that Mr Burrows was the dark underside of Sunningdale. I remember noticing from the school list that he was the only master without a university degree and thinking that this explained it, as though having BA or MA after your name somehow inhibited the thrashing urge. No doubt Mr Fox knew perfectly well just how far Mr Burrows went and it did not greatly trouble his urbane mien. The thump of the cane was too far from the private side to rattle the Meissen china. Yet there were rumours (or perhaps we invented them ourselves) of dark negotiations among the staff. It was said that Edward Lane Fox had been declared exempt from beatings by Mr Burrows after a plea from the cricket master Mr Sheepshanks that he could not possibly be

expected to bowl his left-arm spinners in the crucial match against
Ludgrove if he was still sore from the night before.

If Greenways had had a whiff about it of Evelyn Waugh's Llanabbas
Priory, Sunningdale was an upmarket version of Beachcomber's
Narkover academy, where the headmaster Dr Smart Allick and most
of the boys are obsessed with gambling in all its forms. I rather fancy it
may have been the scent of the turf which clinched my father's
decision to send me there – an expensive sacrifice, since the £84 a
term must have consumed a large slice of his income. But on Parents'
Day he certainly found himself in company he recognised. The
Queen's trainer, the awesome Captain Boyd-Rochfort, had sent
his twin stepsons there, both later to become trainers themselves,
Henry Cecil being the leading classic winner of his day. Our local
trainer, Noel Cannon, whose filly Festoon won the Thousand
Guineas the year before Boyd-Rochfort's amazing triple classic
winner Meld did it and whose stables, Druids Lodge, on the windy
downs beyond Stonehenge we passed on the way to Salisbury, had his
boy there. So did the Queen Mother's steeplechase trainer Peter
Cazalet and the great Newmarket figure Bernard van Cutsem who
trained the immortal Park Top for the Duke of Devonshire.

But more remarkable still was the racing mania of the staff. Sunningdale must be the only prep school where there was a half-holiday every
day of the Royal Ascot meeting in order to allow the assistant masters
to frolic in the Silver Ring while the headmaster paraded gravely in the
Royal Enclosure. There was something deeply strange about the sight
of their grey toppers lined up on the sideboard in the headmaster's hall
until the morning's lessons were over. For the rest of the day we were
left in the care of those few masters who had no inclination or no
entrée to Ascot, notably Mr Burrows and Mr Marriott, the science
master, alias Moses Maggot, who was clearly unsuitable. By contrast,
R.G.T. Speer, the tall fair-haired young master who taught me Greek,
was just the right sort. When he ran off with the Assistant Matron Kitty
Dean, he gave up full-time schoolmastering and became the stipendi-
ary judge at York races. Even the school doctor, Dr Duncan, was a
racing man. When I was lying in bed with asthma or gastric flu or
whooping cough or measles or German measles or some combination
of the above as I did for much of the year, especially in the spring term

(Mrs Fox's claim about the health-giving properties of the air on the heath turning out to be false, in my case anyway), we would look over the racing pages together and he would ask my advice, as I had already acquired a small reputation in this line, based on my in-depth study of the *Sporting Life*. I followed the ups and downs of their resident tipsters and matched my own performance against theirs in the paper's challenge trophy awarded to the sage whose nap selections over the season offered the best return on a £1 bet. I could never come anywhere near the *Sporting Life*'s own Man on the Spot or the Scout in the *Daily Express*, though I could jog along in the pack with Warren Hill, Augur and Solon. But my reputation with Dr Duncan was based not so much on the occasional winner I gave him as on the wealth of jargon about breeding which I had picked up from Audax in *Horse and Hound* (the classical choice of pseudonyms was a pleasing relic of the early days of sporting journalism, the era of Nimrod and Pierce Egan's *Boxiana*). So while Dr Duncan was listening to my chest and in between his asking me to cough or say aah, I would wheeze, 'Those Owen Tudor colts never stay much beyond a mile' or 'French three-year-olds can't handle Epsom.' All of this knowledge was strictly theoretical. I had never been to a proper race meeting and I have always been incapable of telling the difference between one horse and another, nodding sagely when someone else says, 'I don't like the look of his head' or 'He's nice and deep in the quarters.' Just as Mr Burrows provided an invaluable lesson in the merits of keeping one's head down, so Dr Duncan offered useful early opportunities in the confection of bullshit.

Sunningdale was almost as addicted to snobbery as to horseracing, here as elsewhere the two passions being lovingly twined. Every Hon. and Viscount was accorded his full title. The country-house atmosphere was further inspissated when Patrick Howard, youngest brother of the Earl of Suffolk, brought his nanny back with him after the holidays. Nanny, a sweet and gentle girl, became an invaluable member of staff, staying on long after Patrick left and establishing a little sanctum where she attended to numberless sewing, repairing and ironing tasks and offered a cosy refuge to the tenderer boys, no doubt recalling to some their own nanny's room at home where they had taken shelter from draughty passages and chilly parents.

It was Patrick Howard who christened me Mount Everest because I spent so much of my first few terms in bed. The more time I spent in the sickroom, the more germs I picked up. The £84 my parents were shelling out might as well have been spent on treating me in a high-class clinic. Not that the Sunningdale sickroom with its extensive views of Mr Fox's lawns and shrubberies was anything but high class. The food was delicious, and extra delicacies, not to mention toys and games galore, were delivered by the silent green Harrod's van to my most regular fellow patients who were all born to the purple – Adrian Berry, son of the proprietor of the *Daily Telegraph*, David Verney, son of Lord Willoughby de Broke, and, a less frequent inmate, Michael Cranley, in later life as Lord Onslow the gadfly of the House of Lords. We had every blessing that fortune could shower on us, except the ability to breathe. David Verney had a deluxe blow-football set and we spent hours puffing down the hollow plastic tubes, partly in the hope that this would improve the performance of our own tubes. Our sickroom was also thick with the fumes of Potter's Asthma Cigarettes. Cranley put in a request that we be allowed to try Craven 'A' instead of these footling herbal cigarettes, on the grounds that the medical profession certified them as good for the throat, but Matron wouldn't have it.

The clientele was thus already of the toppest notch when Mr Fox achieved his greatest coup. 'Boys,' he announced one morning, 'His Royal Highness Prince Michael of Kent will be joining the school next term. He has expressed a wish to be treated as an ordinary boy and so he will be known as Michael' – which, as Nichol pointed out, wasn't ordinary at all since the rest of us were known by our surnames. On arrival the Prince himself quickly spotted this fact and asked to be called Kent instead. Shortly after his great announcement, Mr Fox called me into his study and told me that I had been selected for the honour of being Michael's dormitory prefect. This post carried no special duties beyond telling noisy boys to shut up after lights out. We had no firepower to compare with Mr Burrows's nuclear deterrent. However, Mr Fox's barely suppressed excitement communicated itself to me and I was in a highly nervous state when the Prince reported for his first night in our dorm. He seemed a shy and amiable sort, a sleepy personality remarkable only for his mother's piercing eyes which when supplemented by a naval beard enabled him to make good commercial use in later life of his resemblance to the last Czar. After a week or so, during which he seemed quite at ease, he began to develop a peculiar habit not shared by any other nine-year-old boy I had come across. He would take off his clothes and stand stark naked on his bed and then jump up and down vigorously for about ten minutes. He would do this as regularly as a trout rising at dusk. The rest of us watched the ritual with curiosity rather than derision, marvelling in particular at the spectacular way the princely willie flew up and down. However, it was a decidedly odd performance and taking my duties as royal protector rather seriously I asked for an interview with Mr Fox.

'It's Kent, sir.'

'Ah yes, now how's he getting on?'

'Well, he's all right most of the time but every night he takes off all his clothes and jumps up and down naked on his bed for about ten minutes. Sometimes he goes on doing it after lights out. So I wondered whether that was, you know, all right, sir.'

Mr Fox did not answer immediately. His tortoise–gravedigger countenance remained imperturbable.

'Every night, you say?'

'Yes, sir.'

He paused again. In fact there was a long silence.

'Perhaps I shouldn't have said, sir.'

'No, no, Mount, you did quite right to come and tell me.'

'Thank you, sir.'

'I don't think there's any cause for concern. In fact, you must expect that sort of thing from—' He paused once more, unwilling perhaps to suggest that a royal background was liable to produce oddities of behaviour, and then corrected himself to '—in a situation like this.'

'Yes, sir.'

'But let me know if there are any further developments.'

There were none. Kent gradually desisted from his evening bouncing and drifted out of my life, though not before his scarlet-and-blue dressing-gown cord, carefully nametaped 'HRH Prince Michael of Kent', had got packed in with my luggage at the end of term. My father snaffled it and tied his own dressing gown with it for many years. This appropriation did not derive from any great interest in the royal family, for he had none, and at my last school concert he warmly embraced Kent's mother, Princess Marina, under the impression that she was someone he had danced with before the war.

As with many headmasters, Mr Fox's manner became increasingly theatrical, his pauses stagier, his tortoise-head so motionless, his gravedigger features giving so little away that it seemed almost miraculous when he spoke. He rose beautifully to the great occasion. Once a week during break the whole school played a rough variant of Rescue on the large stony area running down from the classrooms to the railway line known as the parade ground. In other schools this might have been a casual pick-up sort of pastime, but at Sunningdale not much was left to chance and so this brutal hounding down of smaller or slower boys as they slithered and skidded on the harsh surface had official sanction and assistant masters would look on from the high ground near the clump of firs and rhododendrons that hid the tin school chapel, smoking and swapping jokes. It was, though, not from this group of bantering ushers but from the school house that Mr Fox came forth at his stately tortoise gait and stopping at the top of the parade ground called for silence.

'Boys, I have sad news. His Majesty the King died peacefully in the night.'

No announcement has ever moved me more. I can at a pinch remember where I was when Kennedy was shot or when the Twin Towers crumbled, but the fear and awe that those events inspired in me were not in the same class as the death of a middle-aged man with a stutter who smoked too much. I remember the precise spot on which I was standing, about ten yards in from the railway fence and rather less from the lower end of the gravel where the playing fields began. It seemed to me an inexpressibly sombre moment. We were all of us caught up in a great drama, in our dark blue jerseys with the Eton-blue V round the neck and our grey flannel shorts or longs (being lanky, I had already graduated to longs and been ticked off for presumptuousness by Cranley who was lankier still). History was now and England. These sentiments were so deeply sunk in me – and remain so still – that I found it odd when I began to meet boys, both cleverer and stupider than me, who didn't feel them at all and regarded the monarchy with derision or indifference. My abject conformity of spirit was even then coated with a smartass veneer, but coated was all it was.

That same conformity of spirit overcame me when we trooped off to the tin chapel in the woods where Mr Tupholme who taught geography and maths was waiting for us, disguised as a clergyman in a surplice hastily thrown on over his tweed suit, a more bilious shade than Mr Fox's tweeds. Tuppy was, I think, a lay reader but normal boys found it hard to take his sermons to heart and longed for the service to be over, especially the full matins on Sunday. In summer the heat built up under the corrugated iron roof and the air became stifling. Boys were liable to faint, more liable still according to legend if they put blotting paper in their shoes. Any boy who came over seriously queer had to be escorted out by a member of staff, starting with Matron, then the next one by the Assistant Matron, the next one by Nanny, the next by the most junior master and so on up the staff. The dream of the more subversive spirits was to exhaust the supply of escorts until there would be none left except Tuppy and so the next boy who feigned faintness would bring the service to an untimely end. Even on the hottest days of early July this ambitious scheme never quite came off, although once the number rose high enough for Mrs Fox to be called into action. I was perhaps the only boy in the school who enjoyed chapel so much that I desperately tried to stay on my feet even when my legs were giving under me and my body was damp with sweat.

How sharp and indelible then was the sensation of place, the impress on the memory of exactly where you were standing when something happened. It is a grossly indecent thing to recall but I cannot help dredging up the precise spot on the lower walk below the verandah on the far side of the house, just before the path turned up through the rhodies to the aforesaid chapel with its whitewashed corrugated iron roof, rather like some mission hut in old Malaya, the spot at which Mr Ling told me I was the cleverest boy in the school and might get a scholarship. This was in one sense not such a revelation. Sunningdale was a small school with only seven or eight boys in the upper sixth and I usually finished first or second in exams.

But coming from G. A. Ling this was a papal pronouncement. He was an elderly man, as were most of the masters, had fought in the Great War and had his right arm shot to pieces. Ever since he had been writing with his left hand but his writing had never improved. He kept stubbing the chalk against the blackboard and breaking it as he wrote in stuttery erratic characters so indecipherable that it was sometimes hard to be sure whether he was writing in Latin or Greek. He was also unappealing to look at, with a permanent sour expression on his thin pouting ruddy face, watery eyes behind thick glasses and, when out walking as now with me, a muddy green tweed cap perched forward on his bald scalp. He lacked anything in the way of charm to make up for these visual deficiencies; the nearest he came to humour was a scarring sarcasm and if he had any affection for his pupils he hid it well. Thirty years earlier he had taught the young Quintin Hogg who remembered him as the best teacher he had ever had. He still was the best. By the age of twelve we could write Latin verses as well as we could English and in our spare time we did Aristophanes. So when Mr Ling uttered this judgement of my abilities, it took hold of me in the most odious and ineradicable fashion, reinforcing every supercilious fibre in my being. I was ruined. Subsequent failures, demotions and rejections, thick and fast though they came later on, especially in my twenties, dented but never quite destroyed that insufferable overvaluation of my abilities that Mr Ling implanted on the lower walk just before the forest of *Rhododendron ponticum* began. That was my Fall.

Another little epiphany took place the far side of the playing fields just between the sightscreen and the pavilion, behind the green iron machine that sent such stinging slip catches. Here were the dusty benches where we smaller boys had to sit and watch our First XI play some other school in the rhodie belt, all within a few miles of Sunningdale – Ludgrove, Scaitcliffe, Lambrook, Earleywood, Heatherdown, St George's Windsor, every thicket of pine and *ponticum* seemed to shelter an expensive prep school. Like all dictators, even the benevolent sort which he largely was, Mr Fox was keen on enforcing mass attendance at public occasions. So there was no question of playing truant. We passed the time as best we could, inflicting Chinese burns (Joe Laycock, son of my father's old commanding officer Lucky Laycock, could twist your skin so fiercely that you thought he would tear it apart), or better still, with the aid of the sun and a magnifying glass, real burns on one another's bare arms and legs, or scratching messages in the dust with the point of an old cricket stump, or fooling around on the slip-catch machine pretending that it was a raft or a submarine. Then there came an unexpected diversion. From further down the bench a strange fluent burbling came to my ears. It was a commentary on the game but one which imparted an almost foreign excitement to the desultory proceedings out in the middle. This commentary seemed to go on for hours, unstoppably, like the song of a bird in the mating season. It came from a freckled, beaky-nosed boy with hair the colour of dark tan shoe polish. So enchanting was the sound that I remember turning back to front so that I was facing into the privet hedge that bordered the ground and finding that the effect of the commentary was even more mesmerising if you weren't actually watching the game. This was, I think, the first time that I became conscious how in certain departments art could be superior to life.

Fifty years later Henry Blofeld is plummier, more measured as he describes the pigeons fluttering above the Mound Stand or the red buses in stately procession past the Vauxhall end. Yet he has undeniably trained on. Seldom has early promise, you might think, been more exactly fulfilled. But there is another story. Not long before we left Sunningdale and went on to Eton together, Henry developed a startling gift for playing the game, first as a wicket-keeper, then and more extravagantly as a batsman. He played for the Public Schools at Lord's and, with Sir Donald Bradman applauding from the Pavilion, scored a century as only P. B. H. May and M. C. Cowdrey had done before him. From his angular, rather ugly stance, all hips and elbows, he developed an ability to hit the ball anywhere he wanted without thinking about it. It was a style more Antiguan than Etonian and he was confidently expected to play for, perhaps even to captain, England, as Etonians used to. Then cycling up to the cricket ground for net practice one afternoon and talking over his shoulder to a friend, Henry ran slap into a bus full of French tourists and woke up, he claims in the morgue, with a smashed skull and other severe damage. He was lucky to wake up at all. He did play cricket again – in fact won a blue at Cambridge and made a first-class hundred – but he was never quite the same. The instinctive gift had gone. The gods had had second thoughts, or rather returned to their first ones.

Slowly my health improved and for the first time I spent more time in class than in the sickbay. But there was a sad consequence, at least I think it was a consequence. It was now during the holidays, especially the first few days of the holidays, that I became breathless and helpless. This caused my parents a distress they had not bargained for. It was as though my bronchial tubes were registering a transfer of loyalty. My real life was now lived on the school stage, while home life had retreated to the wings, becoming comparable in its grubby, untidy chaos to the actor's dressing room. And Sunningdale, being a beautifully organised school, knew how to mimic home comforts.

Between the railway line and the little hut where we did biology (exiled from the main block as though to demonstrate the social inferiority of the sciences) there was a patch of ground which had been dug over and subdivided into little garden plots. Two or three boys would share each miniature allotment. Towards the end of the spring term, we would sow our seeds, some of us further dividing our plots into two: radishes, cress and lettuce in one half, nasturtium, French marigolds, love-in-the-mist, larkspur, clarkia and California poppies in the other. There was a clear advantage to those whose parents were first-rate gardeners like the Lytteltons and the Lane Fox brothers, two of whom, Martin and the much younger Robin, went on to become garden writers and designers, but most of us could show off a fine riot of colour by the time of sports day in July. I remember the tremble of pleasure on returning after the spring holidays and seeing the little rows of seedlings to be thinned out. But even this innocent diversion had its perverse side-effect, for when I came home again I could no longer muster much interest in our own borders where I had once been such a willing little helper. Like some prisoner long penned in the gulag, my patch inside the wire had become my real garden.

My attention was now so intently focused on school life – even more so when I progressed to the steamy hothouse of College at Eton – that I became inattentive and offhand at home. I did not notice (or

My father with Henry
and Virginia Bath and Diana

care) that we seemed to do things together as a family rather less now, that my mother went for walks by herself across the downs, that my father disappeared for long periods of the day without much explanation. The car would putter off down the Codford road and the house would become silent. Which suited me fine because I could settle down to my holiday algebra or Book V of the *Aeneid* without being disturbed.

Soon after I went to College, a new neighbour moved into a handsome manor house a couple of miles up the Wylye Valley from the millpond that Greenways had claimed as the school bathing pool. Diana, as befitted her name, was a superb steeplechase rider and dedicated to foxhunting as to any dangerous sport that came her way. In the war she had driven motorbikes for the Army. In peacetime she was a serious competitor in the Monte Carlo Rally. But hunting was her thing. Diana the huntress looked unnervingly like her prey. She was a sparkling foxy-faced beauty who made the room come alive before she opened her mouth. She was also a duchess, still, just, being separated from the Duke who had decamped with the harbourmaster's wife in Kyrenia. Soon Diana Newcastle was the star of all the local parties. After a year or so, she took over the Wylye Valley hounds. From being to my eyes at least a rather mangy pack, they took on an unexpected glamour. Even their coats seemed glossier, their hound music sweeter. When years later I first read *Mr Sponge's Sporting Tour* (so enjoyed by my father while recuperating in the library in Alexandria), the character of Lucy Glitters seemed like Diana to the life. She would call in at the Malt House on her way home from hunting, still in her hunt livery with her glossy boots, dark velvet coat and snowy stock, shaking her hair free as she took off her black cap. I had never seen anyone so dashing, or so dangerous. It was like the glimpse of the fox at the bottom of the garden, there one minute and then gone again.

We were discussing not Soapy Sponge but Anna Karenina, my father and I, and he said 'How can someone your age possibly understand adultery?' I must have been about fifteen at the time and would never have dreamed of claiming that I understood anything at all in that department. There was something fretful about the way he said it, as though the whole business, whatever it was, had become too much for him. He said no more on the subject and I didn't want to hear any more.

When he died, thirteen years after my mother died, Diana was almost the only one of his old friends who came to his funeral. She eventually was divorced from her duke, but she never remarried.

DIFFICULTIES FOR GIRLS

THE NOTICE BOARD at the Gridiron Club wasn't the sort of notice board that people stuck notices up on much. At the beginning of term there would be the details of the club's opening and closing times posted by the barman, a quiet and courteous man who was, oddly enough, called Mr Barman (had his name nudged him towards his occupation, or had he seized on it as a convenient alternative to his original name which was embarrassing or unpronounceable? My grandmother's butler Mr Butler raised the same question). Now and then some member would offer a bicycle or a beat-up Mini for sale. There might even be a flyer for a college concert or for the Bullingdon point-to-point. But stuck out in the dim passageway behind the service hatch, it was not a notice board that encouraged the free exchange of ideas. So my attention was instantly caught by the quotation written out in a hand that was both neat and relaxed. I knew who must have written it because I had been queuing behind him at the bar before lunch when he was asking Mr Barman for drawing pins.

Public schoolboys go forth into a world that is not entirely composed of public-school men, or even of Anglo-Saxons, but of men who are as various as the sands of the sea; into a world of whose richness and subtlety they have no conception. They go forth into it with well developed bodies, fairly developed minds and undeveloped hearts.

It is not that the Englishman can't feel – it is that he is afraid to feel. He has been taught at his public school that feeling is bad form. He must not express great joy or sorrow, or even open his mouth too wide when he talks . . .

E. M. Forster, 'Notes on the English Character'

A spasm of rage seized me, all the more violent because I kept it to myself. Bloody Forster, who the hell was he to lecture us about how to feel? He could only fall in love with policemen, and married policemen at that. What made him think he was entitled to set himself up as an expert on the human heart?

As I came back into the dining room, I saw Andrew Osmond smiling quietly to himself and not at what someone at his table had just said. Andrew was a tall, attractive character, unquestionably handsome with crinkly hair and a profile that could only be called chiselled. He had been a National Service officer in the Gurkhas and you could imagine him sitting in the officers' mess amid the regimental silver with this detached smile on his face, always a little apart and inscrutable. In fact he wasn't really quite like that. As a comic actor, he had only to come on stage at the Edinburgh fringe for everyone to corpse. After Oxford, when he was studying in Paris before taking his Foreign Office exam, he did not hesitate a minute before responding to a call to come home and invest his entire legacy, £450 to be precise, in a new satirical magazine which three old Shrewsbury schoolfriends – Richard Ingrams, Christopher Booker and William Rushton – were planning to start. He thus became the sole proprietor of *Private Eye* before it became *Private Eye* – Ingrams wanted to call it *Bladder* but Rushton vetoed this because his grandmother was dying of a bladder disease. So it was entirely in Osmond's quietly subversive character to put up this prissy quotation rebuking all the young public-school men in tweed jackets who were at that moment arguing about the right way to cut the Stilton or whether to fill the afternoon by taking in a scope at the Regal or the Scala. I have never heard anyone outside the Grid refer to a film as a scope.

Andrew went on to manage *Private Eye* after he had stopped owning it and Peter Cook had become the largest shareholder. Finally he joined the Foreign Office after all. When stationed in Rome, he became friends with his immediate boss Douglas Hurd, and they began to write thrillers together, very successfully, until Hurd went off into politics. Later Andrew settled quietly in Burford with his handsome American wife Stuart and died badly young, of a brain tumour I think, as quizzical as ever. He seemed to have life more or less measured for size and was not inclined to make too much of it. But the Forster quote struck its mark. I wonder whether it stung anyone else as much as it stung me. But then perhaps nobody else in the club was going around with quite such an undeveloped heart.

The Grid occupied a couple of shabby rooms over Barclays Bank in the Cornmarket. I had joined it at the urging of Henry Scott Stokes whom I was doing French with. Henry was a rather solemn person, an old Wykehamist (no, I am not going to say where *everyone* was at school, but in his case it is relevant). His family was something to do with Clark's shoes. The Clark's factory was in Street, Somerset, not all that far from Uncle Grig's factory in Bristol, so I was rather chagrined when Henry hadn't heard of Lennard's, which I had thought a rather major concern. 'You ought to join the Grid,' Henry said, 'lot of first-rate chaps there, all public-school men of course.' Snobbish as I was myself, I could not believe that anyone could actually say such a thing and for a time 'all public-school men of course' became my phrase for describing any more than usually stuffy institution, something of which there was then no shortage.

Henry took me fishing on the River Test, on a stretch of water belonging to his godfather who was the head of Barclays Bank. It was a blistering hot day, much too hot to fish on. We had flogged the dazzling clear water for a couple of hours. Not a trout in sight. Then we drank the two bottles of Liebfraumilch that had been cooling in the keepnet. The only thing left was to strip down and have a swim. We floated gently downstream (the water was hardly deep enough to do strokes in), pausing now and then to remove the duckweed from our Y-fronts, heedless in our stupor of the water bailiffs who would have arrested us if they had come upon our sacrilegious splashing.

'You know, this is the most expensive fishing in Europe,' Henry said.

'The most expensive swimming,' I corrected drowsily.

Not exactly Brideshead, but then Henry wasn't Lord Sebastian Flyte. After Oxford he joined the *Financial Times* and went to Tokyo where I think he married a Japanese girl and passed out of my life. These idle aquatic excursions with people I hardly knew and often, like Henry, never got to know better seemed to fill quite a lot of my first two years at the university. We went up the Thames in a launch with David Dimbleby at the helm because he knew about boats, through the daisied meadows past the sites visited by Matthew Arnold's Scholar Gipsy, ducking as he had under the chopping rope at Bablock Hythe. We messed around in punts on the Cherwell, sat shivering under Magdalen Bridge on May Day morning, straining to hear the choirboys singing on the top of the tower, with the morning mist still on the water. In Eights Week we lolled on the upper deck of the college barges (now all sunk, burned or demolished) with their white balustrades and gay coats of arms watching the serious oarsmen scud past. Pretty much everything we did could have been and was done by Victorian undergraduates a hundred years earlier. We might have bumped into the Dean's daughters rowing Dr Dodgson down the stream.

> All in the golden afternoon
> Full leisurely we glide
> For both our oars, with little skill,
> By little arms are plied.

Why wasn't Lewis Carroll doing the rowing himself? Too busy thinking up Red Queens and White Rabbits, I suppose. But the most Victorian thing about our excursions, unlike Lewis Carroll's, was the almost total absence of girls of any age. It was not merely that I did not know how to feel. In those years of moony chastity I did not know any girls to express my feelings to.

There had been opportunities which a feistier person would have seized. Only a few weeks into our first term, my cousin Judith Pakenham had given a tea party in her room at Somerville to introduce her intake to a few males she had managed to dredge up. Judith's friends sat shoulder to shoulder on her bed with the latecomers crouched on the floor, these delectable and terrifying creatures with the static crackling off their sweaters and cardigans, and the occasional glissade of black stockings, and the crumpets toasting on the gas fire: Margaret Callaghan statuesque even when squashed between the slender and laconic Auriol Stevens and Susan Wolff with her marble-bright brown eyes and her alarming laugh, and the minxy Caroline Seebohm who couldn't ask you to pass the milk without making you blush. On the male side, Judith had whistled up a few distant relations and some childhood friends from the days when my uncle Frank was teaching economics and they lived in North Oxford, but we were a dismal crew, stammering, gawky and using unnecessary long words whenever we did manage to get out a sentence.

Even in this unalluring male chorus I must have stood out for my total ignorance, not just of sex (it went without saying that on that side of life I was a blank), but of the elementary techniques of chatting up, or even chatting. After the second crumpet (how ironic that those spongy rondels were the only sort I could deal with) I made my excuses and fled back to our little all-male circle: Dimbleby, Harrod, another schoolfriend the caustic John Spicer, who had been in the Army with two new additions, Michael Beaumont and Giles Havergal. We non-combatants made a joke out of their having done their National Service and been made men of, but it did make me at least feel inferior. Compulsory National Service had come to an end the year before, but it was still possible to volunteer and I had not volunteered, arguing to myself that it would have been pointless as I was bound to fail the medical. Logical, I suppose, but not exactly glorious. Giles was six foot three, ramrod straight and at first sight, like Andrew Osmond, unblemished officer material. He had been in the Coldstream which his brother Malcolm was to command. All this concealed a capacity for the outrageously camp and a lifelong devotion to the theatre. For more than thirty years he ran the Glasgow Citizens' Theatre and transformed it into a European mecca of theatrical adventure.

Among Giles's first stagings was a Christ Church college production of *Murder in the Cathedral* in a church just behind the High Street. *Murder* is a mostly male play with the women relegated to the chorus, perfect for us. Dimbleby was First Knight (quite a big part). I was Fourth Knight (a small part). Michael Beaumont was Third Tempter, another future director Gavin Millar First Tempter. The Knights wore jerseys and football socks painted silver to imitate chain mail,

then changed into dinner jackets for the final scene after the murder. This turned out to be my final stage appearance, lamented by nobody, least of all me, as true to form I forgot my lines on the second night.

It was shortly after this production that Giles took me aside. He had a serious concern for the wellbeing of others which he has never lost.

'You don't seem to go out with anyone,' he said.

'Umm,' I said.

'I think you ought to, you know. You don't want to get too solitary.'

'I'm not,' I said. 'Anyway, what about you?'

'Well, I do take Auriol out,' Giles said. 'Anyway it's different for me.'

'I don't see what it's got to do with you.'

This conversation annoyed me even more than Andrew putting up the E. M. Forster quotation. I was annoyed because I knew they were right. I was hiding away like someone with a disfigurement who is pretending that he is doing everyone a kindness by not showing his face.

I certainly could not claim to be burying myself in work. Of the three subjects I was supposed to be studying – Politics, Philosophy and Economics – it is hard to say which I was learning least of, not to mention the extra mathematics which was a nasty surprise. All the stuff I had happily left behind three or four years ago – trigonometry, vectors, logarithms – came back to haunt me. On top of this came symbolic logic and the propositional calculus with all its dismal apparatus: the tilde, which I knew only as harmless decoration to

the n in señor, meant 'not', as in not-p $= \sim$p; the horseshoe on its side
meant 'if p, then q'; and the big black **V**, alias 'vel', meant either/or.
'Or' was a big thing in Oxford philosophy. The only known
published work of Oscar Wood, our philosophy tutor at Christ
Church, was an essay in *Mind*, the philosophers' journal, entitled
'Alternative Uses of "Or"', a work which was every bit as indeter-
minate as its title. Several years later he produced another paper, this
time for the Aristotelian Society, entitled 'On Being Forced to a
Conclusion'. Oscar looked like a cherub who has been spoiled by
claret. He was simultaneously charming and miserable. To many of
his pupils he became a lifelong friend. He and I never quite clicked.
My kind of laziness wasn't his. Besides, I found the linguistic brand of
philosophy then in vogue as dry and sterile as those who taught it. In
my prelims, on the college's peculiar crabbed scale of marking I scored
a miserable *vix satis minus* for philosophy and *vix satis double minus* for
economics – 'not satisfactory minus' and 'not satisfactory double
minus', the latter being one step above *non satis*, or in plain English
'fail'. My breaking point came in a New College lecture room where
Professor A. J. Ayer, the legendary seducer and wit, was lecturing on
the problems of induction. In his quick, desiccated voice, he invited
us to consider an imaginary universe in which time was split up into
an infinity of separate instants, none of which had any connection to
the next. In such a universe how could we induce anything? It was
intolerably stuffy in the room. The leaded windows were all shut,
perhaps were already rusted up in Matthew Arnold's day, and flies
were buzzing against the panes as desperate to get out as I was. If this
was philosophy, I could do without it and it could do without me.
After the lecture was over, I went back to Christ Church and called on
my college tutor, Roy Harrod.

'I don't think I'm getting anywhere with PPE, well, philosophy
really,' I said. 'I think I'd better go and read something else.'

Roy looked up with his mild grave look which was almost a smile
as though he knew a joke was coming.

'Oh well,' he said, 'I expect you're right. What would you like to
do instead?'

This took out of my sails any wind I had. I had expected a heartfelt
plea not to desert PPE, perhaps even a reassurance that I was among

the most promising pupils he had ever etc. This placid acceptance of my diagnosis took me aback. I mumbled something about going back to French and German which I had got in on. And so I became what was grandly described as a linguist and soon found myself immersed in medieval French philology which was twice as dry as any bit of PPE and reading *Madame Bovary* for the third time.

My German tutor, David Luke, was a pale, ascetic-looking man then in his mid-thirties. His face was almost hairless, by contrast with the long-haired cat he cradled in his lap while listening to me read my weekly essay. As I stumbled deeper into the imagery of Goethe's *Faust* Part One, he and the cat would lean further and further back in his horrible orange easy chair of modernistic design. This appearance of effeteness amounting to terminal exhaustion was misleading. Luke was a marvellous translator, perhaps the best Englisher ever of Goethe's poetry. And among Nietzscheans he was a virtual superman. As soon as he got on to the lecture platform, he threw himself into a passionate exposition of his hero, waving his lecturer's billiard cue like a Wagnerian spear although he had no slides to point to. While I was enjoying one of these breathtaking performances, I noticed another undergraduate further along the bench so overcome with mirth that he was stuffing the sleeve of his gown into his mouth. From student theatricals I recognised that this was John Wells. Even then there was no mistaking his floppy forelock and weird piccolo player's lips, soon to be immortalised in Willie Rushton's figure of Little Gnitty, the knight with the crumpled sword who has adorned the cover of *Private Eye* for forty years. This first sighting of Wells was typical, not least because he became a lifelong friend of David Luke and often consulted him when translating a German play. His wild cackle could alarm the unwary because otherwise he spoke in such a quiet confiding mutter, but it always had within it a note of appreciation or affection.

Wells was the son of a clergyman who became Rural Dean of Bognor and he himself was clergy-boned. Even when he had become something of a showbiz celebrity mingling with Princess Margaret and Peter Sellers, he still went about disguised as an old-fashioned prep-school master in a dung-coloured tweed jacket and trousers too heavy for the time of year. Later on, he was much mocked in the pages of *Private Eye* for social climbing, but when I met him it was usually with a decayed clergyman or a disgraced schoolmaster or actor now unemployable or a mysterious figure from the heyday of the Third Programme. Nobody could have been less stuck up or less inclined to forget people and places he had once been fond of. His fiftieth birthday party lasted three days in order to accommodate the throng of old friends.

It must have been about then that he contracted the non-Hodgkin's disease which he held at bay for a decade and which then came back at a gallop. His last weeks in the Charing Cross Hospital were more crowded with appointments than a doctor's surgery, clergymen being strongly represented at all levels up to Archbishop Runcie. The priests felt it their duty to crack jokes with the second funniest man of his generation (after Peter Cook) and were too shy to offer the spiritual comfort John said he wouldn't mind a bit of. His normal confidential mutter was now so inaudible that I had to lean down to him like a doctor listening to a patient's chest in order for him to tell me that the one exception had been Dr Runcie who said: 'John, if I may get a bit professional for a moment . . .' Weak as he was, the thought of this roused one last faint cackle.

Wells was the classic example of how making girls laugh was the way to bowl them over. The confiding quality of his speaking voice gave his imitations and anecdotes a particular intimate charm, avoiding any suggestion of stage performance. It was as though only your company could draw out of him this latest example of life's absurdity. His love affairs were not only numerous and complicated, they seemed to range all over the country. More than once I have been walking down the high street of a strange provincial town and there, quite unexpectedly, would be John in his dung-coloured ensemble scurrying to or from a rendezvous with some intolerably pretty girl but always happy to stop for a cup of tea or a look at the parish church.

'Despite his grand connections,' *The Times* intoned in its obituary of him, 'Wells was always on the political Left, partly due to the influence of the former *Daily Worker* political journalist Claud Cockburn' – which though not exactly untrue somehow misses the point, giving the impression of Cockburn conducting conscious-ness-raising seminars on economic policy. What Wells, like

Cockburn, was on the side of was mischief. The great cause he was associated with was that of Arnold Bennett's the Card: that of cheering us all up, or if that sounds too chirrupy, of reconciling us to our absurdities and so to one another. He could not help humanising the targets and his targets could not help liking him. Mary Wilson once said she would like to bite him and Richard Ingrams for writing 'Mrs Wilson's Diary'; she came to be a friend. Similarly, he helped turned Denis Thatcher into one of the immortals along with Jeeves and Molesworth. In his generation he carried on the enterprise begun by his friend John Betjeman, that of teaching the English to be fond of each other and of the places where they lived. Far from being snobbish, I should have thought the two Johns did as much as anyone to undermine class hostility.

When I switched to modern languages, I thought, or persuaded myself, that those four terms doing PPE had been a complete waste of time. What a farrago of nitpicking and logic-chopping I had been wading through, or most of the time not wading through. The curious thing is that, looking back today, I realise that during that brief period of intermittent attention I picked up, almost unwittingly, half the mental furniture that, scratched and battered no doubt, I still use. From the elementary economics that did stick in my head, I more or less grasped the basic laws of supply and demand. No doubt I could have picked them up quickly enough if I had ever helped run a fruit and veg stall, but my rarefied upbringing had left me a commercial innocent. Then, from the voluble torrents of Isaiah Berlin's lectures on political ideas, I picked up the insight, which amazingly seems to have evaded scholars for several millennia, that political principles may be equally admirable and yet conflict with one another and there is nothing we can do about this except live by making untidy compromises and trade-offs between them.

Above all, from J. L. Austin, that astringent philosopher with his unforgettable rasping voice and unforced wit, I understood that philosophical problems are very often invented by philosophers themselves. From Plato to Ayer, their warped jargon and their crude and dishonest assumptions have time and again prevented them from seeing that ordinary language copes pretty well with reality and enables us to say most of what we want to say. Far from being trivial, this 'ordinary-language philosophy' cleared the trivia out of the way, leaving us free to talk directly about the serious things. Austin's lectures were so crowded that when he came in he had to pick his way through a black sea of gowned undergraduates. He was listened to with an intentness I can never remember being part of before or since. Although his asides could be very funny, we did not dare to laugh too expansively for fear we might miss a beat in the argument and when he finished and strode abruptly out of the room the hush remained unbroken for a moment or two as though we had been holding our breath the whole hour and had forgotten how to breathe out. 'That's the real thing, isn't it?' Alasdair Clayre murmured as we straggled out into the High Street. Alasdair was famous as the cleverest boy ever to come out of Winchester or anywhere else and I was flattered that he should confide his reverence to me, including me in the magic circle. Austin died, not yet fifty, while I was still at Oxford, and though I had never exchanged a word with him I remember being shocked that such a light could be so rudely snuffed out. I tried to re-create him a bit as the philosopher W. R. Scrannel who pops up in some of my novels but it is a crude reproduction of the real thing.

Although we did not know it, what we were living through was the twilight of the Oxford don. This was the last period in which the same English university contained such a line-up of spellbinding lecturers, and the last period too when university lecturers enjoyed a decent professional standard of living. More important, there was an intimacy then between teachers and students which has since dimmed, for reasons I do not quite understand. A lucky undergraduate could have coffee with W. H. Auden in the Kardomah café, lunch with Maurice Bowra in Wadham or dine with Raymond Carr in New College or Warden Sparrow in All Souls.

And on Sunday morning there was sherry with the Cecils. At about a quarter past twelve, we would make our way up St Giles to the clang of church bells. Turning off the Banbury Road into Linton Road, ducking the blossom – it always seemed to be fresh and springlike outside, in contrast to the sherry-fumed fug inside – we could already hear the machine-gun stutter of Oxford voices pattering out their hasty orisons. Of the room itself I can remember little, it was too full of people. There was, I think, a screen of darkish green, behind which David or his wife Rachel would dart to fetch another bottle or perhaps, at a later stage in the proceedings, to bring out their youngest child, Laura, then in her early teens, with all the reverence and anxiety appropriate to the handling of fine china. It was even then obvious to the dullest observer after five minutes' conversation with her that Laura, except for her delicacy of feature, was not fragile at all, being robust and caustic from an early age. David's readiness to confide his anxieties about or, but only if pressed, his pride in his children was one more aspect of the way he treated everyone with an immediate presumption of equality. Salons tend to become cockpits where the weak are swiftly and mercilessly defeathered. What hell it must have been to be plumped down without proper introduction at supper with the Goncourts or lunch at the Algonquin Round Table. Linton Road was not like that. David and Rachel were friendly and welcoming to all-comers and this rubbed off on the all-comers, encouraging me to regard people I had met there as established friends and rush up to them in other milieus and find them cold and dreary. It was in fact these little moments of family anxiety – David and Rachel were great fussers – that my memory first dredges up rather than the baying of the lions of Oxford – Maurice Bowra, Hugh Trevor-Roper, Enid Starkie in her red-and-blue outfits like some besotted football fan, Iris Murdoch, Isaiah Berlin, all of them jammed together between sofas and chairs, holding their ground with loud rapid-fire talk. Interspersed with these sturdy figures wandered the tall, thin Waugh girls, Teresa and Margaret, whose appearance of vague uncertainty was as misleading as Laura's ethereal pallor.

David's own ethereal appearance had done his reputation no favours. An image of fragility and aristocratic frivolity lingered in certain cramped brains and as Goldsmiths' Professor of English Literature he had become the Enemy to the Leavisites. When he turned down Kingsley Amis's thesis (as did his fellow examiner), he became the representative of the effete Old Guard and the subject of one of Amis's most telling imitations, all languid vowels and lisping consonants, generously lubricated with a torrent of spit (it was true that on a good day, if the dais was close to the seats in the lecture hall, in a moment of high emotion David's spit could reach the third row). He himself was distressed that Amis should, understandably, be so bitter against him and lamented that 'the thesis simply hadn't worked', a point of view which in a more detached moment Kingsley himself would endorse. In fact, it always seemed to me that there was less division between the rival camps than the Leavisites pretended. David Cecil's sense of the moral was just as robust as theirs and his favourite writers overlapped with theirs. His famous gift for enthusiasm is what comes back to me now as my mind returns to the slender figure cocking his head to one side, insisting on pouring out the third glass of sherry, thrusting the bottle forward with an abrupt gesture as though his elbow was being jogged by some unseen agency. He talked with his whole body and listened with the same physical commitment as he threw back his head to let rip his gurgling jay's chuckle. I have never met anyone who laughed with his legs as he did. The convulsive piston-like motion of the knees beneath the tweed trouser could rattle the change in his pockets. Even situations which in theory should have contained this urge to throw himself so physically into the conversation failed to curb him. Driving me from Salisbury station over the downs to Cranborne, he would repeatedly turn from the wheel to quiz me in the back seat. What was the most shameful profession for one's son to go into? It was possible, we agreed, to talk with pride of 'my son the bookie', 'my son the MP', or even to say with a certain insouciance 'my son is cleaning lavatories at the moment', but what about 'my son has just joined a leading firm of undertakers' or 'my son is doing very well as a traffic warden'? At each fresh suggestion, he turned his head right round to see my reaction, while another articulated lorry hurtled towards us over the brow of the hill.

The politics didn't help. Although David had not the slightest interest in politics, his being Lord Salisbury's younger brother had him tagged as a High Tory. At that period in Oxford, most other universities too, any hint of conservative views was to be covered up or laughed off. Whatever party might be in power in London, throughout the post-war period students and teachers stuck to the progressive consensus, an adherence which culminated in the refusal of the dons to grant Margaret Thatcher an honorary degree though she was a Somerville graduate, the only time a Prime Minister has ever been denied one. During the 1959 election campaign which happened while I was there, the smart thing was to say that one remained loyal to Hugh Gaitskell though he had sold out to the right. Only when graduates voted, as they do in elections for the Chancellor of the University, did the Conservative candidate have the sniff of a chance. Harold Macmillan was elected Chancellor the year after he had been returned to power and we stood at someone's window in Canterbury Quad to watch as he processed past in his black-and-gold robe. As he came by, Auberon Waugh led us in a chorus of 'God bless our glorious Chancellor' and Supermac raised his cap and looked up with a droopy eye. Being a connoisseur of cynicism, no doubt he had a shrewd idea of what contempt we held him in.

Bron had arrived a year after me, to join his sisters, in the autumn of 1959. He had been in hospital for months recovering from the dreadful wounds he had suffered when he accidentally peppered himself with his own machine gun while serving with the Blues in Cyprus. He had lost a lung, a finger and two ribs, leaving a terrifying cavity in his shoulder which was to become infected at recurring intervals in his life and send him back to hospital for long stretches to have the wound drained. He remained gay, unperturbed and re-morseless, without an ounce of self-pity or indeed pity for anyone else.

For some reason we had got it into our heads that he had been permanently paralysed in the privates too. We had no evidence for this. Perhaps it is a whisper that always goes round when someone suffers multiple wounds. Bron somehow got wind of our believing this and taxed me with it which I had blushingly to admit. Subsequent history was to provide abundant proof that he was intact in that region. But Bron was delighted by my illusion, almost as delighted as when he discovered that I was also under the illusion that the doctrine of the Immaculate Conception meant that the Virgin Mary was conceived supernaturally, without any sexual activity. Bron's stay at Christ Church was brief. His performance in prelims was even worse than my own and he made no effort to stay on and take them again. He may well have already been sent down when he led us in serenading the new Chancellor. He went off to London, took lodgings in Half Moon Street, made an instant hit as a novelist and popular journalist and married Teresa Onslow, sister of my inky fellow asthmatic Michael Cranley, on the strength of his first earnings. It was as though he thought his time would be short and he had better make the most of it. Despite puffing smoke in the doctors' faces and drinking all the decent wine he could lay his hands on, he survived another forty years, to the perpetual delight of his friends and distress of his enemies, for he kept both friendships and enmities in good running order.

It is curious considering how close Bron had come to death and how uncertain were his prospects of long-term survival that we should have had such an easy relaxed time in his rooms, listening to him sing 'If I were King of the Boeotians' from *Orpheus in the Underworld* or tell the story of how his uncle Alec's first marriage was annulled on grounds of non-consummation. Sometimes I too would be asked to sing a solo, some air from Gilbert and Sullivan or *Annie Get Your Gun*, in order to demonstrate to incredulous newcomers that it was possible to sing a whole song through without ever hitting the right note, not even happening to connect by accident as I slid up and down the scale. The fame of this remarkable gift of mine spread, so that Charles Campbell, later the presiding genius of the Neal Street Restaurant, would ask me over to his room in Brasenose College to show me off to a new audience.

There was a feckless gaiety blowing through the quad that year, as giddy as it was shortlived. Bobby Corbett joined Bron in showing us the sort of good time we could not have dreamed of even if we could have afforded it. Bobby was the son of the Chief Scout and former Governor of Tasmania, Lord Rowallan, a rather solemn figure never happier than when showing off the collection of narwhal horns, South Sea island carvings and other gifts he had received from grateful

Tasmanians and scouts around the world. Bobby's frolics were
financed not by his father but by his benefactor, Colonel Collins,
the most amiable of bachelors. The Colonel had walked out for years
with Bobby's mother, Jo Grimond's sister, they had played in the
mixed doubles at Wimbledon together and it was an unsolved
question whether he was Bobby's father or not. Either way, Bobby
set out to scatter as much of the Colonel's cash among his friends as he
could. There were lunches for twenty at Wilton's or the Mirabelle, or
the Bell at Aston Clinton, or the Elizabeth in Oxford. He bought
drawings and pastels by Rossetti and Burne-Jones and gave them
away as birthday presents. There were sodden shooting parties at
Rowallan with terrified beaters cowering in small fir plantations as
cackhanded undergraduates blazed straight at them. And through all
these delights, there was the enchanting burble of Bobby's conversation, as high-speed as any Oxford don's, a stream of hair-raising gossip
and art-historical scholarship, the salacious story of some laird's
conception being followed by a searing inventory of his dining-room
furniture. The pace was too hot to last. I don't think Bobby really
meant to hang on for the duration. This brief rekindling of the pre-
war spirit was snuffed out at prelims. Bobby and Bron and several
other impatient spirits moved on, leaving behind a certain feeling of
deflation, much like a small port after the fleet has sailed.

My defection from the PPE school was not entirely forgiven.
When Roy Harrod retired ten years later, his old pupils gave a dinner
for him at the House of Commons. Obviously I was not invited as I
had failed to stay his course, but Henry said I could come along as a
friend of the family. As we sat down, I saw Oscar Wood on the other
side of the room. He had one of his miserable spoiled-cherub grins on
his face. Suddenly I realised it was me he was grinning at. Then as I
fiddled with my place card I saw why. Written on the card in Oscar's
tiny precise hand was: 'Mr W.R.F. Mount soi-distant pupil of Sir Roy
Harrod. Hilary Term 1959 Econ prelims *vix satis double minus*'. In
Oxford malice springs eternal.

Roy's star pupil was Peter Jay, son of my mother's best Somerville
friend Peggy Garnett and of Douglas Jay, Wilson's President of the
Board of Trade, these days remembered mostly for having said 'the
man in Whitehall knows best'. He was talking about diet and

education, so he might just as well have been saying the same thing today when the man in Whitehall never stops telling teachers how to teach and children what to eat. Douglas could scarcely have been less like my father, being teetotal, tight-fisted, fiercely competitive, a brilliant scholar and puritanical about everything except sex, the only thing my father was puritanical about. But the two of them hit it off and the chattering brood of Jays often came to stay at Chitterne. Peter had inherited some of his father's traits, with an extra dose of good humour thrown in, which defused his reputation for being the second cleverest boy at Winchester after Alasdair Clayre. When he left Oxford and joined the Treasury, he was frequently described as the cleverest young man in England. But he remained a bouncy, friendly character whose conspicuous brilliance inspired remarkably little resentment. Unlike me, he plunged headlong into the wonderful world of PPE and in no time his conversation was peppered with jargon borrowed from the economics as well as the philosophy. Tildes and vels, the Law of Excluded Middle, the Multiplier Effect and the Concept of Marginal Utility would be remorselessly applied to subjects like which pub we should go to, or whether A was really sleeping with B, or if it was right to call Three No Trumps with no hearts to speak of.

He was assisted in these manic excursions, at a slightly lower voltage, by his friend Hugh (Tiggy) Stephenson, who I suppose must have been the third cleverest boy at Winchester, a drier, more austere character with a strongly developed critical faculty – he once crossed the High Street in order to tell me that no normal human being would think of wearing the double-breasted suit I was wearing. Tiggy rose to succeed Peter as President of the Union, but it was not because of this that they came into my life – I only went to a Union debate once and, like the legendary aesthete in the trenches, didn't care for the noise or the people.

What brought us together was that Peter was going out with Margaret Callaghan, daughter of his father's old Labour colleague, and Tiggy was going out with Auriol Stevens, and Margaret and Auriol were just setting up together in lodgings at 76 Woodstock Road with Caroline Seebohm and Susan Wolff. Caroline was at that moment the girlfriend of Roger Smith, a dashing leading man in

Oxford theatre who was supposed to have gipsy blood – certainly his dark compelling features looked in need of an earring. And Susan, well, somehow Susan found herself going out with me.

To say we were opposites is to put it very mildly indeed. Susan was as intensely lively, ebullient, argumentative, self-confident and Jewish as I was droopy, languid, hesitant and C of E. She was also as liberated as I was inhibited, as typical a product of her alma mater, the fearsomely progressive Frensham Heights, as I was of mine. She was reading Psychology and Physiology and I had barely passed a science O-level.

For me 76 Woodstock Road was a realm of liberty, at once enchanted and alarming, of doors half open and glimpses of bra straps being fastened and girls wandering around in pyjamas with blue-and-white striped mugs of Nescafé, and boyfriends crouching at mirrors which were too low for them, slowly shaving and talking at the same time about what was in the papers. They all knew about things of the moment, like sanctions against South Africa and who was going to be elected to the National Executive Committee of the Labour Party. All I knew about was the sonnets of Ronsard and the bloodlines of Derby winners.

Susan took me up to London in her duck-egg-blue Morris Minor convertible (I hadn't passed my driving test yet) to meet her parents in their flat in Cottesmore Gardens. Eric was a lawyer and Camille was a GP. They greeted me with great friendliness but also a certain bemusement. A couple of their cousins dropped in for a drink, just back from Israel, later on so did another friend, possibly a cousin too, Eric Estorick who had an art gallery and had written a life of Sir Stafford Cripps. They talked about the fighting in Jerusalem and then about the fighting in the Labour Party. Later on, a dark slender young man appeared who Susan told me had been exiled from South Africa along with most of his friends, which is why they got on to talking about the latest tightening of the pass laws. It is hard to exaggerate how inadequate I felt to cope with these worlds full of such energy and bitterness. My upbringing seemed criminally escapist. Everything I said sounded woefully naive.

The next day back at Oxford I went round to 76 Woodstock Road and apologised for being so pathetic. Susan was not inclined to varnish her words.

'Oh, my parents really quite took to you,' she said. 'They said they'd never met anyone like you before – they thought you were a character straight out of P. G. Wodehouse.'

It was painfully clear that, although the girls at 76 Woodstock Road were kindly enough, they thought that Susan had a dud this time. Frances Kaldor, the brilliant daughter of Harold Wilson's favourite economist, once said at a picnic beside the ruins of Minster Lovell, when either she had failed to recognise me or had not realised that I was within earshot: 'The extraordinary thing about Susan is that she can fall in love with *anyone*.'

They might seem liberated to me, but free and easy would not be the right way to describe any of them, except perhaps Caroline. If they were the first generation of Somerville girls to take sex in their stride, they all still regarded love as a serious engagement.

'It isn't being in love unless you really believe it's going to last for ever,' Susan said as she was driving me out to Witham Woods in the blue Morris Minor. I had just failed my driving test for the third time. The only consolation was that Peter Jay, who had never failed anything, had failed his, which he confided to me as though confessing to incest.

'I don't see why,' I said. 'Couldn't it just be a brief encounter which would make it all the more intense and passionate because you knew it wasn't going to last?'

'No,' she said. 'You're missing the point. You both have to *believe* that it's going to go on for ever, otherwise it's phoney.'

'Oh,' I said, 'I'm not sure I can manage that.'

'No, you probably can't,' Susan said, not unkindly.

As that winter and spring wore on and we made more excursions in the Morris Minor, I became aware that this was not just a theoretical impediment. Clearly at sex itself I was *vix* or possibly *non satis* – not much improvement on Bron's Uncle Alec – but with practice that might in time be rectified (Uncle Alec had married again, possibly several times, and became a legend in the sack, at least by his own account). But the shortfall in the affections looked like a more deepseated problem, which would present a challenge to any prospective partner. Kingsley Amis wrote a novel entitled *Difficulties with Girls*. My story at this period would have been called *Difficulties for Girls*.

Susan's parents bought us tickets for a fancy-dress opera ball at the Dorchester Hotel. By the time we got to Nathan's the only suitable costumes they had left were Madame Butterfly and Lieutenant Pinkerton. We both thought we looked rather good: Susan a bright-eyed, back-combed Butterfly almost engulfed by her kimono, I a tight-laced, pink-faced Pinkerton. To our annoyance we finished only third in the fancy-dress competition, behind a rather vulgar Carmen and Don José and a winsome Hansel and Gretel. The chairman of the judges was Benjamin Britten and when he handed us our trifling prizes, he murmured 'A rather fine Pinkerton, I thought,' which miffed Susan, but I explained that was simply the way his fancy lay. Never having been to the opera in question, or any opera at all for that matter, I read up the plot with interest and found a certain kinship with Pinkerton, the faithless moral lightweight. Butterfly's views on love, by contrast, seemed alarmingly close to Susan's.

Soon after the opera ball Susan got appendicitis and was rushed into hospital. Ten days later when she was due to come out, I rang Cottesmore Gardens to arrange a date. I got on to Eric.

'I don't know how you dare to ring up now. I just cannot believe that my daughter is going out with someone like you.'

'How do you mean?' I mumbled.

'You didn't go and visit her in hospital, you didn't even telephone us to find out how she was.'

'I sent flowers,' I mumbled.

'Flowers aren't good enough. I expect Susan will forgive you because for some inexplicable reason she seems to be fond of you, but her mother and I won't forget this in a hurry.'

This onslaught completely floored me. My view of being in

hospital was that when you were in it you were out of action, off the board. I was taken to see my mother in hospital, but I probably wouldn't have thought of it on my own. The whole world of hospital visits and telephone calls was a foreign language. Perhaps the same could be said of the language of the affections as a whole. I listened with furtive envy as Caroline described how she and Roger had these historic rows but 'we always make them up in bed afterwards'. Both parts of this dramatic process seemed utterly beyond me. I was like a small iceberg floating south into warmer waters with a little survey station on top of it, inside which the team were drinking cocoa and monitoring the passing tundra, blissfully unaware of the hazard they posed to passing shipping.

Susan remained bewildered by me, and from time to time exasperated. Like her parents she had not come across anyone like this before. Though she was tenacious in her affections and did not like to admit defeat in anything, I cannot help thinking that it was something of a relief when I finally said that – well, what exactly did I say? I know at least that it did not involve the word 'relationship', because it was clear that the failing was all on one side. Within a year of our parting she married the slender dark exile from South Africa, moved to an old manor house in Walton-on-Thames and has remained happily married in Walton-on-Thames ever since. That same year after they all left Oxford Margaret married Peter and Auriol married Tiggy. David Dimbleby nearly married my cousin Georgie. Bron did marry Teresa, and Simon Boyd married my cousin Alice.

Only twenty years later when I wrote a book about the history of marriage did I come to realise quite how extraordinary it was that so many of my friends should be getting married at the age of twenty-one or twenty-two. This flurry of splicing in the very early twenties was quite exceptional in English history. If we leave out the atypical early betrothals of the aristocracy, the average age of marriage in all classes and for both sexes was always around twenty-six, sometimes later, as it is again today. What explained the sudden rush to the altar or the register office in the early 1960s? The glib explanation was that this was the only way that couples could legitimately enjoy sex – 'licensed now for embracement', in Betjeman's phrase. But that is surely the opposite of the truth, because this was the very moment at which the barriers to premarital sex among the respectable classes were being trampled down – certainly at 76 Woodstock Road. Nor do I think it represented some sort of flight into bourgeois tranquillity. On the contrary, I remember thinking at the time that these early marriages were born of a rather delightful adventurous spirit, an impatience to try out everything that life had to offer. It was all part of the Sixties, not an escape from that semi-mythical, unrepeatable decade. I think so still, even if some of those marriages ended in divorce, as three out of the four 76 Woodstock Road ones did, though in the case of Margaret and Auriol only after twenty-five years and half-a-dozen children.

Whatever inspired this urge, the inspiration escaped me. Getting married at that date was as far from my mind as going to fight in Vietnam. Instead, I drifted off into calmer waters where less was expected of me. Mary MacDougall was at Somerville too and reading PPE, but she could not have been more different: tall, gawky–elegant, shy and hesitant but also extremely sociable with an astringent wit inherited from her alarming Boston grandmother, sceptical about most things, completely uninterested in current affairs, of the public sort anyway. Far from regarding marriage as the ideal state, she said she could not imagine getting married at all unless it was possible to get divorced at a moment's notice. This wariness, she candidly admitted, came from the unsatisfactory example of her parents' marriage, or rather the example of her father. Jack MacDougall had in his day held what seemed to be even then the almost official title of cleverest boy at Winchester and had been quite a successful publisher at Chapman and Hall, his star author being Evelyn Waugh. But retirement and cheap red wine had soured him. His enchanting wife May and three daughters were powerless to shake off his low spirits. Almost his only friend now seemed to be Waugh and these ill-humoured elderly gents would go off on jaunts together from which they returned to menace their families. Waugh dedicated *Love Among the Ruins* to Jack and they corresponded about their miseries. 'I am very sorry you have the accidie,' Waugh wrote. 'I don't think the cure really is new and varied activities. I think God sends these times to remind us that there is no rest except in Him' – not, I think, the kind of remedy for depression that Jack was looking for. For my part, I found Jack MacDougall

rather easier to deal with than Eric Wolff, since he had no expectations of decent behaviour. And whether staying with the MacDou-
galls in their pretty house on the slopes of the Hog's Back or
wandering round Oxford and Kensington with Mary, I felt quite
at ease and imagined if I thought about it at all that she felt similarly
relaxed. Which once again showed my total absence of self-
knowledge. Mary was the first person to point out how impatient
and gloomy I turned as soon as anyone showed their emotions – 'You
really can't bear people not being ordinary.' This was the logical
sequel to E. M. Forster's indictment: if the Englishman had been
taught not to show feeling, he would naturally expect other English-
men (which of course included Englishwomen, who were not to be
allowed any special privileges or exemptions) to be taught so too. A
properly conducted society was a damped-down milieu, in which
feelings tended to be extinguished for sheer lack of practice. I should
have had at least a glimmering of all this. But icebergs have no learning
curve, and once again I was startled as we were walking down
Ennismore Gardens and Mary said suddenly, apropos of nothing,
'You don't really care about anyone, do you? I mean, not just me.' I
said that wasn't true, not true in the slightest bit. But even as I was
saying this, I could see how hard it would be for anyone to believe
me, least of all someone as sceptical as Mary.

The Malt House was sold soon after I left Oxford. The house seemed
to be sinking back into the hillside, unlived in and uncared for. My
father was indifferent to, perhaps even rather liked, this Tennysonian
decay, but he was short of cash and the £4,000 he got, though not
much of a price even then, would keep him going for quite a time.
My sister and I could not bear to watch our home mouldering away.
Even the plumbing was beginning to fall apart, bringing down with it
showers of plaster, sometimes larger lumps too. I was in a state of near-
catatonic escapism, not yet then dubbed denial, and took no part in
selling the house. The clearing up was left to Francie, who arranged
for the larger pieces of furniture to be stored at Wasing and took the
smaller bits to her flat off the Fulham Road. I took only some of the
books and a few ornaments. Neither of us had the energy to feel in the
least possessive.

My father moved into a room in Oakley Street, Chelsea, which is the long street leading down to the Albert Bridge. I had briefly stayed in a house there a year or so earlier and he had told me then that 'everyone lives in Oakley Street once in their lives', and he was delighted to prove this true in his own case. He had already made this part of London his own, having previously lodged at the Polish Naval Officers Club round the corner on Chelsea Embankment. It was Archie Colquhoun, the famous translator of *The Leopard*, who had put him on to this strange establishment overlooking the Chelsea Physic Garden. The club had been set up after the war by some sort of grant from the British government, still suffering the odd twinge of guilt from its treatment of the Poles. On Tuesday nights a young lady in a purple frock played Chopin in the bar. Another evening there was Polish dancing, or so we were told by the melancholy Polish officer who ran the place, hoping to make us prolong our stay. Most of the guests were not Polish at all, just people like my father and Archie looking for a cheap place to stay. That was how I thought of London when I first came to live there full time – as a place where nothing was quite going according to the original plan and people were making the best of a situation they had not intended to be in. Even now, although we have been living in the same house for thirty-nine years, I still sometimes experience a little twitch of apprehension that any day I shall be plunged back into that sort of improvised existence.

If I had had any plans, they would not have included starting my life in London as an Embassy nanny. Two summers earlier I had looked after a couple of pre-teen American boys at Deauville and word had spread that I was a reliable help, although my duties at Deauville had not extended much beyond babysitting for Ricky and Kenny when Ric senior and Mary Ohrstrom were at the races or the casino and carrying the picnic basket when they weren't. Mary was a bubbly Texan, from the Murchison oil family, and played the part with exuberance although she was pregnant with her fifth or sixth child at the time. Responding to my obviously orphaned state, in the end it was she who was mothering me more than me nannying her children.

Anyway on the strength of this reference, I was hired to teach English history and manners, including cricket, to the three children of David and Evangeline Bruce who had just moved into the American Embassy in Regent's Park. Suddenly there I was ensconced in the garden wing of the enormous mansion that Barbara Hutton had donated to the American nation with a bottle of Bourbon at my bedside and nothing to do except set out the cricket stumps on the vast lawn, since David Junior, Nicky and the eldest, Sasha, a dark coltish fifteen-year-old, had a real nanny who looked after them most of the time. David and Evangeline had a limitless and glittering circle of friends and were charm itself to me, but their children seemed ill at ease with them. As we played our desultory games out on the huge sward, the boys cross-batting the ball baseball-style despite my repeated instructions on keeping a straight bat, the Bruces' guests – British politicians, American senators, other ambassadors, sometimes film stars like Gregory Peck – would come out on to the terrace for pre-lunch cocktails. They seemed miles away. It was as though our little game was taking place out in the middle at Lord's or the Oval. Now and then I would be roped in to make up the numbers at table and would find myself, a bit sweaty and out of breath, sitting down next to Mrs Rockefeller or Mrs Annenberg. When the waiter came round, being left-handed I always found it awkward to help myself and the serving spoon would swat their big hairdos, as brittle and finespun as the Embassy chef's amazing sugar palaces. I felt like a tutor in a Chekhov play, one of those superfluous individuals who fills an empty chair and everyone is rather kind to because they can see at a glance that he doesn't count. 'Oh this is Ferdl,' Evangeline would say, lending her irresistible Virginia drawl to the Austrian diminutive of my name (although she wasn't Austrian, in fact partly English). 'The children are unrecognisably delightful since he came' – which they weren't in the slightest, only rather puzzled and uneasy at living in this mansion and not seeing their parents much.

For me, though, it was a wonderful carefree summer, almost like Oxford going on into grown-up life. My only anxiety was whether the Bourbon bottle was a one-off or whether it would be replaced when I had finished it, which it was, the next night. In the evening I would go out to see friends, a few times to a debutante dance usually given by people I had never met, which meant putting on my dinner jacket. As I strolled out through the wrought-iron gates and down the

Outer Circle under the limes and chestnuts, I no longer felt like a Chekhov tutor but rather like a young blood in Thackeray out for an evening's gaming, although usually it was a question of a rather stilted pre-dance dinner with complete strangers in a flat in Albert Hall Mansions.

In September the children went back to school in America and the next time I saw Sasha she was grown up, at a party her parents gave for her at the Embassy. She must have been about twenty by then and had become as charming-looking as her mother, but she still seemed awkward and a bit detached, as though the party was nothing to do with her or she wished it wasn't, but then plenty of girls having parties given for them look like that. Like her brothers she wasn't finding life easy. They were part of the first generation that got seriously messed up with drugs. Sasha in particular tangled with a series of bad characters, druggies and art forgers. Finally when she was twenty-nine, she married a man who turned out to be the worst of the lot, a Greek national called Marios Michaelides. They had been married only three months when she was found bleeding to death under a cedar tree at the Bruce estate in Virginia. Her father, one of the greatest smoothers-over in American history, managed to have her buried without an autopsy or any criminal investigation. Then a couple of years later, David himself died, and Evangeline and David junior got the case opened. Michaelides was eventually indicted for murder, and incidentally bigamy, but he had already skipped back to Greece and was never extradited. Evangeline threw her energies and a great deal of money (much of it inherited from David's first wife, Ailsa Mellon, who had died in a plane crash over the Bermuda Triangle) into founding a series of projects in Sasha's memory, most of them to assist the black and poor young people of Washington. Sasha Bruce House and the Sasha Bruce Youth Network have become north-east Washington's safety net for drop-outs, so she is remembered abundantly. I would never have guessed that she would have such a sad life when she was yelling at her brother, 'No, David, that's not the way you do it,' and scampering after the ball across the enormous lawn into the distant shrubberies. David and Evangeline were so benign and thoughtful to me that I never properly took in how distant they were from their children. David bequeathed me two pairs of white buckskin trousers and when I got married Evangeline gave us a double-blossomed cherry tree.

Then my London wanderings began. Over the next few years I squatted in a basement in Campden Hill Square belonging to the Harrods, then in a rather damper basement in Knightsbridge belonging to a couple who weren't getting on at all well and I had to leave when they split and were going to sell the house, then in a boxy mews-house cottage off the Fulham Road which I shared with my Oxford friend Henry Berens. Number 21 Bury Walk was a strange miniature dwelling, filled with violent feral paintings of occult and magical subjects. Our landladies, Guinevere and Jacintha Buddicom, had taken an interest in such things when young and had known Aleister 'the Beast' Crowley. The Buddicom sisters and their brother Prosper had been close childhood friends of George Orwell, and Jacintha and Eric Blair (as he then was) had been semi-sweethearts through their teens. In old age she claimed that when she was twenty and he was eighteen he had assaulted her and torn her skirt and this had put an end to their friendship which had not been renewed till he was on his deathbed, partly because she was not aware that he had changed his name to George Orwell. That may be. Orwell could be rough with girls and at six foot four he was nearly eighteen inches taller than the diminutive Jacintha and might well have terrified her so that she never wanted to see him again. But I suspect he might also have been put off by her quirky pantheism, already well to the fore in her teens – she told her shocked housemistress that she was willing to worship the Christian god for a week or two, so long as they could pay honour to other gods as well. Certainly on the evidence of the pictures on the walls of 21 Bury Walk, by her middle years she had become decidedly freaky. We met her and her sister Guinny only once, when they came to settle the handover of the house – two little old ladies who looked as if they had never had an evil thought between them.

Here I lived downstairs a life of gloomy chastity which Henry upstairs did not. Many an innocent debutante had her early experience of love surrounded by nightmarish canvases of snakes and apes copulating in orange and purple jungles. The upstairs room was just big enough to fit a double bed in. The boxroom I occupied downstairs next to the kitchen was not only tiny but had an overhanging ledge which you hit your head on if you sat up too suddenly in bed, a further deterrent to dalliance if any had been in prospect. Behind the smallest imaginable kitchenette was an even smaller room with twin bunks in it suitable only for children but occupied for some months in the early part of 1963 by Tara Browne, the Golden Child of the Sixties, and his equally tiny girlfriend Nicky MacSherry. Tara was the adored younger son of the tearaway heiress Oonagh Guinness. By the age of fifteen he had been everywhere and got to know everyone like the Beatles and the Stones. His charming blond elfin face was devoid of malice or indeed of any expression much. He had the impersonality of an angel. He and Nicky came and went mysteriously. I never quite understood how they had ended up with us in the first place when they could have afforded infinitely more spacious premises. Some row with Tara's mother or his trustees perhaps. Most of the time I was scarcely conscious of their being there at all. In the morning towards eleven they would tumble out of bed in their rompers, looking like illustrations to Wee Willie Winkie as they foraged for cornflakes. They seemed so ridiculously young that I could not really believe it when the year after they stayed with us they got married and Nicky had a son – I can't remember in which order these things happened. Tara was still only eighteen. Then they had another son and the year after that Tara was killed driving his Lotus Elan at 100 miles an hour with his girlfriend (not Nicky) through the traffic lights at the bottom of Redcliffe Gardens, aged twenty-one. The day after he was killed John Lennon was sitting at his piano and saw the news in the *Daily Mail* and composed the song 'A Day in the Life', which includes the bit about the boy racer who fails to notice that the lights have changed.

A complete life in its way, I suppose, unless you happened to be the person living it. I can't say I knew Tara any better when he left than when he came, although we had been sleeping only about six feet apart for several months. Roughly the same distance, in every sense, as I had been from James Stobo.

My own family had broken up but not widely dispersed. All three of us were living within five minutes' walk of the King's Road. My sister, almost as vagabond as I was, lodged first in Markham Square, then in Pelham Court, then shared a flat on the corner of Oakley Street overlooking the river (so she too had fulfilled my father's dictum), and finally settled further down the Fulham Road in a house in Lettice Street which was as charming as its name suggests. My father meanwhile had moved on to live with Connie Bainbridge in a modern mews cottage in Cadogan Lane.

Connie was an exotic import into our family, as exotic in her way as my aunt Betty whom she had known quite well when young. Née Constance de Pinna of the family who owned the well-known de Pinna stores in Manhattan, she was the bad girl of the family and had been left out of her father's will. Her mother, though, was still around, living in an enormous apartment on Park Avenue. By now in her eighties, Mrs de Pinna had recently taken up abstract painting and was turning out giant canvases in violent colours which were selling well. The paintings were three times her size which was tiny. Connie too was a tiny figure, just as feisty as her mother, in appearance halfway between a sphinx and a Pekingese, both of which were in stock at 23 Cads Lane, as she had a passion for Empire furniture and small snuffly dogs. She had been married four or five times. The fifth time depended on whether you counted (she certainly did) her affair with the film director John Huston. She worked with him on the set of *The African Queen* and has a credit as 'Costume Designer except for Miss Hepburn's clothes', which were designed by somebody else. Fans of the film will recall that nobody except Katherine Hepburn is wearing much to speak of, on account of them having to tow the *African Queen* through the mangrove swamps.

Connie's more accredited former husbands were of less interest than her friends, who included a fair slice of the New York intelligentsia after the war. As you manoeuvred past the gilded sphinxes and pyramids and eagle-clawed armoires into her dark low-ceilinged sitting room, you were likely to find yourself being introduced to the composer Virgil Thomson, or Alexander Calder, the mobile maker, or even to Gore Vidal. Years later when I was working for the *TLS* and came to know Gore as a contributor (he would sometimes send us the articles that were too wicked for his old friends at the *New York Review of Books* to print), he developed the fantasy that Connie was my real mother and I had invented my Pakenham background in order to get on in the world. You had to see Connie and me together to appreciate the full sauciness of the conceit.

She looked after my father as devotedly as she could. I dread to think what would have become of him without her. Throughout those years when I came across him walking through Chelsea on his way to the library or, more likely, to the Queen's Elm or the Chelsea Potter or the Princess of Wales, he looked well turned out, even debonair, ruddy-faced, with his flowing white hair carefully brushed and a scarlet or white scarf tucked into his overcoat, in his last years carrying the silver-knobbed cane Connie had given him for his sixtieth birthday. You had to come up quite close to catch the look of sadness. To me the sight of him walking among strangers, living so near me and not with me, was always disturbing, as though a part of me had escaped and could never be recaptured.

I am not sure that he actually drank any more in the last ten years of his life after my mother died, but the drink seemed to damp him down more, reduce him to incoherence earlier on if it was a bad day. Once or twice I have tentatively swapped notes with other people whose father or mother had taken to the bottle. Our experiences had little in common. In their families, drink brought on rages, unpredictable or repulsive behaviour, sometimes physical violence, almost always verbal abuse, visits by the police or to the police station. We had to endure none of this. My father tended rather to slide into a state of sodden sweetness, perhaps while telling in a meandering fashion one of his favourite stories which he told so crisply when he was sober. Though it was a melancholy decline for him, and a depressing process to watch, we never loved him the less, nor vice versa.

To start with, I was stiff and awkward to Connie, resentful in fact. Even years later when I got engaged and took my fiancée, who like my mother was called Julia, to meet my father at Cads Lane, she swears that I had not warned her of Connie's existence and she was startled to meet this tiny figure coming out to greet her with the same friendly welcome that she had always given me. Connie was probably kinder to me than she was to her only child Toddy, her son by her last husband Emerson Bainbridge. In fact I had every reason to be pleased when she and my father decided to get married (there had been a brief break-up a few months earlier which must have taught them that they were better off together). I think my sister was pleased too and we were both there at Chelsea Town Hall on the day. The wedding did not take place, however, without one last piece of fraternal meddling. My sister reported that Uncle Grig had warned her to look out because Connie was a grasping woman. Funny, I reported back, that's just what Uncle Bill warned me. The advice was of course entirely beside the point, since my father had little or nothing to grasp. As it turned out, Connie could not have been more generous to both of us, and she made my father's last years bearable if not happy. I would go round to Cads Lane for duck à l'orange on Sundays and now and then my father would give me lunch at the Queen's Hotel in Sloane Square, once the haunt of Augustus John, or at the Wilbraham Hotel round the corner, which was the haunt of nobody, or we would go up west, to the Ladder Club in St James's where pre-war belles would perch on high stools to show that their legs were as good as ever, or to the French pub in Soho where we might catch a glimpse of Francis Bacon. In most of these venues I was deeply uneasy. They formed no part of my long-term flight plan in search of respectability. Jeffrey Bernard recorded that after his first visit to Soho he thought, 'This is where I want to spend the rest of my life.' I thought, 'Get me out of here.' I was going in the opposite direction from most other people in the Sixties, against the flow of the traffic.

My father's health began to decline noticeably. He suffered several bad falls. A spell in the Holloway Sanatorium dried him out and he looked briefly splendid again, but the hospital could offer him no alternative to fill the day. When he died after another fall and a severe stroke (I'm not sure which caused the other), my grief was staunched a little by relief. The light had not quite gone out of him, nor the fight, but they were dimmed. As the years go by, I think about him more not less, quote him, imitate him more – the way he would drop his hands at the wheel in a traffic jam as though dropping the reins of a racehorse whose path is blocked by other horses, the way he would ask any stranger with an Irish accent which part of Ireland he came from, the way he would stare into the distance like a prophet who has had a glimpse of the Promised Land. I inherited that habit and his long sight too.

Quite soon after I came to London I met Sarah Goldsmid and Henrietta Guinness, probably together, as they always were together. And probably at a dance. They were invited to every dance, so even if you only went to a couple of dances you would be likely to meet them. Sarah was tallish with chestnut hair and a round face that was really quite ordinary until she smiled and made you feel she had been waiting all evening for someone to say what you had just said. Henrietta was petite with a dirty laugh which she unleashed when anyone used an affected word like petite. 'You'll have to come and stay at Somerhill,' Sarah said. 'My mother's desperate for more young men. I produced five last weekend and she's still not satisfied.' 'My mother's desperate too,' Henrietta said, 'but she's such a snob I only know about two people she'd have to dinner.'

Somerhill is the house you see when you come over the brow of the A21 just after the Tonbridge turn-off, an enormous Jacobean pile standing on the opposite hillside. Harry and Rosie Goldsmid entertained there on a scale the house cannot have experienced since the Earl of Essex's widow sported there in 1613. The dark panelling glowed with Sisleys and Vlamincks and enormous Rothkos and the guests did their best to glow too. Harry was Tory MP for Walsall South, so there would be a sprinkling of his colleagues – Christopher Soames would come over from Tunbridge Wells, Duncan Sandys would pay heavy compliments to Rosie with whom he had had a fling, though flinging does not sound the right word for that formidable slab of old red sandstone. There would be some snazzier American visitors connected with showbiz, Sam Behrman the playwright and biographer of Berenson and Duveen, the film director Stanley Donen, the legendary scriptwriter S. J. Perelman who afterwards wrote a cruel sketch based on his weekend at Somerhill. There might also be English writers from Harry's vintage, Cyril Connolly, Sacheverell Sitwell, Anthony Powell, Isaiah Berlin who had been at Balliol with him. Not all these guests could be relied on to make the party go. When Rosie asked Connolly to tell one of his celebrated anecdotes, he snapped, 'I'm not a performing seal,' and relapsed into a silent grump for the rest of the meal. Harry himself was capable of flooding his end of the table with gloom, not lightened when Rosie could be heard barking at the other end, 'Sir Henry's in one of his moods tonight, I don't know why he bothers to come down to dinner.' During the day Rosie looked like a plump piece of Dresden china but when she lit up a small cheroot after dinner she was a woman carousing in a Dutch painting. She combined huge generosity and unquenchable appetites with ferocious opinions which made her husband appear the limpest liberal. Harry had been unstoppably brave in the war, accumulating even more medals than his brother General Jackie Goldsmid. He was also extremely well read in several languages and had a fine library in what was said to be the longest room in Kent, though I doubt it. It was a standing joke that Cyril Connolly was not to be allowed into the library unaccompanied, as he was supposed to be light-fingered even for a bibliophile. In fact I never saw anyone read a book in the library, which was given over to ping-pong. It was on this ping-pong table that I played the great violinist Jascha Heifetz. As I am writing this, I am also reading an article by Paul Johnson in the *Spectator* on the subject of hands. He ends the article by saying, 'I would also like to know more about the hands of Jascha Heifetz, who to my mind was the most spectacular executant in all music, producing a continuous series of sounds of a special kind never heard before or since. Was there something equally special about his fingers?' I ought to be able to help Paul out here, but unfortunately I can remember nothing about Heifetz's fingers, only that he played an orthodox defensive game, all backhands and crouching over the table, and I won 21–13 and he was very nice about it.

Sometimes one or two Pakenhams would come over. Bernhurst, the house that my uncle Frank by-now-Longford had inherited from his aunt, was only twenty minutes away. I scarcely knew any of them and had never been to Bernhurst. There being eight children, they were a self-contained bunch and anyway Frank's sisters did not seek out his company. The sisters were fond of each other and regularly telephoned one another when unable to make physical contact, but they regarded their sole surviving brother with amused detachment as something of a freak and unsuited to normal human life. To his younger sisters Mary and Violet he had dispensed unwanted advice, especially about boyfriends, a subject on which they thought they knew rather more than he did. In my few meetings with him to date, I felt much the same. He was certainly friendly and showed interest in what I was doing or might do next, but somehow one could tell that he would have shown exactly the same interest if I had never met him before and was never likely to meet him again. He was famously indifferent to material things too – clothes, decor, food – and to the arts – music, novels, pictures. All this could be credited to his ascetic nature. His inability to distinguish between human beings obviously made him the perfect prison visitor, since he genuinely did not judge a serial murderer any differently from a nun. Yet coupled with his fascination with celebrity and success, it certainly gave his company a wintry quality. Almost his first remark would be 'And who would you say was the most successful of your generation?' When Powell's *Dance to the Music of Time* began to gain popularity, Uncle Frank claimed that the character of Widmerpool was based on him, which is not a thing most people would wish to claim, but suited his book perfectly since he was both claiming to recognise himself in the villain, thus advertising his humility, and also laying claim to the only character in the book who was becoming one of the immortals. In reality he possessed more of the characteristics of Lord Erridge, the narrator's ascetic, high-minded and annoying brother-in-law. That he never claimed to be the original of Erridge suggests that he had not actually read the books. On the other hand, I do remember catching sight of him, by then in his late eighties, jogging in a filthy old tracksuit through the lanes of East Sussex – a spectacle which cannot help recalling the scene at the end of Powell's novel when Widmerpool collapses and dies of a heart attack while on a run with his acolytes.

But then I imagine that saints quite often possess Uncle Frank's traits, not excluding publicity mania. And to see him standing ill-shaven with a piece of sticking plaster flapping from cheek or forehead and the wind blowing his wisps of hair across his specs on a platform in the winter months waiting for the connection that would take him to Dartmoor or Wakefield was, for me at any rate, to experience a feeling not of kinship but of unwilling admiration.

It was not hard to pick holes in the logic of the causes he promoted so doggedly as a penal reformer. If Myra Hindley were genuinely contrite as he claimed, then surely she would wish to spend the rest of her life not agitating to be released but on her knees begging forgiveness, which in any case was God's, not Uncle Frank's, to bestow. His protestations that he was just as sensitive to the sufferings of the victims and their families never quite carried conviction. All the same, I could never help feeling that his insistence on the Christian imperatives, however lopsidedly applied, did make his country a less hard-souled place.

He was too restless to be the ideal weekend guest, at Somerhill or anywhere else. Although always glad to take the measure of any social occasion, however grand or frivolous, he would soon long to be somewhere else. For his grandson Benjy's wedding he had been persuaded that he must stay the entire weekend at the new in-laws' house overlooking the Solent. But as he stared disconsolately across the rolling lawns, a light suddenly went on inside his head – Parkhurst! And he was on the next ferry to the Isle of Wight to pay a call on one of the Kray twins.

A more likely visitor from Bernhurst was Frank's second son Paddy, who was his favourite in so far as Frank was capable of making any such distinction, being boisterous, sporty and capable of keeping the company amused for hours on end – all qualities which Uncle Frank admired and envied, in particular Paddy's low golf handicap. Sarah's boyfriend, the exuberant and caustic David Winn, was an even better golfer, good enough to play in the Amateur Championship. The two of them would humble the great seaside links of Kent and Sussex – Sandwich, Rye and Deal – before coming back to Somerhill to intimidate and beguile the company with their fearless backchat.

At this stage Sarah and Henrietta were doing their best to fit in with their parents' wishes, Sarah the more graceful and submissive of the two. The young men who had to be imported in such quantities were all likewise agreeable and suitable, mostly lawyers or bankers with an eye for the main chance already nicely developed. Even the one who did seem a bit vague and unfocused, Stuart Wheeler, eventually accumulated a vast fortune from his spread-betting firm and bought a castle in Kent the size of Somerhill. But the girls were different, not rebellious but unquiet, nagged by a sense of their inadequacy for the world from which their inescapable wealth was sheltering them. 'Of course we'll never actually *do* anything,' Sarah said. They were caught between generations, not yet expected to go to university and pursue a serious career, but already well aware that the life mapped out for them was not enough.

Yet on the surface high society had brought off the most brilliant reconstruction of its pre-war heyday. The great country houses were reoccupied after wartime requisition and lit up again for coming-out and coming-of-age balls. Londonderry House in Park Lane survived long enough to house one last whirl before the wrecker's ball. I crashed the party, egged on by John Wells, and looked down from the balcony to watch Benny Goodman give a final tootle on his clarinet for the jazz-crazed Alistair Londonderry. In a *cottage orné* down by the river at Cliveden, I lolled on the sofa and through the open French windows listened to the band playing in the marquee on the lawns above. Beside me was a girl I had only just met and was not getting to know better. As we were talking about whether boys or girls looked better in jeans, an urbane middle-aged man tiptoed past us purring, 'Please don't let me disturb you.' This was Lord Astor's tenant, a Harley Street osteopath called Stephen Ward. The girl, it now comes back to me, was called Frances Eliot, later to marry Charlie Shelburne whom I had last seen being birched bare-bottomed in Lower School. The sofa was the one that, the next summer, Jack Profumo first got to know Christine Keeler on, no doubt also with Dr Ward tiptoeing past.

That summer too I danced with Rose Dugdale at her own dance at the River Club. Through the long white gloves her mother made her wear her grip was like a man's. We took a breather out on the balcony and looked across at Battersea Power Station. It was a steamy July night and I said something smarmy about the night and the party. 'It's a complete and utter waste of money,' Rose said but not indignantly – in fact she gave one of her gurgling laughs, not unlike Henrietta's. A man passed behind us carrying a couple of drinks. I nodded at him and said he was a friend of mine from school. 'He's a completely pointless person,' Rose said. These were early days in her career. She had not yet burgled her parents' home as a dummy run for her more celebrated robberies on behalf of the IRA. But already the subversive energy was visible, at this stage being defused by her irresistible merry chuckle.

I asked Sarah if she would like to go with me to Ireland for a few days to stay at Pakenham Hall, alias Tullynally, the original name which my cousin Thomas Pakenham had just reinstated. David Winn was doing something else, so she said there was nothing she would like better, which with her gift for illuminating the most ordinary phrase made me feel that my hesitant, almost offhand suggestion came straight from heaven.

'We're going on a boat trip,' Thomas announced. 'Down the Shannon for two days. Desmond Guinness is bringing his party and Patrick Forde's bringing his own boat.'

After breakfast Desmond Guinness appeared in the Tullynally library with his terrifying blue eyes blazing.

'I hope you don't mind, I've brought my stepfather.'

It took me a second or two to work out who this stepfather was. Desmond's mother Diana from whom he got his blue eyes had run off with Sir Oswald Mosley and a couple of years later married him in the Chancellery in Berlin with Hitler and Goebbels as witnesses. And here coming through the door behind Desmond's German princess wife Mariga was the old monster himself – great horse teeth gleaming in the morning sun, bounder's moustache now flecked with grey but his general sense of confidence in his destiny quite unimpaired by years of internment, exile and popular loathing.

'Christ,' I muttered to Sarah, 'I'm desperately sorry about this. I'm sure we can get out of it.'

'No, no, I don't want to make a fuss.'

'But Sir Henry will be furious when he hears.'

'No, I'm sure he'd say we Jews have got to stop being so absurdly sensitive.'

'Well, if I was the leader of Anglo-Jewry I'd be bloody cross if my daughter went cruising with Mosley.'

'Don't worry, it'll be fine.'

My only hope was that when we got to the jetty Sir Oswald might be allotted to the other boat. But nobody else seemed to think it odd or offensive that he should be included in the party, still less that it might be especially embarrassing for Sarah Goldsmid. Pakenhams are not notable for their sensitivity on these or any other matters. When we arrived at Carrick-on-Shannon, Mosley was not only assigned to the boat we had already climbed into but occupied the prow seat, so that his great bulk obscured the delectable views as we chugged past wooded islands and ruined abbeys. The Leader maintained a pretty steady flow of comment on public affairs, evincing little interest in the passing scenery even when the river suddenly swelled out into a great shimmering lough. Having spent most of his life attuning his views to his milieu of the moment, he did not of course speak about the menace of coloured immigration on which he had recently been so eloquent in Notting Hill and was to return to in spades, so to speak, in his last election in Shoreditch in 1966 where once again he was slaughtered and lost his deposit. Instead, we were treated to cloudier expositions, on the need for European unity, on the future of Irish agriculture.

But when we stopped for the night at a pub in Athlone, he opened up while we were having a glass of Guinness in a corner of the snug: 'There was never any violence at our rallies until the Communists tried to break them up. Our supporters wanted to hear what I had to say, so they naturally resented any interruption. But we had the Biff Boys to steward the meetings. They were a fantastic bunch, very fit, the best sort of chap. They stood no nonsense.' The years melted away as he continued to rhapsodise over the Biff Boys. His eyes were as blazing as his stepson's and his presence seemed to fill the entire snug. Yet behind us at the bar I noticed a couple of elderly locals conversing quite unmoved by the Superman on song, demonstrating the unrivalled ability of the Irish to distance themselves from a tricky situation.

There was not much room upstairs in Athlone. Mariga shared a bed-and-breakfast with Sir Oswald, perhaps on the grounds that nobody else fancied the prospect. Years later, I heard that in the night he had tried to get into her bedroom but had collided the landlady who was on the prowl or, according to another account, Mariga herself had managed to fob him off. In the course of a long and relentless sexual career, Mosley was said to have seduced both his sisters-in-law among hundreds of others. A stepdaughter-in-law was fair game.

The next day, after we had finished boating we drove down to Desmond's castle in Co. Kildare. After dinner Desmond announced that there would be a fencing display in the hall. The Irish fencing champion, a local boy by the name of Cochrane, would take on Sir Oswald Mosley. Despite having one leg a couple of inches shorter than the other as a result of a flying accident in the Great War, Mosley had been runner-up in the 1931 British épée championships and was very nearly picked for the Berlin Olympics. The hall was lit only by candles casting a ghostly light on the two fencers in their white uniforms and masks, Mosley a head taller and several stone heavier than the slender Irishman. Not the least unsettling feature of the contest was that as they saluted each other, kissing their swords, Mosley was announced as representing Great Britain against Ireland.

Fencing is a desperately silent sport. The shouts of 'en garde' and 'hit' that punctuate it only emphasise how noiseless the fencers' manoeuvrings are. For long periods it seemed that the only sound was the squeak of Mosley's surgical boot on the wooden floor. Under the flickering candlelight it was the eeriest of spectacles. I felt even more uncomfortable than I had being cooped up with him on the boat. Sarah said she wouldn't have missed it for the world.

When she got back to Kent, she was reunited with David Winn and the two of them went out sailing with Paddy Pakenham in his dinghy. They had to be towed out to sea by a motorboat because they could not sail against the incoming tide. They got about four miles out heading towards Dungeness, perhaps not so far. The sea was calm and there was very little wind and what there was kept changing direction. They were about to turn for home when the boom swung right over and tipped them all into the water. The boat went over with the mast pointing to the seabed with all the sails on it. Paddy swam underneath and pulled out the life jackets and the oars, but they could not right the boat, so David and Sarah sat astride it paddling it in the direction of the shore, with Paddy swimming behind steering. David kept them entertained by a string of funny stories. They shouted at several passing boats with no luck. Darkness fell and the weather turned cold and windy. Paddy managed to get the boat upright and cut away the sail with a penknife, but by now the waves were breaking over the boat. At about two in the morning David, who was thin as a pencil, got very cold and quickly became unconscious and died. A few hours later Sarah lost consciousness too. At about 9.30 in the morning Paddy decided to swim to shore to get help. It took him a couple of hours, so they must still have been some distance from the shore. Harry and Rosie commissioned Marc

Chagall to design a window in Sarah's memory. I am not usually a Chagall fan but the east window in Tudeley church with its ultra-marine sea and the sunlight flooding in through the side windows would make you catch your breath even if you had never met Sarah. I always meant to apologise to Harry for landing her up in the same boat as Sir Oswald Mosley, but the moment had passed.

Quite soon after Sarah died Henrietta took up with a dashing boyfriend, Michael Beeby, described in one gossip column as Britain's 'best-known beatnik', though he wasn't either really a beatnik or especially well known. They disappeared to the South of France in Henrietta's red sports car and had a horrible crash. It was said that she was never the same again, though people always say such things with hindsight. Then she fell in love with a sous-chef and set him up in a restaurant, in Ebury Street I think. The person she saw most of was her hairdresser Stewart Hiscock who was extremely nice and they became partners in a hairdressing salon. In between all this, she had a series of breakdowns and ended up in St Andrew's, Northampton. This was the place where the poet John Clare had spent the last twenty years of his life. It was later renamed the Northampton General Lunatic Asylum for the Middle and Upper Classes, I suppose to exclude destitute labourers like Clare, and it was still operating at much the same social level in the 1960s as a private charitable hospital. I wrote and asked if I could visit Henrietta and take her out (that was how formal things were then). The Superintendent wrote back: 'Miss Guinness's behaviour is liable to be unpredictable and even violent, so I suggest that you do not leave the hospital precincts as there may otherwise be embarrassing incidents'. This letter was shattering, even more shattering in fact than my first sight of her in the hospital day-room, ghostly pale, damped down, resolute and trying to be cheerful. It was the first time I had visited a psychiatric hospital (my father had not yet agreed to be dried out at the Royal Holloway) and I found it hard to handle that succession of sights which were to become familiar: at first the reassuring lawns and flowerbeds with patients reading or playing chess under a large tree, then the impersonal corridors, the splash of blood on the doorpost, the stifled wordless cry from somewhere, the glimpse of bedlam through the glass panel in the door of the locked ward. Then the quiet tea in the Copper Kettle (the nurse on duty had relented about us going out), the chainsmoking which scarcely stopped for the scones and cream, the spreading sense of desolation.

When she came out, she seemed to be relatively calm but did not, I think, particularly want to see her old friends. Much later she fell in love with an Italian medical student ten years younger than her and they went and lived in his home town, Spoleto, where they got married and she had a daughter. But the depression returned after the baby and she jumped off a famous medieval bridge outside Spoleto. The *Daily Mail* published a picture of her body lying 250 feet below in the shallow waters of the River Tessino. The body was scarcely distinguishable from the weeds and stones. The newspapers, even *The Times*, ran articles about 'the Guinness curse', although there are an awful lot of Guinnesses and quite poor families clock up multiple tragedies too. Nor did her contemporaries who survived, got married to suitable husbands and brought up several children necessarily find a smooth path. Many of them got knocked over by the accelerating juggernaut of divorce. Of the half-dozen girls I remember best from that dancing summer all but one also had severe episodes of drink or depression later on.

For me the city then scarcely existed outside the patch between Sloane Street and the Earls Court Road. I knew no other London and regarded a journey to Islington or Hampstead, let alone south of the river, as an excursion to the provinces. Chelsea was already getting written about. Mary Quant and Biba had opened up. But it was still possible to rent a basement or an attic off the King's Road for nothing very much. And here roosted several odd acquaintances from Oxford, such as the mysterious and reclusive Nicholas Tanburn. Nicky spoke so softly you could scarcely hear what he was saying and it was unnerving when his face broke out in an impish, slightly sinister grin, often when nobody had said anything funny. His intelligence was of the dry, unforgiving sort which made him a natural don, but he drifted away from postgraduate work to set up in a flat in a rather down-at-heel house in Redburn Street. Here he lived off I don't know what – some people said that his mother was connected to the Salmon family who owned the Lyons corner houses, but no such information was offered by Nicky himself. He took me round the corner from 6 Redburn Street to introduce me to two students at the Royal College of Music he had got to know (no clue of course as to how, he was reluctant to reveal even that they were girls).

Number 21 Redesdale Street was measurably more run down than 6 Redburn Sreet, and its basement damper as basements always are. The two students were like opposite heroines in a Victorian novel: Caroline Broughton, always known as Tam, fair, ravishingly pretty with an instant charm and a saucy drawl, and Katherine Pring who was dark and handsome with green eyes and a black mane and a strong pre-Raphaelite profile. Tammy was studying the piano and Kathy was a singer, which I somehow thought should have been the other way round, because Tammy was so ebullient and Kathy so quiet and reflective. For a while we went around as a foursome, from Redburn to Redesdale or vice versa or to one of the King's Road cinemas, as though this was all the world there was. We were an odd foursome, or rather I was an odd member of it, being so tone-deaf. Once or twice when the two of us were alone because Tam and Nicky had gone back to Redburn Street, I asked Kathy to sing and because she was a mezzo-soprano and Kathleen Ferrier was the only mezzo I had heard of she would sing for me, softly, half mockingly, a little bit of 'Blow the Wind Southerly' or even 'My Bonnie Lies Over the Ocean'. Even though she was singing so softly, not wanting to strain her voice because her teacher Ruth Packer had told her that this was the worst possible thing for a young mezzo, perhaps for any young singer, the effect was overwhelming. The whole basement seemed to be brimming with this effortless resonant sound, making the cups rattle on the draining board.

Knowing nothing about the singing world, I had assumed that Kathy would go on to teach music or sing at recitals of lieder and church music. I was startled when she told me she was going to be an opera singer, she seemed so reticent and unhistrionic. But quite soon after she graduated from the Royal College she found a slot at an opera house on the Continent, Geneva I think. By then we had split up for the usual iceberg reasons and Tammy told me that she had got married not long after she went abroad. It was nearly ten years later after I myself had got married and I was walking down St Martin's Lane and there was Kathy's name up on the ENO boards outside the

Coliseum playing Preziosilla the gipsy girl in *La forza del destino*. That was the first time I heard her sing in public. Then the following season we saw her as Carmen with Alberto Remedios as Don José. This was the greatest role she sang at the Coliseum and she sang it off and on for several seasons. To Wagner lovers she is better known for the leading mezzo roles she sang in Reginald Goodall's version of the Ring, Fricka and Waltraute. But we saw her only in Verdi and Bizet.

The voice was every bit as thrilling as in the basement at Redesdale Street but I was amazed to see this earthy, sluttish vamp striding about the stage barefoot and part of the time bare-breasted, with her black mane sweeping her suitors aside. She was flamboyance personified. How could I have so misread her, so utterly failed to catch a glimmering of what she was capable of? But then I knew nothing about her, she was as reticent as I was. Our friendship was a mutual non-disclosure pact. Appealing for sympathy, I told her it was difficult to be taken seriously with a red face like I had because people always thought you were so cheerful, and she said, no, I had a rather sad face, which greatly cheered me. But then she had a certain sadness about her too, though I never said so. Perhaps that was why we got on. By then I had passed my driving test and had bought from a friend for £100 a 1948 scarlet Triumph Roadster. This dashing vehicle with its swishing lines and dickey seats later achieved television notoriety as Bergerac's car. I could not afford to have either its brakes or its steering repaired and so I rumbled very slowly and nervously round Chelsea and South Kensington at the wheel with Kathy alternately sliding up against me and then, as we swung uncertainly round a tight corner, slithering off across the front seat which was a single bench of ancient cream leather, our hesitant progress on the road mirroring our progress off it.

It was many years later that Tammy told me, as though she was reminding me of things I must know already, how difficult Kathy's early life had been, how unhappy she had been when she was sent off to boarding school after her mother remarried, how the other girls bullied her, how long it had been before her talent was spotted and what a triumph it had been for her to get to the Royal College. Of all this I was quite ignorant. To me Kathy showed not a trace of emotional scarring, still less of the resolve she must have needed to carry her through.

When I wander down the King's Road, which isn't very often as we live up the other end of town, I find that even the ghosts have been ethnically cleansed from the area. The big supermarkets and chain stores have displaced the old amateur boutiques. The Duke of York barracks is a shopping centre. The flower children are long gone and I was never remotely one of them anyway. The decayed patrons of the Potter and the Markham have been displaced by a sharper, more commercially rewarding crowd. Nobody drives down Redcliffe Gardens at 100 miles an hour – or at 20 miles an hour in a 1948 Roadster. No music student could afford to rent even a shoebox in Redburn or Redesdale Street any more. I mourn none of this. All I regret is the way I misspent my youth, misspent meaning missed and pent up. It was a miserly withholding of which I am the more ashamed the more I think about it.

I drifted off along with Henry Berens to a maisonette above a garage in Pavilion Road, just behind Sloane Street, then when Henry got married, to an attic off the Earls Court Road, and finally to a roomier first-floor flat in Earls Court Square, the original of Patrick Hamilton's Hangover Square and still living up to its name twenty years later, certainly in my case. With each move I became a little more reclusive and feral, a little less rewarding to know, behaving a little worse and getting even less pleasure out of it. The low point comes when making someone else unhappy and not minding, or not minding enough, is your normal state of mind, almost the way you know you are still alive. There were only two things I thought might save me. One was going to America, famous for being the place to go if you wanted to get away from yourself. I tried that first. The second was getting married. I somehow knew, though I knew virtually nothing else worth knowing, that marriage was the last refuge of the undeveloped heart, the warm-water port that welcomes every iceberg. Marrying Julia was the end of my early life and the beginning of my present. It is impossible to recollect the present because it is still going on, which is why I do not intend to say anything about it here. Though two Julias have made my life, in this book there is only the first one.

After my father had his stroke, he lay unconscious in St George's Hospital, breathing with a clanking rattle like an old goods train. The doctors said he was unlikely to survive more than a few days and it would be better if he didn't because his brain was so badly damaged that life would not really be worth going on with. So I am not sure why they bothered to transfer him down to Atkinson Morley in Wimbledon which was tops for brain surgery. Going through the motions, I suppose. Anyway Atkinson Morley was where he stopped breathing. I went down the next morning to tidy things up.

'Would you like to see him?' The enquiry sounded strange, somehow reproachful, although I don't know what else the nurse could have said. Perhaps I was meant to have been quicker to make the request myself. Yes, I said, and followed her down the passage to the mortuary chapel. Dr Atkinson Morley had made a fortune in the hotel business in the 1850s after qualifying at St George's and he had left a large slice of it to finance this place out on Copse Hill as a convalescent home where patients could escape the smog and stench of Hyde Park Corner. Every Wednesday two black horse-drawn buses brought the peakier patients down here from St George's and took the revived ones back again, together with fresh fruit and veg from the gardens of Wimbledon. It was a high-tech hospital now but there was still something of the convalescent home about the pillared portico and the ivy-covered Second Empire façade, although my father only had a one-way ticket on the black bus.

How much smaller he looked, and pale as he had never been in life. The pallor brought out a refined, almost Spanish quality that had been hard to see in his ruddy old face, or perhaps that was just the waxiness. He had not been dead more than eight hours, yet it was already hard to imagine that he had ever been alive. I bent down to kiss him. What comes back to me now with a rush is not just the sadness and how cold his forehead was but the sense of being so terrifyingly alive myself, awash with sorrow, guilt, relief, resentment and half-a-dozen other things at once. For the first time I could see why people used to think (still do, I suppose, though not much in England) that at death the soul flies out of the body like a bird and migrates, perhaps only for a time, from the dead to the living, perching where it fancies. These days the cognitive scientists put it differently. Professor Douglas Hofstadter talks of 'loops of consciousness' that float free of the dead person and attach themselves to the mind-patterns of the living, so that there is 'an interpenetration of consciousnesses'. I prefer the migrating bird. Anyway that was how I felt, as though in Dr Atkinson Morley's chilly chapel I had myself taken on all my father's memories and habits of thoughts and affections and jokes – in a diffused and diminished form perhaps but still retaining enough power to break through my defences and become part of me. People often speak of feeling very strange after losing their father or mother. Even if they have got on badly with their parents or not seen much of them, they find themselves disoriented and vulnerable in a way they had not expected. They suppose it is because for the first time they really know themselves to be alone in the world, literally desolated. But I think there is even more to it than that. The direct experience of death as of birth has the power to open us up and expose our hearts. We feel at once intensely fragile and intensely alive. Now I had that direct experience as I had missed out on it thirteen years earlier when I lay dry-eyed on my bed at 50 Zugspitzstrasse after receiving the telegrams about my mother. I had felt a similar rush of feeling three months earlier in Queen Charlotte's Hospital when I held our first child in my arms, the awkward intensity recognisably the same though then provoked by joy rather than sadness. Mortality is as precious as it is tragic. How hard-hearted and dull-souled we would be if we were immortal. That is why the gods on Mount Olympus were so callous and bored, moved only by lust and anger, rather like a gated community of pop stars, emerging only at intervals to ravish and dazzle us lucky mortals. 'Birth, and copulation, and death, That's all the facts when you come to brass tacks,' sings Sweeney Agonistes. It seems quite enough to be going on with. These encounters with mortality, incoherent, wordless or nearly so, unmanning, mysterious, shake us out of our carapaces. How alike are the groans of love to those of the dying, the Consul in *Under the Volcano* mutters to himself at intervals during his last day on earth, and the phrase has stuck in my mind and still comes back to me at inappropriate idle moments, queuing for the check-out or sitting in the carwash. After my father died and we had our children, I never felt so cold again.

FORGING AHEAD

DEAR MR MOUNT,
I am disappointed to note that I have received no reply to my letter of February 19. As you will be aware, your overdraft has increased to a worrying extent over the past few months and at close of business on Friday stood at £2,143. The Bank of England has been anxious for some time now about excessive levels of borrowing in the economy and we would therefore appreciate an early reply explaining how you propose to remedy the position.

Things were getting desperate. It was flattering to be told that the Bank of England was worried too, but writing the Governor a letter to say how sorry I was to have caused him any anxiety would scarcely stave off the prospect of a row of bouncing cheques. It was remarkable that Barclays Bank, Salisbury, should have extended such a huge facility (not the right word surely; 'difficulty' would be the mot juste) to someone who had no money at all. At today's prices £2,143 would be £20,000 or more.

I had discovered the reason for this unusually easygoing attitude. The last time my father and I had had an interview with Barclays to discuss our financial problems I managed to read the bank manager's notes upside down across the desk and what the notes said was: 'W.R.F. Mount is the heir to Sir William Mount, Wasing Place, Aldermaston.' This clearly implied handsome expectations in the Jane Austen sense. That entirely erroneous impression can only have been fed to the manager by my father, an inveterate fantasist on this subject as on others. My peep across the manager's desk offered a useful insight into the gullibility of practical men. Nobody outside a bank who knew my father for five minutes would have thought his information on any such topic even faintly reliable. Anyway, as a result all through university and beyond, Barclays had treated me as a gilded heirling whose every whim must be accommodated with a reverent chuckle. Now the fantasy had worn thin and the reckoning had come. Something must be done.

Another Oxford acquaintance, Christopher Gwinner, had a flat round the corner from me, at 96 Oakley Street (where else?). There he gave strange dinner parties in honour of grand elderly ladies such as the famous decorator–hostess Nancy Lancaster. The elderly ladies were flattered to be made the centre of attention once again but something about the occasion would leave them – and indeed the rest of us – puzzled and unsettled. Christopher would be well aware of this and, sounding not particularly disappointed, would ring up the next day for a post-mortem: 'It was a disaster, wasn't it? She didn't enjoy herself at all.' His love life was equally uphill work.

'Do you know how many girls I've asked to sleep with me this year?'

'No, how many?'

'Thirteen.'

'And how many said yes?'

'Two.'

Like most other people of our age, he seemed anxious to settle down. For a time he went out with Q. who had gone out with quite a few men before him.

'Do you think I should marry Q.?'

'How should I know? Do you love her?'

'Oh yes, and we get on awfully well together.'

'Well then?'

'I just can't bear the thought of someone at the wedding reception saying Oh I slept with her in July 1961, and the other chap saying Oh really I think I must have had her about six months after that.'

Quite a bit later, two or three years, he fell in love with the beautiful olive-skinned Lorna, who was born in Singapore but whose parents were of Dutch descent.

'Do you think I should marry Lorna?'

By now I was getting fed up with this role of marriage guidance counsellor, one for which I was hopelessly ill equipped.

'How on earth can I say? Do you love her?'

'I really do, we get on amazingly well. But do you think everyone will go around saying Gwinner's married a half-caste?'

'No, I don't think they will,' I said wearily.

He managed to overcome this imaginary obstacle and married Lorna and was as happy almost ever after as someone of his mordant melancholy was capable of being.

Christopher's father, Commander Clive Gwinner, was said by Christopher to be the second most unpopular man in the Royal Navy (in fact he was a much decorated submariner hunter), but Christopher himself was a winning jester with his giant specs and big lips and fruity laugh, resembling some stand-up comedian who could hold his own in a Lancashire working men's club. He liked to remind me of the insecurities of his Jewish side.

'The only things worth collecting are small gold boxes.'

'You mean snuff boxes and so on? I think they're rather horrible objects.'

'Of course they are, but they're the only valuables small enough to put in your pocket when you have to crawl across the frontier in the middle of the night.'

As we passed the Ascot laundry on our way to play golf, Gwinner pointed to the smoking chimney of the laundry's boiler house and said, 'We honestly thought it was just a laundry, we had no idea that there were people in those vans, but of course they never believed us afterwards.'

He had already charmed his way on to the City pages of the *Daily Mail*, having made friends with the paper's proprietor, Lord Rothermere, through one of his grand dinner ladies. When I confided to him how desperately short of cash I was, he said, 'Don't worry, Esmond will give you a job like a shot, but you'll have to go down for a weekend at Daylesford first. He's very lonely since Annie left him and went off with Ian Fleming. It doesn't help that those James Bond books have been such a hit. Esmond feels a bit out of things.'

I was deeply impressed by this airy rundown of the situation. How could Lord Rothermere with his hundred newspapers be out of things (it seemed unimaginable that I should ever be on Esmonding terms even if I survived this terrifying weekend)? We tootled down through the Cotswolds in a second-hand two-seater that Gwinner had just acquired, a Morgan I think. As he ground through the gears and the engine did its best to imitate a full-throated roar of the sort expected, he added further details. Esmond was the third son of the first Rothermere, who was the original of Lord Copper in *Scoop*, and brother to Lord Northcliffe. Between them at one time or another Northcliffe and Rothermere had owned most of the newspapers in Fleet Street, dwarfing the Beaverbrook empire. Northcliffe, 'the Chief', had died raving mad and childless and Rothermere's two elder sons had been killed in the first war. So Esmond, aged nineteen and then a lieutenant in the Marines, became heir to the lot. His father bullied Lloyd George into taking him as an aide to the Versailles Peace Conference. Aged twenty-one, he became the youngest member of the House of Commons, succeeding in that role Oswald Mosley who had been elected the year before. Rothermere told the new Prime Minister Bonar Law that unless Esmond was given Cabinet rank he would withdraw the support of his newspapers – an empty threat, as Rothermere was a hardline Conservative and had nowhere else to go. Esmond never got a job in the Cabinet, though his father nearly wangled him the throne of Hungary, but that didn't quite work out either.

Daylesford, the house he had bought just after the second war to please his second wife, the one now married to the creator of James Bond, lies in one of the softer folds of the Cotswolds. Warren Hastings's father was rector there, and before the Hastings family slipped down in the world they had once owned the estate. As a boy, Warren Hastings had dreamed of reclaiming his own. The dream grew on him all the time he was governing Bengal and hoovering up the wealth of those steamy plains. Even during his agonisingly protracted trial for corruption and extortion, he was still waiting for the opportunity to buy back Daylesford, which in the end he did. Rothermere as a latterday nabob had filled the house with pictures and furniture to do with Hastings and the Raj.

The moment we screeched to a halt on the perfectly raked gravel, I was aware of the manicured desolation of the place. There was nobody in the hall, and the servant who let us in scuttled away as if he feared he might have made a mistake. The smaller sitting room we were not so much shown into as gestured towards was the impersonal sort of place you could have spent the rest of your life reading back numbers of *Country Life* in. The atmosphere did not exactly warm up when our host finally appeared. Immensely tall with sad blue eyes, Esmond greeted us with every possible friendliness, yet was unable to conceal a pervasive gloom, as though he had just come from the bedside of an old friend who was not expected to last long.

Other guests straggled in, all men and almost all connected in some way with his newspapers, old schoolfriends who sat on the board, managers at various levels, and a couple of journalists in the shape of Gwinner and me. The only person not actually on the payroll was a stockbroker called Kingsley who had played Davis Cup tennis and had been Esmond's partner when they won the Monte Carlo doubles in 1925. In the gents, there was a picture of them in tennis gear, Esmond tall and handsome, Kingsley half his size, looking nippy and vole-featured. Kingsley, by now like Esmond in his mid-sixties, had a perfectly good wife and family in Surrey but he usually came on his own. No doubt he had a perfectly good first name too, but I never heard it used. At dinner he would be stationed halfway down the table, apparently in order to relay Esmond's remarks to the junior members of the party, a quite unnecessary service as Rothermere's voice was carrying, even in its chilly way resonant.

'Lloyd George liked rascals, you know. He didn't care for respect-able people.'

'Esmond says Lloyd George liked rascals,' Kingsley would go.

This relaying slowed the conversation down, as though we were at an international conference with interpreters. Unfortunately Kingsley did not provide a service in the reverse direction which would have been more useful, since Esmond was a little deaf. So if one of us said, 'What about Churchill, did Churchill like rascals too?' there would be an awkward pause while Esmond asked his nearest neighbour to repeat the question before replying, 'Yes, Churchill liked rascals too, that's why he and Lloyd George got on so well.'

Kingsley would resume service. 'Esmond says Churchill liked rascals too.'

Occasionally Kingsley would add glosses of his own, for the benefit of new readers as it were.

'Esmond and Winston tried to prevent the Abdication, you know.'

This was a perilous departure from the script, for while Rothermere was exquisitely courteous to all his other guests (and called them all by their first names), he made an exception in Kingsley's case and regarded any independent comment from him as out of order.

'What's that, Kingsley?'

'I was just telling them, Esmond, how you and Winston tried to prevent the Abdication.'

'Rubbish. We did nothing of the sort.'

'Esmond says it's rubbish,' Kingsley loyally reported, although it was a more or less true summary of the facts, as Rothermere and Churchill had been the leaders of the 'King's Friends'.

All the same, Esmond had a sweet side which had not been effaced by half a century of being spoilt rotten. He was mostly liberal in his views, inheriting none of his father's rabid instincts, and did his best to live down the first Rothermere's flirtation with Mosley and the notorious *Daily Mail* headline 'Hurrah for the Blackshirts!' He was also well aware of his own shortcomings.

'My father was cold to me and I was cold to my own children.'

'Esmond says his father was cold to him and he was cold to his children but of course it's not true,' Kingsley glossed, struggling with the demands of relaying the party line and in the same breath loyally dissenting from it.

The lack of any women guests gave a muted, listless tone to proceedings. On Saturday morning the weekend seemed to stretch before us to the end of time. After breakfast Esmond took us on a walk round the lake. This picturesque *étang* had been created by damming the stream that ran down through the park. It was plagued by leaks and breaches in the dam. Esmond had had it drained and lined with PVC. Even so, the water level was sinking, or at any rate that was how it looked to Esmond's anxious eye. The delightful panorama of the vale of Daylesford stretching before us which had so entranced Warren Hastings had lost its power to distract him. We circled the lake for a second time, vainly trying to convince him that the rim of blanched vegetation marked the time when the lake had been deliberately drained and not a more recent seepage.

On Saturday evening the local nobs were invited over to a session in the house cinema where a new West End release, rushed down from London by despatch rider, would be shown. The viewers were arranged in the functional low-ceilinged room according to status: Esmond and Lord Blandford and Michael Astor and Loelia Duchess of Westminster and Mrs Niarchos in the front row, then the directors and senior managers of the *Daily Mail*, then Gwinner and me and any other junior staff and behind us at the back the Daylesford servants. The film was carefully chosen to appeal to the front row. We saw, for example, Anthony Asquith's *The Yellow Rolls-Royce* rather than *Last Year in Marienbad*, which also came out at the time. Even so, the front row seemed to have no idea how to behave in a cinema, or perhaps they regarded Esmond's cinema as merely an extension of his drawing room, so that at times it was difficult to distinguish the soundtrack from the dribble of upper-class chat in front of us.

'Sheemie says he's not speaking to Boofy after what happened at Chatsworth . . .'

'No, that was his second wife, his first wife was a Wardell-Yerburgh . . .'

One later weekend at Daylesford, the Saturday was the final of the World Cup, England versus Germany. None of the other guests had the slightest interest in football, but it was agreed that as a matter of social duty the party ought to watch the match, and a big television was wheeled into the cinema. Once again the commentary was intermittently drowned by the babble of the *gratin*, Loelia Duchess of Westminster being especially loquacious, though it was not then but on another occasion that I heard her utter the immortal remark 'Anyone who takes a bus after the age of thirty is a failure.' This remark has since been attributed to other legendary battleaxes including Margaret Thatcher and I suppose the Duchess may not have originated it, but I did hear her say it in the interval at Covent Garden, when I was summoned by Rothermere at short notice to make up a party to see Fonteyn and Nureyev in *Giselle*, another event that failed to engage her full attention. As the match progressed to its memorable climax, the non-fans talked more rather than less, having by now seen quite enough football to last them to the next World Cup and beyond, and so it was that we must have been almost the only household in England which failed to hear clearly Kenneth Wolstenholme saying, 'They think it's all over. It is now!'

All this would suggest, correctly, that Esmond did not have his finger on the pulse of the masses. He was perfectly competent at making money, but he was animated by few of the vulgar passions that fuel a successful press baron. While Northcliffe Newspapers grew fat on the profits of their provincial chain, the national titles dwindled into flimsy and insignificant sheets which were beginning to lose a lot of money. Esmond was unsuited to embark on any draconian programme of reform, being an unregenerate old-fashioned paternalist. He was reluctant to hear a word against the printers who were loathed by everyone else in Fleet Street for their bloodymindedness and envied for their enormous pay packets. All he would allow his managers to do was to reduce the number of pages, which inevitably accelerated the slide in circulation. But he remained assiduous in helping people out and giving the young a leg up, which is how I came to start work as a leader-writer – well, the leader-writer – on the *Daily Sketch* on 4 January 1965 at a salary of £2,500 a year, three times what I had ever earned before. Getting the *Sketch* job in this fashion established a pattern in my life which became a regular one. Every time I actually applied for a job, I failed ignominiously to get it. If there was any question of sending in a CV or undergoing a competitive interview, I was done for. My only avenue of survival was personal recommendation, my only method of arrival the parachute. I lived on the oxygen of influence.

The *Daily Sketch* had doom written all over it. Hobbled by gentility – or rather by Esmond's terror of being associated with the extremes of vulgarity – it was selling less than a million copies and heading south, long ago having given up all hope of catching its soaraway rival, the *Daily Mirror*. The *Sketch* was a tabloid for housemaids in an age when nobody except its proprietor could afford to employ housemaids. The editor, Howard French, took delivery of me with good-humoured resignation, like someone receiving a hideous vase from a rich aunt: 'Well, old boy, we could do with a bit of education round here.' Howard had been with the company for years. He looked like

Osbert Lancaster's Lord Littlehampton with droopy shoulders and a
luxuriant grey moustache of a type seldom seen in England since the
1890s. In the street he wore a bowler hat and a navy-blue raincoat
which gave him the air of someone performing an unpopular but
necessary public function like a bailiff or an inspector of some kind.
Unlike most editors I have known, he had an austere attitude to the
perks of office, his view of public transport being diametrically
opposed to that of Loelia Duchess of Westminster: 'Always travel
by bus, old boy, keeps you in touch with the people.' Years after I left
the paper, I would sometimes see him standing in all weathers at the
bus stop outside the Reuters building, looking quite unlike anyone
else in the queue. On the editorial floor too, he seemed detached
from the mayhem, wandering in his navy-blue cardigan with a
disconsolate mien down the narrow path between the desks. New
Carmelite House was an imposing, fairly modern building, smart
enough for the group's management to have chosen it for their HQ.
But the *Sketch* had managed to reduce the floor it occupied to the
cluttered squalor common to all newspaper offices in old Fleet Street.
I was squeezed into the assistant editors' room, a box enclosed by
reeded glass about twelve foot square which already had four desks in
it. In the corner, the sports editor was in conclave with an ancient
black man of dignified aspect who turned out to be the great West
Indian cricketer Sir Learie Constantine. 'One of them's writing the
Learie Constantine column for tomorrow but I'm not sure which of
them it is,' explained the politics editor, Louis Kirby, who had been
detailed to look after me and had been writing the leaders until I
arrived. Lou had black hair, a ruddy face and a naughty grin. He was
one of eleven children from Catholic Liverpool and like the Beatles
had the knack of making a slow, faintly mournful Scouse voice sound
seductive. He himself already had five children and was at present
carrying on with the delicious Heather Nicholson on the Diary. The
Diary table was only about two feet outside the glass door to our
office, so when Heather was reduced to tears by the strains of the
affair, I could hear her sobbing about three feet behind my head
before she came in to have it out with Lou. The absence of privacy
was overwhelming. Lou was also in charge of the specialist correspondents and when he called one of them to give him a rocket or, on

a couple of occasions, the sack, the victim would be sat down so close to me that I could feel him trembling while I pretended to be immersed in some galley proofs or reading the latest *New Statesman*.

On the dot of eleven o'clock Lou said, 'Time to show you the ropes.' He took me across the road to the White Swan, better known as the Mucky Duck, and gave me a pint of Guinness. 'It chills the stomach at this time in the morning, doesn't it? That's why you need a chaser.' So we each had a double Scotch to warm us up. Then we went back for the morning conference.

'Why haven't we got a story about the flu epidemic?'

'John says there isn't a flu epidemic, Howard. The BMA's quite positive about it.'

'Look, old boy, everyone's got the bloody flu, my secretary's got the flu, my wife's got the flu. Readers will want to know why we haven't got a story about the flu epidemic.'

After conference Lou said we ought to go out to lunch to celebrate my arrival. David Campbell, the mercurial young features editor who was about my age, came with us, complaining that he hadn't been able to get out for a jar all morning. As we sat down, he downed a couple of large Scotches, so we had two gin and tonics each to keep him company. In the Forum restaurant in Chancery Lane we had a couple of bottles of Muscadet with the moules marinières and some red burgundy with the boeuf stroganoff and then a couple of brandies rather quickly because David had to get back to start remaking the early features pages. It was a real skill on a popular paper then, designing and pasting up a run of pages, so that each page looked enticing in a different way. David would toss discarded schemes into the wastepaper basket with the groans of a frustrated artist. Then we had evening conference.

'Where's the flu epidemic story? I don't see it on your news list.'

'John says he can't make it stand up.'

'Well, tell him he's got to bloody make it stand up. Either we run a story or we get a new medical correspondent.'

John Stevenson, the medical correspondent, was a cheerful character with crinkly hair and specs who always bounced into the room shouting, 'Stand by your beds.' He became almost my best friend on the paper. I never guessed that he suffered from intermittent depression. He did talk of going to work on another paper where they took medical matters seriously, but he never did.

After conference I produced my piece. It was about the New Year fare rises on British Rail and Harold Wilson's instant dismissal of Dr Beeching. It was 225 words long. Later leaders might be up to 250 or even 300 words, depending on space, never more.

'That's bloody good, old boy. Strong, don't you think it's strong, Lou?'

'Very strong, Howard,' said Lou who had confided to me that he was longing not to have to do the leaders any more.

We went out to the pub to have a couple more G and Ts to celebrate my first contribution to the paper. Then I excused myself and went home to Earls Court and wasn't quite sick. Oddly enough, I don't remember feeling sick during my early days at the *Sketch*, not like I had so often felt sick at Oxford after overdoing it. What I did have quite often was a terrifying pumping feeling as though my heart was making a run for it. I would get this feeling without warning as I came out of the pub door or skipped to dodge a paper van hurtling round the corner to catch the first-edition train. Even now the sight of a newspaper van rattling down the street on a wet night has the power to revive that sensation of apoplectic panic.

I had none of the essential gifts of a genuine newspaperman, such as cheek, ratlike cunning (the first essential according to the late Nick Tomalin), insatiable inquisitiveness, or the ability to ask awkward questions. But I could turn out a tolerable leader to order – a skill not highly regarded among true reporters, Comment being in their eyes only one rung above Gossip, but luckily indispensable on even the least ambitious paper. If ever you want to know what an expensive classical education fits you for, it is for writing 250-word leaders in a tabloid newspaper. Years of imitating the Odes of Horace, translating the orations of Cicero, construing Book V of the *Iliad* – all these come together to instil the lapidary and laconic skills required. It was a relief to have discovered a branch of journalism that I could manage. In my only previous experience of Fleet Street – a nine-month stint as dogsbody on the *Sunday Telegraph* Albany column – I had been mystified by the trade. My boss, Kenneth Rose, had briefly been a schoolmaster at Eton and something of the schoolmaster clung to his witty–prickly persona. He was a legendary diner-out and clubman, which was a useful cover for his subversive and scholarly biographies of Curzon and George V. As in the case of his rival Philip Ziegler, the Establishment had become so accustomed to regard him as one of their own that they failed to notice when he removed their trousers. But I was not made for the Gossip trade, even the refined end of it as practised by Kenneth. I trembled every time he told me to ring up some general to ask whether it was true he was about to be made colonel-in-chief of his regiment or to ask some ancient diplomat if he had any recollections of Ribbentrop or Ernest Bevin. Nor had I the slightest clue how to compose any item in a style that Kenneth would tolerate. Every paragraph I submitted was either too stale or too vulgar or just simply 'didn't make a par'. On the *Sketch* by contrast, every-thing I offered was greeted as a masterpiece. The sterner sort of schoolmaster had always been quick to denounce my fatal facility. Here facility was the name of the game, in fact a much apter name than when used by the manager of Barclays Bank, Salisbury.

Admittedly Lou had managed to acquire the same skills free of charge at Coalbrookdale High School. On top of that he could at a moment's notice compose the most vivid and poignant tribute to any much-loved personality who had inconsiderately died half an hour before the first edition was due off stone. Gradually I acquired some of the dark arts of colour writing but I could never come close to Louis Albert Francis Kirby, and certainly not after drinking the equivalent of eighteen units every day. What I did realise was that the only way my liver and I had any chance of long-term survival was not to clock on until after lunch and to leave as soon as my piece had been approved, which made for a shortish working day. Besides, I tended to run out of things to say in pubs, more from an ingrained stiffness than because

I was the only person on the paper who had been to university, let alone a public school. With all my expensive education I seemed to be spending most of my time with two classes of people who had never been near higher education: debutantes and popular journalists. Both categories I found a lot more congenial and less pleased with themselves than my fellow graduates, especially those working on the better class of newspaper. These days the tabloids are full of graduates and most upper-class girls go to university. It would be nice to think that both institutions are more refined as a result but I rather doubt it.

After a few months of these featherlight duties I began to fear that my sloth would catch up with me and I needed to offer the paper a bit more if I was not to be on the receiving end of black looks as I swanned in so late and swanned out again so early. Ted Heath had just been elected leader of the Conservative Party and it was coming up to Harold Wilson's first anniversary as Prime Minister. How about an interview with each of the three party leaders? I suggested. Splendid idea, old boy, responded Howard, sounding under-whelmed but aware that this was the kind of thing he ought to be encouraging.

I tackled Jo Grimond first. He was still on his summer holiday in Orkney. Couldn't I send him some questions and he would post me the answers? Not exactly the face-to-face grilling I had envisaged, but it was a start. Harold Wilson, by contrast, was only too eager to give me a personal *tour d'horizon*. He received me at the bizarre time of 9 p.m. on Saturday night in the study at Number Ten which was darkened because most of the lighting system had fused. The atmo-sphere was rendered more sinister still by the fact that the Prime Minister was wearing a large black eyepatch. The single lamp that was still functioning gave a weird cinematic effect. It was as though I had tracked down some war criminal in his last redoubt. 'Sorry about this,' Harold Wilson said, gesturing at the eyepatch, 'I've got a rather nasty stye in my eye.' He was charm itself. When my tape recorder ran out and I couldn't work out how to load the fresh tape, he and his press secretary fixed it in no time, showing that his talk about the white heat of technology was not just a figure of speech. 'First-rate questions,' he said at the end as he shook my hand and adjusted the eyepatch which had begun to slip down his cheek. I began to think that I might have a future as a political interviewer.

The following Tuesday I had a 6.30 slot with Mr Heath in his flat in Albany. 'Sorry, I'm afraid there's a bit of a queue. Would you like a glass of sherry?' His private secretary handed me a bumper of Tio Pepe and sat me down in an anteroom lined with watercolours and political cartoons. Twenty minutes later he came in and said the photographers were taking ages and gave me another bumper of sherry. Then a quarter of an hour after that, he said that something that couldn't wait had just come up and it would be better if I went away and came back in half an hour. So I walked across Piccadilly and knocked on the door of my friend, the budding impresario Michael White, who had just rented a flat in Duke Street to impress other impresarios. Michael gave me a large gin and tonic and then said, 'I expect you'll need another one if you're going to see that awful man.' Then I returned to Albany where the thing that had just come up was still going on, so I had another bumper of sherry. The sherry tasted awful after the gins. Finally, 'Ah he's ready for you now.' In I went and there was Ted in a jersey that was too tight for him and a fractious air. 'I expect you'd like a glass of sherry,' he said grumpily. I took the glass and put it down with a clump on the little glass table in front of me. It didn't quite break but he jumped up like a dolphin and wiped the surface with his handkerchief before whisking a little rubber coaster under my glass. I was so unnerved by this implied rebuke that I began my questions in the wrong order, starting with one about Rhodesia, then darting off on to taxation, then back to Rhodesia, then asking whether he got much time for sailing now before another question about the Import Surcharge, or was it the Selective Employment Tax? Worse still, after the best part of a bottle of sherry, not to mention the gins, I was finding it hard to concentrate on his answers. After he refilled my glass, I stopped taking notes at all and began staring vaguely at his grand piano. There was a pause. I had lost anything resembling a thread. Struggling to find words of any sort, I mumbled something like 'Do you think that Mr Wilson has to some extent . . .' It was going to be a long time before I got to the end of that sentence and it was almost a relief when he interrupted me and said, fixing me with a glare that combined loathing and contempt, 'I didn't realise this was going to be such a superficial interview.'

Naturally none of this found its way into the pieces I submitted to Howard French. Each in its way was largely fabricated. The Jo Grimond one implied without actually asserting a rather congenial physical meeting, while the Heath encounter sounded like a lively ding-dong in which I gave as good as I got.

'First-rate copy, old man,' said Howard, not so much twirling his moustaches as massaging them. 'Only trouble is, we would have to run them next week and we don't have a slot for a three-parter because we've just managed to get Ann Sidney's life story, dull girl of course but she's the first British Miss World ever and we're putting on 100,000 extra copies.' No more was heard of my interviews, or of my interviewing anyone else.

The following Monday my old Deauville employer Mary Ohrstrom invited me to have dinner with them at Claridge's. Rising from the lower depths of Fleet Street to the haunts of the plutocracy was a strain rather than a relief. Changing into my dinner jacket in the gents at the *Sketch* I felt ill-fitted for either milieu and would much rather have been at home watching TV. Nor was I cheered up when I came into the Ohrstroms' suite to see, to my complete surprise, the tall figure of my present employer and patron Lord Rothermere. The evening turned out to be an awkward one all round. Mary seemed to be getting on badly with her husband Ric senior and made the friction worse by responding with girlish giggles to Esmond's lumbering compliments. After dinner Ric played old Cole Porter numbers on the piano, banging the keys and singing along in a raucous voice which took the sophisticated charm out of the lyrics. While he was hammering out the twirly bits on the keys, he bawled at the rest of us to sing along but there were no takers. Mary took me aside.

'Oh it's so embarrassing, Esmond's such a flirt. I do wish he wouldn't, it upsets Ric so.'

As usual I completely failed to decode the situation, being stupefied with embarrassment at my employer's crass behaviour. So I was astonished when only a few months later the *Daily Sketch*, which always gave prominence to Harmsworth family doings, as though it was their private court circular, which indeed it was, reported on page three, 'Lord Rothermere weds', and there was a picture of Esmond and Mary coming out of the register office. He being about eighteen inches taller than she was, the photo bore a slight resemblance to the picture of Esmond and Kingsley in the gents at Daylesford, although obviously they weren't in tennis kit. I was dazzled by the speed of the disentangling. A Mexican divorce had apparently enabled Ric to marry his long-term mistress, which left Mary free to hitch up with Esmond who was a mere thirty years older than she was. To me they seemed the most ill-assorted couple you could imagine, both of them in their different ways capable of generating a fair amount of unease but not, as it turned out, in each other. She bought a yak to graze in the park at Daylesford, because Warren Hastings had brought a yak back from India. Its mournful posture in the middle distance was somehow reassuring. I began to feel a certain kinship with the yak as I too was now the boss's pet.

After a couple of months at the *Sketch* I was now and then given a feature to work up into an article with my name on it. 'Here's one for you, Ferd. Some screws at the Scrubs say George Blake's being given special treatment. Looks like a good tale.'

The letter, signed only 'Five Prison Officers', did indeed tell an extraordinary tale. They alleged that discipline at Wormwood Scrubs was now so lax that prisoners regularly hopped over the wall for a weekend with their girlfriends and that the spy George Blake, who was serving the longest sentence ever handed down by a British court – forty-two years – was being given the most lavish special privileges, including afternoon tea off Dresden china in his beautifully carpeted cell with his fellow spies John Vassall and Gordon Lonsdale and the notorious fraudster Kenneth de Courcy, alias the Duc de Grantmesnil, along with an Irish bomb-maker by the name of Sean Bourke who was the editor of the prison magazine, puckishly entitled *New Horizon*. The prison officers enclosed several copies of the magazine to show how it was running a campaign to whitewash Blake, deploying the old argument that spying wasn't really a crime. It was a scene straight out of *Porridge* (then not yet in existence), with the role of Grouty being played by the appalling Blake, whose sentence was popularly supposed to reflect the forty-two British agents whose deaths he was responsible for. I gave the story the full *Sketch* treatment under the headline 'STRANGE . . . GEORGE BLAKE'S NEW FRIENDS', although in truth the letter was so lurid it did not need

much embellishing: 'Tea cups clatter in the cell of George Blake, the man whose treachery placed the lives of many British agents in jeopardy . . .'

'You don't think we ought to check whether it's all true,' I enquired when showing the piece up to Lou Kirby.

'No, no,' Lou said, 'that would be fatal. They'll just deny it, might even slap an injunction on us.'

So out it came and very stirring it looked. The prison Governor instantly denied there was any truth in the report and denounced the *Sketch* for not having checked the facts. That was to be expected. What was less expected was that Sean Bourke made a formal complaint to the Press Council. In the subsequent inquiry he produced evidence to show that both the letter and the copies of *New Horizon* that had been sent to us were forgeries. Everything alleged in my article, he claimed, was false. He had never planned any campaign with Blake and de Courcy to whitewash Blake's crimes; he had never drunk tea in Blake's cell and had never been in the cell at the same time as de Courcy. As we had no evidence at all to back up the letter and prove the magazines genuine, the Press Council had no alternative but to uphold Mr Bourke's complaint and deplore in the strongest terms the 'irresponsible conduct' of the *Daily Sketch*. To my surprise nobody on the paper, except me, was the least bit chastened. Everyone else continued to believe that what the warders had said was true, or near enough to the truth to have been worth printing.

As a result of some organisational reshuffle, I was moved down the corridor to share an office with Fergus Cashin, the paper's star columnist. Fergus was a brawny great Irishman with twinkling greeny-blue eyes. He looked like a horse-coper in a Jack Yeats painting and he wrote in a wild overblown way that burst the bounds of tabloid prose, sometimes achieving an almost Joycean level of incomprehensibility. We shared a secretary, a handsome distracted girl, who didn't bother to distinguish whether the call was for Fergie or Ferdy before passing one of us the phone.

'Is that you then, I'm amazed you're still alive after last night,' I would hear a smoky woman's voice breathing down the line.

'Who's that? This is Ferdy,' I would say stiffly.

'What are you putting on that snotty voice for, my darling?'

Three or four weeks after the Press Council had roasted us, I heard about the Aberfan disaster on the morning news. By the time I reached New Carmelite House Fergus was on his way to South Wales. By five o'clock his copy was pouring in to the copytakers: 'Black, awful, awesome Friday. The day a slag cinder mountain moving in a river of filth turned this valley into a valley of tears. Never, ever has there been such a tragedy. Wars and even the most bloody explosion of nature have never been so selective in their slaughter,' and so on, no doubt until the copytaker uttered the immortal dampener before going on to a new sheet, 'Is there much more of this?' There was. In the centre spread alone, the phrase 'valley/vale of tears' occurred three times. All the same, I found myself near tears as Lou showed me the copy he had so brilliantly woven together for the splash. Although I tried to conceal it, he could see how moved I was. 'It's not that good,' he muttered, embarrassed by my failure to maintain the proper hard-boiled composure but a little touched himself as he took the copy from me. Later he married Heather and had two more children, then a few years after that he interviewed another girl called Heather for work experience and married her instead and had two more children, making nine in all, his two latter wives being known as Heather One and Heather Two. At his funeral in 2006 – he reached the improbably ripe age of seventy-seven – his final father-in-law in a touching tribute praised Lou's faithfulness. On the face of it, not exactly the right word, but I knew what he meant. His capacity for fondness amounted to a kind of faithfulness, loosely construed.

The day after the Aberfan disaster, George Blake hopped over the wall and escaped from Wormwood Scrubs with the help of a nylon rope ladder and an ingenious accomplice on the outside. The accomplice was Sean Bourke, who had been released on parole that summer. They had concocted the plan while they were together in the Scrubs. The escape was all the more scandalous because the furore about lax prison security had been going on for months after the separate escapes of the train robbers Charlie Wilson and Ronnie Biggs. The Governor of the Scrubs had begged the Home Office to transfer Blake to a maximum-security prison, but the Home Office refused and at the time of his escape Blake was still in D wing, the easiest part of the jail to escape from. The nation was too preoccupied by the terrible news of Aberfan to take very much notice of Blake's escape, until he turned up in Moscow with Bourke. The subsequent report into prison security by Lord Mountbatten, not to mention Bourke's own account, *The Springing of George Blake*, confirmed that pretty much everything the five prison officers had alleged was true, down to the Bokhara carpet in Blake's cell. Sometimes the worst thing about irresponsible journalism is that people refuse to believe it.

The *Sketch* continued to coast downhill, but by then I had been transferred to a similar role on the *Daily Mail*. Lord Rothermere, now enjoying something closely resembling happiness with his third wife, proposed this to me as though conferring a post of almost unimaginable power and prestige. In fact, the *Mail* was going downhill, if anything, even faster than the *Sketch* and was as out of date as the coal fire in the grate of the office I took over from my predecessor George Murray, a man of great age and charm who had started work in the same office thirty years earlier, the day after the Reichstag fire. The office I inherited was panelled in light oak with bookshelves inset in the panelling. On the shelves were pre-war books on world affairs with titles like *The Stormclouds Gather* by legendary foreign correspondents such as Wickham Steed and G. Ward Price. I had fallen into a time warp. As I poked the fire and waited for the lady in the apron to bring round tea and biscuits, I might have been about to compose a thoughtful leader on the League of Nations or the crisis in Manchuria rather than grappling with the miners' strike and the prices and incomes policy. It could not last. The truth was that I had merely been winched across from one sinking ship to another. And it was not long before the survivors of the wreck of the *Sketch* joined us in the new combined paper which was to be called the *Daily Mail* but was to be a tabloid. All of which sounded like and was a desperate measure. They would have closed both papers if it hadn't been for Esmond's son Vere Harmsworth who had just taken over from Esmond and didn't want to be remembered as the chairman who trashed the family heirloom. By some mixture of luck and judgement, the new team had hit upon the right formula in advance of its time. To read the back numbers of the early tabloid *Mail* is in one sense to step into a world which now seems almost as remote as the 1920s. 'Coloured man to read news' is one headline and he was only going to read it on radio. Princess Margaret lights up a cigarette at Wimbledon, Christiaan Barnard transplants hearts. But the actual format of the paper is amazingly familiar, and has changed hardly at all in the succeeding thirty-five years or so. Some of the main contributors have lasted most or all of that time, such as Patrick Sergeant and John Edwards and Nigel Dempster and Keith Waterhouse and Ian Wooldridge and Andrew Alexander. I have to concede through gritted teeth that the credit goes to the editor who came with the other survivors from the *Sketch*, David English. As a rule, great editors are not lovable, and English was a great editor. His choirboy grin concealed, well, didn't really conceal an arctic temperament, for if as Graham Greene said every novelist needs an icicle in his heart, a successful editor needs a small iceberg.

The new paper gradually righted itself and began slowly to steam forward. The same cannot be said of all its staff. Quite a few found the demands now placed on them too intense to bear. The managing editor, John Golding, at best a nervous, even frantic character, disappeared. At first it was feared that he had absconded with the petty cash, but everything seemed to be in order. For a few months there were reports that he had been sighted, at various resorts on the south coast, or with a mysterious companion. Then the trail went cold, and we concentrated on more famous people who were disappearing at the time like Lord Lucan and John Stonehouse MP. Then my friend John Stevenson disappeared too. And he was found, or rather his body was, sitting bolt upright on the slopes of Box

Hill. His depression might have had that tragic result in any circumstances, I suppose, but it was not exactly an encouraging sign. I
decided that somehow or other I had to get out. The trouble is that
the demand elsewhere for my services was invisibly small. I tried to get
some academic job teaching politics, but Reading, Brunel and the
LSE all made it clear that they wanted someone who was both
younger and had a respectable academic track record. I decided at any
rate to commit myself to change things by going part-time. I would
wander in two or thee days a week to do the leader, which naturally
reduced my pay but enabled me to con myself into thinking that I
wasn't exactly *on* the *Mail* any more.

At least this dribbling existence came to an end in a spectacular
fashion. 'Here, come into my office and have a look at this, and don't
say a word.' David English could scarcely keep the grin off his face.
This was one of the times that I did warm to him, when he was hot on
the scent and his icy calculating self was swept to one side. He showed
me a letter from Lord Ryder of Eaton Hastings, the chairman of the
National Enterprise Board, to Alex Park, the chief executive of the
then nationalised British Leyland company. At first I couldn't make
much sense of it. What was all this stuff about special payments and
the Secretary of State nodding them through? 'It's the biggest slush
fund in the world,' David chortled. 'Look here, eleven million quid
last year, even more this. BL are having to bribe the bloody foreigners
to buy their cars.' As I got the hang of the whole pile of documents,
David's enthusiasm took hold of me too. I was talked through them
by his deputy, the irrepressible Stewart Steven, who was mastermind-
ing the story. Stewart loved conspiracies and scandals. He was one of
several to have discovered the present whereabouts of Martin Bor-
mann. Some people said that he was an undercover agent for Mossad,
a rumour which he encouraged at every possible opportunity. He had
been born Stefan Cohn in Hamburg and had come to England as a
six-year-old refugee. He adopted the most outrageous parody of an
English gent wearing loud pinstriped or Prince of Wales check suits
and talking in a fruity toffish voice. With his shiny black built-up
shoes and his exuberant whoops of 'Preposterous, my dear fellow,' he
was irresistible. I have never met anyone who enjoyed being a
journalist more. Carried away by Stewart's gusto, I rushed off to

compose a suitably stirring leader to accompany the story: 'There can be no excuses. British Leyland's practice of bribery is illegal and immoral. And it must stop. The hypocritical face of socialism has replaced the unacceptable face of capitalism. If this is "National Enterprise", it is the enterprise of the Artful Dodger.'

One of my better efforts, I thought. Stewart's front-page story, headlined 'WORLDWIDE BRIBERY WEB BY LEYLAND', was even more striking. The next morning there was a glorious explosion all over Fleet Street. Every paper followed up our exclusive, the broadsheets with sombre leading articles no less condemnatory than the one I had written. We were basking in self-satisfaction. There was just one tiny snag. British Leyland did not deny the authenticity of the heap of documents we had produced – how could they? But Don Ryder did deny and deny most strenuously that he had ever written the letter round which the story centred. The letterhead was not his normal one; he never put 'Lord Ryder of Eaton Hasting Bt', since he was not a baronet but a knight. Nor, I uneasily realised as one who pretended to know about such things, did any other peer ever include the lesser honour of baronet in his address. Nor, Ryder continued, would he ever have allowed a letter to go out with three gross spelling mistakes: 'recieved', 'fundamently' and 'dagerous'. The letter was a crude forgery. By the evening of the next day, a discontented middle-ranking BL financial executive called Graham Barton confessed to the forgery. Calamity. David English offered to resign. Stewart Steven offered to resign. I couldn't offer to resign since I wasn't on the staff any more. But it was at my leading article that Jim Callaghan directed his fiercest fire during Prime Minister's questions the following Tuesday: 'I thought both the presentation of the news and the comments that were made in the editorial were a contemptible display of political spite.'

By now morale at the *Mail* was so shattered that we scarcely noticed how carefully Callaghan had avoided denying the charges of bribery. Other MPs were so keen to stamp on the bleeding corpse of the *Daily Mail* while they had the chance that they missed the chance to quiz the government on the substance of the accusations. I took my shattered little lance off and did nothing very much until I was rescued from sloth and penury by Alexander Chancellor who had just become editor of the *Spectator* and needed someone to write about politics. At 56 Doughty Street I was cosseted and indulged. Part of Alexander's genius as an editor was that once he had chosen his writers he let them rip. Quite soon I had forgotten all the traumas and humiliations I had endured while slaving in the Rothermere galleys, including this last and most humiliating of all.

Thirty years later, government files obtained under the Freedom of Information Act revealed that the British Leyland story was in all essentials true. Soon after the forgery was exposed, Denis Healey, then Chancellor, told a handful of colleagues gathered over lunch at Chequers that 'there was no doubt that bribery had been going on for years on a large scale in the Middle East and Africa and that organisations responsible to government (including defence sales and nationalised industries) had been involved'. About 10 per cent of overseas trade involved practices which would be considered improper in Britain. A private report to ministers established that Leyland had been running an offshore slush fund based in Lausanne, especially to sell overpriced Land Rovers to the Saudis. This report was hushed up, with the agreement of Jim Prior, the Opposition spokesman. Such payments became explicitly illegal in 2002. But they still go on apparently, from BAE Systems to the Saudis, according to a scandal that went on running hot and strong into the last years of the Blair government. In November 2006, the Attorney-General instructed the Serious Fraud Office to discontinue its inquiries into the allegations of bribery, on the grounds that these inquiries might prejudice national security, or in other words were likely to annoy the Saudis so much that they might not only cancel defence contracts worth billions but also undermine Allied efforts in Iraq.

Ever since, I have been rather sympathetic to people who are conned by forgeries, or by fraudsters. It is so easy to be fooled when you want to believe. David English survived to edit the paper successfully for many more years. Stewart Steven went on to become a respected editor of the *Evening Standard*, as did Lou Kirby. The Prime Minister and the Leader of the Opposition both attended Stewart's memorial service. Old Fleet Street was always good at rehabilitating its rogues, and rightly so. Journalism was never meant to be a respectable trade, which is why I landed up in it.

SELWYN AND KEITH
AND MARGARET

'You will find Selwyn a very modest man.' It sounded unlikely. The general picture of Selwyn Lloyd then was of a stiff-necked, prickly, rather off-putting figure. The description of him came from my boss Michael Fraser, who had known him for years (they had both been to that dour academy Fettes College, along with Iain Macleod, though not all at the same time). It was Fraser who had picked me out to be Selwyn's personal assistant on his inquiry into party organisation. Well, perhaps picked out is overdoing it – I was the junior recruit at the Conservative Research Department and so far hadn't been given anything much to do, apart from churning out a few pamphlets for party workers, so I could easily be spared.

I trotted along Old Queen Street and Petty France the short distance to Selwyn's flat in Buckingham Gate, 230 St James's Court. Although purpose-built in the 1890s for the humdrum purpose of service flats, St James's Court is one of the most exotic buildings in London. Outside it is a mixture of redbrick Tudor and Pont Street Dutch, but its inner courtyard is a riot of faience friezes in bright jade and primrose, telling Shakespearean tales with elves and fairies and caryatids all over the place. It is as though this startling exuberance was deliberately designed to compensate for the impersonal apartments, the gloomy passages and stairways and the workaholic lives that would be led in them. Selwyn's was the first politician's flat I had ever visited and I was struck by how cheerless and functional it was, a machine for living in, a couple of armchairs, a drinks cupboard, a signed photo of the Queen, a signed photo of President Eisenhower from pre-Suez days, a rather anaemic drawing of Selwyn himself, not much else. To be fair, he can only have been there a few weeks. It was no more than three months since Macmillan had thrown him out of Number 11 in the Night of the Long Knives. But he never did much to lighten the place up later and I never noticed him take the slightest interest in his surroundings.

The moment he said hullo, I could see exactly what Michael Fraser meant. Selwyn was wearing his standard indoor kit, beige cardigan, the grey pinstripe trousers of his double-breasted suit made of a cloth which always looked heavier than anyone else's suit and tennis shoes to rest his feet. He had a ruffled, sad look as though bad news had only just reached him and it was an effort to be as friendly as he wanted to be. Above all he gave off a pervasive modesty, in which the only element of pride was a pride in being inconspicuous.

Being sacked was not the only disaster that had overtaken him. At the age of forty-seven, he had married Bae Marshall. The marriage lasted only five years. I don't know how you pronounce Bae (Bee I expect) because he never spoke of her. She was the daughter of friends who lived just across the links at Hoylake from Dr Lloyd's house at 27 Stanley Road, overlooking the famous short 13th hole described by the poet Patric Dickinson as 'jiggety, tricky, witty, deplorable', which is surely too many adjectives for a hole on a golf course. Bae was half his age, Selwyn himself was highly apprehensive about the wedding and Selwyn's youngest sister could see disaster looming. It was not just the disparity in ages. Selwyn was still essentially living with his parents at Stanley Road, lodging in London in a flat in Eccleston Square belonging to his political friend Bill Aitken. He had never had a serious girlfriend. And he really wasn't at ease in the company of women. In fact this was almost the first thing I noticed about him, because along with me from the Research Department to help out came Michael Fraser's assistant secretary, Diana Leishman.

Diana was the nearest I have ever seen in the flesh to the ideal girl described in the early novels of P. G. Wodehouse. She had hair the colour of ripe corn, which gently bounced like corn blowing in the breeze, a tip-tilted nose (essential for Wodehouse heroines) and a beaming smile that made strong men go weak at the knees. There was a suggestion of plumpness about her figure, just the suggestion, no more. I could not help looking up every time she came into the room. I also could not help noticing that Selwyn did not. He was not in the least frosty to her, in fact they got on very well, and after our assignment was finished she stayed on to be his private secretary. But her presence did not stir him.

At the time Diana and I signed on, the only person doing Selwyn's secretarial chores was Bill Aitken's son Jonathan, who had just left Oxford and came in a couple of days a week to help out. I was sitting in one of Selwyn's oatmeal-coloured armchairs when he appeared for the first time.

'Jonathan!' Selwyn leaped up. His face, his whole being was radiant. His affection was so immediate, so intense, that I could not help being overcome by it too, although I knew Jonathan a bit and was already suspicious of him, mostly because he was so appallingly handsome, as dazzling in his way as Diana was. He had been a slow starter with girls – he had even asked Noel Picarda to act as a sort of Cyrano to ease his path with one of the belles of Lady Margaret Hall, the last man anyone would choose for such a delicate role – but now Jonathan instantly bowled over anyone of either sex.

As was natural with any man who had stayed a bachelor until his late forties, the political world speculated and lucubrated about what Selwyn was like in that department. Lady Pamela Berry, wife of the *Daily Telegraph*'s proprietor and a hostess who picked up Tory MPs the moment they got into the Cabinet and then tossed them aside like used napkins after they fell, claimed that Selwyn had told her he did not much care for sex. The same could not be said for Pam Berry who for a time was famously energetic, several journalists and politicians who frequented her salon graduating with honours. Among them was my old mentor Malcolm Muggeridge who had been deputy editor of the *Daily Telegraph* for a time in the early 1950s and went out with her for a bit, a high-end office romance. 'Went out with' is the right phrase for once to apply to the day trip they took from Scarborough during the 1952 Conservative Party Conference. They spent the afternoon up on the bee-loud moors round Fylingdales (no early-warning station then to spy on their manoeuvres). They returned to the Grand Hotel for a well-earned tea. As they walked through the lounge, the assembled journalists could not help noticing that the back of Lady Pamela's cashmere twinset was still covered with sprigs of heather in full bloom.

Such excursions were not up Selwyn's street. On the other hand, it is not clear whether he was ever gay in the active sense. Tony Booth, the 'scouse git' in *Till Death Us Do Part* and father to Cherie Blair, claimed that as a young man he was walking along the Mall one night and Selywn emerged out of the shadows and recklessly asked him back to Carlton Gardens for a drink. I don't put much more credence in this story than in Lady Pamela's, because Selwyn seemed to me too shy to say or do such things. In fact his shyness was the most remarkable thing about him. It was the shyness of an old-fashioned bachelor, a category which rightly recognised that there were men – and women too – for whom reticence and celibacy amounted to a sexual programme as valid as any other. Modesty in every sense of that interesting word.

I do not mean that Selwyn went in for false modesty. In fact he didn't talk much about himself at all. And when he did, he was utterly realistic. He possessed, as few public men I have ever met, an exact appreciation of himself. His patience, tenacity and hard work were not to be undervalued. But he did not pretend to talents he did not have. He spoke with little facility and wrote with less: a speech or an article meant discarded pieces of paper scrumpled all round the room. He never got round to writing his memoirs, which he said he was going to call *A Middle-Class Lawyer from Liverpool*, because that was how Harold Macmillan referred to him during one of their frequent spats. Supermac also called him 'the Little Attorney'. Bernard Levin in his celebrated Taper columns for the *Spectator* called him 'Hoylake UDC', because Selwyn had been chairman of his local council throughout most of the 1930s. He was used to being patronised. He didn't care. He was proud of the things he was patronised for being.

His loyalty was what he was most praised for, but this too was a form of condescension from those who found loyalty a quality of limited value in their own lives. He was loyal to Anthony Eden and never expressed any resentment that he had been led into a course of deceit by that vain, hysterical, serious-minded prima donna (can you be a serious-minded prima donna? Yes, I think you can and Eden certainly was). A few months before Eden married his second wife, the cool and witty Clarissa Churchill, Selwyn had been a guest at a house party given by John Wyndham at Petworth, which included Clarissa. He had been horrified by the way everyone present had said how ghastly Eden was, while Selwyn stuck up loyally for his boss. When the engagement was announced, the others desperately tried to cover their tracks, but Selwyn had no malicious words to swallow. As it happens, a year or so earlier, my father too had met Clarissa at a party in Wiltshire where she had a cottage at Broadchalke called Rosebower.

'Do you think I should marry Anthony Eden?' she asked quite out of the blue.

'Well, that's surely for you to decide,' my father said primly, no keener than I ever was to be conscripted as a marriage guidance counsellor. In any case, he did not know Clarissa that well.

'Everyone keeps telling me I should, but the trouble is he's such a bore.'

In fact the marriage was a huge success. Three years on, Eden, by then Prime Minister, had been triumphantly returned to office after a general election campaign in which he was deluged with bunches of daffodils by adoring female fans. Soon afterwards he had scored another triumph at the Geneva Summit. He had retired to Broad-chalke for a well-deserved rest. By chance my parents' friend Tony Rumbold was his Private Secretary and lived only a few miles away. Pop-eyed, genial Rumbum was, like Eden, a keen tennis player and had been boy champion at San Sebastián when his father, the famous Sir Horace Rumbold, had been Ambassador in Madrid. Eden wanted a tennis four and my father, known to be an all-round athlete, was summoned to make it up. He borrowed my Dunlop Maxply racquet and bought a pair of tennis shoes. He had not played for years but he was worried less about his game than about his appearance, the Prime Minister being a notorious dandy, and he bought some new hair cream to give him the same slick grey locks as Eden's. We crowded to the door to see him off to this Summit tennis party with as much trepidation as though he was setting off to sail the Atlantic single-handed. It was a steamy hot August day. The other side of Salisbury Plain in south Wiltshire the afternoon seemed steamier still. My father was rather dreading meeting Clarissa again, but my mother reassured him that she would have forgotten all about their earlier conversation. He was dreading the Prime Minister's forehand too, but what he had not foreseen was that as soon as he got on court all the flies in Wiltshire, multiplied in the sultry weather, made a beeline for my father's hair, seduced by his fragrant pomade. He looked like the Old Man of Three Bridges whose mind was distracted by midges in Edward Lear's limerick. Wherever he went on court he was blinded by this cloud of winged creatures, while there were, literally, no flies on the Prime Minister.

The irony is that the Edens' marriage, begun in such an unpromising atmosphere, was so long and happy, while Selwyn and Bae's was so short and miserable, leaving behind a daughter Joanna whom they both adored. Historians often blame Eden's Suez disaster on his wretched physical health at the time. Perhaps they ought also to blame Selwyn's Suez on his miserable state of mind at the time, because that was precisely the moment when his marriage was finally breaking up, after Bae had been in a bad car smash with her lover, later second husband. Dick Crossman described him as looking 'harassed and bedraggled' at a meeting to discuss Israel just before the Suez operation. But even if Selwyn had been at the top of his form, I suspect he would have stayed loyal, while inwardly agonised that he was being dragged into the kind of dodgy conspiracy that was alien to him.

As I sat there in Buckingham Gate making notes for our own little operation, old colleagues and their new replacements rang him up to thank him for taking on this thankless and menial task of reviewing the organisation of the Conservative Party only a few weeks after being sacked in the most humiliating manner possible, after nearly seven years as either Foreign Secretary or Chancellor.

'Good morning, Chancellor, I trust you are happy in your work. Yes, I know I'm mad to take it on, Reggie, but thank you for your good wishes.'

Then, turning to me, 'They're like young bullocks, you know, these Maudlings and Macleods jostling blindly for position, can't see a yard in front of their noses.'

So off we went, Selwyn and I and usually Diana and sometimes a large bluff official from Central Office called Rex Bagnall who, after two whiskies, always told me that I ought to go into the Berkshire Yeomanry which he had served in with my uncle Bill. It was a strange odyssey. We travelled mostly by train through what turned out to be the hardest and longest winter of the century. We sat opposite each other in heatless first-class carriages as the train rumbled through endless snowscapes. All too often the train screeched to a halt and we rubbed the windows to see where we were: Selwyn in heavy black overcoat and paisley muffler reading Georgette Heyer with the book held up to his extravagantly flared nostrils.

'I expect you don't approve of this sort of thing,' he said, waggling the book at me with its dust jacket of Regency bucks doing something dashing in a carriage.

'I'm afraid I haven't read her.'

'It's jolly good.'

'I like *The Scarlet Pimpernel*.'

'Not the same thing at all.'

As we were waiting to change trains at Darlington, a man approached us out of the darkness. 'It is, isn't it?' he said, shaking Selwyn warmly by the hand. Selwyn did not demur, standing there bareheaded in the freezing cold, rather embarrassed by the attention, so the man continued. 'Wait till I get home and tell the wife. I've always wanted to meet Mr Duncan Sandys.' Selwyn continued to shake hands gravely, not wanting to embarrass the fan. It was not until the man had said goodbye and disappeared down the platform that Selwyn broke out into his chuckly laugh, like a bird talking to itself in a bush some way off.

At our destination, the stationmaster, forewarned by the Area Agent at Central Office, would be there to greet us (there were still stationmasters then). Sometimes he would be wearing a bowler hat or a buttonhole. At Crewe Junction he was wearing a bowler hat *and* a red carnation. I had been transported into a half-vanished world. I remembered reading that Stanley Baldwin used to take the nation's political temperature by consulting the stationmaster at Worcester. That was before the war but this was 1963, *Lady Chatterley* and the Beatles and so on, and I had strayed into a provincial England that I had no idea still existed.

The hotels we stayed in hadn't been done up for years. For those of an earlier generation their names tweaked memories of long-gone heydays when the place was full for race days and the assizes: the Black Boy at Nottingham, the Blossoms at Chester, the White Hart at Salisbury and then, in the great provincial metropolises, the Midland at Manchester, the Adelphi at Liverpool where Sir Jock Delves Broughton took an overdose after being acquitted of the murder of Lord Erroll, the Station Hotel at Newcastle where you could hear the hooting of the Edinburgh expresses deep into the night. And the unvarying meals, the prawn cocktail and the tournedos Rossini and the rusty claret and the ancient camembert served from an enormous sideboard carved with motifs of local legends – Robin Hood or Chevy Chase – the sideboard itself encrusted with legend, a greasy label claiming that it had once stood in the dining room at Belvoir Castle or Hardwick Hall. Across the enormous market square, you could see the vast soot-blackened gothic town hall and the covered markets piled high with fluffy toys and sausages and black pudding, and the statues of great Victorians who had saved the manufacturing classes from ruin or disorder – Cobden, Peel, the Iron Duke. In the mornings we would sit in the chilly function room and Selwyn would listen to the complaints of the local Tories – well, often they were so respectful you could scarcely call them complaints.

Only once do I recall anyone actually criticising the government, as distinct from Central Office, for the management of the party (too remote, the pamphlets they send us are useless and so on). This was at a lunch given in Selwyn's honour in Huddersfield where a long-jawed young man in a bow tie got up and made a scorching attack on

Macmillan's loose and irresponsible economic policy. This was Andrew Alexander, then City editor of the *Yorkshire Post*, and it was the first trumpet call I heard in the battle between the Wets and Dries which was to consume the Tory Party for nearly thirty years. Had I but recognised it, I was in the position of someone hearing for the first time in about 1825 that the Corn Laws were ruining the country. By implication if not by open invitation, he was encouraging Selwyn to take up the banner and wave it in favour of sound economic policies and against Macmillan's beguiling heresies. After all, was Selwyn not the first martyr of monetarism (as we didn't call it then)? I suppose that title really belongs to Peter Thorneycroft whom Macmillan had sacked as Chancellor for pretty much the same reason, namely refusing to splash taxpayers' money around. But Selwyn with his air of provincial probity and prudence was a much more telling emblem of sound money than Thorneycroft who seemed a bit raffish and fruity. When Andrew Alexander had finished, Selwyn just smiled and said, 'That's a most interesting point of view and I shall reflect upon it with gratitude.' This encounter came in February 1963, quite late on in our travels, and by now I was familiar with Selwyn's guiding principle: 'We must show no hard feelings, we must just keep smiling' – and he twisted his face into a hideous parody of the politician's instant smile. He was in short playing a long game, inconspicuously but beautifully. Even so, Macmillan remained suspicious that Selwyn might be stirring up trouble and sent him little notes enquiring as to the 'exact status' of his investigations. As Macmillan stumbled deeper into the mire, there was Selwyn dutifully, uncomplainingly, not merely in the wilderness but in his quiet way making it blossom.

But to think of the party (either Labour or Conservative) as any sort of wilderness is to fall into a misleading anachronism. At that time the Conservative Party was not the shrunken hollowed-out thing that all political parties have now become. It was still a large and prosperous organisation, with a couple of million members, an agent in every winnable seat and some that were not, area agents and trade union organisers and women's officers and above all the support of every local businessman worth his salt. There they were, straight out of the pages of J. B. Priestley, well advanced in middle age for the most part, with waistcoats and watch chains, wool merchants in Bradford, steelmen in Swansea, carpet makers in Kidderminster, fireworks manufacturers in Halifax – these last a couple of brothers or perhaps cousins, who wore identical brown suits and who both sported brown bowler hats. And as we drove through the narrow rainswept Pennine valleys and over the Derbyshire Dales and across the Welsh valleys, we caught glimpses of their works, huge grimy piles, some with broken windows and rags stuffed in them but still operational because we could see the lights through the grimy panes, and when we stopped to look at the map we could hear the hum of the machines. They were cheerful and spoke in their local accents, without any attempt to sound posh, but now and then I thought they seemed a bit gloomy underneath, as though they knew their day was going. They were all still making things but their margins were melting like butter in the sun under competition from the Continent and the Far East. When I travelled the same routes to the North a decade later, the railway line passed through industrial wastelands with roofless workshops, scenes of desolation as grim as any I have seen in the rustbelt of the USA or East Germany after the fall of the Wall. The ghastliness of the spectacle was immediately due to the strong pound shattering British exports and also to a crazy regulation under which business rates were levied on any disused workshop that still had a roof on it. But it had all been a long time coming and I don't think those elderly gents in their waistcoats and watch chains would have been surprised if they had lived to see it. The big bonhomous Area Chairman who showed us round Manchester cut his throat rather than go under.

To me, reared on the soft slopes of Salisbury Plain and gently watered at Eton and Oxford, this was a new world, more strange and entrancing than my first sight of Italy or Greece. It is hard to exaggerate how deeply dim and unfashionable anything to do with provincial England had become by then. The *Manchester Guardian* had fled to London out of sheer social embarrassment. The grandchildren of the old mill-owners and brass-founders and ship-owners and ironmasters had all gone south a generation or two earlier, the Palmers of Jarrow (whose yard's closure had provoked the Jarrow March), the Millers of Preston, the Greens of Wakefield (inventors of Green's patent boiler), the Mayalls of Mossley – all of them far removed from the muck that had made their brass. And

now with Selwyn I was meeting the stay-behinds who were still minding the shop.

They recognised the Little Attorney as one of their own, someone who had gone to London but had not become in the least stuck up and who never pretended to be someone he wasn't. 'He's a good chap, Selwyn, he takes an interest,' Rex Bagnall said, and told me, by way of contrast, how he had once escorted Macmillan to a party function in Cardiff. They had chatted all the way down from London in the car and when they got to Cardiff Rex got out and went round the back of the car to open the door for Supermac, who shook him warmly by the hand and said 'How nice to meet you' without the slightest glimmer of recognition.

I fancied that I had discovered the real England and returning to London between these excursions found my old haunts rather effete and even dull, in fact as dull as the provinces were considered to be by people in London at that time.

In the depths of January I went to a party given at the Hyde Park Hotel, and in the doorway to the ballroom met Bobby Corbett, whom I hadn't seen for ages. After his brief spectacular passage through Oxford, Bobby had become an indispensable and inimitable fixture on the London scene, knowing everyone and everything about everyone, and still dispensing hospitality at a reckless rate. I told him that Selwyn and I were going round the country reviving the Tory Party. He could scarcely contain his mirth.

'Poor dears, they simply haven't the faintest idea what's going to hit them.'

'How do you mean?'

'There's a court case starting in a couple of weeks that's going to blow the whole government sky high. They're done for, totally done for.'

'What sort of case?'

'Oh it's just a black fellow being had up for assault, but the point is he's going to spill the beans about a girl he knows and who she knows.'

'I don't see how that—'

'You just wait and see, my dear,' and he swept on out of my sight still chuckling.

By now our wanderings were nearing their end, but there were a few nooks and crannies of the country to be ticked off. Snow was still thick on the ground as we journeyed through East Anglia, staying with the Area Chairman, Colonel Joly de Lotbinière (an amiable moustachioed figure – most of the area chairmen had moustaches still), at his home on the edge of the park at Ickworth. I remember walking out across the grass to look at the great house with its amazing dome and feeling a sensation of enormous happiness as my feet crunched through the frost-tipped snow. Of all my ups and downs until I was married, I think my most carefree days were those spent with Selwyn, though we really didn't have much in common and he could become quite tetchy when I was at my most languid and lackadaisical. It was already spring by the time we went on one of our last excursions to stay with Selwyn's friend Alan Lennox-Boyd in order to do Cornwall. Here I was on home ground because Alan's eldest son Simon was an Oxford friend and was already married to my cousin Alice. It was for this reason that I felt a curious and shameful sense of apprehension that my friends would not see the point of Selwyn, would regard him perhaps as a bit stiff and dull, which he was capable of being. If he felt he was being got at, he would put up the shutters and play the part that was expected of him, refusing to reveal his more puckish, sympathetic side. This fear turned out to be a fantasy and the weekend went like a breeze in the Boyds' rose-pink toy castle overlooking the Lynher estuary. Diana and I were quartered in two little turret bedrooms up a steep stair. Somehow I thought we must bump into each other on our way to and from the bathroom we were sharing. She would brush against me without meaning to in that narrow passage and I would steady her with my hand and – but no such thing happened. I saw only the whisk of her white nightdress with green sprigs on it and the flounce of her golden hair and she was gone, leaving a fragrance of Pepsodent in the passage. The following year she married a stockbroker who was already baldish and not otherwise much to look at, I thought sourly as I stood at her wedding in the doorway of the Hyde Park Hotel, probably the same doorway where I had stood with Bobby the year before, and wondered how she could. However, her husband became chairman of the Stock Exchange and a great patron of the arts and conservationist of the landscape, and they had four children and she obviously knew what she was doing. She has just become High Sheriff of Essex.

No luck on that front, but perhaps the Selwyn Lloyd report would startle the nation and, as well as rehabilitating my master, in a small way make some sort of name for me. As the snow melted and spring came late and slow, we finished our odyssey and began to sift through the heaps of notes and memos in search of some hard conclusions that could be built into a respectable monument to our labours. It was not an easy task, since the dissatisfactions of the party faithful mostly amounted to no more than a general feeling of staleness, of the government being tired and out of touch, of ministers not bothering with them. In short, it was end-of-regime time and Macmillan with his weary manner, his obsolete moustache and the grouse-moor image which he went out of his way to cultivate was the embodiment of it all. I have read with some amazement recent attempts to rehabilitate Macmillan as a dynamic and purposeful Prime Minister. That was not how he seemed at the time, except where his own career was concerned. None of this was anything to do with our report, and Selwyn more than once anxiously speculated whether we weren't going to be launching the most appalling flop.

Which we were, though not for the reasons we thought. For as the timetable of our inquiry was ticking towards its conclusion, the timetable of another affair was pursuing its remorseless course.

On a December afternoon while we were travelling through the snowbound Derbyshire dales, a West Indian salesman fired five shots at a girl at the window of a mews flat behind Harley Street (shots which one overexcited commentator later said rang round the world like those that killed President Lincoln or the Archduke Ferdinand). The lovesick John Edgecombe missed Christine Keeler, but he landed up in the Old Bailey and on 15 March was sentenced to seven years. By now London was awash with rumours about Christine and her protector 'Dr' Stephen Ward (he had no British qualifications) and the man Ward had introduced her to at Cliveden, Jack Profumo. Only a week after Edgecombe was sent down, Profumo had been grilled in the small hours by seven senior Ministers and the following day made a statement to the House of Commons stoutly protesting his innocence.

Selwyn was one of the Conservative MPs (the only one not a minister) who went to see Profumo, an old friend of his, and sought reassurances that the story was untrue. Selwyn then passed these assurances on to the Prime Minister. I think Selwyn had convinced himself that the whole thing would blow over. In any case, he always said, in his unworldly way, 'I don't see how Jack could have had the time.' The only cause he himself had for anxiety was that the anaemic portrait on his wall turned out to be by Stephen Ward who doubled being an osteopath with drawing his patients' portraits (trebled I suppose would be the better word in some cases, since he was finding girls for them too) and he wondered whether he might be roped into guilt by association, though no less likely member of the Cliveden swimming-pool set could be imagined.

It took another two and a half months for Profumo's defence to be finally cracked, by which time nobody could talk of anything else. It was in the afternoon of 5 June that Profumo's letter of resignation was published.

Our report was scheduled for release at 1630 hours the following day. Price one shilling, the Selwyn Lloyd report was a slender, unpretentious thing, deliberately kept at half the length of its much more formidable predecessor, the Maxwell Fyfe report of 1949. The report's reception was, to put it mildly, rather muted. *The Times* asked in a second leader, 'did it really require an investigation of some seven months to establish what even some of Mr Lloyd's supporters would regard as self-evident?' On a different tack, but just as acerbically, the *Daily Telegraph* began its leader:

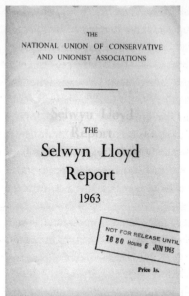

THE

NATIONAL UNION OF CONSERVATIVE
AND UNIONIST ASSOCIATIONS

THE

Selwyn Lloyd
Report
1963

NOT FOR RELEASE UNTIL
16 30 HOURS 6 JUN 1963

Price 1s.

Mr SELWYN LLOYD's report on Conservative party organisation records with prophetic justice complaints that pronouncements from the top of the party are often badly timed. Few key workers in the organisation, with Mr PROFUMO's resignation still ringing in their ears and Miss KEELER otherwise prominent in the news, are likely today to feel vast enthusiasm for energetic improvement of the machinery for presenting the party image to the people.

How peculiar now seems that old convention of putting people's names in capital letters, as though the editor was terrified they would be misread as someone else's.

Miss Keeler was indeed prominent in the news. Selwyn's television dates to launch the report were postponed, never to be rearranged. He was rueful, but more upset on behalf of the Profumos to whom he remained very close – Jack Profumo read the first lesson at Selwyn's memorial service. Yet he must have reflected at some point what an untrustworthy lot he had fallen among: Eden, after all, had not been exactly forthcoming with the truth to his own Foreign Secretary. Macmillan lavished him with tokens of friendship – encouraging Selwyn to use Chequers, for example, because he had no country house of his own – yet all the time he was pouring out an endless stream of patronising complaints to his intimates about how useless and unimaginative Selwyn was. And now he had been used as an intermediary to reinforce Profumo's lies in order to help the Secretary of State for War cling on to his job.

Selwyn even lived long enough to see the first evidence of his protégé Jonathan's in-and-out running, when Aitken narrowly escaped being convicted on a charge under the Official Secrets Act. Yet

Selwyn stuck loyally to them all. Whenever he went down to Sherborne School to see his darling daughter Joanna, he would call in on the Edens at Broadchalke where he was received with open arms. His biographer Richard Thorpe can find only one trace of Selwyn showing any signs of regret over Suez. This was when he confided to Michael Astor that it had been a mistake to have been so charmed by Eden. But that was in the immediate aftermath of the affair. Thereafter he held to the line that what they had done could not properly be described as collusion and that in any case their actions were honourable because they were in the national interest and it would have been dishonourable to have revealed them. I think he even believed it.

On my birthday three weeks later I got a letter from Selwyn typed, as always, beautifully by Diana.

Dear Ferdy,

This letter is rather belated, but I am sure you will understand the reason.

I must thank you very very much indeed for all your help over the Report. You sustained manfully the physical hardships and six months of being messed about by a difficult taskmaster. You were a tremendous ally. I am only sorry that our joint effort was submerged by the other affair.

With many thanks

Yours ever Selwyn

Well, it was a nice letter, which is why I quote it. But it is interesting for another reason because it indicates, in a delicate fashion, just what a deciding moment that 'Other Affair' was, not least for Selwyn himself. From the moment that Profumo got up in the House of Commons, the 'Macmillan must go' movement gathered volume and momentum at frightening speed. The moment any party leader is mortally wounded, even the doziest member of the pride wakes up and goes on the prowl. In those weeks after 6 June, Selwyn had nothing to do in the official Parliamentary sense, nothing, that is, except to conspire. Macmillan's prostate operation at the beginning of October provided an unmissable opportunity to get rid of him, but the Other Affair had already done for his credibility as an effective leader. What a shambles it was. I remember thinking, if Bobby Corbett could tell me the shape of things to come back at the end of January, how on earth had the Prime Minister with all the powers at his fingertips allowed the mess to drag on to disaster all the way into the summer?

Selwyn threw himself into the succession battle with an unabashed brio, quite unlike the reticent, cautious figure I had travelled round the country with. He was one of the first to press Alec Douglas-Home to stand and was confident from the first that his candidate would win, telling Jonathan Aitken so, who in turn told Randolph Churchill who laid off his massive bets on Lord Hailsham as a result. At the party conference Selwyn was in and out of Home's suite at the Imperial Hotel, Blackpool, and later was a constant visitor to Home's official residence at 1 Carlton Gardens. He was standing at Home's elbow as the dissident rivals Hailsham, Macleod and Powell came on the phone and when Hailsham said to Home, 'If you take the job it'll be a disaster and I'll have to denounce you in public,' Selwyn took up another phone himself and said, 'It'll look like sour grapes, Quintin.' He was, in short, an energetic conspirator. Of course he hoped that his preferred candidate would give him a job (Home in fact made him Leader of the House), but also he did feel that Home was the only one of them whose judgement was not fatally poisoned by ambition. Certainly Home was just about the only front-line politician he spoke of without a tinge of contempt. Iain Macleod's brilliant piece in the *Spectator* about the 'magic circle' has fixed in the minds of historians and journalists the idea that the struggle to succeed Macmillan was a conflict between the progressive wing of the party and the stuffy old toffs. But I think there was another divide, at least in Selwyn's mind, between the straight and the devious, and seeing it that way he spoke for plenty of the people he had been listening to all through that long hard winter. He was not, after all, a right-winger by temperament. He had started life as a Liberal, not surprisingly as he came from a long line of Anglo-Welsh Methodist doctors and ministers. And he retained a core of distaste for the more brutish side of Tory life. Sir Cyril Osborne, a notorious hanger and flogger, had demanded an interview during our inquiry and ranted on for hours about immigrants and why wouldn't Rab Butler call him Cyril. At first it looked as though Selwyn was listening with non-committal politeness. Then I noticed that his whole body had gone stiff as a board. When I returned from ushering Osborne out, Selwyn did a kind of little dance on the scarlet and blue carpet of the Research Department, chanting, 'Thank God the man's gone.'

History to the defeated does not merely not say alas or pardon; history sneers and patronises. Selwyn, according to his obituary in *The Times*, though of course 'a loyal servant', 'lacked the sensitivity to adjust to criticism and the imagination to carve out original policies of his own' (twaddle as a matter of fact – Selwyn in his couple of years at the Treasury was more innovative than any other post-war Chancellor except Nigel Lawson). The sophisticated and statesmanlike Macmillan, on the other hand, 'was preoccupied with the broad issues of foreign policy'. Selwyn seemed slow-footed by comparison as Supermac shimmied off into the blue yonder leaving poor old Celluloid to carry the can. Macmillan's memoirs are comically self-serving, as he repeatedly quotes from his own Diaries: 'Selwyn tired . . . seems to have lost his grip . . . Strange apathy has overcome him . . . I shrink from the task . . . I have made up my mind where my duty lies . . . terribly difficult and emotional scene . . . in the end things worked out pretty well.'

What went wrong of course was that Macmillan became impatient. With his congenital love of the flash gesture, he could not accept the slow grind and the inevitably painful costs involved in defeating inflation. It is hard today, now that it is taken for granted that the defeat of inflation must be the prime goal of economic policy, to understand quite how nonchalant Macmillan was about its dangers. His mind was still stuck in the 1930s and he was thirsty for reassurance that he could pump money into the economy with impunity. For this reassurance he leaned heavily on Roy Harrod, the last of the great Keynesians. Much of the summer holidays of 1958 and 1959 I spent in Norfolk with Henry and we would cycle to the postbox through the cornfields, proudly carrying his father's letters to Number Ten. Billa in her subversive way liked to pretend that the PM would toss her husband's letters straight into the waste-paper basket, but Macmillan's diaries show how again and again it was Roy who egged on his natural expansionist tendencies.

We can see now that just as Suez marked a watershed in the conduct of British foreign policy, so the day Macmillan sacked Lloyd and the others marked a watershed in domestic policy. Before that date, the actions of the British government, though they might often be mistaken, seemed to have some kind of weight behind them. After, they appear more like gestures of impotence, with no settled purpose, dictated by the last by-election or opinion poll. By comparison, Selwyn, 'limited' and 'inflexible' though he might be, possessed qualities of realism and steadfastness and common sense which sprang from recognisable principles. A little more inflexibility would not have gone amiss in those years of postponement and delusion. The paradox is that the most dramatic incident in Selwyn's public life remains the Suez collusion. Yet I can't think of any politician since the war who showed more consistently that a politician can be an honourable man.

I was in Blackpool too that frenzied week in October. Most of the Department went up there. 'It's like a staff outing to the seaside,' Charles Bellairs said. Charles was my immediate superior, a Research Department veteran who had survived from the great days of Maudling, Powell and Macleod. He was a character of immense sweetness, much too gentle to think of going anywhere near the House of Commons, with a voice which swung between an amused gurgle and a high squeak. For me it was the first taste of Blackpool and of party conferences. The broad sands, the distant sea, the tawny glitter of the Tower with Reginald Dixon at the organ of the Tower Ballroom, a familiar radio sound from my youth, and inside the ugly sprawling redbrick palace of the Imperial Hotel the sound of hearty, mirthless laughter and the stench of self-importance filling the air. We CRD officials saw little of all this as we sat in a little back office next door in the Park House Hotel preparing the Daily Conference Notes under the direction of Oliver Stebbings, a figure of stately weight, not unlike Mr Perkupp the office manager in *The Diary of a Nobody*. During the sandwich break we dutiful Pooters listened to far-off tales of life with S.B. as Stebbings always called Stanley Baldwin. Then the second evening I escaped from the Park House Hotel to see the fun. Hugh Fraser, already a revered figure in the party, had married my cousin Antonia the week my mother died (she had brought her wedding dress to the hospital to show my mother) and it was he who had put in a word to get me into the Department. He was fourteen years older than Antonia (part of the reason why the marriage eventually fell apart, in that way though not in others like Selwyn's break-up). Anyway, Hugh and Antonia had asked me to have dinner in the Imperial Hotel. It was a huge party at the big round table in the middle of the dining room. The other guests seemed rather slow in showing up and I sat nervously studying the menu with nobody to talk to. Then suddenly with whoops and halloos and the strong aroma of Trumper's Bay Rum hair oil that accompanied old-style Tory MPs in came Hugh's cronies, what might be called the White's Club faction. Maurice Macmillan, the Prime Minister's son, and Julian Amery and his wife Catherine, Macmillan's daughter, and half-a-dozen others.

'I think Quintin's odds-on now.'

'Odds-on to go for it?'

'No, odds-on to win. We were in Sister Agnes just before I caught the train and the old boy's rooting for him.'

'Randolph's already going around handing out these badges with Q on them.'

'If anyone can balls it up, Randolph will.'

The Macmillan detachment had come straight from the Prime Minister's bedside. Macmillan had initially decided, three weeks before the conference, that he would not lead the party into the next election. He had even told the Queen so. But then he wavered and wavered again, and by 7 October he had firmly decided to carry on and fight the election, then suddenly that night his prostate had flared up and the next morning he had to leave the Cabinet halfway through. The same evening he was admitted to King Edward VII Hospital and had a catheter inserted into his bladder. In those days, when laymen knew much less about anything medical, he assumed that this meant he would have to resign. In fact the obstruction was not malignant and he was perfectly fit again after a longish convalescence. But with his instinct for melodrama, he convinced himself that he was mortally ill, and played the part for all it was worth. To his Sovereign who came to visit him he was the adoring subject nearing death. To his son and son-in-law he was the enfeebled monarch bequeathing them one sacred task, at all costs to stop Rab Butler from succeeding him.

These breathless emissaries lost no time in getting stuck in to the wine and spirits, rising every five minutes to buttonhole other diners and preach the message.

'Quintin's the only man, he's going to walk it.'

Julian Amery had already done himself pretty well on the train and I think he was confusing me with one of the younger Tory MPs when he urged me in his gravelly voice to 'get on the Hog's back while there's still time'.

We had got through quite a few bottles of champagne by the time the oysters arrived in great silver dishes. Just as the waiter bent down to ask me how many I wanted, a feeling of overwhelming nausea swept over me, so violent and seismic that I was unable to speak as I rose from the table and fled, just managing to get out a few words of apology as I shot past Antonia's chair. Thus ended my part in the great leadership plot.

The next evening I went along to the Winter Gardens theatre to hear Lord Hailsham deliver the Conservative Political Centre's annual lecture. His text was unremarkable, verging on banal, but the theatre was packed mostly in order to hear his final postscript in which he announced his intention to disclaim his peerage and the whole place erupted. Contrary to what most people thought, including Hailsham himself, this opportunity to throw his hat into the ring while actually on stage turned out to be disastrous, reminding the doubtful of his erratic, exhibitionist qualities. Not that Rab Butler or Reggie Maudling did any better with their dreadfully anodyne platform addresses. Only Alec Home enhanced his chances by a neat self-deprecating speech which appeared to remove him from the heaving scrum – 'I am offering a prize to any newspaperman who can find a clue in my speech that this is Lord Home's bid for the leadership.' This disarmed not only the delegates but the journalists, who still had no clue about what was going on behind the scenes. I was as entranced as everyone else by the whole gorgeous seaside drama. I had to survive another forty years of party conferences to see anything remotely resembling it.

While I was in the Research Department I started reading Russian novels and short stories. This was partly because the books I had taken from Chitterne had fetched up on my own shelves in Earls Court, battered now and in old-fashioned translations by Constance Garnett. 'Good morning, Pavel Sergeyevich, I trust you are in good spirits,' that sort of thing. But it was also because the scenery was strangely familiar. Far from being mostly about duels and Cossacks riding through dark forests, the best bits were all about hard-up clerks living obscure lives in shabby tenements – which just about corresponded to my own situation, and what was so appealing about Gogol and Dostoevsky and Goncharov was that they knew how to make such situations absurd and touching. I now had the health and pensions brief at the Conservative Research Department in 24 Old Queen Street, a pleasant old building which at the back looked out on Birdcage Walk and St James's Park and there was birdsong if you opened the windows. But I was on the street side sharing an office with Charles Bellairs.

'You're sitting at Enoch's desk,' he gurgled.

I almost jumped from my chair, as though frightened of catching something. Although this was a few years before his Rivers of Blood speech, Mr Powell already had an unnerving reputation.

'And that', Charles squeaked, 'is the Cupboard.'

He pointed to the large built-in cupboard next to the desk now used for storing stationery and painted a soft blue like all the woodwork in the Department.

'When Enoch was courting Pam, they hid in there to avoid being caught.'

I gaped at this legendary cupboard as though it were the Great Bed of Ware. At first my head was full of images of Enoch in his Superman mode grappling Pam to his bosom, his moustache tickling her nose as they struggled to prevent the piles of foolscap and carbon from burying them. Only now, more than forty years later, have I discovered that I must have misheard Charles (his warble was sometimes hard to disentangle). Though Pam, later Mrs Powell, was a secretary in the Department, it was not she and Enoch who hid in the cupboard but a young Naval officer in uniform who was courting another secretary and who had been pushed into the cupboard by his girlfriend, aided by Pam, in order to avoid detection.

It was a toss-up which of my new portfolios I had less mastery of. Health I knew as much about as you learn from having been in hospital now and then, social security I knew nothing about at all. This did not matter much as the Conservatives were still in government and their ministers were spoon-fed by their civil servants and felt little need of our services. There really wasn't much for us to do. I would wander out for a pint at the Two Chairmen at the end of the street with two other malcontents in the Department and then stroll round the lake in St James's Park, watching the mournful pelicans doing just about as little as I was doing.

In the afternoons I took to reading the *British Medical Journal*, to hone my expertise on the health side. Its lead-grey covers enclosed a world of grotesque enchantment. Victims of interesting diseases stood stiff and naked in front of the medical photographer to exhibit their blotches, swellings and deformities. The poor quality of the paper turned even healthy flesh to a muddy grey. Some of the patients had their faces blacked out, as if the photo might incriminate them.

Occasionally I wrote letters to the newspapers to rebut Labour slurs about the rate of hospital building or the current level of old-age pensions. 'Sir, Once again Mr Crossman has twisted the true facts. The reality is that . . .'

Then came the general election and Labour won a surprisingly narrow victory, and everything was changed. 'You'll find it much more fun now they've got nobody to look after them,' Charles said. The next morning after the Shadow Cabinet appointments came out, there was Sir Keith Joseph standing at my desk, introducing himself with a flurry of apologies for breaking into my labours, although in fact all I was doing was reading the newspaper and my labours were in any case now to be on his behalf.

With his velvety brown eyes and crinkly black hair, he radiated nervous energy and a heavy cold. He seemed to have a cold all that autumn and with that electric intensity which was so unnerving he made it impossible for you not to be aware of it. There was a flourishing of handkerchiefs, a seismic nose-blowing, an unrestrained show of misery interspersed with a reprise of the apologising. It was as though he was employed to represent the figure of the Common Cold in a village pageant.

This conspicuous rheum did not interfere in the slightest with his appetite for work. On the contrary, it souped up his desire to get on with things, as though he was desperate to complete his task before the cold turned to some more sinister complaint. 'Please write me a paper on it,' he would say after a few minutes' discussion on any subject. He consumed paper like he consumed paper handkerchiefs.

Back I went to Old Queen Street and, it seemed like every night, sent over to him by the last messenger a massive paper on the reform of the National Health Service, or the pension system or the local welfare services, and at our meeting the next morning he had already digested it and was waving it about, tapping it with his pen, almost blowing his nose on it: 'This is a splendid paper, quite splendid.'

I still have a folder full of those papers, beautifully typed on foolscap, full of schemes of breathtaking sweep and complexity, based on an ignorance of the most exquisite purity. There is one chart showing wondrous intersections of dotted lines and branches linking hospital almoners to health visitors and chiropodists to home helps. I had never seen a home help, would not have recognised an almoner even if I knew what they did. All these beings and their budget were to be harmonised under the 'integrated', 'rationalised', 'restructured' framework of an Area Welfare Council. Everything was to be streamlined, co-ordinated and made one as at the day of the Last Judgement.

Where had I got all this stuff from? In part from the pages of professional journals, like the *BMJ* and *New Society*, from Bow Group pamphlets and old White papers and Green papers, but the awful truth is that most of it had come from the top of my head, which is to say from the conventional wisdom of the day. Keith Joseph was inhaling the same ether through his clogged nostrils which is why he loved everything I fed him and called for more paper as lesser men called for more wine. I glowed. Overnight I had become a guru in a small way of business.

There was, however, a snag. After three or four meetings of our mutual admiration society, Keith asked if I would greatly mind if he brought his junior spokesman to our next one – another example of the absurd lengths to which he carried any opportunity for the display of courteous apology. This junior spokesman was a relatively new MP called Margaret Thatcher and not bringing her in from the start was an example of Keith's countervailing quality, a thoughtless, forgetful insouciance amounting to tactlessness, which often undid all the good work of the apologies. Margaret Thatcher had, after all, been junior minister in the Department for the past three years, whereas Keith was a relative novice in the field, so she might be expected to know rather more about it than he did (let alone his assistant) and should have been in there at the first meeting.

This turned out to be her view too. When she came into the room, she immediately made it clear that it had been a mistake to leave her out of things. At the same time, she made a strong physical impression. She was both a little cross and unmistakably pretty, more striking because she was giving off this whiff of umbrage. At the same time she was entirely calm. There was nothing flustered about her. The note of censure in her voice seemed to come quite naturally to her, as did the way she sat so upright at the table. She was then thirty-nine years old and to me then looked more like one of the over-age milkmaids in the chorus of the Bath panto than someone in training to be an Iron Lady, although you could not miss the willpower. Her voice was sharper then than it later became, when she had had voice training to bring it down a semitone after criticisms that she sounded shrill.

To me anyway she sounded unbearably sharp as she began to slice my papers into pitiful shreds.

'I don't see any figures of the cost there. Where are the figures?'

'Yes, yes, we must have figures,' Keith would come in eagerly.

'And what exactly would be the benefits of integrating these two branches of the service?'

'Well, they would be, well, more co-ordinated.'

'That is surely another way of saying the same thing.'

Suddenly the happy warm times were over. I was no longer the in-house guru but the idle apprentice with a hangover. Each meeting became an examination for which I had not prepared, and in which I was distressed to see that my former admirer joined in with all the convert's enthusiasm. Unkind critics asserted that Keith, in the words of Field-Marshal Haig about Lord Derby, like a feather

pillow bore the marks of the last person who had sat on him.
Certainly he was hugely receptive to any new approach that caught
his fancy. He was not unaware of this and he would say, 'I haven't
got an original mind, you know, but I am very eager to listen and
learn.' His capacity to absorb and then reflect the light of others was
not so much a defect as a virtue almost unique among politicians.
Most of his colleagues would have bridled at being corrected by a
bossy younger woman who had only been in Parliament for five
years. He revelled in it.

The curious thing, though, is that in the event Margaret Thatcher
scarcely slowed us up, perhaps because she had not yet thought her
own ideas through on the relevant subjects or perhaps because
ultimately she still thought it politic to defer to her superior, or
perhaps the Zeitgeist of the mid-1960s was still too strong for her.
Together the three of us fiddled away with the machinery of
government, aspiring to manage decline as best we could, 'shifting
the deckchairs on the *Titanic*', the wounding phrase that was just
beginning to become a cliché at the time. There were no larger
possibilities of reform in sight. 'You can't unscramble the omelette' –
another cliché that was trotted out when anyone suggested breaking
up one of the giant monoliths that Lord Attlee had left dotted around
the landscape like those grim statues on Easter Island. And in due
course we ourselves managed to bequeath a few more forbidding
megaliths to the nation. My idea of Area Welfare Councils bore a
disquieting resemblance to those Area Health Authorities which
Joseph, back in office as Social Services Secretary in 1970, was to
establish under the NHS Reorganisation Act – a large unlovely thing
which was soon blamed for all the bloated bureaucracy and general
inadequacy of the Service. It would be presuming to claim more than
the tiniest share of the ignominy; I was only parroting the conventional wisdom; my papers were as deeply dunked in the Zeitgeist as
any madeleine. But when Keith began in the later 1970s to do his
familiar routine of slapping his forehead or groaning with his head in
his hands, the only man I have seen in real life adopt this posture of
despair so common in novels, 'How little we knew – and we meant so
well,' I can at least claim to have been part of the 'we'.

It was quite a time before I saw him again. By then I had been to

America and come back with the extraordinary unBritish idea that as well as all the enjoyable conspiring and manoeuvring, politics could actually be about something, that arguments involving the higher reaches of the brain might come in handy. I began to see that large parts of the political system we had inherited were not natural and inevitable but rather had been thrown together during one of those recurring fits of panic that afflict the ruling class. There were no eternal commandments prescribing that the majority of new homes had to be built and owned by the local council, or that this or that industry had to be nationalised or that the trade unions should enjoy such near-total immunity from the law. Other countries had quite different arrangements, as Britain had had in the past. These things could be reversed or reformed if only we had the self-confidence. What I brought back from America was not anything resembling a new idea, what I brought back was the habit of optimism.

While soldiering on at the *Daily Mail* to earn a crust, I began to write high-flown essays for *Encounter*, quoting Tocqueville and Marx and John Stuart Mill as though I was familiar with every word they wrote. At the *Encounter* offices high above St Martin's Lane, I met the affable, voluble editor Melvyn J. Lasky, who looked like Lenin after a good lunch. He was one of those few editors who is also an enhancer, who can tell you not only what is wrong with your article but how to make it better. He did not go to the lengths of my principal employer, David English, who would sit down with his leading female columnists, Jean Rook and Lynda Lee Potter, and until they had got the hang of it write half their stuff himself like Nathanael West's 'Miss Lonelyhearts'. But Mel could see where your piece ought to be heading and tell you how to get there, offering useful sources to help you along the way. Looking back at those long pieces, the first time I had tried to write anything over about 800 words, I am struck by how often the interesting bits were suggested by him. In his later years Mel was rather shunned by the London intelligentsia partly because he would go on and on and partly because they were ashamed of having anything to do with a magazine which turned out to have been, even indirectly, financed by the CIA. I wasn't in the least bit fussed by that, nor am I now, thinking of some of the press lords I have written for before and since. And anyway I was fond of Mel.

I was fonder still of his assistant Margot Walmsley, a large, affectionate character with big round eyes and a great mass of tousled blonde hair, who called you Darling the moment she met you. Margot had had a tragic life, both her husband and her only son had committed suicide, and she threw herself instead into giving parties once every month or two, which were the first thing approaching a literary salon I had ever come across in London. She had a top-floor flat in Earls Terrace, Kensington High Street, on a controlled tenancy which meant that the landlord did not bother to install any improvements like an entryphone. At the same time, the other tenants complained if the front door was left open on party nights and so the drill was, as each guest rang the bell, for Margot's tousled head to appear at the third-floor window, crying Darling and chucking down the key wrapped in an envelope. Sometimes there would be a delay in her getting to the window and a little crowd would be assembled on the damp pavement looking like a party of carol singers. A. J. Ayer, his stepdaughter Nigella Lawson, Victor and Dorothy Pritchett, Peregrine and Claudie Worsthorne, Paul and Marigold Johnson and other obscurer characters who had fallen into Margot's generous embrace, all of them staring upward as though waiting for the Second Coming, until the envelope with the key in it came whistling down, now and then inflicting a flesh wound on its way to the pavement.

It was there in Margot's low-ceilinged attic, over the flagons of Italian wine and taramasalata biscuits, that I first met Shirley and Bill Letwin. They were both academics from Chicago, Jewish by birth, and on intimate terms with the great figures of the Chicago intelligentsia such as Saul Bellow and Milton Friedman, but they had taken up England in the wholehearted way they took up everything – conservatism, lawn tennis, Trollope – and settled in Regent's Park and sent their brilliant only child, Oliver, to Eton and Trinity where he swept the board. This did not mean that they had become in any recognisable way English. Bill still happily recalled his days in the US Navy in the last days of the Pacific war, listening to Peggy Lee singing 'Sentimental Journey', and Shirley retained a raucous caustic wit which was all the more piquant when she was in one of her showy, off-the-shoulder frocks with which her wardrobe was stuffed. One of their charms was their unbridled extravagance. Although Bill was a professor of economics at the LSE, they took a very uneconomical lease on a fine house in Kent Terrace and entertained all their colleagues in style. Here I met the great Elie Kedourie who was shy, charming and implacable and his beautiful wife Sylvia who was as brilliant as he was. Elie, who came originally from Baghdad, spent his life trying to dispel the illusions of the Foreign Office and Chatham House about the Middle East, without much luck. Also round the Letwins' table you would find the saturnine Maurice Cowling who infected the minds of generations of Peterhouse undergraduates with his own dark version of conservatism; Ken Minogue whose book on Nationalism was almost as caustic as Kedourie's; Maurice Cranston, the great expert on seventeenth- and eighteenth-century thought, the original of Penistone in *A Dance to the Music of Time*; and the star of the show, the philosopher Michael Oakeshott.

Oakeshott was an enchanting elfin figure, rather slight with a light but seductive voice. Men sometimes found him a little creepy, women never. He was married three times and was said to have various girlfriends scattered in boltholes in London and around the country. He was sceptical in his views, and not at all religious, thus conforming to my general theory that, as soon as British philosophers stopped believing in God, they started believing in sex. There is no more startling contrast than that between the celibacy, and indeed chastity, of Pascal and Locke and the insatiable appetites of Bertrand Russell and A. J. Ayer and P. H. Nowell-Smith, the author of *Ethics*, who was said to have regarded it as a positive moral duty to sleep with other men's wives.

Oakeshott was outstandingly warm and friendly on first meeting, eager to draw out shy strangers, reluctant himself to be drawn into heavy discussions on politics or philosophy, preferring to discuss the delights of cycling round the Hertfordshire lanes when he was a boy or the brilliance of some old schoolmaster who had taught him Latin.

The one exception to his benign and welcoming attitude to others was, to my great surprise, Isaiah Berlin. He could not stand what T. S. Eliot also had been put off by, Berlin's 'torrential eloquence'. There had too been a famous incident at the LSE, when Oakeshott, as Professor of Government, had to introduce Berlin who was giving the Auguste Comte lecture and described him, in his feline way, as 'the

Paganini of the Platform'. This completely unnerved Isaiah who then gabbled his lecture on Historical Inevitability and began trying to shorten it as he went along, so that the implication of Oakeshott's wisecrack – that Berlin simply rattled off a flurry of high notes which exhibited virtuosity without substance – was fulfilled in the most embarrassing way. It was years later that I realised how violently the whole experience had upset him. I had just written a rather fulsome piece about Oakeshott somewhere and I was queuing at the issue desk in the London Library, when Isaiah buttonholed me, almost shaking with urgency and indignation: 'You were far too kind to Oakeshott, far too kind, the man's a complete fraud, he has no doctrine at all, nothing resembling a doctrine, he has nothing to say.' He went on in this vein until I was rescued by the girl behind the desk asking if these were the books I wanted to take out. This was my last meeting with my mother's old admirer, and if it had turned out to be impossible for him to send courteous messages to her via me when I came to Oxford, I always fancied that the memory of her added a little to the warmth of his greeting when we met.

The irony was that when Berlin died not long afterwards he was reproached by the hard men of both left and right – Perry Anderson and Paul Johnson for example – for precisely the same failing with which he had reproached Oakeshott, the sin of having no doctrine, of not being prepared to stand up and be counted for a definite set of beliefs. Yet the whole point of both Berlin and Oakeshott was precisely that they undermined the idea that a single set of beliefs could provide a coherent and consistent guide to dealing with the world. Not having a doctrine in that sense was for both men the beginning of wisdom. As it happened, each of them did have his own strong personal preferences. Berlin believed strongly in liberty, patriotism and social progress. Oakeshott believed equally passionately in leaving things alone and letting people get on with their lives. But what we remember them for is for teaching us that the world is a complicated place which won't yield to unadjusted dogma. And indeed their mutual antipathy when you would expect them to be soulmates shows how true that is.

At one of these Letwin dinners, two fresh-faced youths appeared. These were Oliver Letwin and his best friend at school Charles

Moore. Both of them joined in the conversation with uninhibited zest. I was struck by how enthusiastic they were and the next time I met Oliver's mother said how they didn't have any of that world-weary attitude that I remembered putting on at that age.

'Yes,' Shirley said in her best wisecracking Chicago manner, 'they're naive as hell. I don't know where Bill and I went wrong.'

'Well, I expect they'll grow out of it.'

'No they won't, they'll stay innocent all their lives.'

I have seldom heard a mother's prophecy better borne out. Both Oliver and Charles later became my colleagues and firmest friends. They have never shed an ounce of their boyish trustfulness. Whenever Oliver gets accused of some gaffe or other (usually for telling the truth) or Charles rides full gallop after some unfashionable cause, I think of Shirley shaking her ponytail and chuckling her throaty chuckle.

There weren't often politicians at the Letwins', and the only one who was a regular was Keith Joseph. Partly he was there a lot because by then he and his wife had more or less split up and he was short of company and the Letwins had scooped him up. I did not reflect on the coincidence that the wives of the two politicians I had worked for had both found the political grind unendurable, but, though both Keith and Selwyn had been profoundly afflicted by a sense of failure, Keith was the harder hit, since he had been married for far longer and was much more the marrying kind.

It was obvious anyway that it wasn't just time that had taken its toll since we last met. The zigzag vein at his temple seemed to throb all the time now and although he was as intense and attentive as ever, he was more disconnected. He would jump between subjects, or switch off altogether, his face assuming an anxious vacancy, as though expecting a message from some medium other than the conversation round the table. He had now permanently adopted the habit of carrying round a little gilt-edged black-leather notebook with attached ballpoint pen. He would without warning make notes at any point during the meal, of some book or writer that had just been mentioned, or more unnervingly of some stray remark which had caught his fancy. Often something quite banal would appear to be completely new to him. In a way, he seemed almost as innocent of the world as the seventeen-year-old Oliver and Charles. Or perhaps it was sometimes that he could not think of any appropriate response except to make a note of what had just been said, the habit having became another nervous tic. More unnerving still was when he held the pen or pencil poised over the notebook, waiting for the next thought worthy of being jotted down.

There was a good deal of this when he coincided with Michael Oakeshott. Naturally Keith with his unabashed seriousness expected that the great philosopher would give him pages worth of useful references and aperçus. It was not that Oakeshott was silent or brusque. On the contrary, he burbled happily about the pleasures of cycling and his excitement when he first got a shiny new Sturmey-Archer gear. Keith's pen would hover disconsolately, his finger holding open the page. The butler would pour more wine, the waitress would bring in the exquisite pudding. Oakeshott would discourse happily about the different sorts of sweet you could buy in the sweetshops of Harpenden before the first war. Still the pencil would hover and still Oakeshott would refuse, on principle, to discuss any serious subject. It was, after all, the nearest thing he had to a doctrine that the purpose of life is to be found in its familiar pleasures. It was a typical tease that the book he wrote before the war entitled *A Guide to the Classics* should be not about Plato and Epicurus but about the breeding of Derby winners, a subject at least in which I could hold my own with him.

Yet Keith did not leave 3 Kent Terrace empty-handed. He had read a great deal all the time he was a fellow of All Souls and now in opposition again he read a great deal more. When he came back into office as Mrs Thatcher's Secretary of State for Industry, he knew exactly what his civil servants needed to read.

He gave them a reading list. This provoked hysterical laughter throughout Whitehall, Westminster and Fleet Street. To give a list of books to read, to *civil servants* – the idea was absurd, fantastical, the biggest waste of time in the world. Joseph was mocked in particular because eight of the titles were books or pamphlets by himself, rather like Elisabeth Schwarzkopf choosing her own recordings for all eight of her Desert Island Discs. Years later, even his biographers seem rather embarrassed and hurriedly add that the civil servants had asked for the list and in any case they had already read most of the books on it and had little to learn from them. Very much the reaction of Chris Patten, then the Director of the Conservative Research Department, when Joseph gave him a reading list, including many of the same books.

I rather doubt in fact whether the civil servants had read half the books recently, or at all, and even if they had, whether they had really hauled in the message. Anyone who had read Peter Jay on the control of inflation would not have made the mistakes that were made at the end of the 1980s, anyone who had read Tocqueville on Democracy in America would not have destroyed the independence of local government as the poll tax did, anyone who had read Adam Smith's *Theory of Moral Sentiments* as well as *The Wealth of Nations* would not have neglected poverty and inequality, anyone who had read Jane Jacobs in *The Economy of Cities* would not have made the appalling mistakes in urban planning that ripped the heart out of British cities. And so on. It is a terrific reading list, none the worse for its mixture of pamphlets and scholarly works, of old and new. In putting together such a list, Keith showed his Keatsian 'negative capability', his ability to absorb and reflect everything he heard and read in order to illuminate the political scene.

As if it was not bad enough to tell people what they should read, Keith would insist on apologising for what he had done. It was this, above all, that gained him the name of 'the Mad Monk', coined by Chris Patten. In theory, we are all in favour of politicians who say sorry. In practice, we (or at any rate political insiders) tend to admire politicians who 'tough it out'; brazenness is often seen as the mark of a big beast.

In this, as in much else, we have fallen away from the exacting standards of the Middle Ages, where on any highway or byway you might trip over a person of high degree, barefoot and clad in sackcloth, crawling on all fours, possibly backwards, in the direction of Canterbury or Walsingham to expiate some sin or other. But these days we find displays of contrition mawkish and embarrassing.

Nor did Keith's return to office fill his sails with fresh confidence. Before a major speech he was said to retire to the gents to throw up (Harold Macmillan had the same problem). To safeguard his fragile

digestion, his special diet became ever more esoteric, consisting
largely of tea, chocolate, British Rail cake and hard-boiled eggs,
preferably chopped. When he tried to persuade the steelworkers to
call off their strike just before Christmas 1979, he was said to be near
tears. The decisions that came out of his departments, first Industry
and then Education, did not always coincide with the principles set
out in his reading list. Again he was said to be too ready to listen to the
custodians of the status quo inside the ministry. Even his most devoted
followers, such as Oliver Letwin who went to work for him as a
special adviser, began to despair of getting him to stick to a consistent
position and see it through. And yet he changed the language of
politics. Twenty years after he finally resigned, all the issues he
obsessed about are now discussed in terms that he made familiar.
We take it for granted that the control of inflation is a matter not for
political manipulation but for strict monetary control carried out by
experts. We understand that the state is not an all-wise, benign master
and that we need to watch all its activities with a close and sceptical
eye. We have no illusions about standards in our worst state schools or
about the feral upbringing so many children suffer. In fact there is
scarcely anything that Keith Joseph worried about that we aren't still
worrying about too.

I doubt whether this can be said of any other post-war politician
who never became leader of his or her party. Rab Butler and Tony
Crosland taught their parties to accommodate to the consensus of the
day. Only Keith attempted something far more difficult, to move
away from the prevailing consensus and establish what he called a new
common ground. When I gave the Keith Joseph memorial lecture at
the Centre for Policy Studies in March 2000, I began by saying that
'Keith Joseph must have been the first serious politician I ever met:
sometimes I think he was the only serious politician I ever met.'

I had ambitions, of an unfocused sort, to be a politician myself. That,
after all, was why I had crept into the Conservative Research
Department in the first place. I did not condescend to dabble in
any of the vulgar pedestrian activities, like knocking on doors, stuffing
envelopes or going to local party meetings. My record of voluntary
activity for the party was a gleaming blank. Despite this, at a point in

my late twenties I decided, by some mysterious process of intuition rather than any logical reasoning, that I was ready, rather like some joint of meat which, though externally unchanged in appearance, has at last cooked through. It wasn't difficult to get on the candidates list. Anyone in the Research Department waltzed on to it. I was given a formal, rather disagreeable interview by Sir Richard Sharples, the MP for Sutton & Cheam, a handsome, saturnine figure who was in charge of selecting candidates. He later reported to Alan Lennox-Boyd that he thought I was one of the wettest candidates he had seen. Sharples retired from the Commons after the next election to become Governor of Bermuda, where he was almost immediately assassinated by Black Power militants not in my employ.

Despite this lukewarm endorsement, I plunged into the peculiar business of getting selected. For months I brooded over the beauti- fully detailed constituency maps and voluminous reports issued by the Boundary Commission which had just finished redistributing all the seats in England and Wales. Did the loss of Blandings Parva to Loamshire West make Loamshire East winnable, had the Liberals driven such fatal inroads in the suburban fringes to make the new seats losable? These base but interesting calculations turned out to be a total waste of time, as Jim Callaghan took fright when advised that the redistribution would cost him dozens of seats and so in a manoeuvre outstandingly squalid even for this, the seamier side of politics, instructed his MPs to vote down the orders bringing in the new boundaries, although it was the government that was proposing the orders. So it was on the old boundaries that I began hacking around the country in my green Triumph Herald convertible seeking some constituency association which could discern the man of steel and destiny beneath my moist and floppy exterior. It was a new English odyssey for me, once or twice passing through the same peeling constituency offices and damp meeting rooms that I had visited with Selwyn five years earlier under less tense conditions. Braintree, Norwood, Nottingham West, Plymouth Sutton, Flint West, New- bury, Wells – how often I have sat in dusty anterooms making stilted small talk with my rivals while in the hall next door we could hear another of our competitors making the audience break out into the kind of comfortable laughter or applause that showed he was stroking

them in all the right places. Sometimes these rivals were shaking as
much as I was. Waiting to be interviewed in Wells, Dr Alan Glyn,
who had already been MP for Clapham, could not keep his white
hands still for a minute. Dr Glyn, who bore a close resemblance to Mr
Pastry on children's television, had achieved immortality in my eyes
during the Hungarian Revolution more than a decade earlier. Ob-
livious of recent political developments, he had been touring Eastern
Europe in his vintage Rolls-Royce with his wife Lady Rosula, who
suddenly saw a menacing cloud of dust in front of them.

'Slow down, Alan, those are tanks.'

Dr Glyn slowed to a crawl to let the enormous column of Soviet
armour pull ahead. A few minutes later, Lady Rosula squirming
nervously in her seat saw another menacing cloud of dust behind
them.

'Put your foot down, Alan. There are dozens of tanks behind us.'

And so alternately accelerating and decelerating, Dr Glyn rode into
Budapest in the middle of the Soviet invasion force.

Despite an unbroken record of immediate rejection, I had a faint
flush of confidence in Wells. With my Wiltshire background, for
once there was a glimmer of truth about my standard opening, 'It has
always been my dearest wish to represent this part of the world.' Dr
Glyn was surely beatable. I had discovered that Piers Dixon, son of the
Suez diplomat Sir Pierson Dixon, did not know how to pronounce
Frome (he called it Froam rather than Froom) which was the principal
town in the constituency, and Bob Boscawen, a Lloyds underwriter of
noble Cornish origin, had been badly shot up in the war and had
received extensive plastic surgery. In an old-fashioned film he would
have been described as the Man Without a Face. If this was to be a
beauty contest surely, I evilly calculated, I must be in with a chance,
not least because I had just become engaged (Julia and I were to be
married in ten days' time) and there was my fiancée in her little pink
suit from Delisse sitting in the front row. Her placement had been the
outcome of a tense debate. Full-blown wives came on to the platform
and were invited to offer a few words of support for their husband,
modestly phrased but suggesting inner strength; Lady Rosula was hot
stuff in this department. Fiancées occupied a sort of limbo. The
association had a right to take a look at them but not to interrogate. So

Julia had one of the most uncomfortable hours of her life, with several hundred citizens of Wells & Frome trying to sneak a look at her by leaning out sideways or making unnecessary visits to the toilet and sneaking a passing glance. All of this came to nothing. The Man Without a Face romped home and I packed it in.

The secrets of my failure were not hard to pin down. My voice was languid. That was not in itself a crippling disadvantage. Local Conservative associations at that period did not resent superior upper-class drawls. What was fatal was that I also spoke much too quickly. A languid gabble may sound like a contradiction in terms, but that was what the effect amounted to and it created a feeling of unease in the audience, communicating all too vividly my inner nervous state. No less damaging, although the time allotted was shortish – typically we were asked to speak for somewhere between five and ten minutes – quite soon I found myself overcome with boredom by the sound of my own voice. This sudden sensation of tedium verging on disgust did not go away with practice. On the contrary, the more often I delivered the latest version of my set speech, the more unbearable it sounded. As repetition is one of the secrets of success in politics, this repugnance would have had to be overcome and for that among plenty of other reasons – lack of social and physical stamina, the general feebleness diagnosed by Sir Richard Sharples – I was clearly disqualified for the struggle.

By the time Margaret Thatcher became Prime Minister I had long ago abandoned any thought of a political career and had happily settled for a life of writing anything that came to hand or mind. So it was a total surprise when her economic adviser Alan Walters rang up on 3 March 1982 and asked whether I would care to come and work for her. Alan spoke in a faintly nasal voice which created a curious effect simultaneously of distance and inwardness so that you felt what you were hearing were some internal vibrations no doubt preliminary to speech as one would understand it but not at that stage intended for the world to hear. The result was that sometimes it took a while to take in exactly what he was saying. And the conversation had gone on for several minutes before I understood that what he was suggesting, or rather what Margaret Thatcher was suggesting, was that I should run her policy unit at Number Ten. The idea knocked me flat.

Although I had ambled around on the fringes of party politics (see above), I had never run anything and had zero experience of the workings of government.

'It's only a little unit,' Alan said apologetically, as though I might be expecting a staff of hundreds. It emerged that in fact the unit was very nearly what it said, i.e. one person, or would be by the time I took it over, consisting as it did of John Hoskyns and Norman Strauss, who were both leaving, and one other.

However, the rest of us could not be expected to know this and it was generally assumed that I was taking control of a small army of advisers.

'Should I take it?'

'Well, you're always going on about what the government ought to do, so isn't this a chance to put your ideas into practice? Won't you always regret it if you don't?'

'But I didn't really get on with her.'

'That was ages ago, wasn't it?'

'Ye-es,' I said, and I knew Julia was right.

The news of my appointment was greeted with general amazement by friends, spiced with sharp disapproval in the case of the more rabid loathers of Mrs Thatcher. 'We'll start talking to Ferdy again when he's stopped working for that woman,' was one of the crisper reactions.

My reasons for accepting the offer are pretty easy to break down: wish to make a difference, fame and flattery and above all curiosity. Whatever else it might be it was an unrivalled opportunity to see the workings of the machine at its core.

The reasons for being chosen are a bit more obscure, but I do now have a fairly clear idea of what they were. The first is to do with Alan Walters himself. Born in England, he had spent much of his adult life in American universities where he had gained a high reputation as a transport economist. Ironically, for one regarded as a right-winger, he is the father of Ken Livingstone's congestion charge. It was in America too that he had learned from Hayek and Friedman his free-market economics and his monetary theory. He had also acquired an American can-do optimism, so that the BBC was not wholly wrong when it referred to him as Mrs Thatcher's American economic adviser.

I had met Alan at the Institute of Economic Affairs where he had long collaborated with Ralph Harris and Arthur Seldon in re-educating a distracted nation in the inexorable laws of supply and demand. The other two shared Alan's cheerful outlook on life. Never was economics less of a dismal science than when they were expounding its benign simplicities. Ralph in a check waistcoat like a stable lad in an early Munnings and Arthur, a short, burrowing creature out of *Wind in the Willows*, injected intellectual self-confidence into a generation of bemused and doleful politicians and commentators. In a political elite obsessed by the problems of managing decline they stood out for their certainty that these problems could be remedied.

It was Alan Walters who was the driving force behind the 1981 Budget which is now generally regarded as the turning point in post-war British economic management. The Chancellor, Geoffrey Howe, after whom the Budget came to be named, was opposed to the last to Walter's proposition that taxes must be raised, even in such a severe depression, in order to allow interest rates to come down and so get industry moving again. Again and again, Alan knocked on Thatcher's door trying to stiffen her nerve against the Treasury. But in reality he had already persuaded her and Howe gave way under her relentless assault and, to the horror of half her Cabinet, she got the Budget she wanted.

Nowhere was the uproar more outraged than among academic economists. For even after twenty-five years of the IEA its supporters were still in a tiny minority among academic economists. Which is why 364 of them – including many of the most famous names – wrote to *The Times* to denounce the Budget. I was struck not only by the flatulent and feeble nature of their arguments but also by their intellectual arrogance. And I wrote a rude piece in the *Spectator* (11 April 1981) which I cannot resist quoting a large chunk of, not because of its brilliance but because it helps to explain why I was offered my new job:

Three hundred and sixty-four is an awful lot of economists. You cannot help admiring the heroic scale of the manoeuvre. Imagine receiving the request to sign the letter to Mrs Thatcher condemning her economic policies . . . the Cambridge postmark . . . already the shadow of Lord Keynes implores you to stand up and be counted . . . the covering note from Professor Hahn and Professor Neild: 'for the sake of the country and the profession, it is time we all spoke up'. Oh to be part of that 'we' . . .

Alas, the reception of the great round-robinson can only be described as humiliating. Instead of being treated as serious political ammunition like the bulletin of some uppity stockbroker, the gallant 364 were greeted with a volley of stink-bombs. Most wounding of all, not a single Labour MP bothered even to mention them. In fact, it was a Tory diehard, Sir Anthony Kershaw, who offered them up as cannon fodder to Mrs Thatcher. The Charge of the Light Brigade suffered only minor casualties by comparison. This debacle is certainly not due to abounding public confidence in Mrs Thatcher or her policies. It is due to the low standing of the economist's profession. Dismal? Yes. Science? Well, most people have begun to have their doubts.

Take the opening sentence: 'We . . . are convinced that . . . there is no basis in economic theory or supporting evidence for the government's belief that . . .' Specious already. So long as there are *some* recognised economists who argue that the government's belief is not entirely wrong, then that belief must have some basis in *their* economic theory. The only alternative is to deny that Hayek, Friedman, Walters, Brittan, Budd et al. are economists at all and to assert that there is only one 'economic theory', to wit, the 364 variety.

The 364 go on to prophesy that 'present policies will deepen the depression, erode the industrial base of our economy and threaten its social and political stability'. And very nasty too. Now these prophecies clearly depend on highly contentious economic assumptions. Is an industrial base something fixed? Does raising taxes depress economic activity more than lowering interest rates animates it? But they also depend on equally contentious *political* assumptions about how people will react to the predicted hardships, about popular allegiance and obedience to authority. What the 364 are trying to do is to bolster up these audacious predictions with a professional authority which we simple folk are supposed to accept as scientific like elementary chemistry is scientific.

All unwittingly, this article clearly demonstrated that, though I might not be a trained economist, I was in that department of life at least clearly 'One of Us' – a phrase much attributed to Mrs Thatcher by her opponents to prove her narrow, cliquey approach but not, as it happens, one I ever heard her use. In any case, when I explained to Alan that my training in economics began and ended with a *vix satis double minus* in Oxford prelims, he reassured me that the only bits of economics that mattered were really quite simple and boiled down to the laws of supply and demand. I said yes to Alan over the phone the next day and he said he would tell the Prime Minister who would be delighted. Then silence fell for several weeks. Had she thought better of it herself, or had some wiser counsellor pointed out to her the obvious disadvantages of employing me? Had I somehow made a fool of myself before I had even started? Then the phone rang. It was Clive Whitmore who turned out to be the Prime Minister's Principal Private Secretary. Would I call round at Downing Street for a chat, then look in on the Prime Minister?

I marched down the long corridor. I had been to Downing Street for official receptions for journalists and the like, but previous visits did not seem to soften the implausibility of my actually working there. My interview with Clive Whitmore did not diminish the implausibility. He was a burly, owlish figure whose friendly manner scarcely masked a capacity for impatience, perhaps was not intended to. Had I understood that I would be a temporary member of the Civil Service, that I would be subject to its disciplines, the Official Secrets Act and so on, that the appointment would cease at the general election, though I could be reappointed if the government were re-elected (a possibility which I guessed he thought remote, with the government then in third place in the opinion polls behind Labour and the breakaway SDP which was surging)? I should also understand that I would not be entitled to membership of the Civil Service pension scheme – a question infinitely remote from my mind which was preoccupied not with the problems of retirement but with getting through the next hour and a half. As I sat opposite Clive Whitmore in the stuffy little interview room, I felt as though I was being grilled about the seriousness of an application to take Holy Orders and putting up a poor show. It was almost a relief when he took me upstairs past the

photos of previous Prime Ministers into Mrs T's study. She was seated
in a high-winged armchair covered in some Peter Jones brocade or
chintz. It is traditional to remark on the homely nature of Number
Ten, as a sort of private town house with extras, but because of the
decor and the furniture it is really more like a small private hotel
which has rooms called 'drawing room' and 'study' and 'dining room'
but which aren't at all like these rooms in a private house. So sitting
opposite her in these big-winged armchairs was like having tea with
my aunt Ursie in one of the hotels off Gloucester Road she migrated
between.

'It's a long time since we last worked together, isn't it?'

'Yes,' I said, 'nearly twenty years.'

'Dear Keith,' she said, 'such a wonderful source of ideas. He taught
me such a lot.'

'Me too.'

'We must do something about education.'

I said that was one of the subjects I hoped to have a go at.

'They're getting at him already, you know,' she said. 'The trouble
with Keith is, he listens too much.'

I did not say that this was what I regarded as his principal virtue.

As the conversation wore on, the pieces fell into place. She seemed
to have completely forgotten what she had actually thought of me at
the time, viz. that I was an idle and effete youth who was full of the
conventional consensus mush of the 1960s and who was indulging
Keith Joseph in his fatal tendency to believe the last thing he was told.
Instead, I had been reinvented as a dynamic young research assistant
who had been completely on her wavelength. Successful politicians –
perhaps people who are successful at anything – need to doctor the
past if they are to keep going. In any case I had done a bit of
reinventing myself. When her campaign for the party leadership was
getting under way, I had written a piece for the *Daily Mail* saying
there was no reason now why Margaret Thatcher should not be our
first woman Prime Minister. To be strictly honest, the article was
David English's idea, he rightly thinking that she would turn out to be
a perfect *Daily Mail* icon, but I wrote the thing, and I think it was the
first article in a national newspaper to take her prospects seriously,
although in my heart I was backing Willie Whitelaw at the time. So

that was probably another reason why I found myself sitting opposite her wondering exactly how to ask her, without looking too clueless, what I was supposed actually to do.

'There's nobody here who has any idea how to write a speech,' she said. 'I hope you'll be able to help with that.'

Yes, I said, of course I would, though my primary focus would be on developing policy ideas.

'We always need fresh ideas,' she said. 'But you're such a word-smith.'

She spoke of this quality with the respect due to any expertise, at the same time suggesting that it ranked lowish in the hierarchy of skills, nearer to being a dental technician than a nuclear physicist. There was no doubt that in her mind I was the answer to the speechwriting problem. I thought of myself more as the answer to the policy problem.

So there we were, starting off on a threefold misunderstanding. She thought I had supported her for the leadership from first to last, whereas I had in fact dozily inclined towards Whitelaw; she wrongly remembered me more as the Efficient Baxter than as Idle Jack; and she thought I was going to spend most of my time writing her speeches while I thought I was going to be inventing her policies. Well, I suppose many marriages have started on a worse basis.

Then she jumped about a bit. I had not then got used to the nature of her talk, which was in a curious way both relentless and jerky, so that you could not be sure whether she would stick to the subject in hand until she had driven it into the ground or whether she would abandon it without a moment's warning for some quite different topic, making it difficult to know at what moment to try to break in yourself before it was too late. In private conversation at least, she was not such an incurable interrupter but she did not follow the conventions of ordinary dialogue. At the same time, to get herself heard, she had developed a one-paced assertive tone which she was reluctant to let drop, as though any hint of the tentative or the laid-back might be taken as a sign of weakness. Yet every now and then the eyes switched on – the eyes of Caligula, according to François Mitterrand – and you could feel she was saying something that she set real store by, as she did now: 'Education is only part of it. What we really have to address are the values of society. This is my real task, to restore standards of conduct and responsibility. Otherwise we shall simply be employing more and more policemen on an increasingly hopeless task. Everyone has to be involved. At one time, women's magazines played quite a constructive role. Now they've just caved in. Personal responsibility is the key. That was what destroyed Greece and Rome – bread and circuses. It has to stop, Ferdy, it has to stop.'

I confess I found all this both startling and thrilling. The naked zeal, the direct, unabashed appeal to morality, the sheer seriousness. I could not think of any other Prime Minister in my time, probably not one since Gladstone, who would have used such language in taking on a new apparatchik. There was none of the weary, professional cynicism I was so used to and had myself become so weary of. Smartasses might raise an eyebrow at her jumbling up women's magazines and the fall of Rome. To me this showed an unblinking resolve to look at things as they were. This was the real thing. I promised to do something for her on Renewing the Values of Society, not a phrase I much cared for – I suspect she had picked it up from Keith Joseph. 'Values' was not a Thatcher word (when she famously said on *The World This Weekend* that she was in favour of Victorian values, the phrase had to be suggested to her by Brian Walden). But I knew what she meant.

Before this meeting I had had a drink with John Hoskyns who had said I should get a mission statement out of her otherwise she would be all over the shop and I would be as much at cross-purposes as he had been. I said I had never had a mission statement in my life and wouldn't know one if I saw one. John laughed and said in that case I might enjoy the job. He had started as a professional soldier and then made a fortune in his own computer firm. His mind was essentially systematic and the 'Stepping Stones' that he and David Wolfson had marked out for her when she was Leader of the Opposition had clarified her mind in working out which were the things that needed to be put first if Britain's decline was to be reversed. John had had a crucial part in locking her mind on to the two main priorities: gaining control of the nation's finances and putting inflation on a steady downward path, and reforming trade union law, so that the trade unions could no longer prevent companies from being properly run. But now the great swirling tide of government business had swept across her path, the stepping stones were deep under water and she was irked to be constantly reminded that she needed a Strategy with a capital S. She knew what she had to do. In psychological terms, she had internalised the strategy. The long term was not something to be approached gingerly with a ponderous statement of first principles. The long term started here and now.

John and his even more systems-minded guru, Norman Strauss, found this infuriating. It seemed all right to me, especially as even on this first meeting I grasped how difficult verging on the impossible it was to make her stick to any topic she didn't wish to stick to, especially when she got going on her colleagues. One after another they bit the dust before my eyes. A was hopelessly indecisive, B left a trail of muddle behind him wherever he went, and as for Jim Prior, the Northern Ireland Bill hadn't a hope of working: 'If it had been anyone other than Jim I would have stopped it. If they ever get the Assembly working, both sides will use it to abuse us. But I was so relieved to have got Jim away from Employment I had to let it go. I call him the False Squire, you know, all bluff and red-faced, but all they're thinking about is how to plan the next retreat. That's not why I came into politics. Sometimes you have to retreat as we did with the miners. But only tactically. You have to go forward or you might as well give up altogether.'

She went on in this vein for a good ten minutes, as though I needed to be converted to her way of thinking, or at least needed to have it all spelled out, perhaps because I was a foreigner or had been living in New Zealand for the past five years, rather than a declared supporter who wrote about British politics twice a week. This was never to change. Even after she had been haranguing visitors for hours – diplomats, businessmen, newspaper editors – and they had finally gone and she kicked off her shoes and we had a glass of Scotch together with whoever else in the office happened to be around, she would resume the harangue, as though we had never met before, as though I had not heard the same spiel half-a-dozen times already that day. Her absence of small talk was so unusual that I could never quite believe it and untaught by experience could not resist offering up some small inconsequential remark which, unless it was strictly political gossip, she would bat away as though she had scarcely heard it. It was well known that she was resistant to humour, often had to have jokes explained to her. But she was also indifferent to most of the tricks of paradox, ambiguity, understatement and saying the opposite of what you mean, which pepper the talk of almost everyone else in this country.

Even in that not-so-brief first meeting I became aware that this was going to be a holiday from irony. Not simply was I going to be doing a job quite unlike anything I had ever attempted or even thought about; I was going to be dealing mostly with a character quite unlike any I had ever had close dealings with before.

She did not look so very different from the time I first knew her, a little sharper in the face, the blue eyes more piercing and the voice famously lower, but what had really changed was that the bridle had come off. There was a magnificent lack of restraint, or so I thought on that first re-meeting, as though the best thing about being Prime Minister was that you could say whatever came into your head. This was curiously liberating to her underlings, because if she wasn't watching her words you didn't have to either, or not nearly so much as with some more watchful political operator. I was shocked too, but I confess thrilled, by the brutal way she talked about her colleagues. Actually that was not nearly so unusual as I thought. I didn't then know any politicians intimately enough to know that denouncing their colleagues as traitors, cowards and halfwits is a pretty standard mode of letting off steam. But I had followed politics closely enough to see that she did have one unique quality: tenacity. She never gave up, she never left a subject alone once it had engaged her attention. All this was intensely exciting. And there was, besides, an exhilarating side to signing on with someone who was so detested by the intelligentsia. Jonathan Miller spoke for the whole world of the arts in finding her 'loathsome, repulsive in almost every way' and denounced her 'odious suburban gentility and sentimental, saccharine patriotism'. Lady Warnock confessed to 'a kind of rage' whenever she thought about her. Margaret Thatcher had committed the ultimate sin, of being suburban and proud of it. Nothing better, I thought. At last I was on the right side. I had finally escaped from the soft seductions of Hobohemia. From now on I would be working with serious people who had no pretensions or snobberies. For the first time I would be living something approaching real life, even if I wasn't by a long stretch of the imagination the right person to be living it.

But I very nearly wasn't there at all. I came close to being the shortest-lived Prime Ministerial adviser in recent history. Just as the timetable of the Profumo affair had shadowed the last stages of the Selwyn Lloyd report, so now another, more momentous affair loomed out of the darkness to shadow the timetable of my arrival in Downing Street.

I was aware of the Falkland Islands as a simmering problem making unpleasant splutterings on the back burner. I had, after all, been sitting in the press gallery when the junior Foreign Office Minister Nicholas Ridley returned from the South Atlantic to report on his attempts to persuade the islanders to accept a leaseback arrangement. He was torn apart. I have never seen a minister endure a nastier half-hour from apoplectic backbenchers. But I found the whole business mystifying – the Foreign Office's determination to appease a low-grade police state no less than the obsession shared between Tory diehards and the Argentinians with a few barren lumps of rock acquired in dubious circumstances. When a party of Argentinian scrap-metal merchants landed on South Georgia on 19 March 1982, a fortnight after my first phone call from Alan Walters, I entirely failed to grasp the significance of the move.

Then on 1 April came the invasion. I experienced the same feelings of astonishment and humiliation as everyone else. And in the *Spectator* I went along with the despatch of 'the last Armada' as 'a quixotic but necessary enterprise', adding a few lofty criticisms of the failure of successive governments to be honest with themselves about the future of the islands. But my heart was not in the business. Anyway my mind was on my own expedition into murky waters. As the task force was steaming towards the South Atlantic, I was steaming towards Downing Street. My appointment was announced two days before the recapture of South Georgia, to rather less general rejoicing. Roy Hattersley in *Punch* said I had a gent's face 'in that special shade of pink that comes from moderate exposure to fresh air and the lifelong freedom from pimples and acne that only careful upbringing guarantees' – the opposite of 'the proper Yorkshire working-class red face owned by the Prime Minister's press officer Bernard Ingham', who, Hattersley suggested, ought to offer me some advice on how to survive without actually agreeing with the Prime Minister, because Hattersley thought my views on unemployment and on the police would be unlikely to chime with hers. On the same lines, the *Sunday Times* expressed surprise at my being chosen, claiming that I was 'cool on monetarism', 'soft on law and order' and 'dissents from Mrs Thatcher's Falklands policy' – all of which, I sighed in the *Spectator*, 'only shows how difficult it is to make oneself clear'. This was not the whole truth, because as it gradually emerged, although whatever Hattersley might say I agreed pretty much with Mrs Thatcher about most things, I did dissent from her Falklands policy, or rather regarded the despatch of the task force more as a negotiating weapon than as a fighting one.

But in any case there was no need to make my views, such as they were, known at all. Obviously, now that I was about to be a civil servant my duty was to shut up. I had to stop writing for the *Spectator* and any other paper straight away. And that is what I told Alexander Chancellor, my old friend and patron.

'But you feel so strongly about it all,' he said. 'You've been writing for me for five years and I've never known you so anguished about anything. Won't you regret it bitterly if you don't write about it?'

Slowly he wore me down with his insidious charm and I agreed to write a couple more pieces before my signing-on date in May. Although I tried to preserve a judicious Olympian calm on the page, I was in a turmoil. Should I resign from my new job before I started it? Should I change my mind again and tell Alexander I must stop? In any case, the sinking of the *Sheffield* and the *Belgrano* tipped me over the edge and in terms as careful and hedged as I could manage I expressed the hope that after bloodshed on such a scale it might be possible to arrange a negotiated ceasefire and an honourable settlement. No such nuances were observed on the cover of the *Spectator* which said simply 'TIME FOR A CEASEFIRE' in extra-large type.

I don't claim that this headline echoed round the world like the shot at Sarajevo. But it did make a bit of a stir. The *Daily Mirror* had also called for a ceasefire and the *Sun* had accused it of being a traitor to Britain. So the *Mirror* on its leader page reproduced the *Spectator* headline with a mugshot of me looking gormless, saying, 'If that is treachery, then Mrs Thatcher has just recruited a traitor to Downing Street.' Opponents of the war congratulated me on my courage for speaking out in such difficult circumstances. Supporters of the war – a very much larger group – denounced me for my lack of moral fibre and unsteadiness under fire. One or two readers cancelled their *Spectator* subscriptions, including Kingsley Amis who wrote to Philip Larkin 'that sodding fool Ferdy Mount has called for an unconditional ceasefire before trooping off to advise Mrs Thatcher at No. 10'.

Sodding fool seems a fair assessment. In the first place, a ceasefire was never remotely likely just after ships had been sunk and lives had been lost. There were besides no conceivable terms that the Argentinian junta could accept without being toppled. But, much more to the point, I should have obeyed my first impulse and stopped writing the moment my appointment was announced. It was nothing but vanity to carry on.

Inside Downing Street they had other things on their mind. But Mrs Thatcher's PPS Ian Gow did take it upon himself to bring up the matter. He and the Prime Minister had both read the article and agreed that the article, though bad, was not as bad as the headline. I think they also agreed that at this delicate juncture it would be a mistake to draw attention to any rat joining the ship. There was, after all, considerable distaste in Whitehall, not only in the Foreign Office, for Mrs Thatcher's determination to recapture the islands at any cost. From the Cabinet Secretary downwards, the permanent officials would have preferred a more emollient course. Even loyal Thatcherites like John Biffen were not entirely sound on the issue. The abrasive Jock Bruce-Gardyne sent a note to his friend Sam Brittan on the *Financial Times* lamenting the cost of the whole caper. And Alan Walters circulated a note suggesting, quite rightly, that it would in the end prove much cheaper to offer every one of the 1,800 islanders a million pounds to resettle in Canada or New Zealand. This was one of Alan's few memos that did not find favour with Mrs Thatcher.

In any case, no mention was ever made of my deviation and Ian Gow and I became friends. Ian was one of the more extraordinary figures in Mrs Thatcher's entourage, which was a mixed bunch to say the least. He was MP for Eastbourne and with his old-fashioned three-piece suit and watch chain he bore a startling resemblance to that celebrated Eastbourne medical practitioner Dr Bodkin Adams, whose elderly female patients had a habit of dying soon after they had altered their wills in his favour. After Dr Adams was acquitted of helping the old ladies on their way, he said, 'I am going back to work' – one of my favourite remarks which I quoted to Ian who didn't think it at all funny. In fact he wouldn't hear a word against Dr Adams, who remained a stalwart of the Eastbourne Conservative Association, much in demand at fêtes and a generous contributor to party funds. Ian's manner of speech was deliberately archaic too: 'Pray, may I wait upon you at noon?' But there was nothing old-fashioned about the intelligence service he operated in the House of Commons which instantly picked up and reported back any evidence of disloyalty or disquiet, earning him the sobriquet of Supergrass. Ian was a hero-worshipper, curiously unworldly in a sense. He was not at all rich and he was pathetically grateful when I paid for lunch. He drove me around London in his battered old Mini, peering myopically over the steering wheel while quoting bons mots of Churchill or General de Gaulle – or above all of Mrs Thatcher, whom he unstintingly adored. When asked whether she ever suffered from self-doubt, he said, 'The truth of the matter is that in my experience she is almost always right and therefore there is not a great necessity to admit she is wrong.' He asked nothing more than to be able to serve his own Joan of Arc indefinitely and when promoted to Housing Minister as a reward for his unpaid service at Downing Street he was disconsolate. In fact he never enjoyed ministerial life at all and after only four months in office at the Treasury resigned in protest against the Anglo-Irish Agreement because he thought it was a betrayal of the Ulster Unionists – something which nobody else in the House of Commons would have dreamed of doing. In the cruellest possible way, he turned out to have signed his own death warrant. He was blown up by the IRA as he was starting his car at his home on the South Downs, which was called the Dog Kennel.

After Ian left, Mrs Thatcher felt that she could not ask any of her colleagues to take on the thankless task of acting as her eyes and ears unless he had a large private income. The result was that none of Ian's successors was anywhere near as good at warning her of looming political danger. It is just when Prime Ministers who have been in office for years begin to lose touch that they most need to be told what is happening. If she had had an Ian Gow in the late 1980s, she might not have made some of her more glaring mistakes.

I started work on Monday 17 May. The Friday before, the SAS had made the first land attack, on Pebble Island. The main invasion was to begin at dawn the following Friday. It was a lovely sunny May morning with that last hint of chill in the air which quickly goes. I knocked at the door of Number Ten, as everyone has to do from Cabinet Ministers to the man who's come to fix the dishwasher, there being no tradesmen's entrance and nobody but a bored policeman in the street who has no power to usher you in. So you stand there on the doorstep feeling conspicuous in front of the small knot of gawpers (it was before they gated the street off). Then Fred the ancient commissionaire lets you in and you stand in the hall still feeling conspicuous.

It was amazingly quiet. The largest task force since the Second World War was closing in on the islands. The balloon was about to go up in what even the most gung-ho supporter could see was bound to be an immensely hazardous enterprise and there wasn't a soul about. Throughout the next three weeks what struck me most was the extraordinary stillness of the place.

Here I must say something about the geography of the house, by which I do not mean, in that old-fashioned euphemism, the lavatories, although I do mean them too. Just as all traffic theoretically has to go through the front door, admin, maintenance and clerical no less than high political and diplomatic, so all traffic has to carry on down the long hall which goes the full depth of the building, thus leading to bizarre collisions. A few yards in on the right there is a fireplace, where the Prime Minister is often photographed with other Prime Ministers, their faces locked in a rictus of feigned delight, their hands slowly pumping up and down until the snappers have had their fill, in summer the flower arrangement in the grate lending an exquisite falseness to the scene. On the left is the gents, a key stopover for ministers with weak bladders or who are worried that they look too blown about. It was here that Michael Heseltine stopped off after he had flounced out of the Cabinet room during the Westland Affair

with the words 'I cannot accept that decision. I must therefore leave
this Cabinet.' His colleagues round the Cabinet table were not 100
per cent clear what he meant. Did he just mean this meeting of the
Cabinet or was he resigning? When he stopped off for a pee – news
swiftly retailed by a passing secretary – the uncertainty was prolonged.
Some wondered whether, cooling down in front of the porcelain, he
might change his mind if indeed he had made it up. Mrs Thatcher
herself, though, was in no doubt and had George Younger lined up to
succeed him even before Heseltine had got through the front door
and out into the street where in fact he did announce that he had
resigned. Simultaneously Mrs Thatcher had called a short break to the
meeting and walked next door into the private secretaries' room
where she asked her Principal Secretary, Nigel Wicks, to bring
Younger in to her.

It is the private secretaries' room which is the hub of the place,
rather than the Prime Minister's own office, because he or she does
not really have one, migrating downstairs from the study and the
drawing room to the Cabinet room or in the evening upstairs two
floors to the Prime Minister's flat, a string of low-ceilinged rooms at
the top which amounts to little more than a dolled-up attic. It is a
matter of taste where the Prime Minister is more often to be found –
Thatcher perhaps in the study, Wilson more likely in the Cabinet
room sitting alone at the thick bit of the coffin-shaped table as though
presiding over a Cabinet of ghosts. Ian Gow had a cubby-hole to the
left of the Cabinet room, known rather grandiosely as the Political
Office, out of which he would pop unnervingly to grasp the elbow of
some minister hanging around waiting to go into Cabinet.

Our office was at the front end of the building. You slipped
through a little door on the left before the gents, past Denis Thatcher's
golf clubs and the Downing Street cat, an overfed animal which had
found a warm spot by the central heating pipes, and up a dim flight of
stairs. The first floor was Honours and Appointments. Through a half-
open door you would occasionally catch a glimpse of a pink-faced
brigadier scrutinising the latest list of MBEs (military) or the Appointments Secretary Robin Catford waggling his enormous eyebrows as
he was telephoning some deanery or Oxbridge common room to
arrange a visit to canvass opinion about the next bishop or Regius

professor. You ascended beyond these Trollopian realms to a quiet suite of offices decorated in the dignified but sombre style of Harley Street rooms where an unbelievably expensive consultant gives you the bad news. Waiting for me were the tall and willowy Linda Rust who was to be my secretary and the short and feisty Rose Padwick who was looking after Alan Walters, the poppy and the marigold as I thought of them, or the long and the short of it as Rose put it in her more Barbara Windsoresque style. Like most of the permanent residents of Number Ten they were utterly relaxed, ready to accommodate any tantrum of the temporary inmates with no more than a raised eyebrow. Linda made me a cup of coffee and brought in the newspapers and left me to it.

The silence was deafening. We were too high to hear any noise coming from the street. Behind our room ran the huge warren of the Cabinet Office, in front the great Italianate palace of the Foreign Office shut out the world. I looked in the in-tray. There was a notice from Establishment about my pay which I hadn't actually mentioned before taking the job (£23,500 per annum as it turned out, not bad at all), and a note from Mr Carruthers in Positive Vetting apologising for not having got round to me earlier but he would be ringing to make an appointment. Nothing else.

Suddenly I had a fancy that this was how it was going to be. I would come in every morning for months, perhaps years, and there would be nothing at all to do, but I would keep up a steady front to the outside world saying that the work was very interesting though the hours were rather long. Wasn't there one of those Russian short stories where this was the plot? Perhaps it had already been agreed that this was the kindest way to cope with the embarrassment of my presence. Rather than undermine morale during active hostilities in the South Atlantic or sour the aftermath of victory by a bad-tempered bust-up, I would be kept on ice up here on the second floor until a suitably dull moment, over the Christmas holidays perhaps, when it would be agreed that the appointment had not worked out. Some tactful formula would be found – mutual agreement, health grounds, etc.

There was a cough at the door. A friendly unobtrusive cough. A Jeeves cough. It was John Vereker, who had been until half an hour earlier the sole member of the Policy Unit. John was on secondment

from Overseas Development. He was a quick-talking, merry character, now and then showing a flicker of pomposity as though
rehearsing for his later career as Permanent Secretary and then
Governor of Bermuda but easily teased out of it by Linda and Rose
who, if all else failed, would refer to his bald patch. Like quite a few
high-flyers in the Civil Service, he came from a rather classier
background than most of the politicians he served (the Verekers of
Co. Galway, not that either of us would have dreamed of mentioning
such a thing and only an obsessive genealogist like me would have
known it), so that he added a certain social self-confidence to his
having passed all the exams that quite a few of his political masters
could not have.

'John, where on earth do I start?'

'Well, first you insist on seeing all the papers.'

'Won't they just send them automatically? After all, John Hoskyns
and Bernard Donoughue [my equivalent under Harold Wilson
whom I had also had a drink with] said they kicked up the hell of
a fuss and insisted they saw everything, so won't all that just carry on?'

'Certainly not. The change is an opportunity to stop sending you
all the Most Secret stuff. What you need to do is go and see the
Cabinet Secretary and say the Prime Minister was most insistent that
you had access to all the papers.'

'She didn't actually say anything about it.'

'Well, she would have if she'd thought of it. Then you need to go
and make friends in the Private Office, so they copy the stuff to us
straight away.'

He took me down to meet Robin Butler and the other private
secretaries, Michael Scholar and Tim Lankester. Suddenly from my
austere isolation I became part of a lively band of clerks, handpicked
from the Treasury for quick-wittedness and good humour. Michael
Scholar in particular had the impish grin of a medieval scrivener. It was a
diversion as much as an education to sit beside him and watch him flip
through the pile of paper that came across his desk and then digest, mark
up and present it to his mistress, explaining it so quickly and with so little
fuss that he made being Prime Minister seem quite easy.

The rougher type of Thatcherite – Ian Gow or his later successor
Peter Morrison – would affect contempt for the entire race of civil

servants, calling them 'Martians'. The truth was the reverse, that the staff in Number Ten were decent kindred spirits while some of Mrs Thatcher's *enragés* were decidedly swivel-eyed. The difficulty was to persuade the decent kindred spirits (on the Tory back benches as well as in the Civil Service) that at this particular moment in history the swivel-eyed brigade were worth listening to.

Slowly, under John's tuition, I began to see how we could find handholds in the smooth forbidding walls of the system, while noting at the same time how 'unhelpful' (the civil servant's favourite word) that system was to anyone trying to inject anything in the nature of a fresh approach. The British Cabinet is a superb machine for organising collective responsibility but it is positively hostile to collective thought. Traditionally its principal motive force is to preserve the independence of its feudal baronies and to deny the Prime Minister any role more dynamic than that of chairing its meetings and appointing its ministers. Throughout the Attlee–Macmillan–Wilson years the Prime Minister had a staff no larger than that of the mayor of a medium-sized German town. And although Ted Heath's invention of the Central Policy Review Staff in the Cabinet Office and Harold Wilson's invention of the Policy Unit in Number Ten when he came back in 1974 increased the capacity at the centre, it was still a long way from being a cohesive driving force. For one thing, the Policy Unit and the CPRS were geographically a long way apart. To pay a visit on the CPRS, you had to go down two flights of stairs, walk the whole way through Number Ten, collect a key from Security to unlock the green-baize door through to the Cabinet Office, deposit the key outside Sir Robert Armstrong's office, then collect it again to repeat the manoeuvre on your return. The green-baize door was symbolic of the jealously guarded independence of the Cabinet Office from the Prime Minister's sole control, with the result that it had no political direction at all.

I went to see Sir Robert in his huge office, tripping across the expanses of his vast white carpet. When I said how keen the Prime Minister was that I should see all the papers, he said that of course there would be no question of any difficulty at all. Nothing could have exceeded his courtesy and I wondered if I was being too shrill, but then I remembered what a struggle John Hoskyns had had to obtain the same rights.

I returned to the Policy Unit, rather proud of having secured this arrangement, not to mention having negotiated the green-baize door.

'There doesn't seem to be any problem at all.'

'We-ell,' John said, 'they wouldn't have let you have them unless you asked.'

'So what's next?'

'Have you noticed the messengers?'

'You mean the one who limps and that nice plump one.'

'Yes, not exactly bred for speed. I think we've got some equal opportunities programme going. Anyway, it's no use just waiting for them to come round, especially at the end of the day, because that's when the departments send in their awkward papers in the hope of getting them into the box without chaps like us getting our inky fingers on them. We have to run up and down those stairs ourselves.'

The best thing for the minister with a policy or a bit of news which he knew the Prime Minister wouldn't like was to slip it into the bottom of the red box, so that the Prime Minister would see it right at the end of the evening when she was getting sleepy and might initial it without comment. This ruse didn't always work, but that didn't stop them trying.

Slowly I began to get the hang of the routine. Beneath the unhurried official tempo, there were moments when speed of foot was of the essence. I often found myself breaking into a run down the central passage of Number Ten and running full tilt into distinguished persons coming out of official meetings, on one occasion nearly headbutting the Prime Minister of Italy, Bettino Craxi, at that time regarded as a likely saviour of his country before he was indicted for massive corruption. On another occasion, I had to perform a rapid body-swerve to avoid the members of the Joint Intelligence Committee marching three abreast. After a bit, we managed to develop a rudimentary early-warning system. The Private Office would let us know in advance that MAFF or DHSS were planning to bring over some disastrous proposal at the close of play, six o'clock or later, and we would have a note denouncing the proposal ready to be pinned to it before we had actually read it. In extremis, I would simply scribble directly on the departmental paper what I thought of it. Occasionally one of these papers got through and the red box had already gone upstairs to the flat before we got wind of it. Even then all was not lost. There was a back stairway leading up from our offices to the Prime Minister's flat and it was possible late in the evening to steal up there and deposit our critique in the red box as though it had been there all along. From along the passage would come the aroma and kerfuffle of the Prime Minister making shepherd's pie. This dish, almost as legendary in its incarnation here as in its pairing with Krug champagne at Jeffrey Archer's parties, was certainly the only one I ever had cooked by her, though others claimed she could roast a nice chicken. Even the bona fides of the shepherd's were in doubt, since Crawfie, Mrs Thatcher's diminutive dresser, would when out of sorts claim that in fact it was she who had peeled and mashed the potato and prepared the mince and the Prime Minister only had to put the two together. It was not exactly against the rules to fiddle with the red box once it had gone up. At the same time, I felt decidedly burglarish as I scrabbled through the papers trying to find which one to attach our memo to before anyone came down the passage from the kitchen.

As I clattered up and down the narrow back stairs, I repeated to myself Bacon's maxim that 'all rising to great place is by a winding stair'. There was plenty of domestic traffic on these stairs, too. In the evening I would often bump into Denis, usually in a black tie, off to some dinner of fellow rugby referees or old colleagues in the oil and paint business. From the first I was enchanted by Denis. He was not unlike the figure in the 'Dear Bill' letters, although oddly enough most of the brilliant antique slang deployed by John Wells and Richard Ingrams came originally not from Denis himself but from the supposed recipient of the letters, Bill Deedes, and even more so from Bill's son Jeremy – such phrases as 'HMG' for 'Home Made Gent' which I never actually heard Denis utter. At the same time such human sensitivity as was on offer in the Thatcher partnership came mostly from him. He was the one who was quick to see when someone was feeling bored or left out of things, the first to smooth over an awkward silence. Mrs Thatcher did not appear to mind silence when she had nothing to say herself. I have sat through some chilly meals in which only Denis and I kept any semblance of conversation going, about the early flowering of the daffodils in the park or the cost of taxis, a thankless task really since, if the topic did not catch her fancy, none of the other ministers present would think it worth taking it up either, perhaps because joining in with us would condemn them as trivial-minded.

I would sometimes meet Alfred Sherman on the back stairs too. Alfred already had his reputation as Svengali to Margaret's Trilby firmly in place. He certainly looked the part, squat with fierce glaring eyes and bulbous unhappy lips. He was bald except for tufts of hair sprouting up behind his ears like some dismal sedge growing between rocks. After a drink or two – he did not really drink – he was inclined to turn lecherous. The sight of his fat paws fondling the décolletage of Debbie, our new secretary, at a Downing Street party could have come straight out of a George Grosz caricature illustrating the horrors of Berlin nightlife in the 1930s. Nor, unlike Svengali, were these disadvantages compensated for by an attractive voice. Alfred's voice dripped menace and malice. The heavy tweed suit and bow tie that he tended to wear only added to the impression of suppressed violence.

This violence had not always been suppressed. He had joined the Communist Party at Ilford Grammar School and at the age of eighteen had run away to fight for the Reds in Spain, where he was said to have been both handy and ruthless with a machine gun. After the war he led a superficially tamer life as a Kensington councillor and leader-writer on the *Daily Telegraph*. But he never lost his taste for unpopular extremes and to the end of his days kept in his *Who's Who* entry the fact that he had served as consultant to President Radovan Karadžić of the Serbian Republic in Bosnia, an indicted war criminal still on the run at the time of writing. His principal achievement was as founder Director of the Centre for Policy Studies under the historian Hugh Thomas with Margaret Thatcher and Keith Joseph as patrons. In the end, he fell out violently with Hugh and lost his perch. At this stage he was still just clinging on, despite determined efforts not merely to remove him but to ostracise him altogether.

By the time of the 1979 election everyone in the Leader's Steering Committee already hated Alfred, except the Leader. Francis Pym, John Peyton, Ian Gilmour, Jim Prior, John Davies (imported, rather unsuccessfully, from the CBI) all agreed that 'if we told the truth about the unions we should certainly lose the election'. They preferred the emollient sound of Chris Patten's 'pragmatic approach' to the insistence of Hoskyns and Sherman that telling the public the truth about the unions was the first step to effective government. Debate had to be opened up, not stifled. It was futile, Sherman argued, to protest, as Peyton did, that they 'were against appeasement and confrontation but there had to be a third way'. No such Third Way existed.

Sherman was right about that, just as he was right that in the end the miners would have to be beaten. He was right about quite a lot of things, and was never forgiven for it. People used to say, 'If only Alfred didn't always attribute the worst motives to people, if only he could at least pretend to be nice.' I didn't agree at all. The whole point of Alfred was that he was horrible and licensed to be horrible. He was thus able to say what nobody else liked to say, which was that three-quarters of the Shadow Cabinet wanted to dodge the central issue of the time. They also wished that the Parliamentary party had never elected Mrs Thatcher in the first place and they would like nothing better than to get rid of her at the first possible opportunity and return to a quieter life. Anyone who closely studied the *Guardian* columns by Peter Jenkins and Hugo Young over the period 1979–82 could be in no doubt that more than a few of Mrs Thatcher's ministers were engaged in a sustained whispering campaign against her – she was shrill and inexperienced, simply not up to the job, they were heading for the rocks. I first got a whiff attending the Thursday afternoon lobby briefings for the *Spectator* in the first days of the Thatcher government. Norman St John Stevas, her first Leader of the House, indicated by nod, wink and gesture that he was at best a semi-detached supporter of her strategy. Jim Prior, her first Secretary for Employment, let it be known that he had managed to wean her off her extreme confrontational approach to the unions and that his own modest little bill was the first and only sop to the right. As for the Soameses and Gilmours, they were just patronising, regarding the popping up of this suburban little person as a temporary interruption.

So when Alfred went around hissing that 'Margaret is surrounded by enemies' he was speaking nothing less than the truth. I'm not sure how much difference his hissing made in this respect, since she could already see for herself that this was the case. But his insinuating, unstoppable conversation buoyed her up and gave her intellectual self-confidence. 'Alfred's the leader of the awkward squad,' she would say affectionately. And in the heyday of their relationship she would say whatever he put into her mouth. I remember hearing her give a speech in her constituency on the eve of poll in which she quoted both André Gide and Guillaume Apollinaire, neither of them house-hold names in Finchley.

I too found Alfred's talk invigorating, though he did go on more than a bit. Every Saturday he would ring me up at home and we would speak for an hour or so – the longest telephone conversations I have ever had. 'My mission in life is to educate the Tory Party in the laws of cause and effect,' he would say, and I felt that I was included in that mission. It was always so easy to postpone, to modify, to lose the original thrust, above all to hope that things would turn out all right, if we waited a bit. By comparison, the other approach of expecting the worst, of taking the flak now, of sticking to the strategy, was bleak and unappealing.

But it wasn't just my resolve that needed stiffening by repeated injections of Alfred's sibilant insinuations. I needed to branch out from the Downing Street bunker, and this meant learning the esoteric tricks of the trade. I was, after all, a complete innocent in the arts of management. John Vereker realised to his consternation that I didn't even know how to run a meeting.

'You mustn't just say at the end, "Thank you all for coming, that was very interesting." '

'Why not?'

'Because they'll assume the whole thing's over and done with and they'll totally forget about it. What you must always do is set out a programme of work and arrange a date for the next meeting.'

'Even if there isn't any action that needs taking and you don't really need another meeting?'

'Especially then.'

John also explained to me how suicidal it would be to start ringing up civil servants all over Whitehall and ask them to come in and explain things to me, because their Secretaries of State would get wind of it and think I was conspiring against them to undermine their authority. The thing to do was to go and see the Secretaries of State themselves first and implore them as a favour to lend me their brightest sparks now and then to remedy my ignorance. I set off on this tour of Whitehall, which I dubbed 'my fireside chats', although there was never anything resembling a fire in those dismal ministerial suites, all recently redecorated at large expense in various shades of sand and beige with low squashy sofas and dim lighting, examples of the management style of interior decor at that period, lowering and stifling places, not much cheered up by the glass of whisky which was invariably served at any time after five in the evening. Whisky seemed to be the universal drink in Conservative politics. I have always found it a gloomy drink.

Not as gloomy, though, as most of the ministers who kindly gave me half an hour or more of their time. By now the Falklands had been all but recaptured, no thanks to me, but on the domestic front there was nothing to cheer about.

'The police are ghastly,' Willie Whitelaw said almost before I sat down, 'absolutely ghastly, I can't do a thing with them. Police pay is out of our control now they have this link to average earnings. I thought non-custodial sentences were the answer to the rising tide of crime, but that was a mistake and we've had to backtrack. But sending them inside is not much better. The prisons are awful. They're completely in the hands of the prison officers who are getting an extra £11,000 or £12,000 in overtime, and anyway there's an appalling shortage of them. Probation orders might be the answer except there's a frightful shortage of probation officers too and they're hopelessly under left-wing influence.'

His oyster eyes brimmed as he continued this catalogue of lament – the BBC was proving very difficult, the immigration of Indian and Pakistani brides was likely to continue for years, whatever controls we brought in, and their families would continue to have divided loyalties. The Commission for Racial Equality was absolutely useless though he had to go on paying lip-service to it.

As I continued on my tour of Whitehall, I discovered that something of Whitelaw's pessimism was shared in every department. David Howell at Transport said that all the public noticed was dirty railway stations and potholes in the road. Patrick Jenkin said he was very worried about industrial production, which was totally flat and showed no signs of reviving. Norman Tebbit had another bill up his sleeve, about secret ballots for union officials, but he was depressed by all the meddling from Brussels, and the corruption, pilfering and sloth that were rife in the nationalised industries. Cecil Parkinson, then fairly new as party Chairman, told me that morale at Central Office had been miserable when he arrived, half the staff of the Research Department had left. There had been a tragicomic misunderstanding about the Stepping Stones group. The Prime Minister was congenitally suspicious about disloyalty and was irked by John Hoskyns telling her that she had no plan, no strategy and no staff. According to Cecil, the Liaison Committee which was supposed to pull the government's whole strategy together had fallen into abeyance because it was chaired by Francis Pym who said openly that he didn't believe in the strategy, so he couldn't possibly proclaim it. Geoffrey Howe told me they had tried to bring out a strategy document a few months earlier but Margaret had stamped on it, and the same fate was likely to happen to anyone who tried to do it again. Keith Joseph said his officials were choking him with cream, deluging him with objections to all his policies. He was beginning to wonder whether vouchers for schools would ever be a practical possibility, although he knew Margaret would not care to be told so. Perhaps they could do something unfrightening to increase the power of headmasters, although how could they exercise real power unless schools had the power to go bankrupt? I said, in my best pompous Thatcherite manner, that we could not duck the subject of education, it was a central part of restoring self-discipline to society. Ah yes, said Keith, but schools were not the whole answer, 'there are these lumpen families, these terrible stories of baby battering. You never read about baby battering in Trollope or Mrs Gaskell, though you do in Dickens. Why is Britain a byword for hooliganism and vandalism?'

Only Kenneth Baker and Michael Heseltine showed any appreciable bounce. Heseltine stalked about the room full of can-do zest, although at the end of our talk he suddenly descended into theatrical self-pity: 'I sometimes wonder why we bother with it all. We work our guts out to get into Parliament. We climb up the greasy pole and finally here we are' – he waved his hand extravagantly at the modernist desk and the squashy sofas – 'and what have we got to look forward to at the end of it all? The order of the boot!'

But it was Kenneth Baker who, although chirpy about his own plans for privatising telecommunications, brought home − or rather brought back to me − the full depth of Tory pessimism. We had had dinner together at the party conference at Blackpool the year before, together with the government's rising young stars, Chris Patten, John Patten (no relation) and William Waldegrave. Baker had decided to relieve the encircling gloom at dinner by suggesting a sweepstake on the result of the next general election. We wrote down our guesses on strips torn off the menu. Kenneth had kept them and he showed me my forecast − 290 Conservative, 270 Labour, 80 Alliance. Mine it turned out had been the most optimistic and I was prophesying a hung Parliament. The Tory MPs had all forecast heavy defeats for the Conservatives. In the event, the result of the 1983 election held the following June was Conservative 397, Labour 209, Alliance 23 − one of the most thumping Conservative victories ever.

We had made our forecasts at a point when morale within the government was slumped in the dumps. There had been a terrible Cabinet meeting on 23 July, the last Cabinet before the summer recess, to discuss public spending for the next financial year, 1982/3, and the cuts that would be necessary to meet the government's target. This, rather than the Cabinet to discuss the 1981 Budget a few months earlier, was the meeting at which the overwhelming majority of ministers openly rebelled. Heseltine said Howe's proposals would cause despair in the cities and electoral disaster. Why not a pay freeze instead? − an idea applauded by Christopher Soames and Peter Walker, who called for more planning. Pym declared that employment not inflation was the issue. Gilmour quoted Churchill: 'However beautiful the strategy, you should occasionally look at the results.' Britain was entering a cycle of hopeless decline. Hailsham compared Britain's state to that of Nazi Germany just before Hitler. But more alarming yet for Mrs Thatcher was the alacrity with which her supposed supporters such as John Nott and John Biffen attacked the policy as profoundly destructive. Only Joseph, Brittan and Howe himself supported the plan. Thatcher was in a minority of half a dozen in a Cabinet of twenty-two.

It is hard to think of any Prime Minister in the twentieth century who has been in a weaker position inside his or her own Cabinet, not to mention the higher reaches of the Civil Service which was almost entirely antipathetic to her personally and to her economic policy. She had to sack the mutinous Cabinet Secretary Sir Ian Bancroft, and the Permanent Secretary to the Treasury, Sir Douglas Wass, was so passionately opposed to her economic policy that he had to be shunted into a sort of internal exile until his retirement, never consulted and left to busy himself with harmless admin, rather the fate I had envisaged for myself on my first day in Downing Street. Robert Armstrong himself confessed that he had some difficulty in picking out bright young officials who 'might be suitable for the work of the Policy Unit' – or, to put it more plainly, who could bear the idea of working directly for Margaret Thatcher. When the caustic and delightful Nick Owen was seconded to us from Trade and Industry, he said they were glad to see the back of him because he was just about the only man in the Department who did not believe that it was the government's job to run industry. At Alfred's instigation, I also recruited John Redwood, Peter Shipley and Christopher Monckton who all had strong links to the Centre for Policy Studies, and I managed to prise Oliver Letwin away from Keith Joseph's side. By now there were half a dozen of us, still a tiny band in the huge expanses of more or less hostile territory.

As far as the Cabinet was concerned, if Thatcher was to survive, the only answer was for her to construct a new one, with the more dispensable wets – Soames, Gilmour and Mark Carlisle – sacked, Prior shunted off to Northern Ireland and replaced by Tebbit, and Cecil Parkinson and Nigel Lawson promoted. These events all took place the year before I shuffled on to the scene. I mention them here only because posterity has a tendency to downplay the appalling weakness of her situation. The Establishment really was mired in pessimism and sloth, reserving what energies it still possessed for smiting her. If she did not smite back, she was a goner. And under any other plausible Prime Minister I imagine that the government would have swung back to all the discredited remedies of the 1960s and 1970s, just as I doubt whether any other Prime Minister would have insisted on retaking the Falklands.

Her position in the opinion polls began to recover rapidly after Port Stanley had been captured. In fact it had started to recover before that.

Out in the country the Labour Party was perceived as unelectable now that the Social Democrats had broken away. In meetings with outsiders there was just the faintest hint of growing confidence. Once a month I went to a lunch for business reps – cars, shipping, insurance and so on. This was invented by Alfred Sherman and entitled the Argonauts, though I am not sure who was supposed to be fleecing whom. What struck me was that these solemn, friendly characters were, on the whole, rather optimistic, even if their own industry – the British motor car industry for example – was having a terrible struggle. For the first time they could remember, the country had a government with a clear strategy and the determination to stick to it.

That was not how it seemed on the inside. Gloom clung to large areas of Whitehall. There was a pre-Budget Cabinet on 3 February 1983 which I sat in on. You would scarcely have noticed much improvement in spirits from July eighteen months earlier. Peter Walker said that the greatest danger was the collapse of morale in the Midlands where they were unaccustomed to hardship. Jim Prior said that Britain was socially and industrially weak and a number of people had given up hope. In one way or another, Biffen, Norman Fowler and Pym argued for a little relaxation here and there. Michael Heseltine conceded that he 'had not thought that the acceptability of unemployment would last this long, but I'm convinced it won't last indefinitely'. The difference this time was that now there was a critical mass of loyalists who were prepared to stick with it. Yet even though the opinion polls showed that the prospects for re-election were brightening, plenty of ministers, even those in sympathy with Mrs Thatcher like John Biffen and Norman Tebbit, continued to think that a hung Parliament would be the most likely result.

About a month after I started, I had begun attending some Cabinets and Cabinet committees, partly out of a touristic fascination to see what they were like. It took me a little while to discover that all I had to do was ask Michael Scholar to ask Mrs Thatcher whether I could go and she always said yes. It was rather like a child asking his mother whether he could stay up late and watch a favourite programme. Strictly speaking, it was against the rules, because only members of the Cabinet were meant to attend. Up to the First World War, the Cabinet had not even had a secretary and the Prime Minister himself took the minutes. In those days it was considered poor form for any other minister to take notes. Something of this informal, secretive tradition still clung to it. We Number Ten functionaries sat on chairs ranged along the wall pretending to be invisible.

These Cabinet meetings struck me as curious occasions, ponderous, oblique, with little open disagreement. Ministers would offer mini-statements of their position, not often supported by arguments, beginning their sentences with phrases like 'It is my considered opinion that . . .' or 'In my judgement . . .' Much of the meeting would be taken up with a *tour d'horizon* from the Foreign Secretary which usually didn't add much to what we had all read in that morning's newspapers. There seemed little predisposition to get down to any close analysis, still less to come to anything like a clear-cut conclusion. In any case, debate on the most important topic was often cut short by the arrival of the lunch hour, not so much because of rumbling stomachs as because if discussion went on until half past one, the media would assume there had been a flaming row. Mrs Thatcher was criticised by her opponents for the bossy way she introduced and summed up the more contentious topics, whereas other Prime Ministers had let the debate run more freely. My impression was that when she didn't give this sort of firm direction (usually because the subject did not interest her) the debate tended to dribble away into the sand. The whole business resembled one of those courtship contests between male mammals, in which there is a good deal of pawing and stamping the ground but not much actual clashing of antlers.

Sometimes in a smaller meeting of some sub-committee, Michael Scholar and I would be encouraged to come and sit at the sacred coffin-shaped table. Then I would find myself within squinting distance of Sir Robert Armstrong as he took notes for the minutes. He wrote in a fine rolling hand, not the revived italic I had been taught by Wilfrid Blunt, but more like the copperplate of Victorian clerks. The trouble was that it seemed to roll rather slowly, not least because he was averse to all but the most trivial of abbreviations, and always referred to ministers by their titles, writing, for example, 'S of S for Scotland: It would be advisable that there should be some room for manoeuvre.' As a result, I noticed that quite often he was well behind the speaker, sometimes still finishing the one before halfway through the next speech.

'Do you want to have a look at Robert's minutes?' Michael said.

'Ooh yes please,' I said, unable to disguise my excitement. For me it was the Whitehall equivalent of a squint at the Dead Sea Scrolls.

And so in the middle of the afternoon I would pop down and together we would sharpen up the somewhat bland typed-up account of proceedings that came over to us from the Cabinet Office. It was not simply that Sir Robert wrote *lentissimo*. He also, like his predecessors, was inclined to smooth over contentious statements and sometimes erase anything that would cause embarrassment if leaked. Yet the Cabinet minutes were the Cabinet's sole authorised method of communication with the rest of Whitehall. Even the Permanent Secretary in each department had nothing else to take his instructions from and when, as often happened, his own Secretary of State gave a rather different account, he had to prefer the version in the minutes. So our meddling with the text in the name of the Prime Minister, though certainly not authorised by her, was rather necessary – or so we thought.

But my first real task, the one I would be judged on, was my promised paper on Renewing the Values of Society. I slotted that in at the end of May and it went down a bomb – on second thoughts, not the mot juste as the bombs were still thudding into the sodden heather of Mount Tumbledown at the time. Perhaps she clasped it to her bosom so fervently because it was a welcome diversion from the grim imperatives of war. Certainly she saw it as her long-term answer to the alienation and resentment that had exploded in Toxteth and Brixton. This was the preamble:

This Government came to power asserting that it is the exercise of responsibility which teaches self-discipline. But in the early stages of life it is the experience of authority, when exerted fairly and consistently by adults, which teaches young people how to exercise responsibility themselves. We have to learn to take orders before we learn how to give them. This two-way relationship between obedience and responsibility is what makes a free, self-governing society. And in the breakdown of that relationship we can trace the origins of so much that has gone wrong with Britain.

If we can rebuild this relationship, we might begin to restore also respect for law and order, respect for property, and respect for teachers and parents. But the rebuilding itself has to be a two-way business. On the one hand, we need to restore effective authority to teachers and parents. On the other hand, we need to offer young people a taste of responsibility and a useful role in society.

A bit schoolmasterly, even plonking, I admit. She didn't mind that, she wasn't majoring in nuance or sophistication. I reprint such a large chunk only because this is the bit she reprinted in her memoirs. It is just about the longest quotation in the whole book, certainly from somebody other than herself. Slightly to my surprise, I was in favour. Just as the Argentinians were surrendering, she set up a group of ministers to carry the programme forward: Joseph, Whitelaw, Howe, Tebbit, Heseltine, Fowler and Neil Macfarlane the Sports Minister. It was called the Family Policy Group – a title some ministers, including eventually Mrs Thatcher herself, thought misleading, when the group's aims could more properly be described as Self-Reliance and Responsibility. In retrospect, I wish that the group had been more rather than less focused on strengthening the family.

Gordon Wasserman of the Central Policy Review Staff, an ingenious Canadian who was married to one of Hugh Gaitskell's daughters, was assigned to marshal all the topics that might conceivably be relevant to the task, and soon I was blizzarded with papers: on truancy, headmasters' powers, school vouchers, parent governors, shared tenancies on council estates, individual retirement accounts, the taxation of husband and wife, the use of school playing fields, community police officers, tax allowances for carers, the role of voluntary action and a dozen other bright ideas.

The next thing that happened was that the whole thing was leaked to the *Guardian*. The speed of the leaking indicated a satisfactorily high level of hostility within Whitehall. I was blizzarded again, this time by the chilly scorn of the *bien-pensants*. We were naive and paternalistic, hopelessly out of touch with modern values. My real aim, according to Polly Toynbee, was to chain women to the kitchen sink.

Nor was this disdain confined to the left and its sympathisers. I bumped into a junior education minister, Bill Shelton, a sleek advertising man who might have served as a model for Michael Frayn's Rollo Swaveley.

'This Family Policy thing – tell me, is it serious or just the usual wank?'

'Serious, I think, but perhaps I had better pass your question on to the Prime Minister.'

All the same, for a day or so I was stricken with panic. Would my pièce de résistance turn out to be an oversized spluttering and very damp squib? But then, one by one, the other newspapers conceded that these probably were the sort of things that any decent government ought to be looking at, even if they didn't go along with this or that bit of it. Plenty of Tory backbenchers liked the idea too. In any case, now that she had scored such a dazzling triumph on the world stage, Mrs Thatcher was in unstoppable mood.

So at 9.15 on a sunny July morning (20 July – our wedding anniversary, which is why I remember the date) I sat down at the Cabinet table for the first meeting of the Family Policy Group, oozing self-satisfaction at every pore. The group were in a cheerful, practical mood. There's nothing like thinking about long-term solutions to cheer you up, when the short-term problems are so intractable. We whistled through the main items, picked out the most promising areas for future work and agreed to meet again in September. As we broke for coffee at eleven, I was as dazed with happiness as a bureaucrat can be.

After our meeting there was a meeting of 'E', the Economic Committee of the Cabinet, which included many of the same people who therefore all stayed in their seats. I stayed in my seat too, although strictly speaking I should have retired to one of the seats along the wall, as the business of the meeting wasn't my baby. So I was still sitting next to Michael Scholar facing the long windows at the far end of the table, the view towards the park now dappled by the thick foliage of high summer.

My attention began to wander, as it often did in these conclaves. Anyway I was a bit drained after launching my own little skiff upon the waters.

'Crrumpff.'

The sound was loud but muffled, not so much a bang as a giant throat-clearing, but loud enough to rattle the windows.

'I'm sure that was a bomb,' Michael whispered to me.

'I don't think so,' I whispered back, 'not enough of a bang.'

What happened next was gloriously English. Whoever it was talking went on talking about Public Expenditure Survey targets. Not a single minister turned round to look through the windows, not that there would have been anything to see, but it would have been an instinctive thing to do. Mrs Thatcher whispered to Robin Butler who rose in an unhurried manner and proceeded at a stately gait to the door. Nobody said a word about the noise.

About twenty minutes later, Robin returned. More whispering. The Prime Minister then told us that a bomb had gone off in Hyde Park and that heavy casualties were feared. She said afterwards that she had noticed that the soldiers had not appeared on Horse Guards for their usual parade. There was then news of another bomb that had gone off in Regent's Park under the bandstand with more casualties. Our children's school was in Gloucester Gate and they played their games in the Park. That was the end of my self-elation.

All the same, when I flip through these old policy papers, I do not repent of that first burst of elation. It would be possible to point to quite a few parts of the agenda that have come to pass over the next twenty years, but one cannot help noticing so many more things that still seem urgent today and have improved little if at all: truancy, family breakdown and the maltreatment of children, standards in schools, low-level disorder and drunkenness, sink estates. In fact what strikes me most is the eerie resemblance that the Family Policy Group's agenda in 1982 bears to Tony Blair's 'Respect Agenda' of twenty-five years later, an indication of just how little progress has been made and how the underlying social problems that had been gathering ever since the 1960s and 1970s had got worse rather than better. Even those of our ideas that were most ridiculed as naive and futile at the time – like teaching schoolchildren how to handle money – have trickled back on to the menu.

Quite soon I began to see that the secrecy of British government had become one of the thorniest obstacles to change. True, the level of secrecy was not quite as tomblike as it had been in the 1950s and 1960s. Ed Shils, the Chicago sociologist who Shirley Letwin used to say was the most evil man on the planet, claimed then that 'the British ruling class is unequalled in its secretiveness and taciturnity. Nowhere else did the elite disclose so little of its confidential proceedings.' Nothing leaked: not the lies the government told about how much it was spending on nuclear weapons, not the reports on nuclear tests, not the details of the Robot plan to let sterling float or even Robot's very existence, not the existence of the Chuter Ede committee on immigration, not the news of Churchill's stroke just after the coronation. When the government tore itself apart after Churchill had decided, entirely off his own bat, both to go to Moscow and to go ahead with the Bomb without consulting the Cabinet, not a word got out. 'A very strange week,' Macmillan noted with some understatement. 'It would be stranger still if the public knew what was going on.'

This tradition of secrecy is dying hard, and it will take more than the Freedom of Information Act to kill it off. Early last year I bumped into Charles Moore, formerly editor of the *Daily Telegraph* and now writing the definitive biography of Margaret Thatcher which is not to be published in her lifetime. 'I've just seen a fantastic paper you did for her about the trade unions, accusing Norman Tebbit of being wet.' 'I can't remember a thing about it,' I said. 'Could I have a look?' 'No, you can't,' Charles said triumphantly. 'It would be against the law.' He was authorised to consult her papers and I wasn't, even though I had written the thing. Nettled by this, I applied to the Cabinet Office for a copy under the Freedom of Information Act. Two months later, I received notification from the Permanent Secretary, Government Communications, informing me that it had been decided that 'the greater public interest is that the information should not be disclosed'. Though the paper was now twenty-five years old, it was still too hot to publish. I could not repress a twitch of pride.

However, informally I was told that they would be happy for me to come and consult the paper *in situ* at the Histories, Records and Openness Unit. Which I did. It was a strange and rather delicious experience to sit in the airless room behind Admiralty Arch with the quizzical eye of the Head of History, Records and Openness on me, in case I should suddenly take it into my head to set fire to the document or eat it.

The paper was six pages long. It was a snorter composed by a younger robuster self I scarcely recognised. I did indeed denounce Norman Tebbit's latest efforts at trade union reform as defensive and limited and urged Mrs T. to press on regardless, to entrench the new picketing code in law, to outlaw secondary action, to enforce ballots before strikes, and to make the closed shop subject to the approval of its members every five years. Our aim should be a trade union movement that was law-abiding, democratic and smaller. Twenty-five years later, more or less everything in that fiery memo has become law or fact. In five years' time it will, I presume, be published anyway under the thirty-year rule. But for the time being its contents remain under lock and key in the Cabinet Office.

British government has always been carried on like this, in a bubble of secrecy which is, I fear, a deceiving comfort to those on the inside. In the 1950s and 1960s the absence of outside pressure meant that government could duck and dither and retreat without fear of criticism or derision. Postponement of the difficult and disagreeable was always a cost-free option.

It wasn't quite as bad as that in the early 1980s. The press was more inquisitive and less respectful. Ministers were readier to lunch with journalists and to sing for their supper. But this in a perverse way made it even harder to discuss difficult and potentially unpopular plans. In conditions of total assured secrecy a certain frankness could flourish among colleagues. In conditions of open discussion in which any plausible proposal had been gone over openly by half-a-dozen think tanks, reforms which would once have been considered daring can be put out to public consultation. But in the 1980s we were in an in-between situation, a twilight zone, in which a Cabinet leak could always be portrayed as part of a sinister secret plan.

The worst possible tactic therefore was to let a controversial proposal, such as fees for schools or for visits to hospital or GPs, surface for the first time in a Cabinet paper. Yet this was just what happened with the notorious CPRS paper on long-term public spending, an enterprise commissioned by Geoffrey Howe, but not under his control.

'Please come down as quick as you can. We've got a disaster waiting to happen.' Michael Scholar was managing to preserve his impish chuckle, but only just.

The CPRS paper which had landed on his desk was due to be discussed a couple of days later at Cabinet. Basically what it said was that, if economic growth limped on at its present rate of 1 per cent a year, by 1990 public spending would consume nearly half of Gross Domestic Product. Britain would become the most overtaxed nation in Europe. The only remedy, the CPRS argued, was to remove large chunks of the social services from the Budget: for example, end state funding of universities, stop welfare benefits rising in line with inflation, replace the NHS with a private insurance scheme, not to mention introducing charges for visits to the doctor.

'Christ, has she seen this?'

'Yes, and she's furious. But as it's gone round, we can't get it off the agenda and, even if we tried, it would be bound to leak anyway.'

The Cabinet meeting when it came was a miserable, sour occasion. Hailsham described the circulation of the CPRS paper as 'the worst mistake the government has made since it came to power'. It wasn't just the wets who wanted the paper off the agenda, Mrs Thatcher was relieved to see the back of it too, although she did not like being forced into burying it and said, 'All right, shelve it then,' in an extremely disgruntled fashion and stalked out of the room after only the most perfunctory wind-up. Her opponents leaked the contents of the report to Mark Schreiber at the *Economist*, but they also spread it about that Mrs Thatcher herself had put the paper on the agenda and was keen to have a full discussion of it. This version found its way into Hugo Young's life of Mrs Thatcher, reinforcing the picture of her as imbued with reckless, messianic zeal after the Falklands. It wasn't quite like that. It is not simply that the crude and unthought-through proposals of the CPRS took no account of the difficulties both of policy and persuasion which would have to be tackled before any such ideas could be seriously put forward. Mrs Thatcher also quarrelled, and rightly, with the gloomy assumptions of miserably low growth continuing into the middle distance. In fact, growth picked up during the 1980s and so public expenditure began to fall not rise as a proportion of GDP. Thus the paper's basic assumption turned out to be nonsense.

You needed to have a wicked conspiratorial nature to slip anything radical through the system. The only person who managed it – and did so twice – was Nick Ridley, the chain-smoking, caustic leader of Mrs Thatcher's gang of four when she first became leader – Ridley, Tebbit, Lawson and Jock Bruce-Gardyne. It was Ridley who in opposition compiled a secret list of the publicly owned industries which would at some point be worth denationalising and of the trade union immunities which would have to be removed if managers were to have any hope of managing. No word of these lists ever got out. Now that both his lists have been finally ticked off, they are all taken for granted. At the time they were dynamite. It was unthinkable that the water industry or the telephones could be denationalised or that picketing of any kind could be made illegal.

His other project was more dashing still. By the time I arrived on the scene, he was Financial Secretary to the Treasury, and he invited me over for a drink. Internally the Treasury is a gloomy place at the best of times with its endless passages and, in those years, acres of linoleum. But Nick's office seemed particularly stygian. The lighting was almost non-existent, the air thick with fag smoke.

'I'd like to show you something,' he said in his insinuating nasal tones, rather like a ruthless baronet about to expose himself to a village maiden. He unlocked a drawer in his desk and handed me a couple of sheets of typescript. 'Nobody else has seen this but Geoffrey, not even my secretary. I had it typed up at home.'

It wasn't a long document. The idea was to abolish tax relief on mortgages, and most of the tax reliefs on pensions and a couple of other lesser reliefs. This would produce billions which could then be spent on reducing the standard rate of tax from 30 per cent to 20 per cent, thus offering incentives for all of us to work harder.

'Gosh,' I said, tribute which provoked his most Sir Jasperish smile. 'She won't like this. You know her obsession with mortgages, and encouraging savings too for that matter.'

'Exactly, that's why she's not going to see it. We're going to work on her year by year, salami-style' – he made a elegant chopping motion – 'offering her something in return each time until we get there.'

Which is what happened. Gradually the tax reliefs were whittled away under Howe and then Lawson and, to a lesser extent, under later Chancellors. Of course the overall effect has been marred if not ruined by the public spending programmes of Gordon Brown's late years as Chancellor. But the essentials of the Ridley Plan – fewer tax reliefs, lower tax rates – have been fulfilled, almost entirely under a Prime Minister who would have disapproved of the whole strategy if it had ever been openly presented to her. That's what I call low cunning.

I was beginning to develop a bit of medium-low cunning myself. First, I discovered the intricacies of briefing the PM. For meetings of ministers, the Deputy Secretary in the Cabinet Office who was in charge of that particular policy area would provide a brief for everyone, explaining in bland and guarded language the pros and cons of doing this or that. He or the Cabinet Secretary would also provide a 'handling brief' for the Prime Minister herself, suggesting how to organise the meeting and some of the salient points she might make. At first, I thought the thing to do was to have a long chat with the Deputy Secretary, explaining what we thought the salient points were. But by the time the material had been put through the Cabinet Office homogeniser the points weren't salient any more and the chances of reaching any remotely crisp conclusions were much reduced. So we took to putting in a snappy little handling brief of our own at the last minute, making sure that it was placed on top of the Cabinet Office one. With a bit of luck, she would read out our marching orders verbatim and give only the most cursory glance at the infinitely more thorough but fatally hedged official handling brief. There was a childish pleasure to be had from sitting behind her trying to look unconcerned, almost bored, with that rather strained expression of detachment affected by ventriloquists of the old school.

But useful though it was, this procedure even when successful only shifted in the desired direction proposals which had already been through the minister's department and had as often as not ultimately originated there. How on earth did you manage to implant a fresh approach in a department resolved to resist anything of the sort by all means short of open rebellion?

Again, as with our sorties to the Cabinet Office, we spent ages talking to the civil servants who had the expertise, usually sparky assistant secretaries around the age of forty. Sometimes we managed to brew up something new, sometimes we could see we were getting nowhere. But our hopes were soon dashed. Higher up the department the deputy secretaries and permanent secretaries would gently shunt the schemes off into the sidings, in the manner so beautifully scripted in *Yes Minister* by Antony Jay (a close friend of John Hoskyns) and acted to perfection by Nigel Hawthorne. Organising a full-scale discussion in the minister's office was more hopeless yet. As soon as the permanent secretary got out his pipe, I could tell we were done for.

Geography, I decided, was the key, as in many if not all covert operations. The target had to be lured off his own ground, denied the support of his *consiglieri*, disoriented and confronted by superior forces. These meetings, convened by an invitation from the Prime Minister which could not be refused, would be given the innocent name of 'seminars'. There would be a disinterested search for truth. The minister's department would of course be fully entitled, indeed expected, to produce some sort of paper, but we, possibly aided by the Treasury, would produce a meatier, tougher one which would in practice form the basis of the meeting because the Prime Minister would read out the questions from it. So the seminar would turn into something uncomfortably like an inquisition.

If this seems devious – well, it was devious – remember that there was no other obvious means of opening up a real discussion of the future of agriculture, say, or the railways. Under the status quo, all that happened was the once-a-year negotiation between the minister trying to increase his budget and the Chief Secretary to the Treasury trying to cut or at worst contain it. No strategic discussion about whether the department was doing the right things or should be doing something different, or less. In a place like the Min of Ag, the incoming minister would soon become a prisoner of the National Farmers Union, as his civil servants already were, and it would be impossible for the Prime Minister to raise any long-term questions such as whether Britain should continue to maintain the wartime Dig for Victory mentality, subsidising livestock to shiver on barren uplands and paying for unproductive bogs to be drained. The system cast the Prime Minister in an essentially reactive role and any attempt by her to be proactive, to give even the mildest nudge to a dozy department, would provoke high-minded mutterings of unjustified interference.

It was not only the Thatcher government that felt baffled and frustrated. It was just such frustration that had impelled Harold Wilson to introduce the Policy Unit during his second spell in office, when he came in vowing that he was not going to let the Civil Service screw him this time. And Tony Blair has turned the whole Whitehall system upside down in a largely fruitless attempt to open up the more recalcitrant departments to fresh ideas. It was, I think, a misconception to give his political advisers the power to order civil servants about. It has created a great deal of annoyance for small benefit and, as we saw in the evidence given to the Hutton Report, it muddles the legitimate channels of government to provide dodgy dossiers and disastrous distortions. The trick is to use the genuine authority of the Prime Minister to get things moving without undermining the authority of the department which has to do the painstaking preparation to ensure that the bright idea actually works in practice.

Hence the seminar. Downing Street was good. The squeals of the minister having his arm twisted would not reach beyond its walls, and there would have been nobody from his own staff to know quite how many concessions he had had to make. Indeed, once back in his department he could present these concessions as the result of a vigorous debate in which he himself had taken the lead.

But Chequers was better. Cradled in the Chiltern hills, seduced by the country-house atmosphere, made giddy by the mere thought of being 'down at Chequers', the most suspicious and prickly minister began to melt. It was indeed a seductive excursion, tootling down the A41 with the roof down, then snaking through the surprisingly rural byways of Bucks, larks singing, the hedgerow honeysuckle in full fragrance, and then that moment which never failed to make my heart skip, there at a break in the hedge in the most countrified lane was the little police station and the barrier and the Special Branch man leaning in at the car window to check your details. In a moment you were transported from the world of Bertie Wooster to a bad spy thriller where an unnameable power lies at the end of the long avenue. And that is just how it seems as you crunch to a halt on the gravel circle and Vera Thomas, the redoubtable housekeeper, comes out to greet you. For just as Number Ten is not really like an old-fashioned town house, so Chequers is not like an old-fashioned country house. It may be a genuine Tudor mansion with the hills behind and a rolling park around it, but it somehow doesn't look genuine. That is partly because Lord Lee of Fareham, who gave it to the nation after the First World War, used his wife's American money to strip off all the Victorian gothic battlements and restored the place inside and out, so that its pink brick and cream facings look dazzlingly new. The Lees cleared up the Tudor panelling too, so that it gleams with a plasticky sheen, and they hung the walls with Cromwellian paintings, these too varnished to the hilt. There is a log fire blazing in the hall, you expect to see minstrels in the gallery. Wonderful fleecy towels and unguents in your bathroom as in the best country-house hotels, except there are no guests visible. It is all too perfect and a little eerie. The first time I went I had just been to see one of the old Aldwych farces of the 1920s revived, I can't remember which one, *Rookery Nook* perhaps. The play started with an empty hall with stairs leading up to a gallery and no one on stage except possibly a maid dusting. That is what Chequers is like. But then it becomes much odder as you see women in RAF uniform bringing in the tea or stoking up the fire, and you feel that you have been spirited away to a secret place where nobody will ever find you and terrible things may happen. It was a matter of convenience, economy too perhaps, that the house should be entirely staffed by personnel from nearby RAF Halton. But when you look out of the long Tudor windows and see the security people slowly circling the house at a discreet distance beyond the ha-ha, you cannot avoid a shiver. The only member of staff in mufti is Vera Thomas and you take it for granted that she is a full colonel in the SAS.

'Isn't this a wonderful room? Don't you feel relaxed as soon as you come through the door?'

Mrs Thatcher gives these polite sentiments her usual forceful treatment, as she bustles into the hall, but she carries no conviction at all. She is dressed much the same as she is in Downing Street, one less brooch perhaps and a cashmere scarf round her throat, but there is nothing in the least relaxed about her. The stained-glass window in the long gallery bears an inscription saying, 'This house of peace and ancient memories was given to England as a thank-offering for her deliverance in the great war of 1914–18 as a place of rest and recreation for her Prime Ministers for ever.' That is not at all how

England's first woman Prime Minister sees it. Chequers is a place rather for redoubling one's efforts, for getting back to it all in spades. There is to be no resting, let alone recreation. Meetings continue all afternoon and sometimes long after dinner throughout the weekend, until even her beautifully coiffed head begins to sink on to her briefing papers. It is at this moment that the celebrated tact of the higher reaches of the British Civil Service comes into play. As it is a publicly declared dogma that the Iron Lady requires less sleep than other mortals and is never ever exhausted, it is Robin Butler's role as Principal Private Secretary to rise to his feet, give a yawn and stretch his arms in an extravagant manner like a man using a chest-expander and say, 'Prime Minister, I'm afraid you'll have to excuse me, I'm feeling extraordinarily tired' – at which the rest of us emit various yawns and sighs and say that, for some unaccountable reason, we feel a bit knocked out too.

'You run along upstairs then, and I can get on with these papers.' She makes a show of getting down to serious work as we troop off upstairs, but as I turn off the minstrels' gallery towards my room I catch sight of the little figure down below gathering up her things and going off to bed, her reputation for being indefatigable undented.

There is one evening only at Chequers when the ministers have gone home and only the staffers are left and after dinner she asks Michael Scholar to play the piano which he does beautifully, as a good Treasury man should. Even then she sits upright at her end of the sofa like a schoolgirl on her first trip to the Wigmore Hall as Michael gives us Schubert, I think, possibly Chopin too. Is her mind drifting away to all the things she never speaks to us about, childhood, Oxford, her first kiss? Or is she making a mental note to call Alan Walters about the inconsistencies in the latest money supply figures? Michael tells me that he has difficulty playing now because he has Dupuytren's contracture, that strange complaint that crooks the little finger and often the ring finger too into a permanent clawing position from which it can only be straightened by surgery. Oddly enough, Mrs Thatcher develops Dupuytren's contracture too and I wonder whether there is something in the Chequers air.

As for physical recreation, her proudest boast at Chequers is that she has saved £5,000 a year by turning off the heating in the swimming pool. I doubt whether the thought of actually using the pool ever occurred to her. For someone so abounding in energy she takes less physical exercise than anyone I have ever met. She will delay until the last possible minute the breath of air she takes on the terrace before lunch. The other ministers are out there already, some of them halfway through their gin and tonics. As she comes out, they stand aside with a vaguely uneasy air. Her eager, waddling walk never carries her further than she can help, like a hen who hasn't the slightest desire to leave the coop. Her mother-hen aspect is always to the fore in her concern for her staff, even in the relentless routine of Downing Street.

'You've got a cold coming on, Ferdy.'

'No, I don't think so, Prime Minister.'

'Yes, you have, I'm sure. You need some Redoxon.'

'Honestly, Prime Minister, I promise you I haven't.'

It is 9.30 p.m. and the meeting has already been going on for two hours and I have been groaning inwardly at the mind-numbing tedium of it all and unfortunately one of the groans has escaped.

'I've got some Redoxon in the flat. I'll go and get it.'

'No, please don't, I'm sure we've got some at home and anyway I don't need it.'

'One always needs Redoxon.'

And she shoots out of the room, up two-and-a-half flights of stairs to get me the blasted pills which I don't need, while everyone else in the room looks furiously at me for causing this further delay. It is hard to think of another Prime Minister in British history who would have insisted on interrupting a meeting and going to get the Redoxon herself. In fact, looking back on it, I think going upstairs to fetch it was the most sustained piece of physical exercise I ever saw her take.

But perhaps there was one sense in which the Chequers air did loosen her up a bit, not always for the better. She was more inclined to let her deeper hidden feelings show. And I began to see how infuriating she could be when she was on the wrong side and wouldn't admit it. One of the rather crucial parts of our family policy programme was the taxation of husband and wife. The Treasury had long felt that in the modern world when the majority of women went out to work for most of their lives, it was anachronistic that the taxman should treat them as chattels of their husbands. The obvious thing was for married women too to be treated as independent taxpayers entitled to their own tax allowances if they went out to work. Since the vast majority of women then were fairly low paid, this would create a considerable incentive for wives to work, since the allowance would make a good deal of their earnings tax free. The logic of this also implied that the existing married couple's allowance should be allowed to wither away as an 'anomaly' (as Ken Clarke described it when he was Chancellor ten years later). So married women who didn't work would be left in a much worse condition. Far from chaining them to the sink, as Polly complained, we would be shooing them out of the front door. Surely a policy to support the family should allow married women to choose whether to work or not, especially when they were bringing up children. There was an easy – though expensive – way to do this, by making the tax allowance fully transferable, so that a man with a wife at home or a woman with a house-husband would receive two tax allowances. This is the sort of system that happens in most other countries.

'Margaret, it's the only answer. Surely we believe in choice.'

'It's much too expensive, Geoffrey. I simply can't accept it. I can't let the mill girls of Bolton down.'

'I don't quite follow you, Margaret.'

'Well, there are these girls getting up at dawn and working all the hours God gives, and then they see these women in the Home Counties playing bridge and getting exactly the same tax allowance. I can't have it.'

It was too late to point out that by now there weren't any mill girls in Bolton because there weren't any mills. But anyway as the argument wore on and on I began to feel the depths not only of Mrs Thatcher's loathing of sloth and privilege – well, that was fair enough – but of her indifference to family life. 'Home is where you come to when you've nothing better to do,' as she told *Vanity Fair* soon after she had been thrown out. She was an individualist at heart who believed that effort alone was what counted and it was not for the government to offer any featherbedding or tolerance for those who could not or would not make the effort. In this arcane discussion, which must have gone on for an hour and a half, I began to acknowledge in my heart that there was a harsh side to her view of life which was both her strength and ultimately her weakness. With infinite patience, Geoffrey Howe repeated the arguments: this was what women wanted, it would be a buttress to family life which was under such threat, it was a profoundly Conservative measure. She became ruder and more dismissive, scarcely troubling to listen any more but merely repeating what she had said half-a-dozen times already, until we were sick of the mythical mill girls of Bolton. Leave aside the man–woman aspect, I don't think I have ever seen a boss being so unrelentingly rude to a senior colleague for so long.

Looking out of the beautifully restored bow window with God-knows-whose armorial bearings carved in the mullions, I longed to escape over the hills through the slowly circling cordon of security men. Round the corner at that moment came Denis Thatcher in his red baseball cap and matching golf jacket swinging his eight iron. With evergrowing envy, I watched him line up half a dozen balls and with his short, rather stiff swing despatch them over the ha-ha in the direction of the nearest policeman who began to gather them up as a welcome diversion from the tedium of staring over the parkland.

Denis too seemed like a disconsolate prisoner. In the bad film he would be the exiled ruler whom the SAS were going to parachute back into his homeland where preparations for an apparently spontaneous coup were complete. In reality there wasn't enough time for him to nip out over the hill for a round at Ellesborough because he was on parade again at six.

She was of course criticised at the time for this intense individualism, and her critics seized with glee on her incautious statement that 'There is no such thing as society, there are only individual men and women and their families.' Her defenders pointed out, reasonably enough, that she understood what society was as well as anyone and her governments had spent billions on the welfare state. But what she didn't understand were the intermediate institutions, ranging from the family to the local council, that stood between the individual and the state. To the importance and exact nature of these she had become more or less deaf, which was surprising in an alderman's daughter.

On her instructions I spent a lot of time that autumn with Terry Heiser at the Department of Environment trying to work out a practical method of capping the domestic rates, which had soared to intolerable levels especially in councils controlled by the loony left. Terry was a burly, down-to-earth character, not unlike a football manager of the old school.

'You do realise, if you go down this road, you will be radically upsetting the whole system of local government.'

'It's only going to be temporary, Terry,' I said soothingly.

'Even so, local government will never be the same again.'

But even after we had capped the rates, she was not satisfied. The rates had to be abolished. Nothing less would do. This was a peculiar volte-face, seeing that in her first front-bench post Ted Heath had made her give a public promise that the Tories would abolish the rates and she had hated doing it. But now it had become a crusade, and even her best friends couldn't argue her off it.

'But, Margaret, we've shot this particular fox already', Tebbit said. 'Now the rates are capped, we can forget about them. Anyway, the rates are a decent tax if any tax ever is – they're visible, easy to collect and voters know what to do if you put them up too much.'

'Norman, I can't let those widows down.'

Her new obsession was with the widows living on reduced incomes in large houses who could not afford to pay the rates at their new exorbitant levels. These were rather opposite heroines from the mill girls of Bolton, since they were presumably living on unearned, even if meagre incomes. In any case, they could be offered some specific relief to cushion the impact. But she would not have it. Her unadulterated individualism led her remorselessly to the disaster of the poll tax, the drawbacks of which were obvious to a child of ten. But by now Conservative ministers and MPs had been reduced to such a spineless condition that, although nobody in the history of all the inquiries into the rates had ever regarded a poll tax as anything but a total non-starter, nobody resigned and in the Cabinet only Nigel Lawson bothered to argue against it. By then I had long disappeared from the scene and I have no illusion that any of us could have argued her off it.

Unfortunately her startling success and her relentless personality had a long-term corroding effect on her party. All of her immediate successors carried the individualism further, becoming even more suspicious of local government and reluctant to support the family in any concrete way. Worst of all was the über-Thatcherite obsession with the deserving, 'with people who do the right thing'. They became blind to the fears and interests of the untalented, the unlucky and the mildly slothful. It was not only her own career which was destroyed by the defects of her virtues; her party was blighted for a decade or more. But at least to argue with her or to listen to her pronounce on such subjects was a serious experience. Everyone was intensely engaged and she was much more often right than wrong, her sharp forensic attack leaving no cover for woolly logic and conclusions reached on little or no evidence.

When it came to helping her write her speeches, there were no such compensations. In a rough concordat after our first meeting, I said I'd do two or three speeches a year, the party conference, the Lord Mayor's banquet, the Conservative Central Council. For the rest, I'd leave her to rely on the private secretaries together with the Foreign Office and the Treasury to feed her drafts. It is interesting in retrospect to note how few 'political' speeches she gave each year, compared with the never-ending roster Tony Blair submitted himself to. It is no illusion to think that government in general was much less highly propagandist then. The press officers were keener to supply information than to put a favourable spin on it, many of them being unenthusiastic about the government's approach. In the same way, special advisers did not bustle about lunching and being lunched, explaining to journalists what brilliant things their ministers were doing. As far as I could see, this low-voltage style of doing politics did the government no harm.

But it is hard to convey the full horror of these speechwriting sessions. They would start towards the end of July, though the conference was not till the second week of October, and they would last for anything up to three or four hours. The first draft I served up was simply there to be torn apart and binned, while she began to think what she might actually want to say. At this stage, various characters would flit in and out of the meetings, offering a page or two, perhaps no more than a paragraph. Alfred Sherman would last only a session or two before denouncing the proposed text as trivial and banal and annoying Mrs Thatcher so much that he was told not to come back.

Jeffrey Archer would schmooze his way into one of these meetings, having buttonholed the Prime Minister at a party and told her that he had some brilliant ideas and a wonderful joke that would absolutely make the speech. The joke was brought over by Jeffrey's chauffeur in his Jag. It was typed out on beautiful cream laid writing paper. Five minutes later he rang, 'Jeffrey here. What do you think of my joke?' 'It's wonderful, Jeffrey, the Prime Minister will love it.' In fact it was unusable, being too stale even for the undemanding standards of a party conference. This would make a better story if I could remember what the joke was, but I suppose the point is its sheer forgettability. In any case, Jeffrey's principal purpose in getting into these sessions was to remind her of his existence rather than to contribute anything useful: 'I think the main theme of your speech this year, Margaret, should be to remind the country of the amazing things your leadership has achieved for every single one of us' etc. etc., until the oil was lapping round our knees. Then she would implore Matthew Parris to be pressed into service, which we were all in favour of because he did have some excellent thoughts and phrases. Unfortunately he was usually drafted in too early. By the time the final version was taking shape, Matthew's best stuff had been discarded.

Then there was David Hart. This remarkable figure, the playboy son of a banker and cousin of the austere philosopher H. L. A. Hart, liked to present himself as a man of mystery, in touch with the people whom the conventional Tory stuffed-shirts couldn't reach. In fact, he had been at Eton and lived in an enormous house in Chester Street. He sported a thin Mafioso moustache and grubby tennis shoes under a pinstripe suit – a costume that has since become de rigueur for the owners of avant-garde art galleries. He claimed to have a squad of West Indians on roller skates whom at a moment's notice he could despatch all over London to find out what the word on the street was. When the word on the street was relayed back to us from these Chester Street Irregulars, it often appeared to be indistinguishable from the views of the average Home Counties Tory, though dressed up in the patois: 'Hey man, we don't dig those crazy taxes.' He would turn up at odd hours claiming to have an important message which he must deliver personally to the Prime Minister. She quite liked this, perhaps seeing in him a younger Alfred Sherman.

Like all Prime Ministers, she often felt isolated and longed to see a fresh face who would tell her something different, though David's face and general demeanour towards the end of the day could scarcely be described as fresh. In the later stages of the speechwriting at the party conference, he would haunt the Prime Minister's suite, hoovering up quantities of the canapés and drink provided and crossing out sections of the speech which had already been agreed. I attempted to have him banned as a disruptive influence, but when I went out for lunch I discovered on my return that he had come in and had rewritten part of the text. The party functionaries had allowed him entry, believing that such an outlandish figure must be working in some capacity for security and thus allowed access to all areas.

But the mainstays of the speechwriting team were Ronald Millar and John Selwyn Gummer. Ronnie, a successful West End playwright – famous for his adaptations of C. P. Snow – had first stalked the corridors of power as speechwriter to Ted Heath. He was a portly, fruity figure redolent of the old West End of Binkie Beaumont and Terence Rattigan though much nicer. He had already been responsible for Mrs Thatcher's two most famous utterances since she became Prime Minister: first, thrusting into her hand the Prayer of St Francis – 'Where there is discord, may we bring harmony' etc. – which he claimed she read with eyes misting over and memorised so she could declaim it on the steps of Downing Street; then giving her the line for her 1980 party conference speech, 'You turn if you want; the lady's not for turning.' Ronnie said it had been hell to teach her to get this sentence right. She could not grasp that the first 'You' needed to be stressed, to echo the 'U-turn' in the preceding sentence. Her ear was unfailingly tinny and, though she could be devastating and inspiring in unscripted harangues, the sight of a written text would make her freeze. Even though the words might be of her own devising – in fact she might already have uttered something like them in public several times before – at first reading they would fall lifeless from her lips. It was as though the mere act of writing them down had leached some primeval potency from them, reminding us that political oratory is a far older form of communication than the first scratches on stone or papyrus. After listening to her dismal read-over, Ronnie would jump up from the sofa and, with beseeching arms outstretched, attempt to gee her up: 'Come on, darling, they want you to show you really feel it.' She would look up at him, bewildered but dutiful, the novice on her first engagement in rep.

By Ronnie's side, John Gummer seemed an insubstantial figure: a callow curate alongside a well-dined archdeacon. He belonged to the redoubtable generation of Cambridge Tories that included Ken Clarke, Leon Brittan, Norman Fowler and Norman Lamont, but perhaps because of this juvenile appearance had risen more slowly than they had, being still an assistant whip. His principal contribution to Thatcheriana came in the first conference speech that I worked on with him. As usual, the Conservatives were being accused of wishing to break up the health service. 'Why don't you say "The National Health Service is safe with us"?' John suggested. It was immediately clear that this was not what she wished to say, although she did not actively state this, probably for fear of it getting out that she had refused to say it. But it was impossible to make her say it as if she really meant it. 'The National Health Service is safe with us' – it came out in the listless drone of a hostage reading a statement prepared by her captors – which is what it was.

I soon discovered that Ronnie and John had developed a strong, though mostly cloaked mutual dislike. 'Our friend Gummer reminds me of Sir Richard Rich – you know, the ambitious turncoat in *A Man for All Seasons*,' Ronnie said, as he was driving me off to lunch in his ancient Rolls-Royce. I was worrying too much whether his windscreen wipers were working properly (we narrowly missed a traffic island in St James's Street) to point out that this was a bit, well, rich, since he himself seemed to have effortlessly survived the transition from Ted Heath to Mrs Thatcher. John for his part was constantly urging that we should meet without Ronnie who held up proceedings with his tiresome thespian interruptions. Mrs Thatcher got fed up with him too, but as the time-slots had been fixed in advance Ronnie turned up all the same and, despite being told at the Private Office that the session had been cancelled, proceeded at his stately gait up the stairs and could be heard saying to some passer-by that he hoped he might catch a word with the Prime Minister. The Prime Minister shot behind the sofa, crouching slightly so that she could not be seen, beckoning me to follow her. Ronnie put his head round the door but, seeing nobody in the study, withdrew. His footsteps sounded slower as he went off down the stairs. Mrs Thatcher surfaced giggling, for once resembling less the Iron Lady than Miranda Richardson's Queen in *Blackadder*.

It seemed strange to me that she should be prepared to devote quite so much time to the one speech in the year in which she was assured of receiving a rapturous standing ovation. I reckon that the entire process must have occupied about eighteen hours of meeting time with a full weekend at Chequers before the week of the conference itself, not to mention all the hours I put in drafting and redrafting. The final text seemed almost deliberately conventional – all the smart phrases that Matthew Parris and I thought would take the fancy had long been deleted in favour of the more direct, brutal way of putting things that she felt comfortable with. I was still more surprised to see how nervous she was just before delivering the actual speech each time, far more anxious than before going to address a fractious House of Commons. She lapped up our halting words of encouragement beforehand.

My incomprehension showed how little I really understood about the mechanics of getting and holding power. I learned a little more as the 1983 general election approached. Geoffrey Howe had been put in charge of a small team of trusties – Tebbit, Lawson, Parkinson – to draft a manifesto, with his adviser Adam Ridley and me to pull the stuff together. Adam and I had been Wiltshire neighbours as children (and in proper Establishment style he had been my fag in College). He was famous as a non-stop talker and know-all who could not help telling you at length the quickest way to Norfolk or how to carve a duck, but he was surprisingly easy to collaborate with and the whole process went on along quite easily, since all concerned were determined that the document should be as bland and inoffensive as possible. This was not Mrs Thatcher's view. She kept on sending back the draft with 'Dull, nothing exciting in this' scrawled across it in her manic sprawly hand. The manifesto group then tried to think of a different way of being dull which at least sounded a bit livelier. I offered a few flourishes: 'Couldn't we have a sentence about our magical heritage of moorland and mountain?' I said wistfully. This was greeted with derision, especially by Nigel Lawson. 'Moorland

and mountain' became a catchphrase to describe anything flowery which needed to be cut. The environment was not regarded as a serious subject by Tory hardheads at the time. I kept on pressing Mrs Thatcher to tell them that it was the coming thing, which she at least half believed. But when I went to see William Waldegrave, who was the Parliamentary Under Secretary responsible for green issues in the Department of the Environment, he told me that nobody had spoken to him for weeks.

I wrote four, perhaps five drafts of the manifesto. As it was nakedly political work, I assumed I would have to send it over to Conservative Central Office to have it typed up (in those days gentlemen in the Civil Service didn't type), but Linda, passing through my office, said, 'Do you want me to do that stuff for you?' 'I don't want to get you in trouble.' 'Oh, I typed the Labour manifesto for Bernard Donoughue, so I don't see why I shouldn't do it for your lot too.' She spoke like a kindly aunt joining in some childish game. Who says the British Civil Service isn't flexible?

Up to the last draft there was one big hole, Northern Ireland. Jim Prior had told us that the whole question of getting his new Assembly off the ground remained a matter of the greatest delicacy and he would prefer to draft his own words and settle them directly with the Prime Minister. This was fine by us. The only snag was that the Prime Minister didn't think that Jim's Assembly would get off the ground in a million years and she was deeply reluctant to give her explicit approval to any formula which suggested that it had the faintest hope of success. So every time Prior sent in his proposed formula no answer came back. Time was desperately short. The printers were waiting. Coming out of Cabinet, Jim bearded her.

'Margaret, could you just bear to have a look at what I've come up with on Northern Ireland for the manifesto?'

No she couldn't. But she was cornered. She actually had the dreaded piece of paper in her hands, like a summons served by an importunate bailiff. Then she saw me hanging about.

'Ferdy, would you have a look at Jim's text?'

I stood there with the paper flapping in my trembling hand and Jim's beady farmer's face glaring at me. Words swam up from the page. 'A framework of participation . . . no devolution of powers without . . .' In that disputatious Province where the placing of a comma can mean a mass walk-out followed by riots, blazing buses and half-a-dozen corpses every nuance mattered.

'Seems splendid to me,' I said and passed the paper back to Jim. Everyone was happy. Jim had got what he wanted and Mrs Thatcher had not been forced to say that she agreed with a single word of it.

With these obstacles overcome, the manifesto was ready to go. But was she? On Sunday 8 May, a senior bunch of ministers plus Ian Gow and David Wolfson and me trooped down to Chequers at noon. The official business was to sign off the manifesto. The real question was to decide the date of the election. The local election results from the preceding Thursday were encouraging. The Tories were 10 per cent or more ahead of Labour in the polls, and the 20 per cent or thereabouts that the Alliance were clocking up was more than enough to unseat dozens of Labour MPs. Going to the country seemed the most obvious decision imaginable. So I was startled to discover that Mrs Thatcher was in an abject state of nerves. Would she be accused of cutting and running, or of clinging on to power if she didn't go now? What about the Summit due to be held in America, at Williamsburg, at the end of May? Would it not be a dereliction of duty if she missed it? On the other hand, if she went in the middle of an election campaign, would she not look out of place, a provisional sort of figure, lacking authority? We tried to remember whether Mr Attlee had gone to the Potsdam conference during the 1945 general election campaign. Then what about Royal Ascot which would fall in the last or last but one week of the campaign if the election was held on 16 or 23 June? Wouldn't it look ghastly if the newspapers were full of toffs in toppers and ladies in huge hats while they were stumping the country? Laughable though it may seem, it was the Ascot factor that clinched the decision in favour of 9 June.

But then, as she saw it, it wasn't yet a decision. She was like a child thinking of excuses to get out of something. 'Even if I wanted to call an election, the Queen could hardly be available at such short notice.' So Ian Gow slipped out and rang the Palace, who told him that the Queen would be happy to see her at midday tomorrow. She gave him a cross look and scarcely bothered to thank him for the trouble. Even after she had said goodbye to her guests, she went on muttering in a quiet, tearful undertone, 'I'm not sure it's the right thing to do at all. I shall sleep on it. It's always best to sleep on these things.'

For the only time when I was around (though there must often have been such occasions in the privacy of their boudoir), Denis lost patience. 'You can't do that, Margaret. They've all gone back to town saying it's going to be the 9th. You can't go back on that now. The horses have bolted, my dear.'

Without actually contradicting this unanswerable argument, she sat by the embers of the fire looking glum and put-upon. At last my sluggish civilian's brain began to understand. The decisions that really matter to political leaders are those to do with the getting and holding of power. Other decisions may turn out well or ill. They may cost billions of pounds or hundreds of lives, but for enlisted politicians those decisions are secondary. What matters to them is, Will I still be here after this? And the spectacle of Mrs Thatcher by the huge Tudor grate at Chequers, exhausted by the day's work like Cinders after a hard time from the Ugly Sisters, made me realise it.

We had decided that the campaign should be punctuated by rallies – Cardiff, Harrogate, Edinburgh, Birmingham, Wembley and Manchester. At each rally she would deliver a full-scale speech. The idea was to give weight to a campaign that would otherwise, in the modern style, be dominated by the early-morning press conferences and carefully placed soundbites. So every morning I pedalled down from Islington to go to the 8.30 press conference at Central Office, once collecting a summons for shooting the lights at Trafalgar Square – my only recorded cycling offence. Then I walked back to Downing

Street to spend the rest of the day writing these mega-speeches. Whitehall is a strange, quiet place during an election campaign, like a resort out of season. The civil servants have nothing much to do. The younger ones slip out to cricket matches or write to their girlfriends. The temporary special advisers whose contracts are brought to an end by the election are mostly dispersed round the country with their masters. Only my lamp was burning deep into the night. Each speech was to have a theme: preserving our liberties, the new enterprise society, better public services and so on. I really threw myself into these speeches, trying to give them a sustained argument lightened by vivid phrases which were not too high-flown to make her uncomfortable. In the evenings when she was back from campaigning we would spend an hour or two going over the speech for the next day.

They were strange evenings, usually just the two of us up in the flat, each with a glass of whisky, she with her shoes off but fretful rather than relaxed. Now and then the phone would ring, usually one of her confidants, Woodrow Wyatt most often, to whom she could pour out her complaints about her colleagues, especially Francis Pym, who had just given an interview saying that it would be a bad thing if the Conservatives won the election by a landslide: 'If it hadn't been for the Falklands I'd never have made him Foreign Secretary. He's so weak, Woodrow, and weak men always let you down. Now he's saying we don't want a landslide. What are all our people going to think?' Far from these intimate late-night glimpses showing a softer, more easy-going side to her, they tended to reveal just how steely her inner core really was. She could forgive a personal peccadillo and was generally tolerant about anything to do with sex. Towards her staff, especially the girls, she was thoughtful and even indulgent. But to her colleagues she was hard and unforgiving. 'No, Francis, I can't agree. I think it was a great mistake and I think it is doing a lot of damage.' I could just hear Pym's gloomy, rather grating voice at the other end of the line and I could not repress a little sadistic stab of pleasure although I had nothing against him and his remark seemed harmless enough to me, in fact more likely to make people vote Conservative rather than not. But I could see that from that moment his career was over and Mrs Thatcher's first action on winning the election was to sack him.

But we had no other interruptions. Without the distraction of the motley army of other speechwriters (and anyway she was tired and time was short) we waltzed through the texts. If ever speechwriting came close to being tolerable, this was it. I could not deny that I was rather pleased with my work.

Picture my surprise then when, after every rally, virtually none of the text appeared in next morning's newspapers. Nor were 'my' speeches mentioned in any later history of the campaign, as far as I could see. Nor do any of them feature in the fat volume of Margaret Thatcher's greatest speeches compiled by Robin Harris. Even the texts themselves seem to have disappeared from the archives. All I have to show from the campaign is one fine for shooting a red light on a bike.

Anyway, triumph. Far from the shattering defeat predicted by Mrs Thatcher's bright young sparks or the hung Parliament predicated by me, she waltzed in with a majority of 144. When a government is re-elected, inside the machine there is a sense not quite of a non-event but of business resumed after an annoying interruption – rather the way people troop back into an office after a false bomb alert. Pieces of work which the campaign had provided an excuse for putting in the pending tray now had to be picked up again, new contracts signed, including mine, new postings angled for.

Meanwhile inside Downing Street itself ministers and soon to be ex-ministers were tramping in and out. As I wandered down the main passage, I bumped into them several times as they were coming or going, their faces barely recognisable because they were so transfigured by their fate: Leon Brittan, normally pasty-faced and hesitant of manner, glowing like a light bulb after being made Home Secretary; Willie Whitelaw's rich purple cheeks as white as paper after being sacked from the Home Office and shunted upwards to the Lords. And Cecil Parkinson looking like a leper. Twenty-four hours earlier Mrs Thatcher had been set on making him Foreign Secretary. Now he had just told her that he had been having an affair with his secretary Sara Keays and she might be pregnant. That afternoon the Prime Minister received a letter from Sara's father, the choleric Major Hastings Keays, confirming the pregnancy. Curiously it was then agreed that Cecil should still be in the government but have a less high-profile department, to wit, Trade and Industry, on the grounds that if the victorious party Chairman was not promoted the press would be so amazed that they would ferret out the real story anyway. This rather bizarre compromise seemed unlikely to endure and did not, mostly because the Keays family had become vitriolic towards Parkinson. A pity from Mrs Thatcher's point of view, since as a result, much against her instinct, she had to make Geoffrey Howe Foreign Secretary instead, which was ultimately to tear the government apart and destroy her. This would not have happened if Parky had been at the Foreign Office. Nor, I fancy, would Britain have been sucked into the Exchange Rate Mechanism – or rather into the whole business of keeping the pound at an unrealistic high level which precipitated the necessary humiliation of Black Wednesday. But then Margaret Thatcher had enjoyed enough good luck to be due for a dose of undeserved misfortune.

The next day happened to be the Trooping of the Colour. It had become a tradition that the Prime Minister should invite her staff and their families to watch the parade from the Downing Street stand, along with the Cabinet and their spouses. It was a deliciously odd scene: junior ministers still trooping in and out to hear what she had in store for them, their paths crossed by flocks of small children and Cabinet ministers' wives in best summer frocks, their husbands still exhibiting the emotional shock of the day before, as though promotion or demotion had caused a permanent change to their blood supply. Lunch had already started by the time Mrs Thatcher herself bustled in fresh from the latest round of bloodletting. She immediately began handing round plates of coronation chicken to the children and asking the quicker eaters if they wanted seconds. She was the Little Red Hen in the fairy story who decides she has to do everything herself because nobody else will do it. My son Harry had briefly taken up autograph-hunting and he worked the room, clocking up the white-faced Whitelaw and Parkinson for starters. As I followed him round, I noticed that Ann Parkinson was standing very close to Cecil, as though fearing that if she let him get a couple of yards' start he might be out the front door announcing that he was off to marry Sara Keays – by no means unthinkable as he remained in an agony of indecision for weeks. Then Harry moved on to get a signature from Denis Thatcher. Would it be all right to ask Mark Thatcher for an autograph too? 'I wouldn't bother if I was you,' said Denis, 'the boy can scarcely write his own name' – which Harry thought the funniest thing he had ever heard. In fact, Mark was delighted to sign his name, saying, as he did so, 'Your father was the architect of victory' – the only person, I am sorry to say, who took this perceptive view.

They ought to have been happy days that followed. The second election victory did make a huge difference. It was not simply that ministers, whether the retained ones or new arrivals, had a greater self-confidence that they could shift the status quo. Perhaps more important, their officials became conscious that the Thatcher approach was not simply a blip but might be here to stay a while. It was possible to discern at least the beginnings of a tanker-sized turning circle (Labour experienced much the same phenomenon after their second victory in 2001). And we ventured to hope that the work we were doing was beginning to feed its way into the departmental bloodstream. After various comings and goings the Policy Unit now consisted of eight or nine people, with the addition of Bob Young and David Pascall who had been seconded from industry via the CPRS, which was now wound up as I had suggested. We also had the unpaid help of David Hobson, a former senior partner in Cooper and Lybrand, so with John Redwood's experience in Roths-childs we could at last give a fairly good impression that we knew what we were talking about, without in any sense presuming to dictate the terms of reform – we didn't begin to have the staff or the authority to do that. We were thinking of new previously unthinkable industries and services to privatise – the water industry, gas, telecoms, perhaps even railways. Step by step, the trade unions were coming back under the same laws as the rest of us. Although Keith Joseph had failed to persuade his civil servants to accept education vouchers, we had all sorts of plans to raise standards in state schools and give them real independence. Headmasters and parents, not politicians and bureaucrats, would have the deciding voice. Technical schools would become a reality, forty years after Rab Butler had prescribed them as the third leg of the system.

One by one, the old encrusted monopolies were crumbling as we poked them. No longer would you have to go to an optician to buy a pair of reading spectacles, or hire a solicitor to have your house conveyanced. We were sweeping away taxes on business, giving wonderful new incentives for people to start up on their own. We were nibbling away at the planning process to make it quicker and easier to build new homes. We were decontrolling rents to revive the rented sector and make it easier for people to move to new jobs and gradually, with painful slowness, the jobs were coming back. I had intoxicating plans for restoring the old railway companies in all their glory — the chocolate and cream of GWR, the viridian of the Southern Railway. We would demolish the food mountains and deflate the farm subsidies and bring back the hedgerows and the wetlands. There was no conflict between a leaner state and a greener countryside. The two went together. For the first time conservation would be in the mainstream of government policy. Everything seemed to be surging ahead that autumn.

Yet this was just the moment when I began to experience a nagging discontent. The itch to be somewhere else was intermittent at first and I put it down to tiredness after working flat out over the last three or four months leading up to the election. I also wanted to see more of my family. But that wasn't really it. And you couldn't really speak of a personality clash, because there was no clashing.

On the contrary, I came to admire Mrs Thatcher rather more. She continued to have the capacity to surprise. For one supposed to be so inflexible and dogmatic, she retained an open and attentive mind, at least until she had locked it into position, much more so than politicians who superficially appeared to be more open-minded. It was not my beat but I was fascinated when Tony Parsons, her debonair, chain-smoking new foreign policy adviser, told me that she had asked for a big Chequers seminar on the USSR and was annoying the Foreign Office by demanding papers from every outside expert imaginable. Her turn towards the East was rapid and quite unexpected. It was announced that Hungary would be her first port of call, and by chance I went to lunch that week at the *Spectator* and the Russian Ambassador was there, an urbane fellow.

'Now please you tell me, Sir, why is your Mrs Thatcher choosing to go to Hungary?'

'Well, I don't have anything to do with foreign policy but I can tell you for free I haven't a clue.'

'You are playing games with me. This Iron Lady suddenly become palsy with the evil Communists and you tell me you don't know a sausage.'

'I promise you, I really don't know a thing.'

His Excellency looked at me with baleful frustration, scarcely able to contain his annoyance at the inscrutability of the British. At this moment I was saved by the *Spectator* cook Jennifer Paterson, later TV star of *Two Fat Ladies*, handing round the stew and booming into the Ambassador's ear in her throaty contralto, 'Do you know my brother? He's the British consul in Ulan Bator,' which His bewildered Excellency thought must be some kind of weird British joke but was in fact the truth.

One morning a few weeks earlier, I had wandered into the PM's study to discuss plans for her speech to the Lord Mayor's Banquet. I found her in a steaming rage.

'It's British sovereign territory, doesn't he understand that?' She was shouting down the telephone to somebody in the Foreign Office, possibly the Foreign Secretary. 'Of course I know the President's asleep now. Just make sure I speak to him the minute he wakes up.'

I found this outburst against Reagan's invasion of Grenada thrilling. But I was equally impressed when she dowsed her fury in public and lent Reagan her support in the interests not only of the Anglo-American alliance but of *Realpolitik* (the invasion turned out for the best in the end). Something similar happened when Reagan bombed Libya three years later – a move which she initially thought foolhardy and was on record (in a radio phone-in) as having described as illegal under international law. Again she recovered swiftly. Not only did she give Reagan her public support but, when Conrad Black came down to Chequers to receive her gratitude for saving the *Daily Telegraph* where I was by then writing a column, she denounced him fiercely for allowing wimps like me and his new editor Max Hastings to criticise the bombing. Bruised by this first encounter from which he had expected nothing but flattery, Conrad immediately conceived and stuck to the view that 'Ferdy Mount is so wet you could shoot snipe off him,' though mercifully he made no move to sack me, or none that I observed.

So if she had not lost her dynamic allure, why was I increasingly so keen to get the hell out? There was the grind of course. We had begun the same relentless build-up to the conference speech, this year at Blackpool, and the same wrecking crew of speechwriters was blundering through the same motions. I was deep in the third or was it the fourth rewrite when Linda said, 'Your nephew's here to see you.'

Nephew, what nephew? (My only nephew Archie was barely into his teens.) Then I recalled that a few weeks earlier my cousin Mary Cameron had rung and asked if I could possibly give her son David an interview for the school magazine. I had grunted something unhelpful about being very busy and anyway I was covered by the Official Secrets Act and couldn't say anything at all interesting but I might be in touch. I rang off expecting to hear no more. But unbeknown to me David immediately rang the office himself and made an appointment and here he was, my cousin rather than nephew then just sixteen, looking pink and perky, not yet the size he grew to but abounding in self-confidence. He instantly put me at my ease and his genial chutzpah dissolved my ill-humour in a trice. It would not have taken extrasensory powers to see that he would go far, though not perhaps with the miraculous speed that he did.

It is his audacity – or cheek, to use a homelier word – that has done the trick. It took cheek out of the common run to stand for the leadership of the party after only four years in Parliament, but it took even more to set about transforming the party the moment he won. This was largely a matter of changing the conversation. Instead of talking the whole time about taxes, immigration and the EU, he broadened the debate to include family breakdown, climate change and social inequality – the subjects which people outside politics had been worrying about for years. Having made a few unavailing efforts myself to point out to Tory MPs how far out of touch they were and how they needed to re-engage in precisely this way, I cannot conceal my delight. Especially admirable is the way David is unafraid of being laughed at. He cheerfully disregards W. C. Fields's advice 'Never act with children or dogs' and is photographed looking silly as he whips up a team of huskies or gets down on all fours in a kindergarten. I would never dream of prophesying whether all this will be enough to turf out a government with a handy majority against a background of fairly general prosperity and low inflation and high employment. But what I am sure of is that no other approach would do any better. The limited agenda of the Hague–Duncan-Smith–Howard years never stood a chance. Those endlessly repeated pledges to cut taxes and immigration and to repatriate powers from the European Union looked neither adequate nor plausible. The chutzpah that has pro-pelled Cousin Dave to such startling heights undoubtedly comes from his stalwart and irrepressible father Ian on whom no flies rest, but I like to think that our side of the family can claim some credit for his attentiveness to the real world.

Oh the bloody speech. The whole business seemed twice as bad as the year before, perhaps because we were going round the same hoops again, with Mrs Thatcher wanting to say all the things she had said a million times before and everyone else making footling interjections. It must have been about 11.30 p.m. on the Thursday evening in the Imperial Hotel that I resolved to myself this would definitely be the last time. Just then there was a knock at the door and Robin Butler shimmered in.

'Mr Parkinson would like a word, Prime Minister.'

She shooed us out. We passed Cecil in the passage. His face was a strange grey deathmask colour. The Press Officer at Number Ten had just read over the worst bits of an interview with Sara Keays in next morning's *Times*. This was her response to the statement he had put out earlier in the week setting out the facts of their affair. It was clear that she was not going to go away, but he was.

It was time for me to go away too. I was becoming increasingly tetchy and reluctant to supervise the details of what we were suggesting. I had only promised to stay a couple of years at most. That was probably the useful shelf life of an adviser anyway. Besides, she was beginning to get on my nerves, or I was beginning to get on hers, or both. By November, I was desperate to make a quick getaway, but I knew this would not be possible unless I could come up with a plausible successor. The only one in immediate view was John Redwood, fellow of All Souls, director of Rothschilds, still only thirty-two and a bit other-planetary in manner, but hardworking and enthusiastic.

To my horror, though, he beat me to it.

'I think it's time I moved on, I think I've set the wheels in motion and my best work is done here.'

'Oh dear,' I said, 'that's exactly what I think too, about myself I mean, not you. And I think you would be the ideal person to take over.'

Here our conversation grows hazy, in my memory at least. We both remember John saying something to the effect that this might alter his view, but he also remembers himself asking why I didn't wish to stay on because I admired her so much and got on with her so well.

'Admire her?' goes the Redwood version of me. '*I hate her.*'

I have no recollection at all of this moment, which must have been every bit as dramatic as the bit in *Rebecca* when Maxim de Winter (Laurence Olivier) uses the same words about his dead wife. Perhaps I have suppressed it. But whether or not his report is strictly accurate (and John is truthful as Martians tend to be), he has accurately conveyed my fevered state of mind.

I left Downing Street at the end of the year. By the time of my leaving party my bonhomie was fully restored, as was my admiration for this strange, tense, ruthless but deeply honourable and usually honest woman. It was at my leaving party that Alfred Sherman got drunk and fondled the bare shoulders of the new secretary in the Policy Unit. The promoted Nigel Lawson brought his new wife Thérèse whom he had met while working in the House of Commons library. The resigned Cecil Parkinson brought his old wife Ann. The quarrelsome speechwriters, Gummer and Millar, the latter now Sir Ronald, came. In fact all the Thatcherite top brass were there – Leon Brittan, the Howes, Keith Joseph, Norman Tebbit. Gail Redwood gave Julia a bunch of flowers, murmuring, 'For the power behind the throne,' which annoyed Julia. Even so, the room was only half full, and our three children munching crisps as they ran about the empty spaces only emphasised the lack of crowds and jollity. It was as though the Thatcherites, although firmly ensconced in the Presidential palace, remained a minority tribe which had seized power through a chain of accidents but would never be regarded as legitimate by the majority tribes who would continue to think of them as a bit weird.

It was a fine moment all the same to walk out into Whitehall for the last time a few days later and breathe the damp night air as a free man. It was as good as being told that you don't have cancer any more. In fact ten years later, when I was told precisely that after a disagreeable interlude, I remember thinking, This is as good as leaving Number Ten. Government service is a monastic vocation. However keen you are about the work, you cannot help feeling it as a servitude. The Prime Minister gave me a bottle of Prime Minister's Reserve malt whisky as a going-away present and wrote me a nice letter. The girls in the Policy Unit had a whip-round and bought me an elegant inscribed silver coaster. But the biggest present was liberty.

I was free to speak now, not that I was bursting to (I was keener to do some writing for my own pleasure). Hugh Thomas at the Centre for Policy Studies, now at last disembarrassed of Alfred, having come out top in their titanic power struggle, asked me to give their annual lecture at the party conference at Brighton, and it would have been gruff to refuse. Once more I would be working on a long speech for the conference but at least this time it would be my own. This time too I would not be holed up all day and night in the conference hotel, so I suggested Julia came along as she had never been to a party conference before and Brighton was easy to get to. My oration – 'Property and Poverty: an agenda for the mid-80s' – passed off without incident and was later reprinted in a nice chocolate-and-white jacket. Afterwards Hugh entertained us for dinner in the Grand Hotel, and with the relief of having got the lecture over with I had several glasses too many and became pleasantly embroiled in a conversation about terrorism with the man next to me, a sympathetic character who turned out to be Keith Middlemas, reader in history at Sussex and co-author of a marvellous life of Stanley Baldwin.

'Why', I wondered, my voice rising somewhat, 'don't people who want to change the world try assassination more often? It's so much less trouble to bump off the dictator than to build up a mass movement to bring him down.'

Middlemas reminded me of the incident at Sarajevo and one or two other cases where assassination had not turned out exactly as intended. I retorted that if the Hitler plot had come off, millions of lives might have been saved.

He replied politely but I don't think his heart was in the argument. Anyway it was time for us to go next door to bed at the Metropole. I fell asleep as my head hit the pillow. It seemed only a couple of minutes later that Julia was thumping my shoulder and shouting in my ear. Outside, feet were thundering along the hotel corridor and there was a feverish banging on doors.

'Don't worry,' I slurred, ' 'S jus' young Conservatives, always like this, las' nigh' of Conference.'

She allowed me to go back to sleep, but almost immediately woke me up again. More thundering feet, more banging on doors.

'God, they're a pain,' I mumbled, 'this is the last time –'

We were finally wakened by the telephone at about 7.30 in the morning – Julia's sister Virginia asking if we were all right. It turned out we were almost the only people in the entire hotel who had slept the night through. Everyone else had been evacuated in case there was a second bomb.

We went out into the glorious autumn sunshine. The hole in the Grand Hotel next door was the size of a house. On the forecourt, Cabinet Ministers with ashen faces were wandering about all dressed in the identical Marks and Spencer dressing gowns which had been commandeered from the local branch by Alastair McAlpine. They were a wan, disoriented crew of the undead. Some of them were sitting in deckchairs, as desolate and shocked-looking as though they would never move again. I met Grey Gowrie carrying more deckchairs up from the beach. It was the most appalling weird scene, but it was still the seaside with the gulls flapping and the pier in the background, so there was something oddly domestic about it, like a Stanley Spencer picture of the Resurrection or the Last Judgement, with holidaymakers looking on from behind the police barriers and Grey struggling to unfold the deckchairs.

I wish I had seen Professor Middlemas again to tell him I had changed my mind about assassination. Far from my remarks the night before being brilliantly subversive and original, they were the wet dream of every terrorist thug, one of whom had just succeeded in murdering or crippling a dozen harmless people in their sleep and very nearly assassinated the only politician who, despite our ups and downs, I never stopped admiring.

For none of the things you read about as happening to someone who is drafted in to serve a great man or woman happened to me. I never came to think less of her, as valets are supposed to do. She

remained heroic, intolerable often, vindictive, even poisonous sometimes, but always heroic. Equally, I never became fond of her. That
insistent, harsh concentration could never become endearing. 'I'm
not here to be nice,' she would say, which was just as well. But
working for her was not in the least frustrating. On the contrary, I
sometimes thought it wasn't frustrating enough; she had such an
unguarded enthusiasm for any fresh idea that was served up to her
before it was even partially baked. It is easy to slip into thinking that
some of the things she achieved could have been achieved in a kinder
style and at a lesser cost. I rather doubt it. There are times when what
is needed is not a beacon but a blowtorch.

Hugh liked giving dinners. Nearly twenty years later in March
2001 he gave a dinner at the Athenaeum in honour of Arthur
Schlesinger, the American historian and leading figure of the Kennedy court. Although their politics were far apart, Arthur could charm
anyone and was friends with the Thatchers. Nigel Lawson was there
on his own, over from Gascony where he now spent most of his time,
alarmingly thin after following his own patent diet, no longer the
flesh-creeping fat boy but with the ruined good looks of a retired
croupier. The rest of us, including Gina Thomas (no relation to
Hugh), the London correspondent of the *Frankfurter Allgemeine*,
arrived ten minutes before the Thatchers, and Vanessa Thomas, like
a proper diplomat's daughter (her father was Gladwyn Jebb, the
British Ambassador to Paris who had become a household name for
standing up to the Russians at the UN), had settled us down carefully
next to people we weren't sitting next to at dinner. Naturally we all
got up as the Thatchers arrived. Though it wasn't her party, Margaret
immediately went into Little Red Hen mode and started shuffling us
about into different places, ruining Vanessa's pre-placement by
putting us next to the people we *were* next to at dinner. Naturally
the talk was about old times, how Geoffrey had done this or that,
what Alfred had thought. Now and then she would appeal across the
table to Lawson: 'Nigel, you will remember, I think you were in
government at the time.' She spoke to him as to a dimly remembered
colleague of whom she was quite fond, rather than as someone who
had been her Chancellor for six years and whom she had bust up with
in one of the most flaming rows in recent political history. I wondered

in fact how often they had met since, if at all, and reflected on how reckless you needed to be to give this sort of dinner party, in fact, to give any sort of party involving Margaret Thatcher, the world's least relaxing guest. Across the table from me Denis had fallen fast asleep, but in a neat, self-contained way, his head not quite lolling on Gina's bosom.

'We should have gone on to Baghdad.' It was the trumpet voice of old, undimmed by doubt or age.

'Well, Margaret,' Schlesinger said in his gentle persuasive drawl, 'the UN resolution only allowed us to remove Saddam from Kuwait.'

'No, it didn't, Arthur. We should have gone on to Baghdad. That was the only way, and I told George Bush so.'

'But, Margaret, surely the UN resolution made it perfectly clear,' Hugh Thomas put in.

'No, it didn't. It didn't say that at all.'

'Yes, it did, Margaret.' Suddenly all the old irritation that used to make Nigel Lawson swell and heave in their tenser sessions in the study at Number Ten came back. 'There's no doubt at all. We went in for one purpose alone, to remove him from Kuwait.'

'No we didn't, Nigel. We should have gone on to Baghdad.'

'But, Margaret,' I piped up, feeling it would be wimpish to be left out, 'the UN would never have approved any resolution which interfered with the internal affairs of a sovereign country.'

'That's not the point. The man was a menace to the peace of the region and had to be removed.'

'But the UN resolution said—'

'No, it didn't.'

At this moment, Denis Thatcher woke from his sleep and turning to Gina said, in his most courtly fashion, 'I hope I haven't been boring you, dear lady.'

'We should have gone on,' Margaret said, paying no attention to this graceful awakening.

Well, going on was her strong suit, but it wasn't mine. I always had a weakness for stopping off, a fatal inclination to take the detour. If you want to get on in life, it doesn't do to let your attention wander. Unfortunately, I have turned out to be the sort of person who, as soon as anyone starts talking about 'focus', goes next door to look up the derivation of the word and then finds his eye diverted to 'fo'c'sle'. This butterfly mind I inherited from my father. I remember only rare occasions in my childhood when it was clear that his attention was fully engaged, when he was making mayonnaise or breaking a yearling in the field beyond the beech hedge. His inability to concentrate on practical affairs used to drive me mad. Now that I am older than he ever lived to be, I look more kindly on his willingness to be diverted. He seemed to inhabit the world more fully than people who looked straight ahead. Didn't do him much good. Perhaps it hasn't done me much good either. But I am grateful all the same.

ENVOI: THE DAMSON TREE

M Y FATHER WAS fond of damsons. He liked damson fool and damson tart and once or twice when we had enough of them Mrs Herrington made damson cheese, that delicious sharp–sweet sticky jam which stops just short of being jelly. But what he really enjoyed was getting the damsons. There was a tree on the lawn but it was a thin slanting thing well past its best and a poor fruiter. The sight of it only reminded him of the altogether more wonderful tree in the far corner of the garden whose laden branches drooped over the farmyard beyond the garden wall. This tree did have a fair quantity of damsons on our side, but the droopingest branches hung out of reach over the cowshed at the end of the yard, their bloomy blowsy fruit so thick upon the branch that summer that you could see the purple haze from the terrace outside our back door. The cowshed had an old corrugated-iron roof, sagging and much patched, which should have been replaced years ago. The black paint had been invaded by rust and you could hear the wind sigh through its cracks and holes. We had picked clean all the branches we could get at from our side but the big aluminium pan which we made the jam in was still only a third full.

'If I give you a leg up, will you have a go at that long branch at the end there?'

My father pointed to the branch lousy with damsons hanging so low over the cowshed roof that it knocked against the tin and made it shiver.

'That roof doesn't look at all safe,' my mother said.

'Oh he'll only be up there five minutes and he's so light,' my father said.

There was no way out. My father cupped my sandalled foot and I hoisted myself nervously over the sharp edge of the roof, then knelt to be passed up the floppy basket for the damsons. I crawled across the tin, feeling it twang menacingly under my bare knees. Then it began to dip and sway in a terrifying manner, but I had gone too far to go back. Down below I could see my mother still looking anxious, but not so anxious that she wasn't looking for a viewpoint to take a photo of me up on the roof. It is because of the photograph that I know this happened just after my third birthday, not when I was six or seven as I later came to imagine. This makes it my earliest memory and it was child labour of the most unfeeling sort, every bit as bad as sending little boys up chimneys. But there is the tiny faded picture in the album on the page for 1942, callously captioned 'F. about to fall through the roof'.

I was still a couple of feet short of the magic branch when the roof gave way and I sank at speed through the steamy air of the cowshed. I felt the edge of the tin slash my forehead and there I was standing in deep straw with its fair share of manure squelching over my sandals. I put my hand up to feel the blood streaming down my face and in the same instant I became aware that I was standing next to Mr Stratton's bull, and level with its dark eye and its sandy eyelash. It was a Hereford bull, quite famous for its bad temper, although that may have been exaggerated (perhaps bad temper is a big selling point in bulls). But the best thing from my point of view was that I had landed in the next-door stall and there were three thick steel bars between me and the bull. My father rushed round into the yard to rescue me from a fate which was agonisingly unclear to him, while my mother rang Dr Graham Campbell. Half an hour later I was sitting on a chair in the dining room being given a tetanus injection and eight stitches on my forehead. As the doctor finished sewing up the wound, my mother cleaned the scratches and abrasions on my arms and legs. She looked for some witch hazel to soothe them, but as usual our medicine cupboard, though packed with old bottles, was out of stock of the thing we actually needed, so what she smoothed into the rough patches instead was her universal magic salve, cold cream. As the familiar chill spread over my skin, it was followed by a less familiar sensation which was the warm flush of heroism. I had, after all, done what was expected of me. Anything that had gone wrong was not my fault, and my mother was at that moment making it clear to my father exactly whose fault it was. Though we had no extra damsons to show, I had an impressive *Beano*-style bandage round my head and a misleading aura of audacity to go with it. My crawling out on the roof was, after all, a matter of choice. I could have said no if I didn't mind being thought a weed. My falling through the roof, by contrast, was an entirely predictable event, a question of metal fatigue. It was bound to happen to anyone silly enough to crawl across the roof in its dilapidated state. There was nothing to be done about it. But my coming down in the empty stall and not being impaled on the bull's horns or crushed by its mighty flanks was not predictable at all. It was purely a question of luck. And on the whole, the luck is the bit that counts.

INDEX

ACKNOWLEDGEMENTS

My greatest debt is to my sister, who kept all the letters and photographs. Among the books which have also jogged my memory I am especially grateful to the authors and editors of the following:

Flourishing: Letters 1928–46, Isaiah Berlin, ed. Henry Hardy, Chatto & Windus, 2004

A Divided Life: A Biography of Donald Maclean, Robert Cecil, Bodley Head, 1988

As I was Going to St Ives: A Life of Derek Jackson, Simon Courtauld, Michael Russell, 2007

Keith Joseph, Andrew Denham and Mark Garnett, Acumen, 2001

Siegfried Sassoon, Max Egremont, Picador, 2005

Isaiah Berlin, Michael Ignatieff, Chatto & Windus, 1998

David Tennant and the Gargoyle Years, Michael Luke, Weidenfeld, 1991

The Private Eye Story, Patrick Marnham, André Deutsch, 1982

Everything to Lose: Diaries 1945–60, Frances Partridge, Gollancz, 1985

Five Out of Six, *Within the Family Circle* and *The Departure Platform*, Violet Powell, Heinemann, 1960, 1976 and 1998

Unity Mitford: A Quest, David Pryce-Jones, Weidenfeld & Nicolson, 1976

A Very Private Eye: An Autobiography in Diaries and Letters, Barbara Pym, Dutton, 1984

The Downing Street Years, Margaret Thatcher, HarperCollins, 1993

Selwyn Lloyd, D. R. Thorpe, Cape, 1989

Siegfried Sassoon, Jean Moorcroft Wilson, Duckworth (two vols), 1999 and 2003

A NOTE ON THE TYPE

The text of this book is set in Bembo. This type was first used
in 1495 by the Venetian printer Aldus Manutius for Cardinal
Bembo's *De Aetna*, and was cut for Manutius by Francesco Griffo.
It was one of the types used by Claude Garamond (1480–1561)
as a model for his Romain de L'Université, and so it was the
forerunner of what became standard European type for
the following two centuries. Its modern form follows the
original types and was designed for Monotype in 1929.